338.4778
S948s

Selling Sounds

The Commercial Revolution in American Music

DAVID SUISMAN

HARVARD UNIVERSITY PRESS

Cambridge, Massachusetts
London, England

Copyright © 2009 by the President and Fellows of Harvard College
All rights reserved
Printed in the United States of America

First Harvard University Press paperback edition, 2012

Library of Congress Cataloging-in-Publication Data
Suisman, David.
Selling sounds : the commercial revolution in American music / David Suisman.
p.   cm.
Includes bibliographical references and index.
ISBN 978-0-674-03337-5 (cloth : alk. paper)
ISBN 978-0-674-06404-1 (pbk.)
1. Music trade—United States.   2. Music—United States—History and criticism.
I. Title.
ML3790.S88 2009
338.4'7780973—dc22   2008055620

Contents

	Prologue	*1*
1	When Songs Became a Business	*18*
2	Making Hits	*56*
3	Music without Musicians	*90*
4	The Traffic in Voices	*125*
5	Musical Properties	*150*
6	Perfect Pitch	*178*
7	The Black Swan	*204*
8	The Musical Soundscape of Modernity	*240*
	Epilogue	*273*
	Abbreviations in Notes	*287*
	Notes	*289*
	Acknowledgments	*339*
	Index	*343*

SELLING SOUNDS

San Diego Christian College
Library
Santee, CA

SELLING SOUNDS

Prologue

Marcus Witmark had no hand in the operations of the printing and publishing firm bearing his name, M. Witmark and Sons. He was an immigrant from Prussia, an antebellum slaveholder in Georgia, and a veteran of the Confederate army, wounded at Gettysburg, who moved to New York after the Civil War. In 1883, a few weeks before the end of the year, his bright, mildly obstreperous eleven-year-old son Jay won an arithmetic competition at school and for a prize was allowed to choose from among a printing press, a velocipede, a tool chest, and a baseball uniform. On the advice of his eldest brother, Isidore, age fourteen, he selected the printing press. Together with another brother, Julius, thirteen, the boys started printing New Year's cards, and then business cards, in their home in Hell's Kitchen. A lost printing job taught them the need for "speed and efficiency," and soon they convinced their father to help them buy a steam-powered press. By 1885, Witmark Brothers was a small business operating out of the family home on West Fortieth Street.

The firm began to publish sheet music in 1886 and achieved some notable success with "President Grover Cleveland's Wedding March," penned by Isidore in honor of the president's impending nuptials. Soon sheet music production supplanted all other activities. A photograph from around this time shows Julius and Jay in front of their shop, flanked by younger brothers Frank and Eddie, who later joined the firm themselves. Julius and Eddie hold proof sheets; Jay wears an ink-stained apron. Sheet music covers are

P.1 The House of Witmark got its start at 402 West Fortieth Street in New York, the same building in which Frank, Julius, Jay, and Eddie Witmark, pictured here, were born. Above the number 402 in the middle is the name the firm originally bore, Witmark Bros., before the brothers incorporated with the help of their father. Visible in the window are sheet music title pages, most of which were set in type by eldest brother Isidore. Isidore Witmark and Isaac Goldberg, *From Ragtime to Swingtime* (New York, 1939).

displayed in the window. The boys look into the camera sternly, blankly; the older two reach barely two-thirds of the way up the doorway. Shortly thereafter, the business was rechristened M. Witmark and Sons, so that Marcus could legalize the firm on behalf of his underage entrepreneurs.[1]

Because of the boys' youth, many in the publishing world did not take the young Witmarks seriously at first. Their maturity and experience, however, belied their age. Isidore, who had worked since the age of nine, was avidly entrepreneurial. By the time the publishing venture began, he had sold leather-bound family albums, water filters, hats, women's handbags, and chromolithograph prints; worked as a delivery boy in his father's liquor business; given piano lessons; and apprenticed at a piano factory. The second brother, Julius, was their connection to the world of commercial entertainment. A talented singer, the "Boy Soprano" (as he was sometimes billed) performed with some of the leading minstrel troupes of the era and made a host of friends and contacts who would later be integral to the Witmarks' commercial success.[2] Unlike the rest of the family, the third brother, Jay, was decidedly unmusical, but he possessed a knack for commercial and financial matters, perfectly complementing the talents of his brothers. And so they began: Isidore wrote songs and oversaw the whole enterprise, Julius (and the two youngest brothers) performed and promoted the songs, and Jay attended to the details of the business.

Although this cottage industry division of labor came about fortuitously, it had far-reaching consequences, setting the pattern for a whole new kind of music business. Over the next forty-five years, the House of Witmark took a leading role in shaping what has become known, since the mid-twentieth century, as the culture industry. Although the Witmark brothers' work encompassed all kinds of music, it focused especially on popular music, which it helped elevate to the position of prominence it occupies in American culture today. Under Isidore's guidance, the Witmarks helped transform the way songs were written, promoted, and sold in the United States. In the process, the company absorbed the catalogues of ten other publishing firms, branched off into minstrel show promotion, supplied music to professional musicians, and opened remote offices everywhere from Paris to Melbourne. In cooperation with other publishers that emerged at the end of the nineteenth century, M. Witmark and Sons also guided copyright reform to safeguard music as intellectual property and spearheaded the fight to establish the legal doctrine of performing rights. What the Witmarks oversaw, then, was nothing less than a commercial revolution in music. As culture, commodity, and intangible property, music developed new functions and new meanings at the turn of the twentieth century, and as a result it became stitched into the fabric of the nation as never before.

Two years after the Witmarks got into the sheet music business, another

Prussian immigrant, Emile Berliner, traveled to Philadelphia from his home in Washington, D.C., to give a demonstration of his newest invention, the gramophone, at the Franklin Institute, one of the nation's most august scientific institutions. Although he had no formal scientific education, Berliner had earned a considerable reputation as an inventor, thanks to improvements he had made to Alexander Graham Bell's telephone a decade earlier. Now, four days shy of his thirty-seventh birthday, he had come to introduce his latest innovation: a device to record and reproduce sound. As everyone present knew, Thomas Edison had demonstrated a comparable machine, the phonograph, eleven years earlier, but Edison had become distracted by other projects after the initial acclaim for his device had waned, and subsequently the still-imperfect design had languished. Since then, Berliner had devised innovative means for solving some of the difficulties Edison had confronted, and aided by the work of Charles Bourseuil, Hermann Helmholtz, Edouard-Léon Scott de Martinville, Charles Cros, Chichester Bell, and Charles Sumner Tainter, Berliner now had a workable prototype.[3]

Both Edison's and Berliner's technologies had at their center a sensitive diaphragm, modeled on the tympanum of the human ear, which registered vibrations in the air caused by sound waves. And both attached to the diaphragm a stylus, whose undulations traced the movements of the vibrating membrane onto a delicate, impressionable surface. As Berliner explained, however, the gramophone departed from the phonograph in crucial ways. The gramophone, for example, recorded sound in the sides of the groove, rather than the bottom, with greatly enhanced volume and reduced distortion as a result. Moreover, the phonograph indented or incised sound into the soft surface of a tinfoil- or wax-covered cylinder, but the gramophone engraved sound into a flat metal disc. Such a disc, which was coated with a waxy, petroleum-based solution, was then processed like an etching: dipped in acid to make a "negative" from which numerous "positive" reproductions could be pressed. The original sounds were revived when the positive disc was played back on a separate device dedicated to this purpose. Edison's design had the advantage of using only a single machine and bypassing the need for processing, but Berliner's promised even more. It afforded superior sound and, unlike cylinders, offered the potential to stamp many copies of an original. These divergences in design suggested different possible futures for the listening experience as well. Indeed, the most up-to-date phonograph, on which Edison had recently resumed work, sounded best through listening tubes inserted into the ears, whereas Berliner's gramophone emitted the sounds from an upturned funnel. That is, with Edison's device, the listener had to come to the sound; with Berliner's, the sound came to the listener. After explaining the technical distinctiveness of his design, Berliner proceeded to possible applications for his novel technology. Some resembled the uses proposed by Edison, who suggested that the phonograph could be a tool for the historic preservation of voices of great singers and orators, the recording of last wills and testaments, and the use of sound reproduction to aid in the learning of elocution and foreign languages.[4] But Berliner also suggested that the ability to reproduce sounds on a large scale could make the gramophone a tool of mass communication; a politician's speech or a religious leader's homily could be stamped into millions of copies. (Radio eventually fulfilled this role better than the gramophone, but many leading figures around the turn of the century, including Theodore Roosevelt, William Jennings Bryan, and Booker T. Washington, did make such recordings of well-known addresses.)[5] More presciently, however, Berliner envisioned that sound recordings could become a source of considerable revenue if only licensed reproductions were issued. "Prominent singers, speakers or performers may derive an income from royalties on the sale of their [recordings]," Berliner told the audience, "and valuable plates may be printed and registered to protect against unauthorized publication."[6] Berliner did not anticipate (or chose not to mention) that the owners of the technology, not the artists, were the ones who stood to reap the greatest financial rewards.

Looking back, one may wonder whether those in attendance grasped the implications of Berliner's presentation. Before Edison and Berliner, every sonic phenomenon had possessed a unity of time and space; it occurred once, for a certain duration, in one place, and then it was gone forever. By embedding time in objects and making possible what the economist Jacques Attali has called the stockpiling of sound, recording technology destroyed that uniqueness. But Berliner's design went further. It introduced a structural and social division between making a recording and listening to it. With Edison's design, access to one assumed access to the other as well; sound recording was something people could *do*. With Berliner's design, a wedge

P.2 Pictured here is the gramophone that Emile Berliner demonstrated at the Franklin Institute in Philadelphia on May 16, 1888. With this device, Berliner extended Thomas Edison's earlier work on the phonograph and gave it a whole new direction. The *Philadelphia Evening Herald* called it a "remarkable performance." Courtesy of the Library of Congress.

was driven between production and consumption; sound recording was something people could *listen to*. On occasion, he noted, ordinary men and women might have recordings made of their voices, and in such instances, as with photographic portraits, recordings would be "taken" in local recording studios, where the means of (re)production belonged to someone else. In the long run, *phonograph,* not *gramophone,* was the term that stuck (in the United States anyway), although for many decades, both devices were known generically as talking machines. Meanwhile, Edison's technology, with which users could make their own recordings, lost out to Berliner's in every other way. Berliner's discs were easier to mass-produce, ship, and store than cylinders, and eventually the commercial strategies used to promote disc recordings redefined the place of music in American life.

Today in the United States, music is all around us. In a way, this state of affairs is unremarkable, for music is a universal form of human expression. Definitions and functions vary widely by culture and epoch, but some form of music is found in every society. From love songs and lullabies to war songs and dirges, certain musical genres appear across the human spectrum, connecting disparate peoples that share little but their common humanity. Indeed, poets, philosophers, and scientists have contended that music is part of what makes us distinctly human.[7]

Music has a long history in the national culture of the United States. Although "President Cleveland's Wedding March" by Isidore Witmark has not enjoyed the longevity of "Yankee Doodle," of which Berliner played a recording at the Franklin Institute, it is fitting that modern music publishing and commercial sound recording both had strong patriotic accents from the time of their inception. Through all the nation's vicissitudes, music has expressed both the richness and the contradictions of the American character. The history of the republic echoes with sounds that have united, sustained, succored, fomented, cajoled, and galvanized in times of both calm and crisis, a richness and complexity that even the most cursory survey evinces. Consider "Roll, Jordan, Roll," Stephen Foster's parlor songs, George Gershwin's "Rhapsody in Blue," Aaron Copland's *Appalachian Spring,* the Dust Bowl ballads of Woody Guthrie, Billie Holiday's "Strange Fruit," and Merle Haggard's "An Okie from Muskogee"—these varied strains evoke the deep diversity in the ways music has been used and understood in American life.

Few have grasped better than Walt Whitman the importance of music in the constitution of American society. The bard of American democracy wrote poetry that is steeped in the spirit, language, and metaphors of music. The words *song, sing, singers,* and *singing* appear more than three hundred times in his verse; and in the titles of his poems alone he used seventy-two different musical terms.[8] "I Hear America Singing," his best-known "musical" poem, is now a staple of the English class curriculum:

> I hear America singing, the varied carols I hear;
> Those of mechanics—each one singing his, as it should be, blithe and strong;
> The carpenter singing his, as he measures his plank or beam,
> The mason singing his . . .
> . . . .
> The delicious singing of the mother—or of the young wife at work—or of the girl sewing or washing—
> Each singing what belongs to her, and to none else.[9]

First published in 1860, this paean to American pluralism and personal industry bears witness to an era before the machinery of the music business was first set in motion. By the early twentieth century, "talking machines" were doing much of America's singing, featuring selections from record catalogues hundreds of pages long, which listed songs in every language from Czech to Chinese. It was no longer true, as Whitman had written, that the song of the young wife or the girl washing clothes belonged "to her, and to none else." By then, most songs were owned and managed by a complex publishing industry, whose primary concern was to monitor exactly to whom the people's songs *legally* belonged. As Whitman certainly knew, people in his time did pay for music occasionally, in the form of concerts, minstrel shows, songbooks, hymnals, musical instruments, and music lessons. But those exchanges bore little resemblance to the commercial culture that followed. By the time Whitman died in 1892, the political economy of music had begun to change, and the commercial exploitation of music ceased to be a small-scale, haphazardly organized endeavor.

Today the music business has grown so large and has permeated our cultural lives so completely that it is everywhere, part of the very air we breathe.[10] Compact discs and iPods are of course commonplace, and these make up only a part of the business. Whenever you hear music in a restaurant or department store, during halftime at a football game, in a movie, on a television show, on an airplane before takeoff, or in a hospital, right before you fall unconscious on the operating table, the music industry is present. One of its most recent manifestations, the musical ring tones of cell phones, is already a multibillion-dollar part of the industry. Even the singing of "Happy Birthday to You" is tied to the music business; because Warner Music Group, until recently an arm of the conglomerate AOL Time Warner, owns the copyright to the song, it is technically subject to a licensing fee when it is sung in a restaurant or bar, on the professional stage, in a television show or movie, or even at a summer camp. (Schools and private homes are exempt.)[11]

From this perspective, the ubiquity of music in American life today starts to seem quite remarkable. In most instances, the music we hear is brought to our ears by some machine that reproduces sounds made elsewhere, at an earlier moment in time. However universal music making may be, in our culture it is now characteristically done by automatic machines. Moreover, most of this music is connected in some way with the commercial economy of the music industry, in which value is gauged according to financial, not cultural or aesthetic, criteria. Music may still have cultural or aesthetic value, but neither governs its commercial production.

In our own times it has become fashionable to declare that music has become a commodity. Like many truisms, this claim obscures as much as it reveals. It tells us nothing, for example, about how music resembles or differs from other commodities, or what aspect of music lies at the core of its commercial circulation. Does its value as a commodity inhere in the composition, the performance, or the sounds, or in some combination of these? To say merely that music is now a commodity tells us nothing about how, when, or why it became one, whether all music commodities function alike, or whether music that functions as a commodity at one moment is always so, uniformly. Commodification is not, however, an instantaneous occurrence, like the flash pasteurization of milk. It is a social and political process, populated by human actors, and one that includes various dimensions and phases. To understand what music commodities are and how they operate, we need to revisit the period when the wheels of commercial music began to turn.[12]

At the turn of the twentieth century, a new musical culture emerged as the modern music industry took shape. This culture included many of the terms and conditions that structure the way we now understand and experience music, and its emergence had worldwide ramifications. The rise of music as big business was a multinational and transnational phenomenon, but one in which the United States had a leading position. Stylistically, the emerging soundscape encompassed a vast musical range, from coon songs to opera. The result was that music in many ways came to be manufactured, marketed, and purchased like other consumer goods—in fixed, durable objects, available in dazzling, unprecedented variety and at a cost affordable to millions of consumers in all parts of the country. Paradoxically, however, music was also becoming *de*materialized at the same time, severed from the tangible realm by the metaphysics of sound recording and by copyright law, which came to recognize property rights in music that were unconnected to physical forms.

By the Great Depression, the creation of a new musical culture was effectively complete, in two complementary respects. First, a transformation had been effected in musical forms and the technologies and practices of making music and as such created a *new* musical culture, in contrast to an older one. At the same time, there emerged a new *musical* culture, with more music everywhere, in contrast to a culture in which music was less prevalent, less prominent. On one level, this transformation marked a change in musical works and practices; on another, it signified the alteration of "a whole way of life," in which music was now a presence in schools, in magazines, on the streets, and in commercial spaces as never before. It was also integrated into other forms of the entertainment business, from vaudeville to radio. Music thus developed as a commodity in two distinct registers. In its primary markets music was produced, marketed, and sold directly to consumers. In ancillary markets, it circulated as capital that could be used by other industries, either as a supplement or as indispensable raw material for other "producers," including vaudeville, dance halls, department stores, cafés, radio, and movies. A complete account of the rise of the music business and its consequences must integrate both dimensions of the new musical culture and recognize the dynamic interrelations between them.[13]

The transformation of American musical culture constituted a departure from the disciplined, skill-based regime of the piano in the parlor in the nineteenth century. The advent of a novel kind of popular music written for the market brought light, catchy songs that were easy to play and sing into the rhythms of daily life, while for many people the growing use of player-pianos and phonographs displaced manual music playing altogether.[14] Meanwhile, opera and other kinds of "serious" music were sold as a fresh form of cultural capital. Indeed, here was a new musical bonanza, bringing more choice and greater access for listeners than ever before, and these contributed to the growth of mass consumer society by promoting the separation between production and consumption and by marketing musical goods in innovative and influential ways. The rising tide of consumer capitalism had submerged within it three basic ideas, which were as well suited to the music business as to any other part of the emerging consumer economy: unending novelty, forever tantalizing consumers with the untasted pleasures of the always-new; the production not only of goods but also of desires; and the promise that consumption was the path to personal fulfillment.[15] Consumers assimilated the idea of music as issuing from an automatic machine (such as a phonograph or player-piano), detached from human labor, and fixed in objects (such as records or piano rolls), portable and storable, and independent of time and place. Music, which had once been produced in the home, by hand, was now something to be purchased, like a newspaper or ready-to-wear dress. All the while, the major producers in the music industry advertised with unprecedented aggressiveness, and they developed inventive marketing strategies to attract retailers and consumers to the rewards of consumer credit. In 1907 a typical trade magazine told merchants, "[Selling by installments] is a means of appealing not only to the *classes* but to the *masses*. In other words, to those who *would not,* or *could not,* purchase goods on a cash basis."[16] Yet to consumers the industry conveyed quite a different message, as in this phonograph catalogue from the same year: "Buying on monthly payments does not [imply], as some seem to think, that your means are limited. . . . [It] does show that you are adopting the latest practical and most efficient method of saving and purchasing."[17]

Music was not like other commodities in every way, however, for its essence was aural experience, a fact that was integral to the commercialization of musical life. In one form or another, sound was the commodity the music industry trafficked in, and as a consequence auditory exposure was inseparable from promotion. In the conclusion to his 1930 book on song publishing (still one of the shrewdest available), Isaac Goldberg stressed that exploitation of the aural environment was a fundamental strategy of the industry: "What you sing and whistle, then, is . . . the result of a huge plot—involving thousands of dollars and thousands of organized agents—to make you hear, remember and purchase. The efforts of [song promoters] assail our ears wherever we go, because it is the business of this gentry to fill the air with music."[18] Notwithstanding his florid language, Goldberg's statement points up a fundamental law that guided the industry's development: the more music people heard—the more the air was "filled with music"—the better it was for business. As one music publisher who was active in the 1920s explained, "If people hear a melody, that would be advertisement. If they do not hear it, there is no way of selling it."[19]

As the new musical culture took shape, therefore, it altered the way music was made and heard, bought and sold, as well as effecting other changes that were broader and more subtle, especially the increasing presence and impact of music in the culture at large. An examination of the way music functioned and felt in people's lives can reveal patterns and tendencies that were characteristic of a specific time and place—what Raymond Williams called an era's "structure of feeling." This concept posits a discernible connection between that which is external, physical, and impersonal (that is, structure) and that which is intimate, intangible, and ephemeral (that is, feeling). This is by no means a claim that a structure of feeling is homogenous or uniform, or that everyone experiences the structure of feeling in the same way. It is possible, however, to perceive similarities and trends specific to a given historical moment that together define the prevailing horizon of expectations for most people.[20]

Once the music industries were filling the air with music, American society *sounded* different than it had a generation earlier. Much of the change was attributable to the thunderous cacophony of mass industrialization and urbanization, but music mattered too. Unlike the sounds of factories, automobiles, and teeming city streets, music was a kind of sound that people actively, consciously produced and deliberately tried to control; it was not a by-product of another function, the way the noise of automobiles was an incidental effect of their use for transportation. All the clichés about the Roaring Twenties and the Jazz Age notwithstanding, the significance of this clamor has long been overlooked.[21] In the minds of many philosophers, however, from Aristotle to Marx, it is, to a greater or lesser extent, through the senses that we humans know and understand the world. Such sensory experience is culturally—and therefore historically—conditioned; what is perceived as noise by the middle class at one moment may represent industriousness or freedom of expression to the working class.[22] The senses inform our worldview, our historical consciousness, our sense of what is or is not possible at a given time.[23] As part of a structure of feeling, the senses help constitute the affective mental apparatus through which rational thought is continuously filtered. As Marx noted, we perceive and understand the world through our bodies as well as our minds; the development of our senses is part of our cognitive formation. "Man is affirmed in the objective world not only in the act of thinking, but with *all* his senses," Marx wrote, and elsewhere he concluded, "The *forming* of the five senses is a labor of the entire history of the world down to the present."[24] And Marx was not alone in drawing this conclusion. In *The Power of Sound* (1880), the polymath philosopher Edmund Gurney began, "It is now generally admitted that our organs of special sense, the channels by which we keep up our constant and various intercourse with what we call the external world, have been formed in past ages by gradual processes in correspondence with stimuli which that external world supplied."[25] A generation later, Walter Benjamin echoed this view: "Just as the entire mode of existence of human collectives changes over long historical periods, so too does their mode of perception." Benjamin was particularly attentive in this respect to the importance of technology, which, he maintained, "has subjected the human sensorium to a complex kind of training."[26]

Earlier in the nineteenth century Nathaniel Hawthorne had grasped the impact of industrialization, when the noise of a locomotive annihilated a sentimental pastoral reverie near Concord, Massachusetts.[27] As Hawthorne understood, sound is an intrusive phenomenon: we can avert our eyes from sights we wish to ignore, but sounds enter our ears whether we want them to or not. If sound contributes to the shaping of the self, then control of the acoustic environment—the "soundscape"—becomes an issue with real social and political consequences.[28] In the eighteenth century, perpetrators of "rough music," or charivari, used music and noise as a form of organized aggression or punishment.[29] In nineteenth-century France the sound of village bells assumed explicit political significance in the mediation of competing claims to power among different villages in the countryside and between the church and the secular state.[30]

Early in the twentieth century, as the music industry reordered the American soundscape, sound was invested with power in new ways. Much depended on which sounds the music industry promoted and which it ignored or suppressed. Its authority derived, in part, from the fact that control of the soundscape is generally an exclusive prerogative in any given space, at a given time: although we can easily process multiple visual stimuli, we experience hearing more than one piece of music at a time as cacophony, aural chaos. The influence of the music business over the sounds that filled the air was fundamental to the industry's impact. Music can comfort and delight, but it can also annoy and distract. The long reach of the music business meant not only more music in more places than ever before, but also an erosion of silence or opportunities for reflection, for being alone, quietly, with one's own thoughts. And it meant the promotion of some music—that of the music industry—over other music. By marginalizing musical production that was not oriented toward the market, the industry rendered such music invisible (or rather, inaudible) or less legitimate.

Indeed, marketing based on sound gave the music industry unique scope and penetration—spatial, geographical, and social—far beyond that of virtually any other industry. Music products were "consumed" by people wherever and whenever the sounds were heard, a phenomenon that encompassed people of all classes, in every part of the country. As a consequence, the soundscape itself became a field of marketing, the aural equivalent of billboards, which first appeared alongside roadways in the same years, but far more pervasive. Sound was also far more *in*vasive, as demonstrated by the debates over radio advertising in the 1920s. These were intensified by the fact that as sound, music, which operated both above and below the level of consciousness, had an affective, behavioral influence on people. Like cradle songs sung to lull a baby to sleep, the modern commercial soundscape used music not merely to please but to produce specific effects, like the purchase of sheet music or improvement in sales and employee morale in department stores. As Oliver Wendell Holmes, Jr., noted of music in restaurants, if it had no effect, it would be abandoned.[31]

More broadly, sound is a means by which the world enters the body. In contrast to the eye, which emphasizes the distinction between the self and the world, the ear brings the self and the world together. Through the eye, you see the world *out there;* you observe it as separate from yourself, perceive yourself in relation to it. Through the ear, you hear the world in your head; it enters *inside you;* you perceive the world from the inside out, as it were.[32] More to the point, in the West the eye has been trained to see rationally—as Theodor Adorno and Hanns Eisler put it, "conceiving reality as made up of separate things, commodities, objects that can be modified by practical activity." The ear, however, has not been conditioned by reason to the same degree. No matter how rationalized the production of the sound going into the ear, it remains an organ conditioned first and foremost by emotional response.[33]

Though order, regularity, and calculability lay at the root of profitable, large-scale production of music, the long-term success of the industry depended on mass consumption. Animated by fantasy and enchantment, mass consumption of music grew out of people's emotional, not rational, reactions to the industry's fare. When these were combined with mass exposure and repetition, the result was to make a phenomenon seem commonplace that was actually radical and extraordinary. The rise of the music industry upended musical culture as it had been known, but within only a few decades changes as radical as the manufacturing of songs and the spatial and temporal separation between the production of music and its consumption had been broadly assimilated. As prevailing assumptions and expectations about music shifted, the normalization of aural commodities obscured the fact that every insertion of the products of the music business into the environment represented an active intervention in the culture—a decision to have this music over none, and to have this music over other possible music.

That being said, the burden of the analysis in *Selling Sounds* falls on the *creation* of the new musical culture and not on its reception.[34] Consumers do not command our primary attention, because the creation of modern musical culture was not a consumer-driven phenomenon. The music industry did not grow in response to the unfulfilled desires of importunate consumers. Although consumers—music lovers—welcomed greater opportunities to hear and enjoy music, we would search in vain for evidence of their initiative.[35] Nor was it musicians who propelled the transformation. Musicians, as a rule, did not make records. Musicians made music—which phonograph companies turned into records that they reproduced, marketed, and sold.[36] The radical reorganization of musical culture in the United States was driven instead by a new commercial class of music makers, including in one form or another entrepreneurs, inventors, manufacturers, publishers, sales agents, advertisers, critics, retailers, educators, and lawmakers. Some were also musicians, others not; some cared deeply about musical culture, others were indifferent. Together, though, they harnessed musicians' creative talents and transformed music—that is, sound—into a versatile and valuable commodity. Not surprisingly, certain technological developments feature prominently in this story, but they alone did not determine its course and cannot by themselves account for such varied developments as the invention of the "hit song," the repackaging of grand-opera music for middlebrow markets, or the mobilization of education, advertising, and law in the service of the music industry.

Emile Berliner died in the summer of 1929, two months before the stock market crash and five weeks after the death of Julius Witmark, the erstwhile "Boy Soprano." The passing of these men coincided with the end of the formative period of the modern music business. By this time, numerous developments, including the advent of radio and the "talkies," had signaled the start of a new phase of commercial entertainment. The consolidation of many of the leading firms in the entertainment business reconfigured the field of the music industry and initiated the era of integrated multimedia conglomerates, whose descendants have grown to mammoth proportions. By 2005, according to one estimate, the "core" copyright industries accounted for 6.6 percent of the gross domestic product, and thanks to the growth in computer software, those industries had become the leading sector of foreign sales and exports for the United States—ahead of chemical products, motor vehicles, aerospace, agriculture, and pharmaceuticals. Indeed, recorded sound alone, not including its value within movies, television shows, or other products, accounted for $8.26 billion of the copyright industries' foreign revenue. "I Hear America Singing" had become "We Are the World."[37]

No element was more important to the growing international prominence of the American music business than recorded sound, the commercial production of which had its origins in the United States but developed transnationally in the early twentieth century. In 1929, on the eve of the Great Depression, the phonograph industry in the United States pressed more than 105 million records and manufactured more than 750,000 phonographs, together valued at nearly $100 million. In the same year, almost 50 million records were sold in the United Kingdom and almost 30 million in Germany, and even such disparate locales as Peru, Finland, Egypt, and Malaya had sales of a million records a year or more. Music, especially in the United States, was now inseparable from the technology and business of mechanical reproduction. Meanwhile, the popularity of recordings sent the American piano business into terminal decline. By the late 1920s, the popularity of player-pianos had faded, and at the end of the decade only eighty-one piano manufacturers remained in the United States, down from a peak of nearly three hundred in 1909. By 1933 that number dropped to thirty-six.[38] The decline of the piano business notwithstanding, however, the music business and the culture industry have continued to grow, and the more they have, the more normalized and invisible their power has become. That is, the more the music industry has filled the air with music, the less remarkable the ubiquity of music seems. The foundation of this peculiarly modern condition was set in the early twentieth century, when the music industry drove a wedge between production and consumption—between making music and listening to it—and invested music with new meaning in such a way that obscured the commercial architecture of the new cultural order. Music entered people's homes and lives in exciting new ways, but this expansion depended on a complex set of social and cultural changes, whose meanings reached far beyond music proper. In order to evaluate the effect of this commercial revolution in music, we must first understand how it took place.

1

When Songs Became a Business

"Where is the song before it is sung?" asked the Russian writer Alexander Herzen. Nowhere, was his wistful answer. But then Herzen, who died in 1870, did not live in the age of the modern music industry, when songwriting and music publishing became complex commercial enterprises. In the decades following the U.S. Civil War, a new musical product transformed American musical culture. It was amusing, inexpensive, portable, and versatile enough to be enjoyed everywhere from baseball games and street corners to private middle-class parlors. This product was the popular song, and its advent marked the beginning of a new era in the political economy of music, by refashioning one of the most basic and universal forms of cultural expression—the song—according to the inexorable logic of business.[1]

"Popular" song did exist before this time, but earlier the term had referred to vernacular music in a general way. Popular song resembled folk song, in today's parlance—"an outgrowth from the life of the people," as one survey of American music from 1890 put it.[2] In the 1890s, however, popular song was redefined as a new kind of aural commodity, unapologetically commercial and distinctively American, heard more and more widely across the soundscape. Other song forms—art song, religious song, work song—did not disappear completely, but popular song became the cornerstone of a broad new musical culture, initiating changes not just in the music people made and heard, but also in the way music was woven into the fabric of people's lives. Popular song was a consumer commodity for the ear. Musically, it constituted an elastic, mutable category, containing at any given moment numerous styles and genres, which themselves changed over time. Commercially, it flowed from the processes of industrial manufacturing and marketing, the most successful products of which were deceptively simple, capable of appealing to people of different classes, ethnicities, and regions. Popular music was a national phenomenon, and its sounds accompanied a broad cultural shift in American society.

Whence the Popular Song?

At the end of the nineteenth century many styles of music rang out across America. Ten thousand military bands, from coast to coast, played an eclectic repertoire of marches, European and American symphonies and overtures, operatic arias, dances, and hymns. The sounds of Italian and German opera, singing societies, symphonic concerts, and street bands filled the air in cities. Musical theater and operetta attracted the white urban middle class; vaudeville, variety, and minstrel shows appealed to a mix of middle- and working-class audiences. Among African Americans in the South, one might hear work songs by day and music that would later be known as the blues by night. English ballads were sung in Appalachia, cowboy songs in the West. Religious music ranged from Moody and Sankey hymns to shape-note congregational singing and, among African Americans, music descended from slave spirituals.[3] Of all these many musical forms, however, none had as great an impact on the emergent musical culture in the United States as the popular song industry.

The business of popular song grew up in the shadow of musical "uplift"— the nineteenth-century idea of music as a means to elevate the mind, body, and character of individuals and the spirit of the nation as a whole. In the home, the epicenter of this musical ideal was a keyboard instrument, either a piano or an organ. Over the course of the century, these instruments became a shibboleth of middle-class identity, grounded in both uplift and the respectability of European art music. By century's end, a large-scale industry producing instruments at every level of price and quality extended ownership to all stations of American society, from the White House, which boasted no fewer than four pianos in the late 1890s, to a family in rural Alabama visited by Booker T. Washington, which was too poor to have a complete set of eating utensils but which owned an organ. In 1894, a writer in the *Leaven-worth (Kansas) Herald* could report, "It's a mighty poor colored family that hasn't got some kind of tin pan called piano nowadays."[4]

Under the guiding hand of men like John Sullivan Dwight, a Brook Farm transcendentalist who became the leading American music critic of the age, the works of European composers, especially Germans, were exalted as "serious music" and most other forms of music were casually or vigorously dismissed. By the end of the century, Henry Lee Higginson, Leopold and Walter Damrosch, Anton Seidl, and Henry Krehbiel were laying the institutional foundations of high musical culture in America. As serious music was "sacralized" as a genteel accoutrement of the bourgeois social order, it found a foil in popular music, which was characterized as everything that serious music was not.[5] An 1895 magazine characterized popular music as "the songs of the day, ephemeral, trivial, and of little or no musical value ..., sung and whistled and played for a few weeks or months, and ... then forgotten."[6] Popular song was not merely the opposite of serious music, though: it was a distinct historical creation in and of itself.

Despite the roughly concurrent rise of the so-called royalty ballad in the English music hall and the occasional popularity of English songs in the United States ("Ta-ra-ra Boom-de-ay" and "Little Annie Rooney" were two of the biggest sellers), the rise of popular song in the United States owed more to the "American system of manufactures" than to influence from abroad or coordinated international initiatives. Although the success of music hall songs contributed to the rapid growth of the music economy in England, it belonged to a different order than did the rationalized production of popular song in the United States. Concentrated in New York City, the industry that emerged was a new, modern kind of business that turned songwriting and music publishing into specialized and standardized occupations. "In the distant past," wrote Harry Von Tilzer, the era's most prolific professional songwriter, "the writing of songs was play, a relaxation from daily cares, but today it is a business and demands businesslike methods." Others in the industry reached the same conclusion, though somewhat apologetically. As one music publisher put it in the *Music Trade Review* in 1904, "The publishing business is like any other line with a variety of goods—pardon the commercial term, but it applies all the same—to offer."[7]

This industry was nicknamed Tin Pan Alley. Like "Hollywood," "Tin Pan Alley" became a metonym for a place, an industry, and a mode of production.[8] Like Hollywood, it could produce works in a variety of styles, unified by a constant underlying operational aesthetic. The exact origin of the nickname Tin Pan Alley is now lost, but it involved Harry Von Tilzer and the songwriter and journalist Monroe Rosenfeld and referred to the cacophony created in the music publishers' studios.[9] Geographically, the industry was first concentrated around New York's Union Square. Then, by the first decade of the twentieth century, publishers' offices moved north to Twenty-eighth and Twenty-ninth streets between Fifth and Sixth avenues—the industry's most famous location. At one end of Twenty-eighth Street stood a combination saloon and Turkish bath, where songwriters and actors could get free sandwiches or, for the price of a glass of beer, a plate of baked beans. Inside the publishers' offices, a reception area could be found, with pictures of performers on the walls; an office; a stock room; and a small, parlorlike music studio, or several, each with its own upright piano, some comfortable furniture, and a carpet or rug on the floor, where songwriters composed, arrangers wrote out transcriptions, and salaried "demonstrators" played songs for stage performers and tried to persuade them to incorporate the songs into their acts.[10] Many of America's most celebrated songwriters, including Irving Berlin, George Gershwin, and Jerome Kern, worked for Tin Pan Alley over the course of its storied history, all turning out the light, lyrical, sentimental fare that was the Alley's signature product.

Tin Pan Alley's essential impact, however, lay not in aesthetic innovation but in the relation between aesthetic forms and the industry's modern capitalist structure. Indeed, no single musical form characterized the industry; over time, it incorporated a variety of genres and idioms. As a business, though, its principles remained constant, clearly embodying the two features that according to Thorstein Veblen, writing in 1910, defined the modern business concern. A firm's production had to rest on the systematic organization and application of knowledge—which Veblen referred to as "the machine process," though he emphasized that it could be found in nonmechanized industries as well. And the fundamental motivation of the business enterprise had to be financial profit, which the modern businessman sought to maximize by manipulating the supply of goods and by other means. "The vital point of production," Veblen claimed, "is the vendibility of the output, its convertibility into money values, not its serviceability for the needs of mankind." What distinguished Tin Pan Alley from other modes of making music was that the *primary* motivation for writing a song was to sell it, not to express some inherently human feeling or musical impulse. Applied to music publishing, this principle measured value in a purely quantitative way— "How many copies of sheet music did a song sell?"—divorced from qualitative (that is, musical or aesthetic) considerations. Songwriters in this regime were workers, not artists, and their output was a vehicle for the amusement of others, not for personal expression. The songwriter-publisher Charles K. Harris advised aspiring songwriters to avoid tunes that were difficult to sing, because they were less salable. As Von Tilzer put it, the songwriter's product was "a commodity, a cash value, and in order to augment the value he must subordinate his own personal tastes to those of the music-buying public."[11]

In many respects, Tin Pan Alley was altogether a different entity from the older music business that it gradually displaced. For one thing, in the antebellum era, music publishing had generally been integrated into other professional activities, not carried on as a livelihood unto itself. Typical was Philadelphia's well-known Septimus Winner (1827–1902), who both engraved and published music, owned a music store, gave music lessons, arranged music for others, and served as music editor of the general-interest *Peterson's Magazine*.[12] For another thing, by the end of the nineteenth century much of the nation's musical capital was consolidated in New York, whereas earlier New York had been only one among many important musical cities in the United States. When the country's largest publishers established a trade organization in 1855, for example, Philadelphia had the greatest number of members, with seven, New York had six, Boston and Baltimore had four each, and Saint Louis, Louisville, Cleveland, and Cincinnati had one apiece.[13]

In this older economy, sales of printed music grew steadily throughout the nineteenth century, but individual songs had little commercial value. Publishers did not generally advertise. Songs were financially risky, in that they were quite labor-intensive (requiring considerable attention to detail) yet delivered returns on very small margins at best. For writers, songs might bring a brief windfall, but they were hardly the basis for a livelihood. The best-known exception to this rule was Stephen C. Foster, the composer of "The Old Folks at Home," "My Old Kentucky Home," and "Camptown Races" and perhaps the first American composer to support himself on the sale of sheet music. Born near Pittsburgh in 1826, Foster distinguished himself by crafting remarkably simple songs and by understanding better than any composer before him how much the popularity of a song depended on its being easily remembered and played even by those with only modest abilities.[14] Even so, the income Foster could earn from his songwriting was neither lavish nor stable, and he is almost as famous for dying poor and broken, a victim of the Bowery, as for his enduring songs. Although his most successful composition, "Old Folks at Home" (1851), did earn him $1,647 in royalties, a substantial amount of money in the mid-nineteenth century, an analysis of his royalty payments for fifty-two published songs tells a different story. Excluding his four biggest sellers, his average royalty was $102, and the median payment for all his songs was only $36.[15] For most songwriters, the situation was even more humbling. Over several years or decades, the work of a Stephen Foster or a George Frederick Root might sell in the hundreds of thousands or possibly millions of copies, but as a rule, a writer who could regularly sell five hundred or more copies of a song was considered a solid success. As for payment, most writers sold their songs outright, for a flat price, and in instances where writers chose to receive a royalty, it was not uncommon for them to be bilked by unscrupulous publishers. Reflecting on the value of songs before the 1880s, Harry Von Tilzer recalled, "I hadn't thought of earning money from them, as at that period one never heard of song writers making fortunes, and there were not many trying to write them."[16]

The publication of original songs, then, occupied only a relatively small place in the music economy. Old songs circulated widely and freely, and among those which sold well, many were imported from Ireland and Great Britain.[17] Indeed, numerous commentators believed that the United States had yet to develop a distinct musical idiom. Typical in holding this view was Reginald De Koven, who was born in Connecticut in 1859 and studied music in Europe before earning a reputation as a composer for musical theater. Notwithstanding the quantitative and stylistic expansion of publishers' catalogues, wrote De Koven in 1897, "it would be difficult . . . to find in the entire output even a very small modicum which, by any courtesy or stretch of the imagination, could be called distinctively or characteristically national

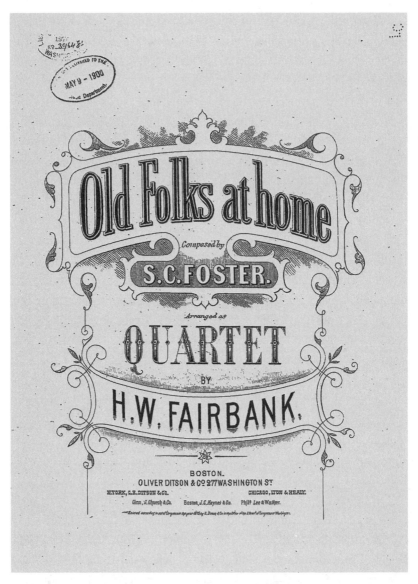

1.1 Stephen Foster, one of the first people to support himself on revenue from sheet music sales, was not well enough known to warrant spelling out his name in full in this 1875 edition of one of his best-known songs. First published in 1851, the song was also known as "Way Down upon the Swanee River." Courtesy of the Library of Congress.

or American."[18] Meanwhile, until the 1890s works copyrighted abroad held the added appeal for publishers of not requiring payment of royalties. With the passage of the Copyright Act of 1891, and with subsequent presidential proclamations, however, publishers were bound to honor foreign copyrights, a proviso that eliminated the incentive to ignore the potential domestic supply of new work. In retrospect, the copyright law also reflected the ineffectual state of established music publishers in the United States. When the law was drafted, publishers of books fought successfully to include a clause requiring that foreign works be reprinted in the United States in order to be eligible for American copyright, lest imports undercut the printing and book manufacturing trades. The music publishers' trade group, the Board of Music Trade, nevertheless appears to have done little to lobby on behalf of its members. As a result, the older, unprotected music publishers faced new competition from abroad, and this ended up diminishing their market share, reducing their relative power in the American music business, and minimizing the obstacle they posed to the new breed of popular music publishers.[19]

The commercial turn in music publishing began in the 1880s when firms began supplying songs for the growing demand from vaudeville, which was quickly becoming the leading form of musical performance in the United States. Mixing skits, dancing, acrobatics, and musical numbers, vaudeville grew out of variety theater, which itself grew out of the minstrel shows. Pioneered by the New York impresario (and songwriter and performer) Tony Pastor, vaudeville was essentially a more wholesome version of variety, aimed at the "polite tastes" of the middle class. Smoking, drinking, and prostitution were banned from theaters, and the most ribald jokes were banished from the stage. At the outset, performers wrote most of their own songs, but as urban audiences grew sharply, even good performers had difficulty writing or obtaining consistently entertaining material.[20]

Up until this time, song publishing had been essentially a passive activity: publishers had songs printed up, then hoped people would buy them. It paralleled, in this way, nineteenth-century print advertising, which was based more on announcing the availability of goods than on stimulating demand.[21] In contrast, the new publishers approached selling with unprecedented aggressiveness. Will Rossiter, whose Chicago firm was established in 1880, be-

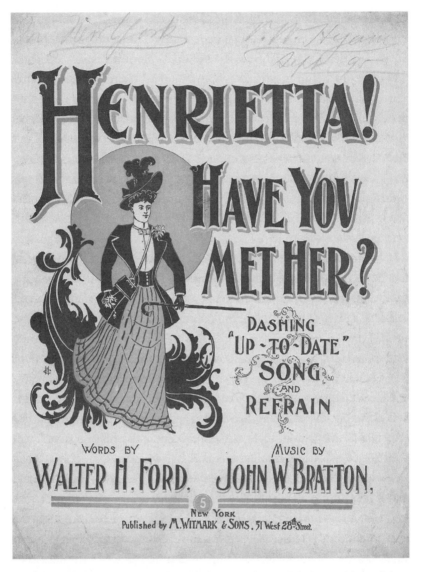

1.2 By the 1890s, modifications in typeface and graphics and the increased use of chro-molithographic printing made sheet music covers livelier and more attractive than earlier sheet music had been, with its relatively drab design. The novelty of modern popular music is underscored by the mention of the "'up-to-date' song and refrain." The Lester S. Levy Collection of Sheet Music, Special Collections, Sheridan Libraries, Johns Hopkins University.

came the first music publisher to advertise in theater trade journals. Carrying bundles of sheet music under his arm, he also journeyed from one music shop to another to sing his songs, and he began to print decorative illustrated covers for his sheet music (made possible by developments in chromolithographic printing), which made his offerings more visually attractive. In the same years in New York, Frank Harding took over his father's "serious" music firm and reoriented it toward popularizing songs that he and others wrote for Tony Pastor's shows. He encouraged local Bowery songwriters to bring him song material, payment for which usually took the form of a few drinks at the nearby bar. Within a few years, his office was a well-known hangout for songwriters.[22]

Meanwhile, the young firms of T. B. Harms, established by brothers Tom and Alex Harms, and Willis Woodward & Company began to enlist the leading performers of the day to introduce and promote their material onstage, often in exchange for money or other compensation—a practice that persisted and grew in importance in the decades that followed. The idea for this in all likelihood came from the British music hall, where much of the repertoire was made up of royalty ballads, songs for which performers received a royalty for singing them onstage. The most remarkable, most important, and longest-lasting of the new firms, however, was M. Witmark and Sons, the firm begun by the young brothers Isidore, Julius, and Jay Witmark (joined later by the youngest brothers, Frank and Eddie). Starting out in business with holiday cards and business cards, the boys had decided to focus their energies on song publishing after the music publisher Willis Woodward reneged on a pledge to cut Julius in on the profits to a song, "Always Take Mother's Advice," that Julius promoted in his act as a minstrel performer. It was not until 1891, however, that Julius incorporated into his act a song that vaulted the Witmarks to the level of a major publisher. They had purchased the song "The Picture Turned toward the Wall" for fifteen dollars a few years earlier but had initially declined to promote it. When Julius added it to his act and sang it around the country, however, it sold thousands of copies and brought the young Witmarks respect from their elder rivals in the business. Indeed, the song's popularity inspired another publisher to issue a song with an almost identical title, "The Picture with Its Face toward the Wall," to which the Witmarks responded with a lawsuit for copyright infringement;

their subsequent legal victory buttressed their reputation as serious competitors in the field.[23]

Around the same time another of the key architects of Tin Pan Alley was beginning his career as well. In the mid-1880s an aspiring songwriter named Charles K. Harris rented an office in Milwaukee, outside which he hung a sign: "Banjoist and Song Writer. Songs, Written to Order." The reference to the banjo signaled his familiarity with minstrelsy, "written to order" suggested his responsiveness to public taste—a quality he capitalized on effectively over the years that followed. Unlike the best-known minstrel songwriters of that time, however, he was not a performer, and although he was ignorant of written notation—a fact he boasted of in his autobiography, as a badge of his divergence from "serious" music—he played well by ear and showed a creative, energetic drive in cultivating demand for his material.[24]

Harris achieved modest success by placing some of his songs with traveling performers, and in 1891 he established his eponymous publishing company. His big break came in 1892–93 with "After the Ball," a defining moment in the creation of the new musical culture. In his *History of American Music* (1908) W. L. Hubbard, the music critic for the *Chicago Tribune*, expressed a typical judgment about the song when he wrote "It may be said that it was this song which really started the popular song craze as we know it today." Indeed, no song had ever sold so many copies so fast and so widely. Departing from the era when a "successful" song sold hundreds or maybe thousands of units, "After the Ball" sold hundreds of thousands—perhaps, as *Munsey's Magazine* reported in 1895, more than a million.[25] Moreover, it was truly a national hit. Before this, very few commercially produced songs achieved real national popularity. What thrilled audiences in one area of the country did not necessarily excite those in another, and although a song might enjoy popularity in different regions over a few years' span, that popularity did not derive from a national infrastructure designed to promote and distribute music.

The song itself was a narrative ballad, with three verses and a chorus, set in waltz time. Its melody was extremely simple, its chorus easy to remember. Its maudlin lyrics were typical of late nineteenth-century ballads, with a sentimentality that was common in Victorian life. In the song's lyrics, a man recounts to his niece the experience of losing the love of his life when, "after the ball," he saw her kissing another man. The catch—and story songs from this era often had one—was learning many years later that the man his sweetheart had kissed was only her brother. Grounded in nineteenth-century assumptions about home and marriage, the narrative components would have registered quickly with listeners; for some they may even have given voice to their anxiety over conformity with Victorian norms. Cultural resonance alone, however, hardly accounts for the song's tremendous commercial success. Indeed, the traditional Victorian values running through the song lyrics in the formative years of the music business obscured the magnitude of the shift that was taking place in the field of cultural production.

In Harris's view, "After the Ball" was different not only in degree but also in kind, part of a new category of music, popular song, that encompassed numerous styles and genres that were similar in their production and promotion. Reflecting a few years later on the rapid ascendance of this kind of music, Harris explained it as the result of a dynamic change in supply, promotion, and demand: with simpler, singable melodies, songs were more musically accessible; with increased music education, more people could play them; improvements in vaudeville enhanced exposure to songs; and within a few years, phonographs and player-pianos were stimulating demand. "After the Ball" showed in particular, however, that additional consumers of song could be systematically produced through intense, repeated, varied musical promotion. In fact, no song could achieve mass sales without such exposure, Harris claimed in his 1926 autobiography: "A new song must be sung, played, hummed, and drummed into the ears of the public, not in one city alone, but in every city, town, and village, before it ever becomes popular."[26]

Harris learned that the "popular" element in "popular song" rested on distribution—*aggressive* distribution—as much as production, and in the age before mass communications, the main channel for it was the stage. "The real start at popularizing a song is to sell it to the performers," Harris wrote. "If it strikes their fancy, they will surely sing it for the public. Common sense tells one that the bigger the reputation and ability of the performer whose assistance the author and composer enlists, the more chances of its success in catching the public's favor." If necessary, a performer's favor could also be curried with a small weekly emolument. Thus, Harris enlisted one of the era's most successful traveling singers, James Aldrich Libbey, to help promote "After the Ball," in addition to persuading May Irwin to sing the song in her Broadway show, Dick Jose to sing it on the West Coast, and Helen Mora to perform it in vaudeville houses around the country. In many cases, this "enlisting" of performers involved a small weekly payment, and according to one report, Harris claimed he paid fifty different singers a week five to fifty dollars each to include "After the Ball" in their acts. Harris did not altogether invent this strategy of using stage performers to promote songs, but he refined and expanded it. Having James Aldrich Libbey's image printed on the cover of the sheet music, for example, he at once capitalized on the singer's existing reputation and enhanced it, for the mutual benefit of singer and publisher.[27]

The song's most important exposure, however, occurred at the Columbian World Exposition in Chicago in 1893, where it became a fixture in the repertoire of John Philip Sousa, a musical figure of unrivaled cultural authority in the 1890s, whose adoption of "After the Ball" had far-reaching effects. As a bandleader, conductor, and composer, Sousa—the "March King"—was the most revered and influential American musician of the age. Thousands and thousands of people from all over the country and around the world heard the performances of the Sousa band on the Midway, and a great many of them brought copies of "After the Ball" home with them as souvenirs. In this way the song was disseminated far and wide, including in translation into many foreign languages.[28]

"After the Ball" changed the social geography of American music and the basic relation between music and business. Largely as a result of this one song, Harris opened up offices in both Chicago and New York, and in moving to New York shortly after the turn of the century, he personally exemplified the mass migration of songwriters and the consolidation of the popular music business there. Meanwhile, Harris's good fortune inspired a number of other music publishers to try to emulate and build on his success. Important Tin Pan Alley firms established in the wake of "After the Ball" included Joseph W. Stern, Jerome H. Remick, and Howley, Haviland & Co. (all in 1894); Leo Feist (1895); Shapiro, Bernstein & Co. (1896); and F. A. Mills (1897). The mid-1890s, Isidore Witmark remembered, marked "the indubitable beginnings of Tin Pan Alley as a national industry," and by 1900 only

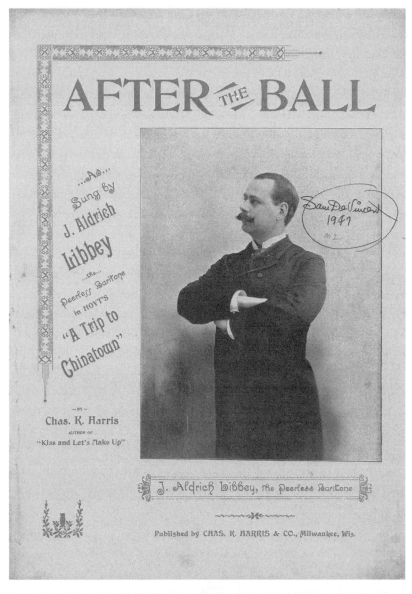

1.3 By enlisting James Aldrich Libbey and other singers to perform his song, Charles K. Harris helped lay the foundation for the systematic promotion of popular songs around the country. For the publisher, printing the picture of a well-known performer on the cover of the sheet music took advantage of the performer's existing popularity; for performers, having their image on the cover of such sheet music enhanced their reputations. Sam DeVincent Collection of Illustrated American Sheet Music, Archives Center, National Museum of American History, Behring Center, Smithsonian Institution.

rarely did a national hit originate in any city other than New York. In Witmark's estimation, these young publishers neither knew nor cared about music, but "they had discovered there was money in popular song."[29]

Tin Pan Alley's principal personnel included a motley assortment of Jews, African Americans, Germans, and Irish, whose previous experience in music, commerce, and theatrical performance shaped the development of the industry in fundamental ways. The number of Jews working in Tin Pan Alley was particularly striking, observable in even the names of the leading publishers. In 1870 the most prominent men in the business had borne names such as John Church, Oliver A. Ditson, Thaddeus Firth, William Hall, William A. Pond, and George Frederick Root. By 1910 most of these publishers had disappeared, and the industry was now led by men such as Louis Bernstein, Leo Feist, Max Dreyfus, Edward Marks, Jerome Remick, Maurice Shapiro, Ted Snyder, Joseph Stern, and Isidore, Julius, and Jay Witmark. Just as the majority of publishers were Jewish, so were many of the leading songwriters. Although the ethnic character of Tin Pan Alley attracted little notice outside the business in its early years, before long anti-Semitic critics of the new popular music seized on the prominence of Jews as, in their view, an explanation for the degraded nature of the music. Typical was the contempt shown by journalist D. G. Arnoth in his visit to a publisher's office. He found the Jewish-run house "cheap, inane, and vulgar," and when a singer "of a pronounced Jewish type" rehearsed a song the publisher was offering, he found, "I had never believed it possible that sounds so horrible and vulgar could issue from any seemingly civilized throat." In contrast, as the social position of popular music and Jews shifted in twentieth-century American culture, many later commentators noted the substantial involvement of Jews in the early music business with more equanimity or celebrated it as a unique creative convergence or a parable of assimilation.[30]

The preponderance of Jews in Tin Pan Alley seldom goes overlooked, but few accounts have explained it in a meaningful way. Rather than ask why Jews were prominent in Tin Pan Alley, we would do better to ask why *these* Jews? A more focused, nonessentialist approach reveals not just a shift from gentile to Jewish songwriters and music entrepreneurs, but also a more complex evolution in the music industry dependent on immigration patterns, professional experience, ideas about showmanship, and the development of heterogeneous ethnic identity. Getting beyond a "Jewish paradigm" for understanding Tin Pan Alley also helps us to appreciate why others who fell outside the white Protestant mainstream of American culture succeeded there as well.

The first notable characteristic of the leading publishers of Tin Pan Alley is that they consisted overwhelmingly of thoroughly assimilated American-born German Jews. In the autobiographies written by Charles K. Harris, Edward Marks, and Isidore Witmark, none of the three mentioned his Jewish background, and Witmark even mentioned his father's membership in "the church choir" before leaving Prussia. Harry Von Tilzer had been born Harry Gumm, to an Irish father and a Jewish mother. (Tilzer was his mother's maiden name; he added "Von" to give it an aristocratic flair.) When his wife died, her body was cremated, a practice at odds with Jewish law.[31] All of them embodied the broad assimilation typical of German Jews in the United States in the late nineteenth century.

Nothing specifically or directly religious animated the entry of these assimilated Jews into popular music publishing, nor were they heirs to a specific Old World tradition of music publishing. A stronger, sociological explanation may lie in what the historian Berndt Ostendorf described as the "cluster of dispositions" peculiar to these publishers' circumstances. The first trait they shared was their youthful vigor; every important publisher of the 1890s was in his mid-twenties when he set out in the publishing business, except a few who were even younger. They included Edward B. Marks (b. 1865), Will Rossiter (1867), Charles K. Harris (1867), Frederick Benjamin Haviland (1868), Isidore Witmark (1869), Jerome H. Remick (1869), Leo Feist (1869), Patrick Howley (1870), Julius Witmark (1870), Joseph W. Stern (1870), Harry Von Tilzer (1872), Maurice Shapiro (1873), and Max Dreyfus (1874). A more salient characteristic, however, was that before going into publishing, a remarkable number of these men had worked as salesmen (an occupation in which Jews were well represented). Isidore Witmark had sold water filters; Stern, neckties; Marks, notions; Feist, corsets; and Dreyfus, picture frames and ribbons. By the time these men entered the music business, they had a deep understanding of salesmanship, and this experience shaped their commercial worldview. They had learned to develop face-to-face relationships with customers, to cultivate interest in novelty, to respond to consumer tastes and desires, and to encourage sales through their personal powers of persuasion. This background in business and sales underpinned the whole of the popular song industry these men built, for they had apprehended that in some ways songs could be sold like soap.[32]

Their commercial identities developed against a German American musical backdrop, for prominent first- and second-generation German Americans were a ubiquitous presence in the musical life of the United States in the late nineteenth century; and in effect, the Germanness of the young publishers of Tin Pan Alley may have done more to establish them in the music business than their Jewishness. Indeed, the German presence in American music was overwhelming: from the concert hall to the vaudeville stage, scarcely any important musical figure of the period lacked an important German connection. New York's leading concert orchestras were directed by German-born conductors Theodore Thomas and Leopold Damrosch, and later Damrosch's American-born son Walter, all three of whom labored to enshrine the ideal of German musical *Kultur* in American concert repertoires. These three also promoted music education and advocated music, especially German music, as an instrument of cultural and spiritual uplift, an effort in which they received important assistance from Henry Krehbiel, the leading music critic of the era, and Oscar Sonneck, the editor, educator, and later, from 1902 to 1917, head of the Music Division of the Library of Congress, both of whom were also born to German parents. Other leading musical figures had German connections as well. The Steinways were born in Germany; John Philip Sousa's mother was Bavarian; Victor Herbert, who was known for his Irishness, had a German stepfather, grew up in Stuttgart, and married a German woman (and he played under Walter Damrosch); and songwriter Paul Dresser (a half brother of novelist Theodore Dreiser) was born to German Catholic parents.[33]

Not only did second-generation German Americans, Jewish and gentile, grow up surrounded by Germans' respect and passion for music, but as children of immigrants they developed a facility for moving back and forth across cultural borders, thereby becoming adept, as the historian Ostendorf put it, "at improvising and innovating, and at negotiating differences." Belonging as they did to both the Old World and the New World, they learned and assimilated what ideas, feelings, and sensibilities moved easily between groups and from one context to another, and this translation became second nature. Among German Jews, these skills are likely to have been even more finely developed than among gentiles, for the Jews belong to three cultural worlds—German, American, and Jewish—not just two. In addition, other characteristics of the German American population may have amplified their transcultural dynamism, including liberal cosmopolitanism, urban orientation, and relative openness to other classes and groups. Indeed, these conditions distinguish the publishers of Tin Pan Alley from the Jewish movie moguls of Hollywood a few years later. Although the latter had also developed skills as salesmen before setting out in the movie business, the founders of the Paramount, Universal, Fox, Metro-Goldwyn-Mayer, and Warner Brothers studios were nearly all first-generation immigrants (only Marcus Loew and the Warners were second-generation) who came from unhappy, straitened circumstances, in contrast to the relatively comfortable starting point of the music publishers.[34]

By the time the Hollywood studios took shape in the 1910s, the Jewish component of Tin Pan Alley had changed as well, as a result of the influx of Jewish songwriters from Eastern European, not German, backgrounds, and from more working-class, as opposed to middle-class, families. Large numbers of Jews from Eastern Europe poured into the United States, especially New York City, around the turn of the century, and these included the families of Irving Berlin, George and Ira Gershwin, Irving Caesar, L. Wolfe Gilbert, and other leading musical figures. Like the second-generation German Jews before them, these men too had grown up in circumstances that rewarded versatility of movement and communication between the home and the street, the traditional and the modern, the old culture and the new. If anything, however, they achieved an even higher level of dynamism, for they lived in and among myriad Jewish communities (Russian, Hungarian, Romanian, Galician, and others), each with its own specific cultural codes—as well as in regular interaction with other immigrant groups (Italians, Greeks, Irish, and so on).[35] As producers of popular songs, neither the German nor the Eastern European Jews created songs with identifiably Jewish features—anti-Semitic denouncements notwithstanding—but they emerged from a field of social relations that rewarded lively, inventive approaches to bridging ethnic and social divisions.

If together these sociological factors help explain the foundations of the popular song business, blackface minstrelsy and the zing of theatrical performance were the catalysts that brought Tin Pan Alley's energies to life. The minstrel show, Isidore Witmark recalled, was one of the Alley's "spiritual and material sources," and at one level or another, the love of minstrelsy and its inherent racial assumptions coursed through the developing song business.[36] What united the three most successful songwriters of the 1890s and early 1900s—Harry Von Tilzer, Charles K. Harris, and Paul Dresser—was not only that each had a German connection (two were assimilated German Jews, one was a lapsed German Catholic), that they all relocated to New York from medium-sized Midwestern cities, and that all moved from professional songwriting into publishing.[37] All three were motivated by their understanding and love of minstrelsy and related forms of theater. As a child Von Tilzer ran away from home to join a circus. He later joined a burlesque troupe and got his start as a writer working for minstrel and vaudeville performers. Like him, Dresser had gotten his start, before establishing himself in New York, with minstrel shows and traveling medicine shows, which combined entertainment with appeals to buy patent medicines.

Even though Harris was never a professional performer, he grew up steeped in minstrel show culture and excelled at playing the banjo, the quintessential instrument of the minstrel stage. As songwriters, all three men were best known for their maudlin ballads, but these were sentimental offshoots of minstrelsy's songs of racial travesty.

Popular blackface theater constituted a pillar of the modern song business in other ways as well. The House of Witmark benefited not only from Julius's career as a minstrel performer (and those of his brothers Frank and Eddie) and from minstrel shows as a vehicle for popularizing songs the firm published. The Witmarks also established a lucrative Minstrel Department, which aided in the production of amateur minstrel shows across the United States. Around 1905 the brothers published the *Witmark Amateur Minstrel Guide and Burnt Cork Encyclopedia,* a book "so comprehensive," according to Isidore, "that for $1.50 a community group could put on a minstrel show commensurate with its facilities, from the simplest to the most elaborate." Another service was Isidore's Minstrel Shows by Mail program, in which organizers or performers mailed in detailed questionnaires listing the size of their group, the number of singers, the capacity of the orchestra, and other information, and the Minstrel Department responded by mailing out a custom-designed show complete with specific songs and gags appropriate to the resources, budgets, and venue of the performers.[38] Thus, while the publishers of Tin Pan Alley may not have invented blackface minstrel shows, they did promote, propagate, and profit from them.

Meanwhile, African Americans were active in the business from its beginnings, but their involvement was marked by uneven power and control. At the turn of the twentieth century both Jews and African Americans were struggling to gain respect and acceptance in American culture, but the two groups were not, as the historian Michael Rogin put it, "moving in the same direction." For Jews, opportunities for economic advancement, social acceptance, and political legitimacy were expanding; for African Americans they were contracting. At a time when many channels were closed to members of both groups, popular entertainment was an important and highly visible exception. Yet the opposite trajectories of blacks and Jews meant that they approached popular entertainment differently. For African Americans, working in popular entertainment was a means of asserting their humanity; for Jews, it was a way to demonstrate that they were a benign presence in American life, capable of acculturation, and sharing in mainstream American values.[39]

In effect, relations between the two groups were complex and overdetermined. Virtually all Tin Pan Alley firms in their first few decades, especially M. Witmark and Sons, trafficked aggressively in "coon songs." These were light musical offerings with "darky" protagonists, often written in "dialect" and usually featuring a grotesque caricature on the cover of the sheet music, and for a time they were Tin Pan Alley's leading commercial product.[40] The vulgarity of this genre's stereotypes notwithstanding, some African Americans actively participated in producing and promoting these songs—including, perhaps surprisingly, men at the forefront of the fight for improved cultural and economic opportunities for African Americans, such as J. Rosamond Johnson (James Weldon Johnson's brother), Paul Lawrence Dunbar, Harry T. Burleigh, Will Marion Cook, and Bert Williams. In the era of Booker T. Washington's accommodationist "Atlanta Compromise," increased racial violence, and the fiction of *Plessy v. Ferguson*'s "separate but equal" doctrine, these men committed to African American cultural production saw no professional options other than the coon song trade, except self-exclusion and cultural invisibility.

Whether they attempted to work within or to circumvent the prevailing cultural order, African Americans faced formidable, complex challenges. One of era's most infamous songs, "All Coons Look Alike to Me," was written by an African American songwriter, Ernest Hogan, although Isidore Witmark, who published it, later took credit for some of the lyrics. In fact, neither the title, the lyrics, nor the sheet music cover were noticeably more offensive than those of many other songs of the era, but when the song became a hit in 1896–97, it emerged as a cultural flashpoint, its title and tune being wielded as potent racist insults. Whites taunted blacks by whistling the first few notes of the chorus, turning the sounds themselves into a weapon of racial intimidation. As a result, the African American press seized on the song as epitomizing the danger of coon songs generally.[41] Although Hogan secured a royalty agreement from Witmark in the contract, which was a more favorable arrangement than many songwriters, black or white, enjoyed, in the end, he is said to have lamented his involvement with the song.[42] At the same time, the Witmarks did publish numerous works by progressive African American musical figures, including Cook and Dunbar's pioneering ragtime piece "Clorindy, or the Origin of the Cakewalk." Isidore Witmark also noted in his memoirs, however, that he broke off relations with Cook when the writer, accompanied by his lawyer, wanted to review the firm's royalty statements. Regardless of the motivation for Witmark's actions, the incident highlights the tenuous position of African American songwriters, for whom publishing opportunities were limited.[43]

Elsewhere around the Alley, there were occasional instances of interracial collaboration among songwriters, as, for example, on the 1903 song "Teasing" by Albert Von Tilzer (Harry's brother) and Cecil Mack (pseudonym of R. C. McPherson), but the scornful words of Theodore Dreiser may have been representative of the industry's general attitude. In a profile of the music publishing business, Dreiser characterized the African American songwriter Gussie Davis as enormously talented but still a "shiftless" "bad negro" —an improvident Zip Coon who would foolishly accept cash payments for his songs instead of royalties. "Doan' want it," Dreiser has Davis saying of a royalty, "Too much trouble. All I want is a little money now and then when I need it." For Dreiser, such an attitude toward profit could only be condemned, as indicative of Davis's low and simple character. Ultimately, no African Americans appear to have worked as staff songwriters or arrangers in any of the leading Tin Pan Alley firms before the 1920s, and some moreover experienced outright theft of their work by whites, some of whom sold songs they heard in African American clubrooms as their own.[44]

Attempts by African Americans to create publishing alternatives pitted them against publishers with vastly superior resources. The most important black-run venture was the Gotham-Attucks Music Publishing Company, established by R. C. McPherson in 1905. Named for Crispus Attucks, the martyred runaway slave of the American Revolution, the firm aimed manifestly at integration, not separation. It published works by both black and white songwriters, targeting both black and white audiences, and its offices were located among Tin Pan Alley's white-owned firms, first on Twenty-eighth Street and later on Thirty-seventh Street. In its seven-year history, the firm's output was modest (between eighty-five and a hundred songs), but a remarkable number of these were successful, influential pieces, above all "Nobody," Bert Williams's signature song. By and large the firms' song lyrics and sheet music covers avoided the "darky" caricatures that typified much of the era's music. Gotham-Attucks, however, faced continued racism in the marketplace —one Memphis music dealer, for example, claimed that his customers would not buy Gotham-Attucks sheet music if they knew that the company was owned and run by blacks—and the company had insufficient resources to compete effectively against other firms' extensive promotional networks. Although later in the 1910s another black-owned firm, the Pace & Handy Music Company, fared somewhat better, it too faced substantial hostility in the marketplace, especially when one if its principals, Harry H. Pace, expanded into the phonograph business.[45]

Meanwhile, beginning in the 1890s, a style of African American music was emerging that precipitated a sea change in American popular culture. The syncopated melodies of ragtime that issued from African American communities in the Midwest quickly became the most popular and the most controversial product of Tin Pan Alley. Critics assailed the music's jaunty, dance-friendly rhythms as crude, salacious, and dangerous. To its most impassioned opponents, ragtime not only made audible, and perhaps inflamed, African Americans' primitive sexuality and lack of bodily restraint; it promoted these impulses in the culture at large, thus threatening the United States with an epidemic of moral degeneracy. In 1904 the World's Fair Committee on Music even banned ragtime from the Louisiana Purchase Exposition in Saint Louis, for fear that it would "demoralize" all the music for the fair. Sexual innuendo in the song lyrics exacerbated the alleged menace, and the use of the piano as the primary instrument in ragtime amplified its pernicious potential. In the ears of its critics, ragtime was a Trojan horse in the Victorian parlor, a fifth-column attack on American virtue. For them, the originality of the music merely confirmed African Americans' inherent "otherness," their immutably separate status in American life. Indeed, some middle-class African Americans, viewing ragtime as morally debased and fearing that it dangerously reinforced negative stereotypes, also rose up in opposition to it. As the Ohio Federation of Colored Women's Clubs had it, ragtime had the propensity "to lower the natural taste of colored people for music and deprive the race of one of its most promising tendencies toward culture." Champions of ragtime, by contrast, saw the music as pleasurable, harmless, and even liberating. For many African Americans, ragtime's celebration of the body formed a salutary counterpoint to the lynching and sexual violence of the Post-Reconstruction era, as well as to the restrictive norms of middle-class "respectability." Moreover, ragtime came *from* African Americans, rather than being imposed on them (as minstrelsy and coon songs had been); and as music that was composed, not improvised, it secured a place for the work of African Americans alongside the music of traditional European composers. Ultimately, ragtime enjoyed enormous popularity, not only in African American precincts but throughout the United States and in many locations abroad as well, and became a central component of the popular song business.[46]

For the publishers of Tin Pan Alley the most important issue was that ragtime was popular and profitable. Some African Americans benefited professionally from this popularity, but the economic power invested in ragtime rested primarily in the publishers' hands. When the best-remembered composer of ragtime, Scott Joplin, confronted this situation, after his publisher John Stark refused to give him a royalty arrangement for new compositions, it led to a permanent falling out between the two men.[47] The music remained associated with African Americans in many people's eyes, but African Americans had no monopoly on the ragtime idiom and therefore had only limited control over its commercial exploitation. Songwriters from a variety of backgrounds began to experiment with ragtime and develop it in new directions, and because of its commercial appeal, publishers began to apply the term *ragtime* to an ever-wider body of music, eventually encompassing practically any music that was new, lively, and exciting.[48] Performers came to understand that just about any piece of music, new or old, could be "ragged," or syncopated, no matter how it appeared on paper, with the consequence that the sound and sensibility of the new popular music resonated far beyond its "natural" boundaries. Ragtime's syncopation thus became a permanent, defining feature of popular music in the United States, although its success did little to affect the distribution of economic power in the music business.

The Song Factories

Although the social relations of Tin Pan Alley informed the development of the music industry to a great degree, its operations and organizational structure derived from the general principles of capitalist enterprise. Armed with the logic of production for profit, industry after industry and sector after sector followed the path of specialization and division of labor.[49] If this was so for the railroads, steel manufacturing, and the chemical and banking industries, it was also so for the systematized commercial production of songs. By 1910 the *New York Times* characterized Tin Pan Alley as a group of "popular song factories," and elsewhere it concluded, "Songs may be properly classed with the staples, and are manufactured, advertised, and distributed in much the same manner as ordinary commodities."[50] The goods themselves fell into a few general categories—parlor ballads, novelty numbers, show songs, dance songs—all produced more or less the same way. No matter how catchy or clever individual songs were, the business from which they issued rested on rational calculation to yield standardized products and to reduce uncertainty and fluctuation in supply and demand.

In Tin Pan Alley, publishers, composers, lyricists, arrangers, pluggers, cover illustrators, and others each served a distinct, defined role. Every aspect of songwriting, publishing, and promoting was broken down into elemental, specialized parts. At the top of the hierarchy stood the publisher, who embodied and administered the growing managerial ethos in the business. His position entailed a variety of complex responsibilities: purchasing songs, helping writers refine ideas, deciding which songs to issue, and designating where and how a song should be exploited. Although a successful song necessarily depended on able songwriting, it was the publisher, not the writer, who stood at the center of Tin Pan Alley's operations. As an editor, a publisher would change a title, add new lyrics, alter a chorus—anything he thought appropriate, as one publisher put it, to transform a bad song with a good idea in it into a good song.[51] The publisher also devised the strategy for promoting a song, which, in the words of one veteran songwriter, was a craft so subtle that it made him "as creative . . . as the composer himself."[52]

The emergence of professional arrangers highlights this division of labor and the consolidation and professionalization of Tin Pan Alley generally. Until the late 1890s, publishers issued only one arrangement of a song, usually a simple score for piano and voice. When a stage singer wanted to perform that song, he or she had to pay someone to arrange it for, say, a ten-piece orchestra (the standard size of the 1890s). If the singer then performed in a theater with a smaller or larger orchestra, he or she had to pay for a fresh score. The person who prepared these orchestrations—Edward Marks characterized him as a musical cobbler—was usually a skilled musician who did this work on a freelance basis and also sold hastily prepared melodies for small sums of money. As vaudeville grew in popularity, competent musicians could always find work writing out arrangements. In the early 1890s, however, this situation changed. In order to make it easier and less expensive for performers to adopt songs, publishers themselves began to hire arrangers to prepare scores.[53] Performers quickly came to expect these "professional copies"—published without covers and on less-expensive paper—and soon they became a regular part of the business, thus leading Marks and other publishers to hire full-time in-house arrangers.

Arrangers' other work consisted of preparing different orchestrations of a song—a "high-class" ballad might be issued in six or more versions, in different keys or for different instrumentation—or transcribing music for songwriters who could not read or write music themselves. Some houses offered custom arranging as well. One songwriter recalled, "You could go to Harms [T. B. Harms and Company] and for two dollars get a frail young man who worked there to make a piano arrangement of a whistled tune or score it for orchestra."[54] In essence, arrangers were the hired pens of Tin Pan Alley—its indispensable semiskilled labor. "They have all the knowledge, but none of the ideas that can be turned into cash," Isaac Goldberg commented. "They're like the swell stenographers in Mr. Babbitt's office: they can spell all the hard words and turn out a snappy looking letter, but they must get all the ideas from the boss."[55]

Around the same time, publishers also began to hire staff songwriters. Having started in the publishing business with one or two successful self-penned songs, many publishers soon found themselves looking around for additional promising material to publish. Purchasing songs selectively from "cobblers" gave publishers flexibility, but it carried the risk that they might lose good material to rival firms. Hiring staff writers reduced this risk. It also significantly increased publishers' expenses, but it gave publishers a steady supply of music to publish and rendered the production cycle for songs more regular, a particularly valuable advantage amid the growing demand for songs from vaudeville and other types of theater. Individual songs composed by writers not on staff retained an important place in the business, especially for smaller publishers who could not afford staff writers, but the internal reorganization had profound long-term effects. The hiring of staff writers increased publishers' capital investment, concentrated more power in the publishing houses, and reduced uncertainty in output. In addition, it shifted the balance of power between the song business and the stage: earlier, publishers had always chased after performers; now performers started to seek out the publishers.[56]

The hiring of staff songwriters also increased the number of people who could hope to earn a livelihood from composing popular songs, although the relationship between publishers and songwriters varied widely. In general, songwriters worked closely with publishers and commanded more respect than arrangers did, but by and large the public paid little attention to them and publishers sometimes treated them as dispensable and interchangeable (not unlike screenwriters in the film industry).[57] "With a few notable exceptions, America's popular songwriters are unknown," W. L. Hubbard wrote in his *History of American Music* (1908). "Such songs are impersonal. They do not bear the stamp of the composer's individuality so much as they reflect the taste of the day." At the same time, a winning songwriter really was *not* like an anonymous factory worker, and publishers knew it. In some cases, good songwriters received a "weekly advance" to sustain them through dry periods. As songwriter Jack Yellen remembered, it was a way "to encourage them, keep them going during the times when they didn't have hits."[58] For very successful songwriters, who earned royalties of three to four cents per copy sold, songs could sometimes bring in considerable sums, and to the public, songwriting came to symbolize the glamour of easy money.[59] Most professional songwriters, however, enjoyed only modest sales, and their contracts afforded them royalties of only one to two cents per copy, plus a small amount, ranging from five to fifty dollars, for the publisher's initial purchase of a song. For the majority in the business, claimed Nat D. Mann, manager of Witmark's Chicago office, there was "not much profit in song writing."[60]

The system at the core of Tin Pan Alley, then, took for granted that the vast majority of the works that the industry published were unprofitable and possessed little aesthetic value. As with book publishing, beginning as far back as the 1850s sheet music publishing was organized around occasional successes; publishers did not expect to break even on every song. For every ten songs a Tin Pan Alley firm issued, nine might recoup only half the publisher's expenditures—which consisted principally of the purchase of the song or payment of an advance on royalties; printing; lithography expenses for the sheet music cover; and—by far the biggest expense—advertising and promotion. This revenue, however, might be enough to cover the firm's fixed costs (rent, wages, and so on), that is, to keep the publisher in business. Then, if one of the ten songs was even a modest success (yielding, say, fifty thousand copies sold), it could cover the cost of publishing all ten tunes and return a small profit.

When asked, some in the business characterized songwriting as driven by inspiration and intuition, but many spoke about it more bluntly.[61] To those who believed that songs were inspired by their writers' real experiences, the songwriter L. Wolfe Gilbert replied: "This is just not so." The publisher Louis Bernstein likewise dismissed this notion: "The public thinks that there is [romance in songwriting], but there isn't." Rather than following some inner muse, songwriters' creations were purely reactive, derived from and bound to the tastes and moods of consumers. In publisher Edward Marks's words, "Song writers are a meretricious race; they write according to the market." A successful songwriter, Harry Von Tilzer explained, was "compelled . . . to study the likes and dislikes of the people who buy popular sheet music," for it was they who determined a song's success.[62]

In this commercial environment, many songwriters plainly understood their products as artificial constructions and their labor as a form of professional manufacturing. When Irving Caesar, lyricist of "Tea for Two" and many other songs, was asked whether words or music came first in his songwriting, Caesar would reply, "The contract comes first!"[63] Popular songs were not "inspired," songwriter Adolph Olman explained: "Writers sit down and deliberately set themselves to the task of writing a song. Sometimes a lyricist comes up with a remarkable idea, but then they sit down and manufacture the song." Olman allowed that "there must be some sentiment in the business, here and there," but its calculated nature was its defining characteristic. "All pop tunes, in my estimation, are manufactured," he concluded. Publishers understood the process in similarly inorganic terms. Louis Bernstein recounted, "[Songwriters] sit down, sometimes mechanically—'Let's go in and write a song.'"[64]

No engineer's instructions prescribed the exact steps in this mechanical process, but in an oft-quoted article from 1920, Irving Berlin offered the next-closest thing, an enumeration of nine inviolable rules for writing a successful popular song:

1. The melody must musically be within the range of the *average voice* of the average public singer. . . .
2. The title, which must be simple and easily remembered, must be "*planted*" effectively in the song. It must be emphasized, accented again and again, throughout the verses and chorus. . . .
3. The ideas and the wording must be [appropriate for] either a male or a female singer . . . so that both sexes will want to buy and sing it. . . .
4. The song should contain *heart interest* [pathos], even if it is a comic song. . . .
5. The song must be original. . . . Success is not achieved . . . by trying to imitate the general idea of the great song hit of the moment. . . .
6. Your lyric must have to do with ideas, emotions, or objects known to everyone. . . .

7. The lyric must be *euphonious*—written in easily singable words and phrases, in which there are many open vowels. . . .

8. Your song must be perfectly *simple*. . . .

9. The song writer must look upon his work as a *business*. . . .[65]

In many ways this list underscores the self-consciously commercial nature of the songwriting business, and the emphasis here on simplicity and universality makes clear the deliberate engineering involved in producing songs for a mass market.

At the same time, however, two of the items on Berlin's list are less straightforward than they appear. Berlin's instruction to write lyrics appropriate for both men and women seems self-evident but obscures the predominantly female audience of the music business and the prevailing orientation of consumer marketing at that time.[66] "Our popular song, in its industrial phase, begins largely under the influence of women," commented Isaac Goldberg, one of Tin Pan Alley's shrewdest critics. "It is women who sing songs in the home. It is women who play them on the piano."[67] John C. Freund, editor of *The Music Trades* and *Musical America,* estimated that women were responsible for 70 to 75 percent of all money spent on music.[68] Beginning in the 1890s, when the New York department stores opened music counters, publishers such as Joseph W. Stern and M. Witmark and Sons sent representatives to give song demonstrations in those overwhelmingly female sanctuaries and subsequently made the department stores a prime outlet for Tin Pan Alley sheet music. By not doing the same, the sleepy old-line publishers placed themselves at a competitive disadvantage that contributed to their being superseded by the young popular music firms.[69] In this respect, Tin Pan Alley was part of the consumer economy generally structured around women already. Notwithstanding this general orientation, however, there was no advantage in alienating men from singalongs (as Berlin knew well), and the performers that the publishers paid to promote the songs were predominantly male.

Production remained chiefly in male hands as well. A few female performers became successful songwriters, but the career songwriters were virtually all men, as were the publishers. The idea of women as songwriters was notable enough, however, for the *Music Trade Review* to run an article on the subject in its 1908 special issue on music publishing. Written by one of Tin Pan Alley's few female songwriters, the article took pains to reinforce traditional, conservative ideas of acceptable feminine behavior. "Oh, no! I am not a suffragette," the article began, "I don't know why I start my article this way, because woman's rights have absolutely nothing to do with the subject at hand." She then argued that there was indeed "plenty of room for women song writers," so long as they put the taste of the public before their own. Echoing male critiques of women's behavior in the marketplace, she declared that a successful woman songwriter must "study" the public taste, "which is just as changeable as—I was going to say a woman's mind—but I will substitute this synonym of changeability for a barometer, which after all, sometimes does keep the same for a day or two each month." The article concluded by reminding women that songwriting for publication "is a business pure and simple," not "a recreation," and that their future in songwriting depended on their understanding this reality.[70]

Berlin's list also greatly overstated the premium on originality in Tin Pan Alley. Elsewhere, he declared, "There is no such thing as a new melody" and asserted that what effective songwriters did was "to connect the old phrases in a new way, so that they will sound like a new tune."[71] In reality, the market valorized sales, not innovation. If a song caught on with audiences, its author often followed it up with a song much like the original, while rival publishers quickly turned out and promoted similar songs on the same theme. Thus, "Meet Me Tonight in Dreamland," a big hit of 1909, led to a host of other "dream" songs, including "I'd Like to Dream in Dreamland with a Dreamy Kid Like You," "In All My Dreams, I Dream of You" "Sweetheart of My Dreams," "Oh! What a Beautiful Dream," and others.[72] In some cases, imitators trod dangerously close to the original. "The Fatal Night of the Ball," for example, issued by a small publisher in Chicago, was almost indistinguishable from Harris's "After the Ball," in numerous respects. The lyrics of Harris's famous chorus ran:

> After the ball is over, after the break of morn
> After the dancers' leaving, after the stars are gone
> Many a heart is aching, if you could read them all
> Many the hopes that have vanished, after the ball.

And the chorus of "The Fatal Night of the Ball" barely diverged from it:

> After the day was over, after the night came down
> After I went to the ball, dear, there's where the deed was done
> Alas my heart is aching but it's no use at all
> I made a false step at the ball.

It is not known whether Harris initiated legal action over this particular song, but many copycat songs did result in litigation.[73] Indeed, because competition was fierce and uncopyrighted tunes were vulnerable to theft, some songwriters muted their pianos by sliding folded newspapers under the strings, to protect their musical ideas before publication.[74]

Formulas, therefore, lay at the heart of song production in Tin Pan Alley and contributed crucially to the creation of a national song business. Although competition among firms stimulated a certain amount of variety, originality, and inventiveness, these qualities were generally discouraged. Standardization, not innovation, was the backbone of Tin Pan Alley. The comedian Bert Williams claimed he did not write songs so much as he "assembled" them, "for the tunes to popular songs are mostly made up of standard parts, like a motor car."[75] Formula-based commercial entertainment did not originate with the song business—in the United States such methods went back at least to the dime novels of the nineteenth century—but Tin Pan Alley, by pursuing this calculated strategy with unprecedented zeal, became a model for the culture industries of the twentieth century. To maximize profits, publishers sought to minimize financial risk and sell to as large a market as possible. Songs based on a previously successful formula appealed to them, because they knew a market for this kind of product already existed. And for consumers, formulas held appeal as well; in a stressful world with a dizzying array of consumer choices, purchasers could know what they were getting and could expect not to be disappointed.[76] This was not mass production in the same sense as manufacturing chewing gum or Cream of Wheat, whose consumers truly wanted to buy an identical product every time. The factories of Tin Pan Alley are more accurately understood as specialty producers, like couturiers or jewelry makers, whose goods, in order to be successful, had to be similar to what came before but always a little different.[77]

This calculated conservatism comes through especially clearly in the how-to books on popular songwriting that proliferated in the early decades of the twentieth century.[78] "Watch the market for the kind of songs that are selling," one guide advised, "and if ballads are in great demand, then write a ballad, and if comic songs are selling, then write a comic song."[79] Charles K. Harris, in his how-to guide, even indicated the preferred musical structure: "The Prelude, or Introduction, should usually comprise four measures of common [that is, 4/4] time, or eight measures of 3/4 time, founded on, if not identical with, the opening bars of the verse melody and accompaniment, closing with a dominant chord, or occasionally a chord of the seventh."[80] Another writer went so far as to warn lyricists to avoid ending any line with "words that have the sound of *k, p,* or *t* at the end."[81] Most of the books encouraged songwriting tyros to conform to a recognized genre, and although there was no definition for what made a song catchy, all the guides agreed that simplicity and familiarity were vital. The point, as Stephen Foster had discovered earlier, was to produce something that people could easily sing, remember, and assimilate.

Invariably, the how-to manuals stressed title, melody, and chorus as the three key elements of a commercially successful song. Charles K. Harris explained, "A really good title is almost everything. . . . It is most essential that the public get their attention fixed on this line at the outset. In this way they retain it in their mind and know what to ask for in purchasing." The title functioned as more than a mnemonic for consumers, however. It was also an essential means of attracting performers, who were indispensable for reaching the public, and they were as attentive (or susceptible) to the lure of a good title as were consumers. An appealing title might jump out at a performer from the listings or advertisements in the trade papers, or it might be the first selling point when the performer visited a publisher's offices.[82] Indeed, some Tin Pan Alley houses employed people whose only job was to formulate catchy titles.[83]

Tin Pan Alley's attention to titles represented a fundamentally new approach to song, following the same contours as the development of other mass-market consumer goods. Indeed, titles were more than a song's packaging: they were also part of its product design. In most cases, the title of a song was the first line of its chorus, and the chorus was the linchpin of a song's popularity. Its repetition within the song could lodge it in people's heads, thus making it the part of the song that people sang, whistled, and hummed. A chorus usually determined a song's "ultimate success or failure," Charles K. Harris wrote; so for songwriters, "the idea is to get to the chorus, or refrain, as quickly as possible."[84] First emerging in American song in the 1840s and '50s, the verse-chorus song form had become virtually ubiquitous by the post–Civil War era. In the mid-1880s, however, professional songwriters began to place greater importance on the chorus, and over the next twenty-five years, song narratives became simpler, verses became shorter and fewer in number, and choruses carried more of the story and music. By the 1890s the most important melodic material was contained in sloganlike choruses, not in narrative verses, and within a few more years the chorus had become, in most cases, almost the whole song. "A few years ago the verses were twice the length they are now," Charles K. Harris told readers in 1906, "To-day, they are regarded as tedious and old-fashioned." The bandleader Paul Whiteman expanded on this point in his book *Jazz* in 1926: "Previous to 1897 every song had to have six or seven verses and each verse had eight or ten lines. Now there are two verses of a scant four lines each, and even at that, the second verse counts scarcely at all. The whole story must be told in the very first verse and chorus and usually there is very little to it anyway."[85]

Indeed, the emphasis on titles and choruses throws into relief a diametrically opposite phenomenon then emerging in American musical life: the collecting of noncommercial folk song. In the pages of the *Journal of American Folklore* (est. 1888), William Wells Newell's *Games and Songs of American Children* (1883), John Lomax's *Cowboy Songs and Other Frontier Ballads* (1910), and other collections, amateur and professional folklorists were documenting hundreds of songs sung around the country, many of which had no formal name or went by different names in different areas.[86] Best-known was the work of Francis James Child, who identified the British folk ballads that he and his followers found surviving in the United States by number, rather than assign arbitrary, extrinsic titles to the songs.[87] Many of the folk ballads were the antithesis of Tin Pan Alley productions: long, complicated, difficult to sing, and lacking choruses. And in contrast to the deliberately ephemeral character of Tin Pan Alley fare, many of these songs had endured for centuries. Thus, the prevalence of Tin Pan Alley's crafted catchiness cast the older music in a glaring new light, in which it appeared premodern, primitive, and atavistic.

If Tin Pan Alley established a new dominant song form, though, it would be a mistake to suggest that the commercial production of songs rendered consumers passive and inert, for some took inspiration from the emerging popular music. Evidence of amateur songwriting is fragmentary, but the number of books on how to write songs suggests that many people were not content merely to have others supply songs for them. Similarly, the thriving shadow industry known as song sharking, which invited aspiring amateur songwriters to have their works published for a fee, also depended on individual, consumer-level initiative. Described by the composer and publisher William Arms Fisher as "the greatest musical fraud in history," the song-sharking business courted novices who paid thirty to seventy dollars per song to a publisher, who feigned interest in his or her talent. Pledging to pair the composer or lyricist with some fitting "partner," the publisher matched the songwriter's work with stock lyrics or melody, which he could use over and over. Even the printing plates were reusable, as were the standard templates for the sheet music title page: the publisher literally just filled in the blanks. Often, publishers even copyrighted these ersatz works—it made them appear more legitimate and enabled the entrepreneurs to exact a commission on the copyright registration fee.[88] On the one hand, it would be easy to conclude that the ultimate effect of the how-to books and song sharking was to induce consumers to participate willingly in their own exploitation. Certainly, the industry benefited from the popular idea that the next great hit could come from anyone's humble pen (or piano), rather than being churned out "mechanically" by an industry hack. On the other hand, the promotion and proliferation of simpler song forms by Tin Pan Alley also democratized songwriting. Whether would-be songsters sought to publish their work or not, they viewed the conventions and codes of the industry as something they could control and use to their own advantage, whether financial, aesthetic, or emotional.

That said, the publishers of Tin Pan Alley institutionalized a concept of "popular music" that was deeply misleading, for however many people sang these airs, Tin Pan Alley's songs did not come *from* the people at all. Rather, the songs were crafted specifically, deliberately, and essentially as commercial products.[89] From the perspective of the publishers and songwriters of Tin Pan Alley, an industry veteran noted, "a song is a clever ad set to music," and the success of a popular song, concluded the critic Robert Haven Schauffler, came from its being "as easy [to grasp] as a soap advertisement."[90] Even if it trafficked in "popular" music, Tin Pan Alley's aim was, quite plainly, to sell songs, not to "give the people what they want." Indeed, the "people" were too vast a group, their desires too variegated for Tin Pan Alley to satisfy; and as the critic Gilbert Seldes noted, the people often did not know what they wanted. Generally, people wanted to be entertained, and to satisfy this yen they were most likely to choose from existing options. Thus, Tin Pan Alley's success depended on selling people not necessarily what they wanted but rather what they would accept. Over the many years since then, the threshold of acceptability has become the degraded standard of the culture industries generally. In a discussion of television more than half a century after the rise of Tin Pan Alley, Commissioner Nicholas Johnson of the Federal Communications Commission tried to disabuse the public of the notion that the cultural economy of the United States was driven by consumer desire: "To say that current programming is what the audience 'wants' in any meaningful sense is either pure doubletalk or unbelievable naiveté."[91]

Unlike the earlier music publishing business, which had existed to link composers with audiences, Tin Pan Alley employed songwriters to produce standardized works that attracted and conditioned a regular audience by keeping its music in the public ear. Publishers expected that most songs were unprofitable; this was an integral part of the system, not an aberration.[92] By the start of the Great Depression, Tin Pan Alley had produced some of the most enduring songs in the nation's musical history, including the work of George Gershwin and Irving Berlin; but for publishers, producing works of aesthetic distinction was really beside the point, a happy accident.

Under the direction of the Tin Pan Alley publishers, an explosion in songwriting took place around the turn of the century. This outpouring remade American music publishing and popular song in conformity with the principles of industrial manufacturing, and the repercussions were felt throughout American society. "The music of the multitude has always been a powerful factor in the social development of nations," the *New York Times* observed, "but only with the past half century has the supplying of it become an important industry."[93] The architects of Tin Pan Alley saw no irony, no contradiction, and probably no pejorative connotation, in the term *music industry*. They enjoyed the music, and they enjoyed the commerce. Whether or not they read industrial trade manuals or consulted with management experts like Frederick Winslow Taylor, ideas from these sources suffused and shaped Tin Pan Alley's music and its business. When Leo Feist died in 1930, *Variety* eulogized his "standards along legitimate Big Business lines." Later, the Roosevelt administration recognized Edward Marks's business acumen by appointing him to the Council for the Coordination of Industry.[94] If we are to understand the phenomenon of Tin Pan Alley fully, however, we must also acknowledge the ways in which, strictly speaking, it diverged from conventional models of big business. Its ownership remained in private hands; publishers themselves directed operations, rather than delegating authority to a class of professional middle managers; and although numerous firms had offices in locations outside New York, the publishers were not multisite operations on the order of the railroad industry.

"Popular music has become a fad from Maine to California," the *Music Trades* concluded in 1907.[95] By that time, New York was the unquestioned powerhouse in music publishing, and the writing and promotion of songs had become highly structured, carefully coordinated activities. As for the songs themselves, they were crafted to achieve broad appeal across classes, regions, and cultures. Initially, in the first decades of the song industry, common Victorian themes—such as hard work, loyalty, home, sexual inhibition, sobriety, and self-control—ran through many of the lyrics, and these familiar themes muted the impact of the profound and dramatic changes taking place. In this respect, the conservative lyrical content of popular songs was comparable to the use of melodrama in cinema in the same years; in both instances conventional, familiar themes and structures offset the radical novelty of the media.[96]

In 1911, however, with the infrastructure of the song business firmly in place, Ted Snyder, Inc., published a song by Irving Berlin that made the cultural break with the nineteenth century plainly audible. It was "Alexander's Ragtime Band," whose insistent chorus epitomized many of the developments in American musical culture:[97]

> Come on and hear! Come on and hear! Alexander's ragtime band!
> Come on and hear! Come on and hear! It's the best band in the land!

They can play a bugle call like you never heard before,
So natural that you want to go to war;
That's just the best-est band what am, ma honey lamb,
Come on along, come on along, let me take you by the hand,
Up to the man, up to the man, who's the leader of the band
And if you care to hear the Swanee River played in ragtime,
Come on and hear, come on and hear,
Alexander's Ragtime Band.

Like any great song, "Alexander's Ragtime Band" resonated on many levels at once. Its words and music laid claim to a connection between past and present—"And if you care to hear the Swanee River played in ragtime"—asserting the capacity of the modern music to absorb what had preceded it and positioning Berlin as the heir to Stephen Foster, the American pioneer of simple, accessible songwriting. Commercially, the song marked a watershed. On the basis of its success, Berlin expanded his professional activities into publishing, first with Ted Snyder and Henry Waterson (the latter a businessman who knew nothing of music and was almost completely deaf), then in his own eponymous firm.

The song also placed syncopated music based on African American rhythms, with all the attendant tensions and contradictions, squarely and permanently in the mainstream of American musical life. Berlin owed a great debt to the musicians who first cultivated ragtime, but this was not in itself significant: musicians borrow from one another as a matter of course, and Berlin's borrowing was filtered through his own remarkable talent. Indeed, his achievement was to mine and refashion a style of African American music for European American song forms, musical practices, and tastes. The result was an archetypal example of American cultural synthesis. Yet such syncretism did not necessarily take place on equal terms. "The best-est band what am" smacked of coon song dialect, and many listeners would have recognized Alexander as a common "darky" name, carrying undertones of the minstrel stage and the plantation. For African Americans, who did not enjoy the same social mobility as Berlin, this kind of cultural borrowing was never so simple: echoes of minstrelsy reinforced negative stereotypes; the three-dimensional richness of African American cultural life was rendered as two-dimensional burlesque; and financial rewards rarely seeped back to the source. At the same time, though, Berlin took ragtime seriously and his inventive appropriation rang with delight in ragtime and the well of creative energy that had produced it.

Like "After the Ball," published almost two decades earlier, "Alexander's Ragtime Band" featured an easily remembered melody, composed by a man who could neither read nor write music. The latter song bore witness, however, to how much had changed. The plaintive strains of "After the Ball" voiced regret and loss, whereas "Alexander's Ragtime Band" was the clarion call of a new musical age, and its lyrics and ragged meter were a conscious expression of the sound of popular music itself—"Come on and hear! Come on and hear!" With their staccato rhythm, repeated over and over in the chorus, these words are a double entendre in the purest sense, both referring to and enacting an aural phenomenon. Rhetorically, they refer to Alexander's band, but orally, they are self-referential, positioning Berlin's song (not Alexander's) as that which is to be listened to and sung along with. As befitted any good Tin Pan Alley song, a similar, less successful song by Berlin followed on its heels a few months later—"That Mysterious Rag." Again, the sound of popular music was, in effect, the subject of the song. "Are you listenin'? Are you listenin'?" runs the chorus; the verses describe a melody so infectious as to induce a mania in those hearing it.

2

Making Hits

The success of Tin Pan Alley in creating and popularizing a new musical idiom was reflected in the countless stories in daily newspapers, mainstream magazines, and the established music press. Many were unequivocally hostile. "One afternoon, when I was watering flowers in the back yard, a boy in the street whistled a tune that I had not heard before," a typical jeremiad began. "The infliction of that tune on my unwilling ears [infuriated me], not only because of its offensive vulgarity, but because there was something in the nature of that mephitic air [that is, song] that made me feel certain I should hear it a thousand times during the summer. And my prophetic soul divined the truth. In the course of a week or two every boy in town was whistling that tune, every other man humming it, and every tenth woman playing it on the piano." The critic then recounted how the song "ravage[d] the country like an epidemic."[1] Another writer deplored the disrespect shown to marriage and "sacred things" in the new music and attributed to it "the deterioration of taste, manners and even morals."[2] Others saved their most vituperative attacks specifically for ragtime (and later jazz), whose association with African Americans and dancing symbolized degeneration and dangerous sexual abandon, or made a point of redefining "music" in such a way as to efface the very existence of popular song.[3]

How should we understand these critiques with regard to the growing commercialization of music? The industrial character and peculiar social formation of Tin Pan Alley account for two of the biggest issues raised. To some ears, the regularity and standardized simplicity of popular songs degraded musical art, and some listeners found troubling the challenge popular song posed to existing hierarchies of race and class. But implicitly or explicitly, critics identified the seeming ubiquity of popular song, locally and nationally—its apparent inescapability—as one of its defining characteristics. And they were right. Tin Pan Alley aimed to reduce uncertainty not only in production but also in distribution, and to attain this goal publishers devised strategies and systems to control where, how, and how often their songs were heard. Vigorous competition in a musical free market was not the goal; making money was, and to achieve it publishers organized a managed market that reduced the risk and protected the investment of the best-capitalized firms. "With the established publishing houses, the work of making a demand for a musical composition has been put on a business basis," wrote Gilbert Tompkins in 1902. "Organization and capital have introduced systematic methods where much was formerly left to chance."[4]

More concretely, the successful creation of such a market depended on overcoming two serious obstacles. First, because many kinds of music were widely available already, publishers had to cultivate in consumers either a taste for more music in their lives, or for Tin Pan Alley songs over other options. Second, building a stable industry depended on high volume sales over time, not occasional flashes of activity, so producers had to promote a steady taste for the new among consumers. This was more than a challenge: it was almost counterintuitive. Older, familiar music had, and has, a durable, established appeal, which Tin Pan Alley needed to offset. By the turn of century, the standard classical repertoire was solidifying into the form that it has today, dominated by works from the mid-eighteenth to late nineteenth centuries and strongly resistant to additions and modifications. Meanwhile, folklore societies and "ballad hunters" were showing that many people were quite happy singing the same old songs year after year, generation after generation. (The popularity of "oldies" radio stations today suggests the same thing.) Thus, publishers set out to create and manage new kinds of music consumers, through an extensive personal and financial apparatus that commercialized public space as it consolidated private musical interests.

As the song industry grew, its strategies and apparatus for promoting its goods became more complex and expensive. Because prices remained stable and in some cases fell, music firms felt greater pressure to broaden the market for their low-cost products (a situation many other manufacturers confronted in the late nineteenth and early twentieth centuries as well). To a far greater degree than soap, shoes, or other mass-produced consumer goods, however, music constituted an important element in local and regional cultures, and the development of national markets undermined these. The large-scale promotion of popular song enlivened the soundscape and brought delightful new sounds into the lives of millions of people, but to some extent, this expansion of the music industry infringed on the limited social and cultural environments and psychic space people had available for making music and listening to it. The issue ultimately was not that the simple, fun, cheap, disposable songs of Tin Pan Alley were inherently pernicious, only that they developed in tandem with a promotional system whose tendency was to crowd out alternatives, a tendency that increased as competition within the industry grew. Music that was serious, complex, or demanding, noncommercial, or bound to local or regional identities and concerns—such music did not disappear, but it was forced to compete in the new musical culture with sounds deliberately crafted and promoted to capture as large a share of the public's attention as possible.

"The Din-Making Drove"

In Tin Pan Alley, what publishers understood was that no matter how clever, how catchy, how timely a song, its commercial and cultural impact depended on its system of distribution and exploitation: who heard the song and under what circumstances. No publisher claimed that a bad song could become a hit, but neither did any believe that a good song became a hit automatically, simply because it was good. Hits did not "just happen," publisher after publisher has explained; they were not essential, irrepressible expressions of the Zeitgeist. Hits were *made*. Indeed, in the music industry's slang, to "make" a song referred not to songwriting but to building a song's popularity.[5]

Before the Tin Pan Alley era, the business of music publishing consisted of little more than printing music and selling it to jobbers, retailers, or consumers directly. Isaac Goldberg characterized pre-1893 music publishing as "passive," "sporadic," and lacking technique, and when large sales occurred, it was "the will of God rather than the will of the publisher." Occasionally some songs did achieve widespread popularity—Stephen Foster's, for example—but it was as a result of happenstance or word of mouth. In the 1890s, however, when publishers became increasingly aware of the potential to cultivate markets by reaching out to consumers, the marketing of songs was turned on its head: no longer would "the public [come] to the song"; henceforth, Goldberg noted, "the song would be sent out to pursue the public."[6]

A song's popularity was built through the process known as plugging. This the publisher Edward Marks defined as "any public performance which is designed to boost sales," but in practice it meant any public performance at all. "A plug's a plug," an industry saying went, meaning that every plug helped and any plug was better than none at all. In effect, successful plugging was an inexact science in which specific experiments mattered less than the number and range of trials overall. "True," Edward Marks acknowledged in his memoir, "we didn't know how many copies any particular public performance helped us sell, but we found a rough relation between the number and variety of plugs we could get for a [song], and its subsequent sale."[7] Although the precise origins of the term *plugging* are obscure, its usage in Tin Pan Alley echoes the word's general meaning. In everyday parlance, to *plug* means to *block* or *fill*—a hole, for instance; in the case of Tin Pan Alley, the hole to be filled was any uncommercialized public space or absence of music in the soundscape.

Underlying song plugging was the basic fact that publishers at that time made their money from selling objects (sheet music) that represented something intangible and ephemeral (sounds). To make sheet music more attractive, nineteenth-century music publishers began to pay more attention to its aesthetic appeal as an object. In the 1820s, pictures and vignettes on title pages started to enhance the visual allure of sheet music, and scores were sometimes printed on pink or light blue paper, to attract female consumers. In at least one instance, publishers even tried to increase the olfactory appeal, by using perfumed paper. Over the course of the century, especially with the advent of chromolithographic printing in the 1840s, the images on the title pages of sheet music became an important part of the visual culture of the nation, and indeed, some of the leading visual artists of the century illustrated sheet music covers for a time, including James Abbott McNeill Whistler, Winslow Homer, and Thomas Nast.[8]

Tin Pan Alley's sheet music also featured elaborate pictorial design, but by the 1890s, publishers had begun to focus on promoting the invisible, intangible sounds of the music. Unlike the leaders of the phonograph record industry, which was developing in the same years, Tin Pan Alley never relied on the external expertise of professional advertising firms, for song plugging bypassed the need for them. Indeed, promoting songs by any means possible, wherever and whenever possible, plugging *was* professional advertising, because the songs literally were advertisements for themselves.

Tin Pan Alley could not create a market, however, for its peculiar kind of goods—popular songs—without the active approval and participation of consumers. They had to do more than tolerate Tin Pan Alley's entry into the music market; they had to enjoy and desire Tin Pan Alley's goods over the alternatives. To achieve this end, publishers had to convert consumers to new ideas about musical experience, which in turn altered the very nature of the public performance of music and blurred the line between advertising and entertainment. Thus, one of the many innovative elements of Tin Pan Alley was the balance it struck between producer-planned consumption and consumer-influenced production, and ultimately between pleasure and coercion. More or less in keeping with P. T. Barnum's "humbug" principle, consumers may have realized that Tin Pan Alley's song pluggers were taking them for a ride, but if they liked a song enough, they did not mind going along as willing accomplices.[9]

Plugging was a two-stage process, moving from local markets to national, and from direct appeals by publishing firms to indirect appeals by surrogates. Each succeeding stage was a test, hinging on audiences' (read, "consumers'") reactions to the song. If they liked it, it proceeded to the next stage, culminating in a national push through the theatrical circuits of vaudeville, all of which could take many months. A given publishing house promoted several songs simultaneously, but these were prioritized, the greatest concentration of energy, resources, and personnel being devoted to the "Number One Plug," of which a major publisher might have as few as two per year.[10] And every year, the onus fell on publishers to excite audiences anew, recasting last season's hit as outmoded and superfluous.

With a new song in hand, they began the plugging process by "trying it on the dog"—that is, testing a song's potential before attempting to exploit it broadly. This started with the printing of five thousand or more copies of a "professional" edition of a song, printed on the cheapest pulpy paper, without artwork. Next, local performers were enlisted to try out the song before the public. For publishers, this was the first check of a song's potential; for musicians, it was a chance to try out the latest numbers. Irving Berlin later recalled the status that accrued to these sheets when he was starting out. "I used to come up from Chinatown where I worked as a singing waiter, to a brownstone building on 28th Street to get the free professional copies from the Leo Feist Publishing Co. Those white professional copies were a status symbol. They made a Bowery busker feel like a real professional singer."[11]

If, according to the performers' feedback, audiences had responded well to the song, the publisher printed trade copies on better paper and with cover artwork, and the real plugging—to *generate* interest in the song—began. The publisher might then sell a thousand or more copies to the trade, generally at a reduced rate, to test the reaction of actual buyers. Many publishers had contracts with small dealers, stipulating that dealers would buy, say, two copies of every new song the publisher issued. Purchased at a reduced rate, these new songs gave dealers an incentive, in the form of a higher profit margin, to sell the newer tunes in preference to older ones. In this way, publishers used the leverage they had with dealers (namely, contracts on which the dealers were dependent) to have them push the latest songs, month after month.[12] Decent sales from this first push to the dealers would lead to the first advertisements in trade publications (aimed both at jobbers and dealers and at performers) and to the distribution of free copies to as many professional singers as possible. These preliminaries launched the next phase, of more aggressive, direct plugging, meaning, more than anything else, relentless live promotion of the song.

For this work, publishers hired young, talented men to push their material in public. These were the "pluggers," and among their ranks at one time or another figured many of Tin Pan Alley's leading lights, including George Gershwin, Jerome Kern, Richard Rodgers, and Vincent Youmans. As one publisher put it, a plugger had to use any means available "to reach the largest possible listening audience with the best song, under the best circumstances, with the best interpretation"—but this succinct description gives no intimation of the ingenious, freewheeling, and wildly diverse tactics publishers and pluggers employed.[13] Live plugging had an air of fun about it— this was, after all, the entertainment business—and to be successful, pluggers had to be energetic and charismatic. Producing "the best song" was the responsibility of the publisher and the songwriter, but the burden of giving "the best interpretation," and in "the best circumstances," fell on the plugger, who was, in effect, a professional entertainer.

Personal appearances took place anywhere and everywhere pluggers could find people to listen to them. They sang at baseball and football games and racetracks and prizefights, in public parks, and at Ivy League dances. In at least one case, pluggers plugged at Sing-Sing Prison, and in at least one other, at a nudist colony on Long Island.[14] They plugged songs on riverboats and in the aisles of New York's elevated trains. Sometimes, one plugger recalled, they sang out of the back of a rented horse-drawn wagon, which was furnished with a piano for the occasion. They also sang at political rallies, where politicians welcomed them as a way to entertain voters.[15] During World War I, pluggers appeared at training camps and in factories. As the plugger Robert Miller recalled, they sang for "shirtwaist factories, lumberjacks, pants pressers—anything and everything. The government insisted on the workers having an hour of relaxation, and again the song pluggers were there." In general, Miller emphasized, "I sang every place and everything that you can think of to make songs for the firm that I represented. You can use me as an illustration of what two or three hundred [other] guys throughout the United States did as well."[16]

Pluggers usually worked in pairs, composed of a singer and a pianist, arming themselves on their excursions with a megaphone and sheaves of chorus slips—small pieces of paper on which were printed the lyrics to the choruses of the songs being plugged, along with the title and publisher of the song. Pluggers passed out chorus slips whenever they performed, and in almost all cases they tried to induce audiences to sing along with the chorus, a practice borrowed from the English music halls. Successful plugging, then, did not consist only of giving a winning rendition of a song; it required audiences' willing and active participation. Meanwhile, the chorus slips served a dual purpose: they enabled audiences to sing along with the chorus and allowed listeners to join in; and they left the members of the audience with a record of the title and publisher of the song. Dependent on audience involvement, suc-

The Great "Trench" and "Camp" Song

There's A Long, Long Trail

Lyric by
STODDARD KING

Music by
ZO. ELLIOT

CHORUS.

There's a long, long trail a-winding
Into the land of my dreams.
Where the nightingales are singing
And white moon beams;
There's a long, long night of waiting
Until my dreams all come true;
Till the day when I'll be going down
That long, long trail with you.

Copyright MCMXVII by M. WITMARK & SONS

"NEW PLATTSBURGH CHORUS"

—FOR—

There's A Long Long Trail

CHORUS

There's a long, long trail a-winding
Into No-man's Land in France
Where the shrapnel shells are bursting,
But we must advance.
There'll be lots of drills and hiking
Until our dreams all come true.
But we're going to show the Kaiser
How the Yankee boys come through.

M. WITMARK & SONS, Publishers New York

2.1 Wherever song pluggers performed, they passed around chorus slips like this one, which helped people sing along with the chorus and left them with a memento of the title, the chorus, and the publisher of the song. Warshaw Collection of Business Americana—Music, Archives Center, National Museum of American History, Behring Center, Smithsonian Institution.

cessful plugging was a dynamic, interactive process, shaped by the rapport the plugger established with his listeners. The success of this process reflects how inclined audiences were at that time to participate and interact with performers, in ways that became exceedingly rare after the introduction of radio in the 1920s.[17]

Although plugging could take place anywhere, pluggers' most important and regular locales were music and department stores, nickelodeons and later movie houses, and restaurants, cafés, and dance halls. A plugger's typical day began around ten o'clock in the morning at the publisher's office, where he picked up bundles of chorus slips and sheet music, for a day of performances in large retail stores. In the mid-1890s New York's famous Siegel-Cooper's, on the corner of Eighteenth Street and Sixth Avenue, was the first department store to install a music counter. Macy's and other department stores soon followed suit, but Siegel-Cooper's remained the largest and best-known music counter in New York. In the big department stores and in five-and-dimes, pluggers performed "demonstrations" of their latest songs, normally at an assigned time, scheduled to avoid conflicts between firms. As Adolph Olman recalled, "At Siegel-Cooper's they'd have at least ten publishers represented there, at one time. The counter was at least 70 or 80 feet long, and there would be a relay of two or three or four pianists. . . . There was one piano. When one pianist played an hour, the next one would come on. But all publishers had their turn singing."[18] Thus, although they probably vied for the most favorable time slots, competition among the pluggers took place in an ordered and organized fashion, as it filled the shopping environment with the exuberant sounds of popular song.

To maximize sales in the stores, a plugger often bribed the salesgirls to push his publisher's songs after a plugging "demonstration." Typical was the experience of Benny Bloom, a plugger for Jerome H. Remick and onetime plugging partner of George Gershwin. As detailed by Hazel Meyer, the greatest chronicler of the Alley's tricks of the trade, at Siegel-Cooper's Bloom would give the counter girls some inexpensive perfume from F. W. Woolworth right before his assigned time to play. This perfume, Meyer wrote, "was always a good investment, for a customer frequently tossed a half dollar on the counter and said, 'Give me six of the latest.' Gratefully remembering Benny's little gift, salesgirls would push six Remick tunes toward the customer. When Benny wasn't there, they'd do the same for Witmark tunes, or Harms, or Shapiro-Bernstein. All the pluggers knew the Woolworth perfume bit."[19] Thus, even under-the-table payments by pluggers achieved a level of standardization. A few years later, the publication of "Ain't My Baby Grand?" attested to the close relationship between (male) pluggers and (female) retail employees. "Dedicated to the Girl behind the Music Counter," the cover of the sheet music read, an oblique bid for the salesgirls' favor and by extension their commercial assistance.[20]

In the evening, from seven until ten o'clock, plugging moved to the theaters, nickelodeons, and eventually movie houses. There, the singer and pianist performed before the regular show and probably again during intermission, and to supplement the plugging visually, the music was often accompanied by "song slides." These hand-colored photographic slides illustrated the narrative or pictorial elements of the lyrics and were projected on a large screen behind the pluggers while they performed. Everything was coordinated with the house projectionist, who probably received some premium for his cooperation. Of course, virtually all of the theaters and movie houses had pianos for the accompaniment of stage performers and silent films. On a good night, an average plugger could reach ten movie houses, or approximately five thousand people. For their part, audiences usually enjoyed the pluggers' performances and viewed them as free additional entertainment.[21]

The "chief electrician" at a Brooklyn theater was said to have devised the first song slides in 1892, and Edward Marks and Joseph Stern initiated their commercial use in 1894 to promote their song "The Little Lost Child." The slides proved extremely effective and soon caught on among other publishers as well. Despite the extra expense, publishers found slides a powerful promotional tool and soon began to include a set of ten to twenty slides with their promotional copies of sheet music. Not only did song slides increase the volume of sales, but the images helped establish a song's popularity more readily. Charles K. Harris found "it was the easiest way to popularize a ballad before the phonograph, player-piano, and radio came into existence. . . . Often within a week after the distribution of the sets of slides to the profession, a song would become a success."[22]

To enhance the realism and associative power of a song, the photographs

2.2 With its dedication "to the girl behind the music counter," this sheet music cover flattered the young female employees on whom the sale of a publisher's music ultimately depended. Song pluggers had other tactics as well, such as presenting shopgirls with small gifts. "Ain't My Baby Grand," written by Lew Brown, Robert King, and Ray Henderson; used by permission of Shapiro, Bernstein & Co., Inc.; courtesy of the Lester S. Levy Collection of Sheet Music, Special Collections, Sheridan Libraries, Johns Hopkins University.

were usually shot on location. "The Little Lost Child," for example, included shots from inside an actual police station. Charles K. Harris boasted that he sent photographers to destinations as far-flung as California, Texas, Alaska, and even the Philippines for his song slides. As advertisements for a song, the slides became even more effective after the introduction of the chorus slide, which displayed the lyrics of the chorus and, just as chorus slips did, enabled the audience to sing along. Vaudeville singers used chorus slides in their performances, and pluggers used them when they performed in movie houses (after the turn of the century). Meanwhile, publishers who could not afford to produce their own sets of original negatives (which might cost as much as $1,500) could purchase stock images for their song lyrics from the ancillary slide supply industry that sprang up.

If illustrated covers of sheet music had begun to create a visual language for popular music, song slides expanded that language. Even more than sheet music covers, the slides made popular songs visual spectacles as much as musical compositions—almost ninety years before the first video aired on MTV. Music and sound were still the focus, but these elusive commodities were easier to sell when they were wrapped up in visual associations and linked to visual referents. E. M. Wickes, an author of songwriting how-to manuals, tellingly described the slides: "They vivify the story and save an audience the mental effort of imagining scenes and actions." Moreover, this visual element came to shape the way songs were written as well. Some song-writers composed with pictorial content in mind; according to Wickes, "Very often persons request to have certain songs sung because they are accompanied by pretty pictures."[23]

For a time, song plugging with song slides and the new medium of cinema overlapped, but use of the slides fell off sharply in the mid-1910s. In a sense, however, their decline had begun a decade earlier with the birth of narrative cinema and the emergence of nickelodeons. The publishers considered early, prenarrative cinema to be little more than a novelty, and in Edward Marks's words it "had lulled the Tin Pan Alley wise guys into a securely derisive attitude."[24] Ultimately, they failed to foresee that audiences would soon look elsewhere for their visual narratives. By the time the complex and visually sophisticated films of D. W. Griffith, Cecil B. DeMille, and others, came out in the 1910s, song slides and their trite stories no longer held much sway

2.3 A precursor to MTV videos, illustrated song slides created a fanciful, often dream-like visual accompaniment for a song—in this case, Harry Williams and Egbert Van Al-styne's "That Slippery Slide Trombone" (1912). A typical set of glass slides included around a dozen original images, the first of which depicted the sheet music cover. An-other (not shown) showed the words of the chorus, to encourage audience members to join in the singing. Music Division, New York Public Library for the Performing Arts, Astor, Lenox and Tilden Foundations.

over viewers. Moreover, these longer films left no time for songs to be inserted into a program as short one-reelers had.

In vaudeville theatres or other venues where singers may already have been performing the pluggers' songs, pluggers themselves did not generally perform. Instead, their work consisted of planting paid boosters in the crowd in hopes of inciting the audience to join in the singing. If one person or a few in the audience stood up "spontaneously" and applauded or sang along when a certain song was performed on stage, Charles K. Harris estimated, "the rest of the audience would surely follow." Although Harris claimed to have devised this scheme himself, he exaggerated the novelty of employing paid plants to support a performance or product. The use of claques dated back to ancient Rome, and they were a staple of the nineteenth-century European opera world. Meanwhile, medicine shows in the United States and elsewhere also made paid plants, calculated to distort the line between seller and buyer, a stock feature in their repertoire of chicanery. Indeed, except for song slides, many industry methods of plugging predated the Tin Pan Alley era; Tin Pan Alley's innovation lay in the systematic and unrelenting way they were implemented, and Harris certainly was one of the first to use paid plants systematically to sell music.[25]

In fact, so extensively did he and other publishers exploit the plants that they soon became a commonplace. A practice that had been stealthy at the outset now appeared conspicuous and humorous—part of the Barnumesque humbug—even to the point of inspiring a song about a plant, "A Singer in the Gallery," published by M. Witmark and Sons in 1895. In some cases, the plugger himself infiltrated the audience; in others he employed an endearing young boy, recruited off the street or out of a Lower East Side synagogue.[26] By the early twentieth century, some contemporaries found the song claques in New York theaters "unbearable." At that time, an audience's (or claque's) enthusiastic response to a number could elicit multiple encores of a chorus or a whole song, which could occasionally be quite disruptive. One *New York Telegraph* writer complained, "First nights are made hideous by so-called 'pluggers' intent on pounding a song into popularity. Audiences are powerless against them. The din-making drove distributes itself judiciously about the theatre and waits its time. The merit of the song makes no difference. Once may be enough for you, but not for the claque. It loves the song for what it is worth in dollars and cents, and whether you like it or not you are compelled to hear it over and over again." Moreover, shows featuring songs by different publishing firms magnified this effect, for each firm would send its own pluggers and they, in turn, endeavored to "outplug" one another.[27]

After the theaters, plugging continued deep into the night at numerous ca-fés and dance halls, where the pluggers either themselves performed or hustled to have their tunes played by a house orchestra. They finished between one and four in the morning. Dinner clubs, featuring music throughout the dinner hours, first appeared in 1907, and a surge in interest in social dancing further reshaped nightlife in the 1910s.[28] These two fashions increased the demand for popular music—and the number of potential plugs, which grew even more when pluggers began using automobiles to travel from one venue to another. On their excursions, pluggers from one house found that their paths often intersected with those of pluggers from other houses, but as with competition at the music counters, these interactions were orderly and good-natured in most instances. As Adolph Olman remarked, "If three or four pluggers got into the same place at the same time, we all took our turns." In the summer, when much of the entertainment life of New York moved out to Coney Island, the pluggers followed. Olman recalled, "There must have been forty places to cover a night. . . . There'd be thousands on the floor, and you'd be up in the balcony up there with a little orchestra and singing through this tremendous megaphone."[29]

Some music halls, such as the Alhambra on Fourteenth Street, had a house orchestra and did not permit pluggers to perform. There, a plugger entreated the orchestra to play his song by buying drinks for all the musicians on the bandstand. This practice could prove costly with a twenty-six-piece ensemble, but the Alhambra's popularity among out-of-towners made it a particularly valuable plug. It "carried [our songs] out to the sticks in the subconsciousness of a tipsy country cousin," Edward Marks explained. Thus, a good performance of a song there could boost sales nationally. Before the era of coast-to-coast vaudeville circuits, the travelers who visited New York and returned home with new songs in their heads or sheet music in their bags served as publishers' unwitting distribution agents.[30]

More than just energy and charisma, however, effective plugging required unremitting persistence (to say nothing of physical endurance). Perhaps no statement reveals as much about the relentless, heavy-handed nature of plugging as the following reminiscence of publisher Louis Bernstein: "During the bicycle races [at Madison Square Garden] we'd have a pianist and singer with a large horn—where they had 20,000 people there—we'd sing a song to them thirty or forty times a night. And the result was that when the people walked out of there they'd be singing the song. They couldn't help it; it was forced down their throat. They'd cheer, and they'd yell, and they'd boo, but we kept pounding away at them. We made songs that way." With the audiences cheering, yelling, and booing, pluggers succeeded in familiarizing them with their songs regardless of the audience members' enthusiasm or interest. An account of plugging strategy by Edward Marks, who claimed he frequented sixty clubs a week in the 1890s, confirms the brutal impression of plugging left by Bernstein's remembrance. Marks also, however, alluding to the women in the audience, implicitly acknowledged the crucial importance of female consumers: "I wanted to get there [to the Atlantic Gardens on the Bowery] before the family crowd went home to put the kids to bed. Louis the Whistler always went with me. Under his arm he carried a bundle of chorus slips, which we distributed among the tables, so that everybody could sing with the orchestra. When there was a real [in other words, professional] singer in the joint, we induced him to sing a solo chorus. Then Louis whistled a second chorus. Finally, we tried to get the crowd in on a third. By the time we were through, our classic was firmly planted in as many domes as were within hearing distance."[31] The ubiquitous chorus slips, the element of a gimmick (performance whistling), the professional endorsement, and above all, the repetition of the chorus—here were many of the most widely used tactics of plugging. All the while, winning over the women ("the family crowd") to a new song was the biggest goal, for they were the consumers most likely to sing it or play it on the piano.

"In the summer of 1918, . . . I came to a music store on South State Street [in Chicago]," the pianist Lil Hardin recalled. "I stopped and gazed at all the sheet music in the window display, wishing I had every one of them, but knowing how impossible that was, I decided to go in and buy one that I had heard so many people whistling on the street."[32] This recollection suggests the way many people must have experienced the new musical culture, although these kinds of minute reactions rarely get recorded. What Hardin's remarks do not indicate are the complex ways that a song came to be whistled on the street in the manner she heard. The work of pluggers and claques was part of this, but the publishers' arsenal contained one other weapon as well: street musicians. Although the business of street music remains one of the least-documented parts of the industry, according to Theodore Dreiser, writing in 1898, publishers worked closely with the manufacturers of the "barrels" that produced music in barrel organs, piano-organs, and street pianos, and with the instruments' owners, to ensure that these mechanical devices were furnished with the latest songs. Pluggers, in turn, paid the operators of the street instruments to play outside a theater after a performance featuring the song the plugger was pushing. In effect, street musicians commercialized the space outside the theater as plants and paid performers were commercializing it inside. Almost all published accounts expressed nothing but scorn for street musicians, yet they persisted in cities around the United States and abroad until the 1910s (and later in some places). Meanwhile, complaints about urban noise attested to their impact. In "The Plague of City Noises," for example, Dr. J. H. Girdner listed street musicians among the "public nuisances" that contributed substantially to the "painful and injurious effect of city noise on the whole nervous system."[33]

Making music on the street was hardly new in the late nineteenth century, but in conjunction with Tin Pan Alley's other promotional sites—from ballgames and bicycle races to department stores and five-and-dimes to cafés and movie houses—street musicians reinforced the music publishers' broad environmental impact. Tin Pan Alley did not simply furnish music in places where earlier there had been none; it reordered these spaces, aurally, to suit its advertising needs. Later, in the 1930s, protests erupted over advertising on radio, which listeners viewed as a commercial incursion into the private, noncommercial spaces of their homes.[34] History records very few protests, however, against the music business's initiatives. In part, the lack of complaint can probably be explained by the growing commercialism of public spaces generally at the turn of the century, of which music was only a single, invisible part. More important, though, was that the music business trafficked in commodities to entertain, and it worked hard to ensure consumers would welcome the novelty and sentiment into their daily lives.

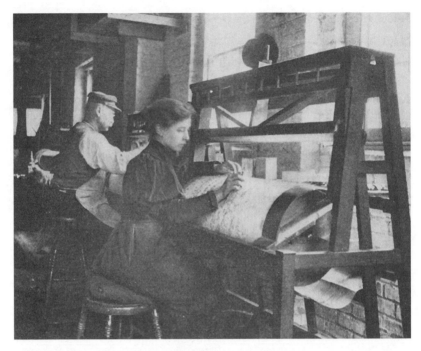

2.4 To fill the streets with their songs, publishers sometimes worked with the manufacturers of barrels for automatic street pianos and barrel organs. Here, a woman makes holes for pins that correspond to the individual notes a barrel organ would play. *Metropolitan Magazine,* Nov. 1898, courtesy of the Library of Congress.

The intensity of Tin Pan Alley's focus on plugging—on promotion through sound—is also suggested by the relative modesty of the industry's use of print advertising. On the one hand, publishers did run notices in the trade press aimed at jobbers, dealers, and performers, and advertisements aimed at consumers appeared on the back or inside cover of sheet music. But compared with piano manufacturers or the phonograph companies, the industry had little involvement with print advertising. The House of Witmark looked down on this means of publicity as crass and unbecoming, and a few firms' experiments with high-profile print advertising were ineffectual.[35] Of all the major publishers, Leo Feist was the most attuned to the use of mass print media. In return for royalty payments, he arranged to have some of his songs mentioned in comic strips in Hearst newspapers and had the choruses reprinted there as well. Occasionally, he arranged for newspapers to write feature stories about a song, and *Printer's Ink*, the advertising trade organ, voted his firm's slogan, "You Can't Go Wrong with a Feist Song," one of the fifty best-known slogans in advertising. In 1908 a controversy over Feist's having planted a newspaper story about his song "Get on the Raft with Taft" swelled his reputation as a master strategist. "What Leo Feist . . . does not know about the science of advertising is hardly worth while knowing," the *Music Trade Review* wrote, "as was demonstrated when he managed to obtain a colossal amount of free publicity by a scheme which would have done credit to any press agent in the country."[36]

Publishers understood, therefore, that the distribution and popularization of songs could be transformed by means that were ready to hand, based primarily on organization and drive. Except for the song slides, plugging was technologically quite simple. There were no public address systems, no electrical microphones, and in the early years, no automobiles. Until the 1910s, the promotion of sheet music had little to do with phonograph records and player-piano rolls, for until 1909 publishers received no royalty on mechanical reproductions of their music. Still, song plugging altered people's social and aural experience of music—the places and circumstances in which music entered their lives and brought pleasure into them. Plugging, however, in its emphasis on novelty and consumption, also changed the nature of that musical experience. These songs existed to be sold, and in many contexts, hearing them was akin to hearing a catchy advertisement presented by a charismatic pitchman. Here was the music business in miniature: the hard sell cloaked in carefree entertainment.

Department stores, which were often at the forefront of twentieth-century consumer capitalism, were particularly attuned to music's commercial utility. As early as 1876 John Wanamaker used an organ at his "Great Depot" to lead customers and employees in song, and by the 1890s merchants were staging musical spectacles, often on the stores' uppermost floors, to attract people not just to their stores but deep within their commerical spaces. Department stores celebrated big events and holidays with musical concerts, as well as arranging music lectures by prominent critics and public appearances by well-known artists, the grandest example of which was probably Richard Strauss's two concerts at Wanamaker's in New York in 1904. Meanwhile, as

2.5a–b These pictures show two views of music at the Wanamaker store in Philadelphia. At top, Leopold Stokowski, center, conducts the Philadelphia Orchestra in 1920 in front of the world's largest pipe organ, installed in the store's Grand Court in 1908. On either side of Stokowski stand guest organists Pietro Yon (left) and Charles M. Courboin (right). At bottom, the store's Egyptian Hall was used as both a piano salesroom and an auditorium for concerts and educational lectures. It had a separate, more modest pipe organ than the one in the Grand Court, a stage deep enough to hold a chorus of five hundred singers, and enough floor space to seat an audience of fourteen hundred persons. John Wanamaker Collection, Historical Society of Pennsylvania.

song pluggers created a cabaret-like atmosphere at the music counters, the large stores provided music on the sales floor as well, which many merchants believed a great benefit to employee morale as well as a boost to shoppers. Often concealed behind screens like backdrops, small groups, individual musicians, or phonographs contributed to the ways commerce drew on the conventions of theatrical spectacle. In some cases, the interpenetration of music and merchandise promoted store sales generally; in others it aimed specifically to enhance the music trade. Responding to a rise in piano sales at department stores, the *Dry Goods Economist,* the leading trade journal for large retailers, reported in 1902 that consumers apparently "delighted" in being able to buy pianos as they would "spool cotton or yard muslin."[37]

One of the principal goals and effects of playing music in the department stores was to ease women's experience in the new commercial environment of the emporium. As a feminine staple of Victorian home life, music was a means to make women feel comfortable and enjoy themselves in department stores. Linking spectacle to cultural enrichment helped the stores achieve this end. Indeed, department stores' commitment to music was perhaps most visible in the auditoriums and concert halls that one store after another built between 1900 and 1920, and in the full-time music directors some hired to oversee musical offerings. In New York the largest included Lord & Taylor, Gimbels, Siegel-Cooper's, and, of course, Wanamaker's (in Philadelphia too). Even stores in smaller cities frequently set aside a special area for musical programs.[38] Although these performances appealed to consumers' sense of cultural enrichment, Wanamaker's concert director G. A. Russell left no doubt as to their design. "Please don't regard me as wishing to picture our place as a philanthropic institution," Russell told *Musical America.* "The aim of Mr. Wanamaker and of M. J. Chapman, manager of the piano department, has been to entertain and educate the public, not only to create a strong appetite for good music, but to improve the desire for it."[39] Thus, department stores used music to further sales of pianos and other music merchandise, as at least one female consumer acknowledged. "The public accepts" auditoriums and concerts in department stores, one woman noted in 1915, "[but] I do not believe it demands [them]." Indeed, music was a means to lure shoppers inside and create an environment that seemed edifying in a way that the crudeness of commerce might not be.[40]

Tin Pan Alley was not directly responsible for many of department stores' musical initiatives, but the stores' use of music complemented Tin Pan Alley's song plugging. Like Tin Pan Alley, department stores used music and the aural environment to promote business. Consequently, the experience of music increasingly became inseparable from the structure and operations of musical commerce. Particularly in urban areas, these commercial musical innovations contributed to a changing soundscape in which the dominant music was the sound of money.

Whether it came from live song pluggers, organ grinders, or department stores, music rang out across the soundscape as it never had before. Certainly, not all within earshot bought every song they heard; if they had, every new number would have been a hit. For the growth of the new musical culture, what mattered most was the infusion of music into an ever-greater range of aural environments. This proliferation of music produced new musical associations in people's lives, new affinities, and especially new expectations, all suggesting that music was an integral part of all aspects of modern life. From serious to silly, the range of moods music could express greatly augmented the number of applications to which it could be put. The sing-along, because of the dynamic interaction it required, played a particularly important role. In the surge of public entertainments in the late nineteenth and early twentieth centuries, including restaurants, dance halls, vaudeville houses, and amusement parks, the sing-along was a familiar occurrence, one that people looked forward to and enjoyed. Regardless whether a sing-along was initiated by a song plugger, audience members who sang along did more than respond to the publishers' bidding. They made music as a group, coming together in a shared social experience. Publishers' marketing strategies notwithstanding, for those who sang along with a thousand choruses, group singing had a more complex significance. As music resounded in more and more environments, sing-alongs involved individuals in a pleasurable, if fleeting, collective process, transcending their identities as individual, unconnected consumers.

Making Hits National

Complementing the methods of Tin Pan Alley to promote songs locally was the development of a system to create and manage markets for its songs nationally, through minstrel shows and vaudeville, thereby extending the commercialization of the soundscape from coast to coast. Before 1900 only minstrel shows had the reach and appeal to spread a song around the country with any degree of effectiveness, and Tin Pan Alley publishers did all they could to exploit this potential. Taking a cue from the circus and the showmanship of P. T. Barnum, one of minstrel troupes' standard practices was the daily "11:45 parade" through the middle of whatever town a troupe was in, to publicize and generate excitement about the show. After the parade, performers routinely sold copies of the music they performed, just as they would to theater audiences at the end of a stage show. With this potential outlet to far-flung consumers, publishers began to employ minstrel troupes' musical directors as unofficial sales agents—in a sense, an extension of enlisting the help of the salesgirls at music counters. Usually payment consisted of a commission on the sheet music the troupe sold, which gave the musical director an incentive to plug that publisher's songs in the show. This arrangement proved so effective for Edward Marks and Joseph Stern that they recruited through the trade magazines "all kinds of burlesque performers, minstrel men, and even medicine show doctors to sell our soul-food on commission."[41]

Publishers also valued and actively sought vaudevillians' adoption of their songs, but before 1900, vaudeville was too unstructured and immature a mechanism for promoting songs widely and systematically. In the 1870s and 1880s New York's biggest vaudeville and variety houses, such as Pastor's and Koster and Bial's, operated individually, unconnected with any larger network of theaters, and booked acts on an ad hoc basis, week to week, rather than by the season. Many performers did travel, but they secured out-of-town engagements by writing letters to theater managers or relying on the help of friends, not through an industry-wide network. Paralleling the managerial shift in Tin Pan Alley, however, vaudeville began in the 1890s, through the agency of Keith and Albee and other impresarios, to organize vaudeville theaters around the country into circuits. Eliminating one of early vaudeville's persistent problems, inconsistent quality, the integrated network of theaters introduced centralized booking, standardizing the shows for all the theaters in the circuit for the whole season.[42]

The vaudeville circuits were divided into two tiers, "big time" and "small time," both of which served important functions in selling songs in the era before radio. The big time featured the more expensive and prestigious performers in more lavish theaters. The greatest of the big-time circuits, Keith and Albee's, included four hundred theaters in the East and the Midwest by 1914. Other important circuits included Martin Beck's Orpheum Circuit, based in San Francisco, and after 1906, the Western Vaudeville Association, based in Chicago and directed by Beck and John J. Murdock. Small time, by contrast, was cheaper, and it generally relied on performers who were on their way up or their way down in their careers. Its value for Tin Pan Alley was its geographical penetration beyond the big and medium-sized cities. The Sun Circuit, for example, comprised two hundred theaters, mostly in small towns, in Ohio, Pennsylvania, and adjoining states, by 1909. From that time until the decline of vaudeville in the late 1920s, the vaudeville stage offered Tin Pan Alley publishers a carefully administered, highly centralized, multi-tiered network through which songs could be funneled to truly national markets and national hits could be created.[43]

Like George Eastman's Kodak cameras or Henry Ford's automobiles, Keith and Albee's vaudeville shows became known for high, standardized quality at an affordable price. Their shows also brought to vaudeville a level of professionalism and organizational sophistication unlike anything known earlier in traveling entertainment. Nicknamed the "Sunday School Circuit," their performances were wholesome enough to be suitable for any audience, anywhere. Sending good, clean acts on the road was part of Keith and Albee's success, but equally important was their rationalized central administration and systematized policing of weak or inappropriate material. They began with booking agents who knew the theaters and the managers around the country and could book acts to suit them. Moreover, theater managers on the circuits then sent back weekly reports to the Keith and Albee offices on the popularity and suitability of different acts. When a manager filed a report about an act that was inferior, indecent, or improper, that act was either cleaned up or eliminated. This system of quality control, therefore, allowed the home office to standardize shows and avoid problematic fluctuation on the road.[44]

Traveling the country for up to forty-two weeks a year, vaudeville performers had the unique ability, in the era before radio, to spread songs systematically across the country. No similar network for mass distribution existed at that time, and publishers used it to turn popular song into a truly national industry. For the publishers of Tin Pan Alley, however, vaudeville's emergence as "a national industry" was not without tradeoffs. On the one hand, vaudeville offered vastly expanded opportunities for plugging and for expansion of the business. In addition to the growing number of vocal and instrumental performances, many other acts required some kind of background music, which publishers also supplied. "Every branch of vaudeville afforded valuable plugs if you knew how to get them," Marks explained. "The music to which the acrobat swung through the air in the opening act, or to which the juggler synchronized the click of celluloid balls on his dome in the two-spot, might stick in the auditor's mind. So also might the waltz to which the high school horse paraded across the then monster stage of the Hippodrome on Sixth Avenue."[45]

On the other hand, the vaudeville circuits diminished publishers' direct, hands-on control and forced them to hire increasingly large "professional" staffs to attract and rehearse performers. Furthermore, plugging on this scale required substantially more capital, a factor that favored the bigger, more established publishing firms and produced, by the 1900s and 1910s, a consolidated national economy that was qualitatively different from the one that had existed a few years earlier. Gone were "the days when the publisher knew every variety [and vaudeville] favorite personally," Marks noted, "and insured singing of his numbers by visiting them in their dressing rooms . . . or treating [them] to pig's knuckles after the show." With so many acts roving the country, the work of having songs placed in the shows of traveling performers now fell on specialized managers and "professional" or "outside" men (so called because their responsibility was to get a song sung by professional performers) and required publishers to set up branch offices around the country to recruit, train, and supervise performers on the road. The Witmarks had probably been the first Tin Pan Alley firm to establish an out-of-town bureau when they enlisted their old friend (and future U.S. congressman) Sol Bloom to run their Chicago office in 1893. Chicago, with its many vaudeville theaters, movie houses, and restaurants and as the starting point for shows traveling through the Midwest, was crucial to the creation of an integrated national market. For a time, the industry veteran Rocco Vocco recalled, "Chicago was the most active place in the country. . . . We could 'make' a song very fast [there]." Louis Bernstein recalled that his firm, Shapiro, Bernstein & Co., had fifteen to eighteen different offices around the country "to maintain contact" with people in the various amusement industries and to ensure that "when we got a song [in a traveling show] . . . somebody [namely, another publisher] didn't jump in and take our song out and substitute" one of his own. Ultimately, Marks concluded, "The expense of professional copies, orchestrations, and professional staffs was great, but the investment bore fruit in sales that would have been incredible in the nineties."[46]

On the surface, publishers and performers had a symbiotic relationship, publishers relying on vaudevillians to popularize their songs, and vaudevillians depending on the publishers for a steady stream of quality material. If a touring vaudevillian had a few weeks off in New York or a dry spell in his bookings, he could always count on a temporary job as a plugger or demonstrator in Tin Pan Alley. Robert Miller explained, "He would walk into a music publisher's office and hang up his hat and say 'I'm working [here] for the next four weeks,' and the publisher gave him the job, knowing that when he went back into vaudeville, this particular singer would sing that particular publisher's songs."[47] In practice, however, it was a relationship of unequal partners, for the supply of songs vastly eclipsed the number of plugging opportunities, and in order to assure that singers would perform their material, publishers began to pay—and pay and pay—performers to place (or keep) a song in their routines.

Generally publishers saw nothing unethical about making payments to performers and objected to it only on financial grounds; it was just "part of the business," one industry veteran explained.[48] In most cases, a performer received cash from the publisher, ranging from ten to one hundred dollars a week, or a publisher might pay a performer's travel expenses, purchase a trunk for him or her, buy fancy gowns for the female dancers, or cover the cost of expensive stage sets. Then again, publishers knew that all vaudevillians were not created equal and that it mattered enormously—and increasingly—which performer introduced a song. Irving Caesar remembered that "Swanee," which he co-wrote with George Gershwin, sold unimpressively after a lavish debut at which an ensemble cast sang, sixty female dancers appeared "with electric lights on their shoes," and music was provided by Arthur Pryor's seventy-piece band, at the mammoth Capitol Theatre, but that the song then became a huge success "within three or four days" of being adopted by Al Jolson. Indeed, when it came to plugging, Jolson was "the greatest power in the business," according to another songwriter; in one instance he was reported to have received a racehorse for plugging a single song.[49] In still other cases, a publisher might arrange for a performer to be compensated in kind, for example by having in-house writers provide the performer with a new comedic introduction for his act. In a practice known as a cut-in, performers were sometimes credited as co-songwriters and paid indirectly, through royalties, a system that gave them an even greater incentive to make a song a hit (but at a higher cost to the publisher). With a performer such as Al Jolson, who was cut in on numerous songs, writers were happy to share credit, because Jolson's endorsement was so effective in the marketplace (although Jolson, it was said, refused to accept material he considered of inferior quality).[50]

This "payola" (as *Variety* termed the practice in 1938) became institutionalized to the point that virtually every vaudevillian collected some weekly "salary" from a publisher, and many performers were taking in more from publishers than from the vaudeville circuit. In the end, though, this system hurt publishers deeply, for they were forced to expend growing sums to edge out competitors without realizing a corresponding increase in performance or sales. By 1914, publishers' aggregate payments to performers had risen so high—reportedly to $250,000 for the previous theatrical season—that the vaudeville giant E. F. Albee, *Variety* publisher Sime Silverman, and the publisher Edward Marks led the biggest and most influential publishers into an agreement to ban such payments by mutual consent. The bylaws of the organization they formed, the Music Publishers' Protective Association, dictated that a publisher would be fined five thousand dollars for violating the no-payment pledge; but as with other attempts at industry self-regulation at this time, the group lacked effective enforcement mechanisms, and blanket prohibitions were ignored or circumvented. In a typical instance, a professional manager would ask an artist if he had a song to publish, and if the artist had something—anything—the publishing house drew up a contract and paid him a cash advance on future royalties. If the artist did not have a song, as "was usually the case," Harry Von Tilzer noted, then the publisher could easily find an older, unused manuscript or have a new song made up for twenty-five dollars. The artist could then be credited as author and a contract drawn up, after which he could receive his advance.[51]

Like Tin Pan Alley, vaudeville was an important transitional component in the emergence of mass consumer culture. In vaudeville an older, localized tradition of theater incorporating audience participation and local cultural identities overlapped with a newer, more bureaucratized and standardized form that had its fullest flowering later in film and radio. Performers carried around the country musical products that were mass-produced in New York but then adjusted and fine-tuned to suit local tastes and expectations. A scripted vaudeville joke from a 1918 sketch ran, "I went from bad to worse, from Jersey City to Hoboken," but it specified that the line could be modified to fit other localities outside the New York area. Although vaudeville sometimes propagated negative racial and ethnic stereotypes, it also served as many people's introduction to the heterogeneous culture of the new immigrants pouring into the country, and it successfully fused the weakening strictures of Victorian middle-class propriety with the more colorful, "rough-edged" traditions of popular theater. Mixing novelty and familiarity, vaudeville did not erase the differences that existed among (or within) audiences, but it fostered a feeling that they had something in common—something that would be expanded and intensified with the explosion of mass entertainment in the 1920s.[52]

If music publishers sought, by plugging their songs in stores and vaudeville theaters, to mold and stimulate consumers, efforts to manage the song market did not end there. In the same years, publishers also engaged in a protracted struggle over pricing. Just as many American industries had found in the late nineteenth century, the free market wreaked havoc on prices and profitability, leading to numerous "crises" and efforts to stabilize prices at "reasonable" levels. Although sheet music sales continued to climb steadily in the first decade of the century, publishers watched in discomfort as the solidity of their retail sales structure eroded. By 1904 the industry was beset with problems: high-volume, low-margin department store sales were driving small music merchants out of the trade. In addition, a few publishers had begun to expand into the business of running the music counters in chain stores themselves. Under this arrangement, not surprisingly, those publishers tended to push their own compositions more aggressively than works from other publishers, and the other publishers naturally cried out against unfairly restrictive trade practices.[53]

By 1907, price-cutting of sheet music became an urgent problem for publishers. Jerome H. Remick & Co. controlled around three dozen music stores around the country and continued to force down prices. In New York the leading department stores, Macy's and Siegel-Cooper's, became locked in a price war that drove prices so low that at one point sheet music was selling for one penny. Publishers' wholesale price at that time was six to ten cents a copy (less than half the wholesale price in the 1880s and early '90s), Woolworth's was selling sheet music for ten cents retail (though for a time it cut prices to five cents), and other, nondiscount merchants generally charged twenty-five to thirty cents.[54]

In response to the price war, five of the leading publishers came together to form their own chain of retail music shops, the American Music Stores, as a means of stabilizing and increasing prices. A short time later, four other leading publishers established their own chain, the United Music Stores. Initially, the joint retail ventures were promoted with a great deal of enthusiasm and optimism. Envisioning that the American Music Stores could become a powerful cartel, one unnamed publisher declared, "We will eventually be the Standard Oil Company of the business, and nothing will stop our growth but the government."[55] However, difficulties involved in five-way management, continued price competition, and the onset of the financial panic fatally undermined the future of the stores, and they lasted only a short time.[56] In the following years, morale in the industry sank to an all-time low as prices plummeted. An editorial in the *Music Trade Review* lashed out against the internecine competition and the loss of "craft" in the industry, charging, "It's dollars, not dignity, that appears to be the slogan of the business."[57]

In the 1920s the rise of radio and the decline of vaudeville undermined many of the older conventions of plugging, but many of the industry's basic precepts have never changed. In the early twentieth century, publishers were working strenuously to overcome the competitive free market for music with a managed market structured around intensive plugging and stabilized prices. This complex system "added tremendously to the overhead of the music business," Edward Marks noted, but it filled the air with the publishers' products and both concentrated and accelerated the commercial song cycles.[58]

What was remarkable here was not the transience of the songs; this was part of their design. Rather than deny this, Irving Berlin even celebrated it in a piece of verse titled "The Popular Song":

> Born just to live for a short space of time,
> Often without any reason or rhyme,

Hated by highbrows who call it a crime;
   Loved by the masses who buy it
. . . . Popular song, you will never be missed,
Once your composer has ceased to exist,
While Chopin and Verdi, Beethoven and Liszt
   Live on with each generation.
Still, though you die after having your sway,
To be forgotten the very next day,
A rose lives and dies in the very same way—
   Let that be your consolation.[59]

No, what was remarkable was the increasing speed with which hits were made and replaced. At the time that "After the Ball" appeared at the Chicago Exposition, a successful popular song remained in demand for two or three years, but by the arrival of the Saint Louis World's Fair in 1904, such songs were "active sellers" for only a single season, and often less. A year later, the humor magazine *Puck* satirized this rapid turnover in a series of "diary entries," written from the point of view of a popular song, recounting its creation, its plugging, its meteoric rise, and its precipitous descent into neglect—all within the span of five weeks. Meanwhile, the concentration of sales grew concomitantly, with more than a hundred songs selling more than one hundred thousand copies each from 1902 to 1907.[60]

To appeal to the widest markets, firms succumbed to greater pressure to produce works that could sell widely and easily in all parts of the country. Consequently, publishers favored anodyne songs whose subjects and sentiments were as "inclusive"—and therefore as unobjectionable—as possible. Such songs were by nature deracinated, unconnected to time and place. They were designed to appeal to audiences in whatever circumstances people heard them, wherever they might be. Paradoxically, however, in the shadow of Tin Pan Alley a musical seed was sprouting that defied this peculiar musical model. The composer Charles Ives drew inspiration not only from European concert music but also from the songs of Stephen Foster, brass bands, the sounds of nature, and the writings of Emerson, Thoreau, and Whitman. By contrast with Tin Pan Alley, whose fungible commodities denied the significance of time and place, Ives wove into his music a deep interest in both concerns, trying to evoke, for example, the feeling of what Central Park sounded like in New York on a particular evening in the 1890s, including the faint sounds of a street band playing somewhere far off. For decades, Ives toiled in obscurity, and many of his pieces were not performed for the first time until long after they were written. He worked for most of his adult life as a businessman in the insurance industry, and many knew him for the influential book he wrote on systematizing insurance sales. By the 1920s, however, he was becoming recognized as a progenitor of American musical modernism. Thus, a composer so marginal that he was not even part of the "serious" music establishment laid the groundwork for thinking about the relation of music, sound, and environment and turned the dominant musical culture of Tin Pan Alley on its ear.[61]

Although Tin Pan Alley is best remembered today for its songs—the several dozen that did not make a quick exit and instead entered into the enduring national songbook—it was perhaps through the soundscape that the industry had its greatest impact. Plugging techniques—innovative, brazen, adaptable, and creative—gave Tin Pan Alley tremendous social and geographical reach. Pluggers made every gathering, from a football game to a prom, a potential commercial audience, and every space, from a commuter train to a prison, a potential site of commercial performance. Indeed, they understood that unlike visual stimuli, sounds are not easily blocked out. They wash over you, and you take them in whether you want to or not. Transforming where and how people heard music, Tin Pan Alley blurred—if not erased—the line between entertainment and advertising. As chorus slips, claques, and street musicians influenced what people sang, hummed, and whistled on their walk home, the line between paid and unpaid performance faded. For the industry it was a distinction without a difference, because all popular songs, in effect, plugged for the industry. In theaters, on the street, at home—in these environments and others, hearing and singing were structured by the hidden architecture of commercial exchange. Melodies functioned as capital, and those who heard them unwittingly became part of a market relationship.

The music business alone was not responsible for this transformation, for other businesses used music as an ancillary component in their operations, including restaurants, theaters, department stores, and five-and-dimes, where song demonstrators enhanced and expanded the resplendent spectacle of consumer capitalism. The omnipresence of pluggers in all public places created a thread linking public activity, amusement, and individual consumer behavior, and in the emerging consumers' republic, national markets could foster a sense of a shared national culture.[62] If posters, billboards, and show windows gave a visual splendor to modern consumer society, Tin Pan Alley gave it a lively musical accompaniment.

A few people complained that the musical innovations of Tin Pan Alley were incursions that they had done nothing to encourage and felt powerless to avoid. Others, however, enjoyed the lively sounds the music business offered. At their best, the songs were catchy and clever and brought real pleasure into people's lives, and through the music people formed meaningful social bonds. At the same time, while the music industry brought amusement into people's lives, it was not connected or responsible to them in any way except through the market, and the national popularity of Tin Pan Alley hits tended to erode local and regional cultures. Both socially and psychically, only a limited amount of air was available to fill with song; people could only listen to one song at time. The music of Tin Pan Alley was calculated to be as broadly appealing as possible, and as its commercial fortunes flourished, other kinds of music, which had trouble competing, grew ever more scarce.

3

Music without Musicians

In the early decades of the twentieth century, musical sounds began to emanate from a new source: automatic machines. To many people's minds, player-pianos and phonographs heralded a great cultural revolution. "The sound-reproducing machine has inaugurated a veritable Democracy of Culture," claimed the *Etude*. A critic in *Current Literature* exulted, "No longer is the world of music barred from those who are unable to pay the tribute of the rich." The impact of such devices on musical culture, estimated the critic Robert Haven Schauffler, exceeded even that of the printing press on literary culture. "Thanks to machine-made music," he predicted, "the time is coming . . . when we shall see as neighbors in the ordinary book-case, such pairs of counterparts as Milton and Bach, Beethoven and Shakespeare." Skeptics raised concerns about the corrosive social effects of mechanical music, but many of its proponents championed it as a vital defense against Tin Pan Alley and the rising tide of popular song. By promoting "good" music, Carroll Brent Chilton wrote in the *Independent,* the music machine could help vanquish "the musical harlotry and Bedlam of the coon song, the Popular Bandmaster's March, the unutterable inanities and vapidities produced by the modern manufacturer of 'popular' music, which vie with our yellow journalism and cheap sensationalism in every form in trying to make the world worse instead of better." Another telling forecast in the *Etude,* however, would prove overweening in its optimism about music education: "The idea that musical mechanical machines will lessen the necessity for good music teachers is about as foolish and untenable as the old-fashioned idea that the automobile would put an end to the demand for horses."[1]

The need for good music teachers, like the demand for horses, never disappeared completely, but it was transformed by the technologies and marketing of mechanical reproduction. The manufacturers of player-pianos and phonographs stood at the forefront of early twentieth-century consumer marketing, and their most effective strategies drew on and expanded the association between music and "respectable" middle-class identity. Indeed, the more adept the manufacturers became at promoting the value of music as cultural capital, the larger their markets grew. Their commercial strategies had paradoxical effects, however, in that they both reinforced and undermined existing cultural hierarchies. They also ushered in a new cultural order in which people became closer to music in some respects and more distanced from it in others. With player-piano rolls and phonograph records, it was possible to hear expert renditions of Beethoven or Verdi in the intimacy of one's own home, at any time. A person could listen to a cherished work over and over, studying and savoring all its complexities and nuances. Schauffler was not wrong, of course, envisioning Beethoven and Shakespeare side by side on the shelf, but such companionable juxtapositions constituted only one dimension of the growing use of music machines. Despite hopes that the enhanced availability of music would fuel musical training, in reality it often meant simply that the actual human labor of making music was now accomplished somewhere else, by specialists.

The phonograph and the player-piano offered listeners access to music apart from the labor and discipline that had underpinned nineteenth-century musical culture; in effect, the advent of these technologies attenuated, reordered, and obscured the social relations of musical practice. Centuries earlier, written musical notation had made it possible to store musical ideas on paper, thus separating their conception from their execution. Mechanical reproduction now made it possible to separate execution from audition, by embedding musical sounds in inexpensive, fungible, durable objects. "I hoard music and speech," read an 1888 ode to Thomas Edison, written from the perspective of a phonograph.[2] In the new regime, musicians performed not for a live audience but for a machine and a roomful of technical experts. Indeed, the very design of phonographs and player-pianos masked their functioning, thus leaving only their effects to ponder. As a result, widespread use of the machines made a signal contribution to the transition from a culture rooted in the values of production to one rooted in the values of consumption.[3]

The Mechanization of Music

The player-piano and the phonograph developed in complementary, interdependent ways. From the vantage point of the twenty-first century, the revolutionary character of the phonograph may appear self-evident, whereas the player-piano now seems a curiosity, an enchanting but insignificant diversion. In 1900 an observer would have said the reverse: then, the player-piano was widely seen as having transformative potential, while the phonograph was generally dismissed as a clever but idle amusement. At that time, both had existed for several years, though neither had much commercial or social standing. In the decades that followed, however, player-pianos and phonographs both became central to the music industry and to musical culture as a whole. From 1919 to 1925 more player-pianos were produced each year in the United States than exclusively manual pianos. By 1923, although the number of phonographs produced exceeded that of player-pianos by more than five to one, the dollar value of the player-pianos was in fact greater. Indeed, the name Victrola, for example, a trademark design of the Victor Talking Machine Company and eventually a generic term for a phonograph, was modeled on the Pianola, a trademark design of the Aeolian Company, the leading manufacturer of player-pianos.[4]

Although the player-piano and the phonograph both reproduced music mechanically, they also differed in important respects. Player-pianos were essentially the descendants of barrel organs and music boxes, whose history went back several centuries. Music boxes were based on the concept of a rotating drum with protruding nubs around it that plucked the teeth of a tiny metallic "comb"; in the case of a barrel organ, similarly, nubs on a cylindrical drum opened or closed organ stops according to a preset musical pattern. The player-piano departed from these earlier technologies in that it was driven by a pneumatic motor (usually powered by foot pedals) and its musical patterns were incised into perforated paper rolls, not fixed on a drum. In the most common type of player-piano, these rolls did not produce "recordings" as phonograph records did. Each roll was a set of instructions, an algorithm based on a musical score, directing the piano to play certain keys in a certain order. It did not determine the speed or volume of the playing, or other nuances; these were controlled through human manipulation, except in the case of the more sophisticated, more expensive "reproducing player-pianos," which appeared later.[5] Reproducing machines were driven by an electrical motor and controlled all pianistic effects, from tempo and volume to pedaling. In both cases, the instrument played the musical sounds anew each time, according to their encoding in the paper roll. The ancestry of the phonograph was different. Culturally, it had its roots in the centuries-old fascination with automata, but its practical development was an outgrowth of the invention of the telegraph and telephone.[6] If the player-piano systematized and mechanized the way the sounds were produced, the technology of the phonograph stored the sounds. As a dam holds back the flow of a river, sound recording stopped the flow of time, yet allowed it to accumulate permanently, a few minutes at a stretch, in the grooves of a cylinder or disc. In this case, mechanical reproduction consisted of reanimating those stored sounds, not of creating the sounds afresh.

In other ways, the player-piano and the phonograph were closely linked, both structuring musical experience in objects, not events—and indeed in objects that could be mass produced and sold relatively inexpensively. This form of music making required no substantial skill or years of practice, but it was not absolutely passive either. At the outset, use of player-pianos and phonographs still depended on some human motive power (foot-pumping or hand-cranking) and supplementary manipulation (such as adjusting the knobs that controlled tempo and volume or putting the tone arm and stylus in place on the record and taking them off at the end). Although pianos too were a kind of complex machine that was operated according to specific instructions (such as sheet music), what differentiated player-pianos and phonographs from the manual instrument was the predetermined outcome of their operation. The musical sounds encoded in sheet music could be followed or ignored; they could be executed well or poorly. The sounds encoded in a piano roll or phonograph record were set in advance and open to only minor variation. Yet at the same time, whether they were intelligently

informed or wholly ignorant about the musical output, the machine operators who used these devices still served an important and active function in
making the musical selections and executing them. (Later, radio users largely
relinquished this role: they selected a station, and someone else determined
the content.)

Even the design history of the player-piano and phonograph reflected the
changing field of social relations. The first player-piano devices were not integrated into the housing of the piano itself, as most people familiar with
player-pianos today are likely to imagine. Rather, they were free-standing
mechanized consoles that users positioned in front of and over a piano keyboard, and housed within the console was a concealed shelf of automated
fingers that depressed the piano keys. Around 1905 the first instruments appeared in which the player mechanism was built into the piano itself, incorporating the same functions as the push-up models but taking up no additional room and concealing the mechanical device in the familiar casing of
the parlor's signature accessory. By 1909 three out of every four players made
in the United States were of this type, a percentage that grew every year until
1923, after which push-up players ceased production altogether.[7]

An analogous change occurred in phonographs. Believing, as the Victor
Company's vice president wrote, that "ladies did not like mechanical looking
things in their parlor," in 1906 Victor introduced its new Victrola design,
replacing the large protruding sound horn with one that was concealed in
the handsome wooden cabinet of the instrument, which made possible the
acceptance of the phonograph as an unobjectionable piece of parlor furniture.[8] Both the player-piano and the phonograph, therefore, underwent a
transformation that twentieth-century industrial designers would later call
sheathing, that is, the modification of product design to hide the instrumental workings of a device in a benign outer shell. (In the 1920s, radio sets underwent the same transformation.) This covering set the user in a new relation to music making, by rendering the effects of the device more abstract,
less grounded in a physical, material process. In so doing, manufacturers
thrust a wedge between the domains of knowledge and use, thereby facilitat-
ing, as Roland Barthes put it, "the conversion of consumption into lifestyle."[9]
Not only was music being made by a machine, but the mechanized process
was obscured.

In popularizing the two instruments, the manufacturers of player-pianos and phonographs had the burden of selling not just one commodity but two: a) machines and b) recordings or rolls. With both technologies, these discrete elements made up a single, integrated system, similar to the interdependence of railway cars and tracks, in which the conveyance and the route, the means and ends, were united—what the historian Wolfgang Schivelbusch would characterize as "a machine ensemble." In the case of railroads, this system transformed both the physical landscape and the ways people experienced it. Trains traveled faster and more economically on tracks that were straight and flat, a consideration that led railroad companies to modify the landscape as much as possible to suit their needs—by boring through a mountain here, leveling one there, grading terrain that was steep or uneven— the result of which was that people, goods, and information moved through the world as never before. With music, the impact of the machine ensemble on the aural environment was comparable, if more subtle. The mechanical reproduction of sounds favored some conditions and was incompatible with others, and these tendencies had profound and lasting effects. In the end, the machine ensemble left the entire soundscape altered by its incursions.[10]

Although the player-piano and the phonograph are most often associated with domestic spaces, the effect of these machine ensembles was hardly limited to the home. In the late 1880s and 1890s, before the development of any domestic market for phonographs, many people attended lyceum-style lectures and demonstrations of the instrument. Meanwhile, commercial agents were placing coin-operated cylinder phonographs, powered by electric batteries, in public waiting rooms, drug stores, hotel lobbies, train depots, summer resorts, and county and state fairs. In some locales, promoters also opened dedicated phonograph parlors, which combined elements of the saloon and hotel or theater lobby, appointed with ceiling fans, potted palms, and banks of phonographs, and later moving-picture technologies like the kinetoscope and mutoscope. Because these early nickel-in-the-slot phonographs required the use of individual listening tubes to hear the recording, they did not alter the aural environment so much as they did the social environment. The same was not so for coin-operated player-pianos—nickel-grabbers they were sometimes called—which started to appear by the end of the 1890s. Beginning around 1910, many of these electrically powered machines were able to switch back and forth between several different rolls, an innovation that makes them precursors to the modern jukebox (which came along in the 1930s). In the 1910s and '20s, coin-operated player-pianos could be found in a broad range of public places, including amusement parks, billiard halls, beer gardens, cafés, confectioneries, cigar stores, clubs, dance halls, drugstores, department stores, groceries, hotels, lodges, lunch-rooms, merry-go-rounds, newsstands, postcard studios, railroad depots, and restaurants. Meanwhile, although the phonograph parlors of the 1890s dis-appeared, phonograph companies continued to promote phonograph music in public spaces, from hotel lobbies to public parks to schools, and dealers regularly set up demonstrations at picnics, parades, and other local events.[11]

If the player-piano and phonograph both moved to the center of the mu-sic industry in the early twentieth century, they entered the industry from fundamentally different positions. In the 1880s and '90s, the player-piano business emerged on the margins of the piano and mechanical and barrel or-gan industries, and its leading firms built on their existing appeal and proven marketing strategies. The father of this business, William B. Tremaine, born in 1840, got his start in the piano business, shifted his attention to mechani-cal instruments, and in 1878 established the Mechanical Orguinette Com-pany. The company produced small, hand-cranked reed organs, whose mu-sic was governed by perforated paper rolls. In 1887 Tremaine established an offshoot firm, the Aeolian Company, which became the foremost popu-larizer of push-up Pianolas in the 1890s and eventually the industry's lead-ing manufacturer and marketer of self-playing instruments and rolls.[12] His son, Harry B. Tremaine, born in Brooklyn in 1866, took over the business in 1898. A man of strong commercial impulses, he proved himself one of the savviest and most influential figures in the growth of the industry. Unlike many industry leaders, who left school at thirteen or fourteen and made their way through luck, pluck, and hard-won experience, Harry Tremaine had had a solid formal education, and he directed the business in accord with the ambitions and strategies of modern, professional, large-scale business.[13]

By 1903 Aeolian was capitalized at $10 million and controlled more than a dozen subsidiaries, including firms in France, England, Germany, and Aus-tralia. Probably most notable about the company's growth, however, was

3.1 In the Eidelweiss, a saloon on Chicago's State Street, patrons could enjoy music from a coin-operated player piano (pictured at right, in 1907) made by the Wurlitzer Company, later a manufacturer of jukeboxes. Richard Howe Collection, Michelle Smith Performing Arts Library, University of Maryland.

Tremaine's unprecedented commitment to advertising. Writing in 1911 in the wake of Tremaine's successes, the industry veteran Alfred Dolge declared that Tremaine's advertising had "stunned" the industry's old-timers. "No one to-day denies him the credit for having blasted and paved the way for the popularity of the player piano," he wrote. One tactic Aeolian used, as Steinway & Sons did as well, was to build a reputation for its products by advertising their placement among people of prominence. By 1901, the company boasted, these included "rulers and royal personages (the late Queen Victoria of England, William II of Germany, Pope Leo III, Porfirio Díaz, president of Mexico), merchants and manufacturers (Philip Armour, John Wanamaker), men politically prominent (ex-president Grover Cleveland), capitalists and people socially prominent (Cornelius Vanderbilt), musicians (Paderewski, Melba, Moriz Rosenthal), railroad and insurance men, bankers (J. P. Morgan), and clergymen and lawyers." Aeolian secured endorsements from numerous prominent conductors and performers, including John Philip Sousa, Ignacy Jan Paderewski, Anton Seidl, and Nellie Melba. While some form of player-piano business developed in other countries in the same years—most notably Germany, which produced expensive, finely crafted machines—it was Aeolian and other firms in the United States that drove the commercial development of player-pianos everywhere. No market was as lucrative as the United States, but Tremaine also marketed Aeolian instruments in Europe, Asia, South America, and Australia.[14]

Tremaine's commercial genius lay in *downplaying* how radical his products were. Instead of emphasizing how sharply they departed from the nineteenth-century musical culture, he used "modern business methods" to promote his instruments as supplementing what already existed. Aeolian's goal was to merge with or integrate itself into the existing piano business, not replace it. The company absorbed five manufacturers of so-called straight (that is to say, nonmechanical) pianos, including the well-known houses of Weber and George Steck & Company, and in 1909, it signed a twenty-five-year agreement to have its player-piano mechanisms installed in Steinway & Sons pianos, to be sold exclusively at Aeolian and Steinway dealerships. Meanwhile, on Forty-second Street in New York, the company built Aeolian Hall, modeled on the old Steinway Hall, which had ceased to present public concerts in 1890 but which had been an important element in building Steinway & Sons' reputation in the nineteenth century. An imposing eighteen-story structure, Aeolian Hall joined Carnegie Hall as the leading venue in the city for symphonic and choral music as well as piano concerts.[15]

The significance and character of the player-piano technology were far from self-evident, however, as is indicated by the conflicting ways people wrote about the instruments in advertisements and public commentary. On one side were those who claimed that the player-piano was easy to use and would revive pianos fallen silent. It gave "the *ability* to *play* as perfectly as the talented musician," a typical advertisement ran.[16] This conceit was best symbolized by the widely publicized trademark of the Gulbransen Company, showing a baby crawling around at the instrument's pedals. If playing the piano had, a generation earlier, been the stuff of character-building discipline, this image proposed that it was now so easy that a baby could do it. At the same time, these machines did require human labor and manipulation, and another approach suggested their continuity with the past—by stressing, in effect, their *difficulty*. According to this view, the player-piano was just a simpler, less taxing way of cultivating the older values, not a degraded form of music making. "The Aeolian is not an automatic instrument. It does not play itself," claimed the leading manufacturer in the business. "The instrument is responsive to [its operator's] every mood and he controls its playing with the same precision and rapidity as the conductor does that of his well-drilled orchestra."[17] In *Woman's Home Companion,* one commentator insisted on the need to develop proper "technique" with the player-piano, while another, in the English magazine the *Sackbut,* maintained that to learn to execute piano rolls well required two hours of practice a day for a year![18] Other commentators clashed over what kind of music was best suited to the player-piano, whether it helped or hindered music education, and whether music made by a player-piano could ever be art, or if it was even music at all.[19]

Some of the most vigorous debates about the value and legitimacy of player-piano music were mitigated by the emergence of reproducing player-pianos, which represented the apex of mechanical piano technology. These expensive, electrically driven instruments played rolls that were said to record a player's performance, having encoded in their paper perforations not just the notes but also all dynamics, tempo, pedaling, and other nuances. In fact, manufacturers exaggerated the degree to which the rolls were pure "recordings"—industry insiders later acknowledged the substantial editing and postproduction processing that went into making each roll—but these instruments did produce breathtaking music.[20] Many of the era's leading performers and composers produced rolls for this extraordinary instrument, including Gustav Mahler, Richard Strauss, Claude Debussy, Maurice Ravel, Camille Saint-Saëns, Alexander Scriabin, and Ignacy Paderewski. Reproducing player-pianos, because of their substantially higher price and jealously guarded proprietary designs, never captured more than a small fraction of the overall player-piano market (at its peak, barely more than 10 percent of the total number of player-pianos manufactured), but they did offer an unrivaled level of verisimilitude, far beyond what phonograph records did.[21] Indeed, these rolls did not simply recall the notes of an earlier performance. They actually produced the sounds again, on a different instrument but with

3.2 Playing the piano once required years of training. The Gulbransen Company suggested that it could henceforth be mastered by a child barely a year old. *Saturday Evening Post*, Sept. 7, 1918, author's collection.

the same thunderous volume and dramatic technique, as if the great performer were sitting at one's own piano bench.

The relation between the phonograph business and the existing music culture was quite different. Rather than stage a revolution from within the music industry, by building on existing hardware, practices, and expectations, as the player-piano entrepreneurs did, the phonograph business intervened in the music business from without. Although the phonograph companies had begun making musical recordings in the early 1890s as an adjunct to promoting the phonograph as a dictation tool, by the end of the century the phonograph's connection with music remained tenuous at best. Coin-operated phonographs appeared in public entertainment establishments, but these were simply novelty concessions, with no connection to the music business, and many of the recordings were spoken monologues, not music at all. A report of the U.S. Census published in 1902 found, "Of the many wonderful inventions during the past quarter century, perhaps none has aroused more general and widespread interest among all classes of people than the machine which talks; and for this reason, together with the fact that it has been widely exhibited, nearly everyone is more or less familiar with the so-called talking machine." It appeared, moreover, not in the section on musical goods but under "Electrical Apparatus and Supplies." Indeed, while acknowledging the phonograph as potentially "of great benefit to the commercial world"—both as a dictation device and as a means of sending oral letters through the mail—this report made no mention of music, commercially produced or otherwise.[22] In the years that followed, however, the *talking* machine became a *musical* instrument. This landmark shift came about not so much because those in the music business discovered the phonograph as the opposite—because those in the phonograph business discovered the powerful, untapped commercial potential of music.

The Musicalization of the Phonograph

By 1916 the Victor Talking Machine Company could tout its enormous factory complex in Camden, New Jersey, at more than 1.2 million square feet, as "the greatest musical center in the whole world."[23] Its musical products could be found on every continent, and its catalogue boasted recordings by the most esteemed international musicians. Yet scarcely sixteen years earlier, when the phonograph had been marginal to the nation's and the world's musical culture, and the man who founded the company in 1901, Eldridge Reeves Johnson, had found himself in a serious predicament. At that time, Johnson had been working for several years as a machinist, designer, parts supplier, and assembler for Emile Berliner's disc gramophone business, and he had recently expanded his small works to meet Berliner's growing demand. Then a legal dispute between Berliner and his marketing agent forced Berliner to withdraw from the business. Johnson bought the rights to Berliner's patents and reluctantly went into business on his own, setting out in the industry with no experience in sales and marketing and facing continued legal attacks from Berliner's erstwhile marketing agent.[24] Although Johnson had done well on the technological and production side of the business, he was uncomfortable dealing with commercial matters and would willingly have sold his stake outright if anyone had come forward with a suitable offer.[25]

To make matters more complicated, the three principal manufacturers in the recorded sound business—Thomas Edison's National Phonograph Company, Edward Easton's Columbia Phonograph Company, and Emile Berliner's company—had for several years been locked in an intense commercial rivalry, and the technological competition between Edison's cylinder-playing format and Berliner's disc-based format persisted. (Columbia dealt in both formats.) Meanwhile, all three companies had undertaken to develop markets in Europe, through subsidiaries or licensees. The most important of these was the Gramophone Company Ltd. of England, established by the American William Barry Owen to license and market Berliner's technology throughout Europe. Thus, on succeeding Berliner in the business, Eldridge Johnson confronted daunting challenges, especially because his rivals had more capital, better name recognition, and greater commercial experience. Even if his disc gramophone sounded better than his competitors' machines, as he was confident that it did, the cylinder phonographs enabled users both to play back prerecorded cylinders they had purchased and to make their own recordings—that is, to be producers of recordings as well as consumers.

In the face of such obstacles, Johnson found his solution in the recordings that users could play on their machines. His endeavor was based on a two-pronged marketing strategy based first on serious musical recordings and second on an unprecedented commitment to advertising, beyond even what Harry Tremaine had undertaken with the Aeolian Company. Notwithstanding the effort to promote the use of the phonograph in offices, most people viewed it as a sound-reproducing novelty on which they might spend a few nickels in an arcade or a hotel lobby, but scarcely worth much more than

The Greatest Musical Center in the Whole World

3.3 This 1916 image of the Victor Talking Machine Company's enormous complex in Camden, N.J., captures both the rapid growth of the phonograph business and the extent to which music had become a product that issued from a "modern . . . steel and concrete" factory. *New Victor Records*, May 1916, Smithsonian Institution Libraries, Washington, D.C.

that. Although National Phonograph and Columbia had developed a small business in prerecorded music, their recordings received no coverage in the music industry. Most of their recordings were made by people with little standing in the musical world, John Philip Sousa's band being the notable exception, but these recordings had only a marginal effect on the status of the business and the medium.

Indeed, Johnson himself cared little for music but came to see that it represented valuable cultural capital. After launching his new company, the Victor Talking Machine Company, in 1901, he secured a stable market position, and eventually a dominant one, by promoting high culture for a mass audience. Victor wooed consumers away from the rival machines by emphasizing not the superiority of its machines or technology but the exclusive content of its records. Through a unique line of recordings known as the Red Seal series, Victor achieved for the phonograph a kind of cultural legitimacy, by associating its machines with some of the most respected musical artists of the era. These specially packaged, specially priced discs attracted both artists and consumers to sound recording as never before and cast all phonographic culture in a new light. To sell machines, that is, Victor pushed records, and to sell records, it promoted high culture.[26] Edison, by contrast, remained devoted to marketing based almost exclusively on sound quality; Columbia followed Victor's lead but never matched the Victor Company's high technical and artistic standard.

Johnson's strategy grew out of a close commercial relationship with the Gramophone Company Ltd. of England. In 1901 Johnson and the Gramophone Company signed a multipart commercial agreement with far-reaching long-term consequences. This agreement, according to which the Gramophone Company could buy up to half the phonographs and parts Johnson produced, created a reliable revenue stream for Johnson's fledgling company at a time when its domestic market was uncertain. Victor was to establish a permanent research and development laboratory, for which the Gramophone Company paid 50 percent of the cost of upkeep and in return was entitled to half the proceeds from patents. Victor also gained the right to use the Gramophone Company's trademark image of a dog listening to a talking machine, accompanied by the caption "His Master's Voice." Meanwhile, the companies agreed to share recording matrices and not to compete with each other anywhere in the world.[27]

The Victor Red Seal series started out in the United States as an import under this agreement. The genesis for the series lay in the Gramophone Company's plan to curry support among top professional musicians and reverse their prejudice against the recorded medium. In 1900 the Gramophone Company hired the young conductor Landon Ronald (later Sir Landon) as a musical adviser, with the intent of using his personal and professional influence toward this end. By 1902 he had enlisted the Covent Garden stars Pol Plançon, Antonio Scotti, and Emma Calvé to join the company's recording roster. Meanwhile, the head of the French branch of the company, Alfred C. Clark, an American who would become managing director of the Gramophone Company a few years later, was sending gramophones and a selection of records to leading composers in Paris, in an effort to attract their support. At the same time, another American, Frederick Gaisberg, who had earlier worked for Columbia and Berliner, came to London to establish a recording program for the Gramophone Company. More than any other single person, Gaisberg was responsible for the recording of leading musicians that followed.[28]

Gaisberg worked simultaneously as what would now be called a recording engineer and as a director of artists and repertoire. In 1899 or 1900 he set out on a tour of Europe to make recordings for the Gramophone Company's fledgling Continental markets. His trip included stops at Leipzig, Budapest, Vienna, Milan, Paris, and Madrid. It concluded with a six-month stay in Russia, where Gaisberg successfully recorded gypsy singers, choruses, and comedians but found that highly regarded professional singers "would not respond to our humble offers."[29] Recalling "what a primitive little affair the gramophone was in 1900," Gaisberg later recounted: "Whenever we approached great artists, they just laughed at us and replied that the gramophone was only a toy."[30] This situation began to change after Gaisberg persuaded Fyodor Chaliapin and other members of the Imperial Opera to make some recordings in Saint Petersburg. There, a local gramophone dealer on the elegant Nevsky Prospekt proposed that to appeal to his aristocratic clientele, the records might carry conspicuous red paper labels in the center, to distinguish them from standard recording fare with its black paper labels. Moreover, to set such records apart further, the company assigned an exalted price to them, the equivalent of five dollars each.[31] When this bit of commercial stagecraft proved remarkably successful in Russia, the Gramophone

Company's home office in London adopted the concept of specialty labeling and pricing for other top-named performers as well, and by 1902, the records were classified as a distinct category—Red Seal or Red Label records.[32]

From Russia, Gaisberg traveled next to Italy, a visit whose consequences proved even more momentous. In March 1902 in Milan, he enlisted the participation of the rising star at La Scala, Enrico Caruso. The twenty-nine-year-old tenor, who had been born in Naples in 1873, had by then sung at Buenos Aires, Monte Carlo, and Saint Petersburg and looked forward to a future engagement at Covent Garden in London. Nothing as yet, however, presaged the phenomenal success he was soon to achieve through phonograph recordings. Indeed, a few earlier recordings he had made for Zonophone and Pathé Frères had attracted little notice. Still, Caruso was promising enough that Gaisberg agreed to pay him by far the largest fee accorded any recording artist up to that time—the princely sum of one hundred pounds for ten recordings. The result was the appearance of some of the most important recordings in the history of the medium.[33]

Above and beyond their cost, these recordings signaled a groundbreaking achievement in music, sound recording, and marketing, whose impact derived not simply from Caruso's prestige but also from the outstanding musical material, the quality of Caruso's voice, and unsurpassed recording values. Together, these elements realized the potential of the phonographic medium to an unprecedented degree and initiated a new era in musical recording. The phonograph was finally beginning to realize its much ballyhooed promise. When the Gramophone Company began to sell the Caruso records throughout Europe, their commercial success elevated both the tenor's and the phonograph's reputation to unknown heights.

In 1903, thanks to the agreement between Eldridge Johnson and the Gramophone Company, Victor started to import and market the Red Seal records in the United States. Up until that time, Eldridge Johnson had done little to distinguish the recordings he sold from those advertised in the catalogues of his rivals, Edison and Columbia. All three companies were selling an assortment of Sousa marches, coon songs, humorous "recitations," and instrumental solos or duets for flute, saxophone, mandolin, piccolo, banjo, and xylophone, along with records having some more utilitarian end, such as entertaining children or teaching foreign languages.[34] At this juncture, however, Victor began to market recordings by eminent European concert artists, recorded overseas. The following year, Victor made Red Seal recordings in the United States for the first time and exported these recordings back to the Gramophone Company. Almost all the Red Seal artists continued to come from abroad, but the establishment of an American recording base permanently shifted the balance of power between the two companies. These records revealed new commercial possibilities for the phonograph, and on the strength of Red Seal, Victor leapfrogged over its rivals and within a few short years redefined not just the phonograph business but the music industry as a whole.

Following the success of Enrico Caruso's records in Europe, Victor's 1903 Red Seal catalogue prominently featured Caruso, in anticipation of the tenor's American debut that fall. From that time until his death two decades later, Caruso remained Victor's most important artist. Although the Red Seal catalogue also contained instrumental music, Caruso and opera constituted the bedrock of Red Seal's success. Opera enjoyed widespread popularity across classes at the turn of the twentieth century, and the early proponents of the phonograph had cited the voices of great divas as among the most valuable sounds that might be preserved. In both Europe and the Americas, opera had a devoted following among the social elite and had long thrived among popular audiences as well, often in heavily adapted or modified forms. In the early twentieth century in the United States, the immigrant and native-born working classes continued to show strong support for opera, immigrants sometimes focusing their attention on performers from their own native region or town.[35]

Opera offered Victor more than a broad-based potential audience, however. Victor's opera-centered marketing strategy depended on the technical specifications of the recording process as much as on aesthetics or culture. Piano music, formerly the cornerstone of American musical culture, did not record as well as opera. "We had to choose our 'titles' so as to obtain the most brilliant results without revealing the defects of the machine," recalled Fred Gaisberg, the pioneering recording engineer.[36] "By selecting loud voices and standing the singer further away from the collector or horn the false tones could be avoided; at the same time the loud, rich voice covered up the surface noise inherent in the disc."[37] Instrumental music never disappeared from the Red Seal catalogue, but technically and commercially opera singers were far more effective.

The problem lay in the narrow frequency range of the acoustic recording process. Some instruments sounded muffled or muted; others were not audible at all. On recordings of vocal music, the accompaniments were usually limited to austere arrangements that lacked the subtlety and richness of composers' original scores. Larger groups depended on heavily adapted arrangements in which tubas and trombones often replaced the cello and double-bass parts, a substitution that made large orchestras sound like modified brass bands. Indeed, such technical limitations help explain why a performer like Paderewski, who had a towering reputation and had traveled around the United States to great acclaim in the 1890s, never became an important recording artist. He did not make his first recordings until 1911, and he remained skeptical whether a machine could capture the power and nuance of his playing. Fred Gaisberg, who recorded Paderewski, concurred in a 1942 autobiography: "Today, knowing better what Paderewski was and the limitations of the gramophone, I am inclined to agree with him."[38]

Sopranos had long been the most highly valued singers—both the highest paid and the most highly acclaimed—but around the time that recording engineers realized that Caruso and other male tenors made the best-sounding records this hierarchy began to change. Caruso was "a recording man's dream," Gaisberg later recalled, "We recorders were always on the hunt for just this type of voice." Caruso was particularly skilled, moreover, at working with the awkward recording horn. Unlike many of his peers who became nervous or disoriented when recording, he sang confidently, never complained about having to do repeated "takes" of a number, and seemed to possess a natural instinct for the nuances to be obtained if he moved closer to or farther from the horn as he sang to modulate the volume of the recording.[39] He was the model of the successful modern musician—as adept at performing for a machine and team of recording experts as for hall filled with opera devotees.

Meanwhile, as both the promise and the problems of the new technology became evident, critics and consumers alike counted technical sound quality as a major factor in their assessment of the phonograph. After a 1904 press audition, one journalist wrote, "The records are not yet free from mechanical defects, but they are marvelously better than they were a year ago."[40] Victor's published endorsements by figures such as Caruso, the tenor Antonio Scotti, and Senator Chauncey Depew conveyed a similar message. Then, around 1906–1908, the sound quality of records stabilized and testimonials to their technical quality appeared less often. Opera singers retained their recording edge, however, and operatic recordings continued to dominate the Red Seal catalogue, constituting well more than half the titles issued until the advent of electrical recording in the 1920s.[41]

Within the cultural field of music, there is a continual struggle over who or what belongs, or does not belong. In the early twentieth century, this clash concerned what kinds of musicians and musical activity would be validated and included within the field. Through opera and Red Seal, Victor expanded the prevailing definition of musicians to include those who made commercial musical recordings.[42] At stake was whether the cultural value that already accrued in music could legitimate the business and technology of sound recording as well. Musical repertoire necessarily affected this outcome. Not only was Red Seal the lead product in Victor's record catalogue, and opera the linchpin of Red Seal, but it was *Italian* opera, which was relatively accessible, that featured most prominently and most frequently. In terms of aesthetics and prestige, Italian opera possessed the requisite critical gravitas, while remaining explicitly entertaining. By contrast, Wagnerian opera, a staple of American opera repertoire in late nineteenth century, was considerably more off-putting.[43]

Although the Gramophone Company deployed Red Seal and Italian opera in much the same way in Europe as Victor did in the United States, Victor enjoyed an added advantage in the widely held belief in European musical superiority, which allowed Victor to present Red Seal as the august embodiment of Old World culture, and, by association, to imbue the phonograph with a level of seriousness and respectability it had theretofore lacked. An advertisement from 1904 highlighted the favorable reception in Germany of Gaisberg's recordings of Caruso and his fellow tenor Francesco Tamagno, the subtext being that favorable judgment in Europe confirmed the value of these records for consumers in the United States. "Just think of it," a Victor instrument catalogue put it, "to hear in your own home the soul-stirring arias and concerted numbers that have immortalized the names of Verdi, Gounod, Donizetti, Mozart, Wagner, Puccini, Leoncavallo and all the other great composers . . . , to hear the masterpieces of music that before the days of the Victor were almost always hidden mysteries, which few indeed could ever know or hope to understand." Elsewhere, a special catalogue showcasing only Red Seal records promised the "actual living voices of international celebrities," now democratically available to "all lovers of classical music and the devotees of Grand Opera, as well as the public in general." In New York, the manager of the talking machine department at the Siegel-Cooper's department store confirmed that customers would pay "fancy prices for the foreigners, especially when these foreigners include such names as Caruso, Giraldoni, Plançon, [and] Calve."[44] By contrast with Tin Pan Alley's unabashed celebration of and dependence on ephemerality, Victor promised consumers the timelessness of serious Art. Publishers embraced the frivolous ethos of popular song, but the phonograph was marketed as a means to a higher end, not an end in itself.

In effect, then, Victor was selling much more than music, and therein lay one of the powerful paradoxes in Victor's marketing. Promoting a series of records of "the world's greatest musical artists" advanced a clear cultural hierarchy. This conformed to a broad pattern, evident particularly since the last third of the nineteenth century, of enshrining art in museums, concert halls, and other formal institutions. In an era of profound economic instability and social unrest, this "sacralization" of art offered a seemingly natural and universal justification for social inequality, as if to say that values and cultural works of some classes were inherently and immutably superior to others'. If the performers and repertoire of Red Seal represented the "world's best," then others—other musicians, performances, genres, and cultures— were of lesser merit. Although Red Seal rested on cultural stratification, however, it also democratized cultural access. No longer was high musical art on offer only in metropolitan centers, where admission to performances was restricted by class, race, or other configurations of social power. It was available to anyone with the money for a phonograph and a recording, which together cost far less than the most inexpensive piano. As consumers, listeners could then do with the music as they wished, and their preference might not involve paying obeisance to a cultural hierarchy.[45]

To the guardians of "high art," quality stood as an inherent attribute that some things had and others did not, but in practice, quality is usually experienced as a relative value. If Victor intended to invest Red Seal with desirable cultural capital, therefore, it would require a foil. To make clear that these records would be systematically differentiated from all lesser recordings—the popular songs of Tin Pan Alley, vernacular "foreign" records aimed at immigrants, humorous recitations, and so forth—Victor enhanced their symbolic meaning through their packaging and pricing. The distinctive red labels and the printing of a separate catalogue enabled the Gramophone Company, Victor, and their respective dealers to claim that these records were qualitatively different from other commercial recordings. As manufacturers, dealers, and consumers understood, records not only transformed the unique moment of a musical performance into one that was repeated over and over; they reduced that performance to an anonymous artifact, which without a paper label or other signifiers was virtually identical to a recording of any other performance by any other performer under any other circumstances. The black disc with a spiral groove in it could contain a rendition by Caruso or by a novelty whistler of bird calls: the material objects themselves were essentially indistinguishable.

If, as Walter Benjamin famously argued, mechanical reproduction stripped the unique work of art of its "aura," the specialty packaging of Red Seal records attempted to create an ersatz aura in its place, as if each disc consecrated a single and singular musical performance.[46] Indeed, sound recordings, especially if well made, were particularly well suited to this semblance of uniqueness because the oral/aural power of the voice could create a feeling of intimacy and presence unlike that conveyed through any other medium.[47] Indeed, the illusion that each disc represented a single self-contained work of art was logical enough and easy to maintain when records were pressed with music on only one side, as was the case until 1908. Notably, however, even after double-sided records became the industry standard, Victor continued to press Red Seal records—and only Red Seals—in their single-sided form until 1923, for no other reason than to present each as a singular work of art. Taken to its logical extreme, this aim even implied a kind of counternarrative to consumer society itself—an illusion of uniqueness based on mass-produced intimacy.

The problem of reconstituting an object of mechanical reproduction as a work of art found a comparable aesthetic response in the domain of photography. Just as Red Seal was intended to elevate a small number of discs above the sea of more pedestrian recordings and thereby ennoble the medium in general, from 1903 to 1917 Alfred Stieglitz published an avant-garde photographic journal called *Camera Work* that attempted to claim a place for photographs as art objects, in contrast to the cheap, "degraded" photographic reproductions then filling the pages of ever more newspapers and magazines. No more than twelve photographs appeared in each issue, printed on fragile tissue paper separated by blank sheets, without titles or legends—all of which were strategies to invest photographic reproduction with the preindustrial value of "craftedness" and mark these photographs as precious art objects.[48] Although Stieglitz confronted this problem in photography from the perspective of an avant-garde artist, not a marketer of consumer goods, his strategy to endow mechanically reproduced works with the value and aesthetic power of conventional artworks bore a marked resemblance to Victor's.

The artificially high prices that Victor assigned to the Red Seal records amplified this intended significance by placing a premium, both monetary and symbolic, on opera and European classical music.[49] Red Seal's power derived in part from the specialty records' scarcity; that is, their value as art stood in inverse proportion to sales. From a marketing standpoint, the Red Seal discs needed to be set apart from other records, and selling the discs at lavish prices was a means to ensure that sales would be restricted. In this respect, these were objects of conspicuous consumption par excellence, their high price constituting a substantial part of their social value.[50] Victor occasionally claimed that the hefty price of Red Seal records was necessitated by the high recording fees the performers commanded, but such claims were disingenuous, because in reality such costs were still relatively minor and were amortized over Victor's other recording expenses. Then as now, retail prices were standardized, rather than correlating to recording or promotion costs.

In this strategy Victor followed the Gramophone Company, whose American-born director William Barry Owen had launched the first records by Francesco Tamagno by taking out a full-page advertisement in the *Daily Mail* bordered by £ symbols, asserting that the cultural value of the records was what made them so dear. Following this strategy in England, the Victor vice president Leon Douglass explained to dealers in the United States the symbolic value of the new records' special appearance and two-dollar price tag at a time when other records cost between thirty-five cents and a dollar. Such records, he wrote in 1903, would "no doubt appeal to a class of people that [had] never been attracted to the talking machine before." Eldridge Johnson described the Red Seal records more bluntly, however, in a letter to the Gramophone Company in 1904. He wrote, "We use them of course almost entirely as advertising," on both sides of the Atlantic. Meanwhile, with consumers Victor advertisements played up the economy of prestige from another angle, following the player-piano companies in listing the representatives of international royalty who owned Victor machines—including the queen of England, the kings of Spain and Italy, the shah of Persia, and the khedive of Egypt.[51]

For Victor and for the industry generally, Red Seal placed the connection between music and the phonograph beyond question. This "musicalization" of the phonograph was affirmed in 1905 in the inaugural issue of *Talking Machine World,* a trade journal launched by the publisher of the leading organ of the music industry. Noting the "fabulous sums" Victor spent to make records by leading vocal and instrumental artists, the vice president of Lyon & Healy, one of the country's top music retailers, concluded, "I think it only just to say that what the Victor people have accomplished deserves credit in large degree for popularizing the talking machine among people of genuine culture."[52] Ostensibly, this was a strategy designed to appeal to the middle class, but in practice it went further. Ranging in price from fifteen to several hundred dollars, a phonograph was a sizable and unprecedented expense, but not one so large as to be prohibitive, even for many working-class families, especially for machines purchased, as many were, on the installment plan. Victor's understanding of this attraction was an important factor for the company in outpacing its rivals. "I imagine," wrote Frank L. Dyer, president of Edison's National Phonograph Company, "that most of our machines are owned by people of poor or moderate circumstances and to most of them, classical music does not appeal." Such assumptions notwithstanding, the feelings elicited by Red Seal recordings could be as intense in a working-class home as in any other. As Studs Terkel recalled, "On a few occasions, [my father] brought home a Victor record and ever so gingerly placed it on the phonograph. It was twelve inches in [diameter] and easily breakable. One side was blank. 'How much did it cost?' My mother was curious. He held up two fingers. 'Dollars?' He nodded. She was furious. My father wasn't much for words. He simply said, 'Caruso.'"[53]

The other half of Victor's marketing strategy, the complement to its Red Seal series, was its tireless, innovative commitment to advertising, which heightened the visibility among consumers not just of Victor but of the phonograph and the music industry in general.[54] Piano and organ manufacturers had long been known as aggressive advertisers, even as far back as the 1830s and '40s.[55] Victor's relentless and original tactics, however, accentuated that bent. Victor spent $52.7 million on advertising from 1901 to 1929, averaging 8.24 percent of the company's annual expenditures, which made Victor one of the most prodigious and best-known advertisers in the world. In 1912 alone, the company allotted more than $1.5 million for advertising. Such an investment established the company as a leading consumer advertiser and showed the power of advertising to build new markets. Although Victor's rivals also advertised nationally—Columbia, for example, ran a few advertisements in national magazines before Victor was even incorporated[56]—Victor from the outset demonstrated an unparalleled degree of innovation and commitment. Indeed, as early as 1903 Eldridge Johnson, who was not normally given to cocksure pronouncements, wrote to his counterpart at the Gramophone Company, "I believe that our goods are the best advertised article in America at present save, of course, some of the household commodities."[57]

In late 1901 or early 1902, with the scarce capital at his disposal, Johnson turned to a professional advertising agency, Powers & Armstrong, one of the new class of professionalized firms that were then remaking consumer advertising. The recently established Philadelphia firm, which was later taken over and renamed by F. Wallis Armstrong, remained Victor's advertising agent for the next twenty-four years. In 1916 the firm took on a bright young adman named Raymond Rubicam, who went on to become one of the leading advertising executives of the century. For three years, Rubicam worked on the Victor account (and others), before moving to another Philadelphia firm, N. W. Ayer & Son, to which Victor switched in 1925. Ayer's other accounts included Steinway & Sons, which the firm had represented since 1900, the pioneering retailers Wanamaker's and Montgomery Ward, as well as Procter & Gamble, the Singer sewing machine company, and Rolls-Royce.[58] More than just hiring a professional advertising agency, therefore, Victor worked with some of advertising's most influential practitioners.

Under the direction of Vice President Leon Douglass, the second-most-important person in Victor's development after Johnson, the company's advertising strategy entailed advertising consistently and as heavily as possible in as many publications as the company could strategically justify. These ranged from national general-interest magazines to specialized periodicals like *Successful Farming, American Boy,* and *West Virginia School Journal.* In newspapers, Victor advertisements announced the availability of new goods, especially records, while in magazines, more visual and more discursive advertisements aimed to generate a "need" for Victor products. In the *Saturday Evening Post,* the most widely circulated magazine in the United States, Victor's prominent advertising gave the company a high public profile, placing the company alongside the largest consumer marketers in the country, far exceeding its actual commercial standing at the time.[59] By the mid-1910s, Victor was one of the top five magazine advertisers in the United States, although in terms of assets it ranked, in 1917, as only the 174th-largest company. In 1923 Victor was the single largest magazine advertiser in the country, the fourth-largest newspaper advertiser, and the first overall.[60]

Both the quality and the quantity of Victor's advertising made a marked impression on contemporary observers. When *Sunset Magazine* held a contest in 1916, for example, asking readers to study the advertisements in the magazine and then write a letter describing what constituted effective and memorable advertising, one prize-winning letter detailed the impact of Victor's celebrity photographs. The effectiveness of the advertisement derived from the images of the Red Seal artists—Enrico Caruso, Nellie Melba, Geraldine Farrar, Ernestine Schumann-Heink—said prizewinner Elinor V. Cogswell: "The reproductions of the photographs of the great musical artists [are], perhaps, the most essential and valuable feature of the ad. It stimulates and increases the desire to hear their superb renditions. To create such desire—to foster such desire—on the reader's part is the aim of the advertisement, and it is successfully accomplished."[61] Contemporaries also praised

3.4 On the back cover of the *Saturday Evening Post*, which had the largest circulation of any magazine in the United States, Victor ran its first full-page advertisement devoted to a single artist. The text emphasizes both the reputation Caruso had in Europe and his exclusive contract with Victor. *Saturday Evening Post*, Apr. 9, 1904, courtesy of the Library of Congress.

the sheer scope, quantity, and regularity of Victor's advertising. As early as 1907 the *Musical Courier,* a leading music journal, declared Victor a "brilliant example of an exponent of modern advertising" and urged all others in the music trades "to watch and study the Victor methods." It chided executives who considered advertising superfluous and cited Victor as an example of the benefits of persistence. It also credited Victor's "publicity men" for having "demonstrated their ability to launch ideas before the public that have, from the very start, shown the earmarks of advertising genius. That accounts for the immense strides made in the Victor business."[62]

Concurrently with its magazine and newspaper advertising, Victor invested heavily in other promotional material, most of which it printed at its own facilities. These publications included a dense, liberally illustrated three-hundred-plus-page hardcover record catalogue, issued annually; monthly catalogue supplements; foreign-language record catalogues; and a regular flow of phonograph catalogues. They also encompassed a few specialty publications, such as the *Victor Book of the Opera,* a handsome hardcover book containing illustrated descriptions of opera plots, translations of arias, and integrated listings of Victor opera records. Blurring the line between advertisement and education, the book was part textbook, part reference, and part sales catalogue. It informed and educated readers about opera, while also inculcating in them an immediate association between grand opera and Victor. Similarly, with their biographical sketches of artists, photographs, suggestions for initial purchases, and more explanations of opera plots, the large annual record catalogues had cultural value beyond a mere listing of available merchandise. Each stood as a virtual encyclopedia of commercially recorded music, containing "all the music in the world," as Victor's promotional copy had it; and indeed, the catalogue contents embraced an astonishing range of material, from Mexican marimba and Hawaiian lullabies to Tin Pan Alley songs about Dixie and addresses by presidents and other national leaders. A vast economy of scope meant that it cost Victor little more to record and produce hundreds of titles in dozens of styles than to produce only a few.[63] All the while, however, Red Seal records were set apart in the listings, printed on special pink paper at the back, to underscore their special status.

Victor advertising also appeared on the sides of streetcars, in shopwindows, and in conjunction with home visits by dealer representatives, all of which helped make awareness of the Victor company—and thus of the music business—a regular feature of life for millions of Americans, whether they were consumers of Victor products or not. And present throughout Victor's advertising, no matter what form it took, was the famous trademark: the white dog, head cocked to one side, listening to "his master's voice" through the horn of a phonograph. If the opera and Red Seal advertisements imbued Victor phonographs with drama, seriousness, and respectability, the trademark dog evoked complementary ideas of loyalty, amusement, and domestication. Here was man's best friend, poised in obedience to his master's voice. He was trained, groomed, and well behaved. He was allowed in parlors. Indeed, the dog's faint reflection in the trademark painting suggests he is sitting atop a polished table. Some scholars have argued that his iconic meaning hinged on an intimation of "fidelity"—the dog's fidelity to his master took the place of sonic fidelity—but to an important degree, whether or not viewers apprehended this play of symbols was of little importance: Nipper was cute, and he was fascinated with the phonograph.[64]

Believing it might make a good trademark, William Barry Owen, the managing director of the Gramophone Company, purchased the picture *His Master's Voice* in 1899 from an English artist named Francis Barraud, who had painted it, probably from a photograph, as a memorial to his recently deceased pet, Nipper. Thanks to the trademark-sharing clause in the commercial agreement between Johnson and the Gramophone Company, Victor began to use the Nipper trademark in 1901, after which it appeared in every promotion and on every object that bore the Victor name.[65] Together, the two companies made this image one of the most widely reproduced and most recognizable trademarks in history. Typical was the enormous sign that Victor erected in 1906 on Herald Square in New York City, showing the Nipper trademark above the legend "The Opera at Home." Seen by an estimated eight hundred thousand people daily, the sign was illuminated by more than a thousand lightbulbs and was reported to be the most expensive in the world up to that time. Situated two blocks from Macy's and two blocks from where the Metropolitan Opera House was then located, the sign and the trademark belonged in equal measure to both these worlds.[66] To contemporaries, the effect of the trademark was clear. A *New York Times* writer remarked in 1910, "One thing has of course boomed the Victor machine tremendously. That is the trade mark, the little dog. . . . Everybody knows the dog, and we all, when he first came out, stopped long enough before shop windows to give him a sympathetic smile and incidentally to read what was said about the

"HIS MASTER'S VOICE"

REG. U.S. PAT. OFF.

The trademark of supreme musical quality
It means the world's largest and greatest musical industry

Twenty years ago the talking-machine was a triviality. Today the Victrola is an instrument of Art. The exclusive Victor processes have lifted the making and the playing of musical records into the realm of the fine arts and rendered them delightful to the most keenly sensitive ear. Opera singers and musicians of world-wide fame are glad to be enrolled as Victor artists.

Every important improvement that has transformed this "plaything" into an exquisite and eloquent instrument of the musical arts originated with the Victor. The Victor plant, the largest and oldest of its type in the world, is the world-center of great music. No other organization in the world is so

qualified by experience, by resources, and by artistic equipment to produce *supreme quality* as the Victor Company. Its products convey more great music by great artists to more people throughout the world than all other makes combined.

The pioneer in its field, the Victor Talking Machine Company today remains the pre-eminent leader. The famous trademark "His Master's Voice," with the little dog, is on every Victrola (look inside the lid) and on the label of every Victor Record. It is your guarantee of the highest musical quality. Look for it. Insist upon finding it. If you wish the best, buy nothing which does not contain this trademark.

New Victor Records on sale at all dealers on the 1st of each month

VICTROLA
Victor Talking Machine Co., Camden, N. J.

3.5 By 1920, when this advertisement appeared, Victor was boasting that its Nipper trademark was a sign of quality and of "the world's largest and greatest musical industry." Author's collection.

3.6 With more than a thousand lightbulbs, Victor's sign in New York's Herald Square was reputed to be the most expensive sign in the world up to that time. The dog alone measured twenty-five feet high. Camden County Historical Society.

Victor." Elsewhere, a writer for *Collier's* estimated that Barraud's painting had by then become the most famous trademark in the world, a claim that Victor trumpeted in its own advertising.[67] By 1916, in an article on famous trademarks, the journalist and novelist Samuel Hopkins Adams asserted that "His Master's Voice" had become "a household word" and that "the quaint little fox terrier at attention before the horn is familiar to more Americans than any of the world's great masterpieces." Meanwhile, Victor told dealers, "If your advertising contained nothing but your name and the Victor trademark you would still be telling almost the whole story, and telling it in a way that *no one could escape.*"[68] A few years later, in the mid-1920s, the Periodical Publishers Association of America issued a pamphlet listing and describing the three hundred most famous trademarks in the world. Nipper appeared first, ahead of Bell/AT&T, Borden's, Westinghouse Electric, Delco, Cadillac, and others.[69]

Before Francis Barraud sold his picture to the Gramophone Company, it looked different, however. As he originally painted it, Nipper was listening to a cylinder phonograph, not a disc machine. Although no one seemed to notice, the painting's title made more sense that way: with a cylinder phonograph, the dog's master could easily have committed his voice to record, but for the dog to hear his master's voice on a disc implied his master was a recording artist or had otherwise gained access to a recording studio.[70] When Barraud offered to sell the painting to Edison's London affiliate, he was turned down, after which he painted a disc phonograph over the cylinder machine and sold it to the Gramophone Company, which in turn made it available to Victor—a potent symbol of the transformation of the phonograph industry as a whole. Thanks to the Red Seal line and its heavy investment in advertising, Victor came to dominate the industry within a few short years, while Edison and his managers stood by flummoxed by Victor's high-class appeal and emphasis on name artists. Moreover, although Edison continued to market the phonograph as an office tool for dictation, his firm did little to promote recordability on home phonographs.

The development of an underground economy of off-color recordings in the 1890s—jokes, songs, vulgar conversations—suggests that some people wanted records that the industry did not offer and would, given the opportunity, make them themselves.[71] Except for sporadic suggestions about throwing "phonograph parties" at which guests would make novelty recordings together, however, Edison did little to follow up his earliest suggestions from the 1870s that consumers might develop a culture of making recordings, instead of merely listening to them.[72] Indeed, such writers as Mark Twain, Arthur Conan Doyle, and Agatha Christie showed more enthusiasm for exploring the possibilities of recording than did the writers of Edison's advertising copy; Twain tried, unsuccessfully, to dictate a novel into a phonograph; Doyle and Christie experimented with phonographs as a plot device. Meanwhile, so successful were Victor's strategies that by 1908 Edison's advertising director was complaining that many of his own acquaintances were purchasing Victor machines instead of Edisons. He attributed the success of the Victrola to its qualitative and quantitative superiority in advertising and a growing reputation among people of means.[73] Edison envisioned his phonograph, by contrast with Victor's machine and its high-class appeal, as a device for the "masses," but in his promotional strategies, including recordings, he neglected or rejected elements of the phonograph to which people might have responded enthusiastically.[74]

Victor's Red Seal recordings and extensive advertising were the one-two punch of the company's strategy to establish a musical market for the phonograph, but contrary to what Victor's marketing implied, most people did not buy Red Seal records most of the time. Victor's advertisements almost never focused on, or even mentioned, the company's vast catalogue of Black Seal records, which encompassed everything from popular songs to political and historical speeches to less esteemed performers of classical music, but these outsold Red Seals almost five to one through 1925.[75] Nevertheless, it was Red Seal–centered advertising that invested the phonograph with cultural value and legitimated it in the eyes of both artists and consumers.

Given the imbalance between sales of Black Seal and Red Seal recordings, one might surmise that Victor would reorient its advertising around the better-selling Black Seals, but such a supposition misses the point; Red Seal boosted sales for all phonograph products. Moreover, even though Black Seal sales exceeded those of Red Seal by a large margin, Red Seal sales were by no means negligible—more than seventy million discs from 1903 to 1925, at a substantially higher price per disc than the Black Seals—and without sizable sales, performers would not receive substantial royalty payments and therefore would have less incentive to make recordings. But as the Gramophone Company's president William Barry Owen put it, for both Victor and its European affiliate, Red Seal was essentially a "high-class advertising scheme." Far from aiming just to preserve art for the ages, the point of this strategy was to use the prestige of high culture to appeal to a broad, heterogeneous market. One remarks with some irony, then, that when Victor established a formal training program for dealers and distributors a few years later, with a curriculum that included salesmanship, orders, and store management, it was named the Red Seal School.[76]

The commercial ascendance of the Victor company was not just a triumph in a war of formats, but a phenomenon with deep cultural reverberations. While this did open up many cultural doors, it closed others, and American life in the twentieth century would likely have looked and sounded quite different if the prevailing technology had enabled consumers to make their own record-

ings. Indeed, during the same years as the rise of Nipper, a democratic revolution was taking place in photography. It was sparked by George Eastman's
easy-to-use Brownie camera, launched in 1900, which enabled ordinary
people not merely to consume but also to produce photographic images.
Eventually, with the advent of magnetic tape half a century later, consumers
did regain the power to make recordings, but by then much had transpired to
reorder people's assumptions and expectations about the prevailing forms,
meanings, and values of music in American society.

The expansion of mechanically reproduced music, and especially of Victor's particular model of it, had deep implications. Through its Red Seal records and unstinting advertising, Victor, with assistance from the American-
led Gramophone Company, became one of the world's most influential
promoters of high musical culture. For Victor, however, this was largely beside the point. Anticipating the advent of the Book-of-the-Month Club in
the 1920s, the Red Seal records were quintessentially middlebrow; they presented an ad hoc assortment of digestible classics as a timeless and definitive
canon.[77] Indeed, notwithstanding the wishes of some contemporaries, phonographic renditions of classical music and opera did not form a beach-
head against popular music; rather, serious and popular recordings complemented each other. On the one hand, the recording industry's vast offerings
could seem like a Whitmanesque celebration of the great plurality of talent
in American life. On the other hand, fundamental to the industry's development was the exploitation and reinforcement of cultural hierarchy.

As the contours of American consumer society became clear in the early
twentieth century, one of its signature elements was the conceit that access to
goods could be equated with the expansion of American democracy. Music
served this idea well, for piano rolls and phonograph records made available
a wealth of music accessible earlier only to a limited, often elite, audience.
Almost invariably, though, the music that consumers heard was modified—
a mere representation of itself. Recordings only several minutes in duration
abbreviated longer works; player-piano rolls adapted anything and everything to the keyboard; "opera" signified any vocal work sung in an operatic
voice; orchestral recordings substituted hardy brass instruments for hard-to-
record strings; and short comic turns stood in for fifteen-minute vaudeville
routines.[78] By encapsulating everything into two-to-four-minute nuggets (the
duration of a popular song) and subjecting it to the same narrow require-

ments regarding what music recorded well, recordings flattened the distinction between styles. Certainly, increased availability often had real benefits for those who heard the music, especially for those barred by geography, race, or other factors from access to urban concert halls. As mechanical reproduction moved to the center of American musical life, however, the course of the industry's development ensured that expanded "democratic" consumption would come at the expense of increasingly managed production. Corporate consolidation and cultural democratization were two sides of the same musical coin.

Unlike Emile Berliner, who sang, played piano and violin, and wrote music, his successor and onetime collaborator Eldridge Johnson never demonstrated a strong connection to music. Johnson claimed to have played the violin as a young man, but not well, and little feeling for music appears to have spilled over into his mature life. When he retired, he kept no souvenirs from his work with the Victor company, not even a sketch given to him by Caruso, an avid caricaturist and the man whose recordings had been so crucial to Johnson's and the company's fortunes. Indeed, Johnson appears to have been essentially indifferent to music and unsentimental about his role in reshaping the American musical landscape. He preferred not to be involved in the music side of the business; he found Caruso and other artists "hard . . . to handle" and disliked what he saw as their propensity to inflate their commercial importance to the business. From the 1920s until his death in 1945, he was well known as a philanthropist. He gave a million dollars, mostly for medical research, to the University of Pennsylvania, where he also served for many years as the chairman of the university's Museum of Archeology and Anthropology. He donated money to the Boy Scouts, the YMCA, and the Episcopal church, sponsored scientific expeditions, and contributed to public libraries, municipal parks, and community centers. He was also a member of such diverse organizations as the Academy of Natural Sciences, the American Academy of Political and Social Science, the American Philosophical Society, the Pennsylvania Academy of Fine Arts, the Zoological Society, and the Pennsylvania Historical Society. In short, apart from his professional activities, Johnson spread his time, energy, and money across a broad range of fields; one of the only areas in which he appears to have shown little interest was music.[79]

4

The Traffic in Voices

The writer A. J. Liebling, born in New York in 1904, made sense of the world when he was a boy by devising his own "small Olympus" of childhood deities. George Washington held the place of Zeus, Lillian Russell shone as his Aphrodite, and Enrico Caruso enthralled him as Pan. Today, it is a platitude that celebrity is the religion of secular society, but for Liebling, at the dawn of the era of modern celebrity, that impression was novel and revealing. "Caruso . . . was a disembodied voice, which is an essential feature of the history of any religion," he recalled. "His, with which I was familiar, came out of the horn, shaped like a morning-glory, of our Victrola. I could not understand what he said, which made it more awesome. Mostly, it seems to me now, he sang, 'E Lucevan le Stelle.' I can identify it, at fifty years' distance, by the place where Cavaradossi sobs. Caruso sobbed louder than any other tenor, and when he did, my father would say, 'That's art. You can tell a real artist by touches like that.'" It was not just the music, then, but the whole social experience of sound that mattered; it was not just the voice of Caruso that made such an impact, but the conditions under which Liebling heard that voice—disembodied, through that peculiar machine, as inflected by his father's commentary. If leaders of the Victor Talking Machine Company and the Gramophone Company thought about Caruso records in terms of their value as cultural capital for consumers, Liebling's recollection reminds us that the records could take on very different meanings once they were in people's homes. There, Caruso's dramatic sobbing could inspire a young mind to think about affect and art, could inform a boy's relationship with his father, and could produce feelings and memories that remained strong and present as the years of a lifetime unfurled.[1]

Victor and the Gramophone Company had sought to make Caruso and the other Red Seal artists inseparable from the public imagination of the phonograph. They had not sought deliberately to create a new model of celebrity, but in effect, this is what they set in motion. The numinous, incorporeal Caruso epitomized not just the phonograph but the power of music and of the voice itself, and as he did, his powers seemed to border on the preternatural. A Victor publicity photograph from 1916 showed Caruso singing into the fingertips of Helen Keller, whose enraptured expression suggested something transcendent about the experience. Studs Terkel later claimed that listening to Caruso records cured him—"where the doctors had failed" —of his childhood asthma. Elsewhere, there appeared stories about stray dogs in Germany who were captivated by Caruso's phonographic voice or a mouse in Atlanta that crept out of its hole only when Caruso records were played.[2]

If the tenor has not always seemed superhuman, over time Caruso's name has evoked a superlative form of greatness, both in and beyond the vocal arts. "He is the greatest tenor since Caruso," Groucho Marx claims of a singer in *A Night at the Opera;* a critic exalted saxophonist Sidney Bechet as "the Caruso of jazz"; a show business veteran remembered Caruso as "the Greatest voice I ever heard," belonging with "many of the personalities acknowledged to be 'The Greatest' in their field," including Jack Dempsey, John Barrymore, and Jascha Heifetz. In Werner Herzog's film *Fitzcarraldo* (1982), a tribe of murderous South American Indians is pacified by the playing of Caruso records on a portable phonograph, mounted on the prow of a riverboat. Indeed, here was a singer of extraordinary powers.[3]

Taken together, these examples attest to the emergence of a new kind of celebrity, launched by the music industry but not altogether controlled by it, and echoing deeply throughout twentieth-century American and global culture. Caruso both embodied and disembodied the aesthetic and technological possibilities of the phonograph. Through the medium of recorded sound, his voice redefined the horizon of expectations and possibilities of vocal expression, while the promotion of his personality and career fueled the growth

4.1 So extraordinary was Caruso's voice that it could move even Helen Keller, who "listened" to him sing the lament of Samson from Camille Saint-Saëns's opera *Samson and Delilah* through her fingers, placed on his lips and throat. According to *Voice of the Victor,* tears welled up in her eyes as Caruso sang, and afterward she whispered, "Wonderful, wonderful." *Voice of the Victor,* June 1916, Rodgers & Hammerstein Archive of Recorded Sound, New York Public Library for the Performing Arts, Astor, Lenox and Tilden Foundations.

of the music industry. No other company had ever promoted a single artist so heavily as Victor did Caruso, and no performer had ever benefited so completely from professional mass media promotion. Caruso was Victor's signature artist, and his success became Victor's. He was the modern music industry's first star, and echoes of his voice resounded throughout American culture long after he was gone.

Gilt by Association

Although it is the movie business that is usually associated with the star system, before around 1910 movie studios did not usually release the names of performers with individual films. Studio heads preferred instead to promote the name of the studio and to avoid giving their employees, the actors, the additional bargaining power that might accrue to public name recognition. In the phonograph business, Thomas Edison, who was a leading figure in the cinema business too, remained narrowly focused on technological quality and actively rejected investment in and promotion of big-name performers. "I propose to depend upon the *quality of the records* and not on the reputation of the singers," he wrote in a 1911 letter. The following year, with the winds of change swirling around his business, he dug in his heels: "We care nothing for the reputation of the artists, singers, or instrumentalists. . . . All that we desire is that the voice shall be as perfect as possible. It is not our intention to feature artists or sell the records by using the artist[']s name. . . . We intend to rely entirely upon the tone and high quality of the voice."[4] Following this strategy, for many years Edison unwisely published catalogues that did not even list records by performer, but only by title and composer.

Edison's rival Victor pursued a different course, in following the newspapermen Joseph Pulitzer and William Randolph Hearst and their proficiency at dramatizing a story by giving it a specific, personal focus. "Names make news" was Hearst's newsroom formula, and Victor put the same idea at the center of marketing music as well.[5] Many singers and performers made records, but Victor advanced Caruso as a symbol of sound recording technology itself—both its artistic potential as a medium and its value as an industry. Beginning in 1903 with Caruso's first American records and his debut at the Metropolitan Opera, his charm and reputation ranked among Victor's most valuable and influential assets. As the fortunes of the tenor soared, Victor benefited incalculably from its investment in his name, voice, image, and personality. He seemed to have the Midas touch, enhancing the wealth of anyone or anything in his vicinity. Edward Bernays, the pioneering public relations strategist, characterized the experience of being around Caruso as "gilt by association."[6]

The new musical culture was one in which celebrity would have a starring role. As Caruso showed, this prominence would be based on two complementary elements, like oppositely charged particles in an atom: the star system and charisma. The first element created or expanded interest in a performer through deliberate, systematic strategies, while the other functioned idiosyncratically, on a subrational level. In contrast to the music industry's sophisticated promotional apparatus, charisma operated outside the structures and values of everyday life and indeed defied them. It was not tied to rational or traditional forms of authority and for that reason offered a release from them. Charisma charted its own course, without respect to law or custom. It paid no heed to worldly responsibilities like work and family and was capable of eliciting intense, even ecstatic, effects. In the case of Caruso, these effects may have been all the more acute for being experienced principally through the ear, then resonating through the body and leaving much else to the imagination of the listener.[7]

To be sure, Caruso was hardly the first musical figure to inspire passionate reactions, and his fame had some important antecedents. Jenny Lind and Franz Liszt, for example, both aroused frenzied excitement on their nineteenth-century tours and benefited from shrewd, conscious professional promotion (in Lind's case by P. T. Barnum, in Liszt's case by himself). Toward the end of the century, Paderewski's towering reputation owed an important debt to Steinway & Sons and the company's prominent use of his name and image in its advertising. In the same years, John Philip Sousa's distinctive stature was the work, in part, of his manager David Blakely, whose canny manipulation of the media was thoroughly modern in both conception and execution. Sousa also came across as a distinctly masculine figure, his marches, his martial dress, and his disciplined codes of performance all contributing to a musical style that diverged sharply from any characterization of music as essentially feminine.[8]

Caruso's fame, however, differed from that of earlier celebrated musical performers. Its engine was the promotion of a specific commercial product. In its strong association with advertising and a single manufacturer, it most resembled the relationship between Steinway and Paderewski, but Caruso's fame was directed with an innovative sophistication and on a scale far beyond what Steinway effected. Moreover, no precedent or analogue existed for Caruso's impact on the culture and economy of the phonograph. Paderewski was a boon to Steinway, but his influence on the perception of pianos, which were already popular and well respected, was marginal. Conversely, Sousa's band made commercial recordings in the 1890s, but these did not factor strongly into his renown or that of the machine. Indeed, only Caruso's fame benefited from being systematically advanced through the retail economy of celebrity-based musical merchandise. "The reputation and popularity of Victor artists is a large factor in the merchandising of their Records," the company explained to dealers, "Their fame is really one of the things you deal in, and yet one that costs you nothing. Therefore, it is to your advantage when that fame is widespread."[9] Victor's advice to dealers regarding Caruso was more direct: "Push Caruso—push his great big name (the biggest in the musical firmament) and his wonderful records for all their worth. . . . He is *the* one artist who stands alone."[10]

For Caruso and a few other recording artists, this new kind of fame carried sizable financial rewards. In 1914 his gross income was more than $220,000. Although live-performance fees made up the majority of his income, the renown of his recordings enhanced his performance fees, and his royalties from recordings were also substantial. From mid-1915 to mid-1916, he earned more than $78,000 in royalties from his recordings in the United States. (His former strong sales in Europe were disrupted by the war.) In 1919 he signed a new contract with Victor, guaranteeing him $100,000 a year plus a royalty of 10 percent of the retail price of his recordings—terms far exceeding those for any other artist. This wealth, in turn, became part of Caruso's celebrity, as newspapers ran stories under headlines such as "Yo Ho! How's $660,000 for Five Years Warbling?" With recording contracts granting him unusually high royalty rates, he may have earned as much as $3 million from his recordings alone. A fortune of that order did not rank with that of a Carnegie or a Rockefeller or even an Eldridge Johnson, but it was exponentially more than performers in earlier eras could have hoped to earn.[11]

Another break from the past was that many people heard *about* a Jenny Lind or a Paderewski, but relatively few ever heard them. In contrast, Victor presented Caruso and other Red Seal artists as an elite ensemble serving at the pleasure of millions of humble consumers. Along with the superior quality of the company's products and the benefits of phonographs as both entertainment and education, Victor offered consumers "the world's leading musical artists" at their disposal. All these themes appeared repeatedly in Victor's advertisements, but among the most prominent motifs was the graphic depiction of costumed Red Sealers singing to a family or a private party in a comfortably appointed private home. These images suggested that owning or listening to records by Caruso and other Red Seal artists was comparable to having them at one's beck and call, while further suggesting that any home where the records were played was infused with their prestige. Indeed, with their artists always pictured in elegant dress, the Red Seal advertisements presented the home as theater, in which consumers were at once impresarios and the owners of box seats. As early as 1907, Victor announced to dealers its commitment to this graphic advertising style, in the belief that artists' pictures were "far more interesting to the general public" and exerted a "magnetism . . . that induces a careful perusal."[12]

When advertisements, catalogues, or posters showed Red Seal artists, Caruso almost always appeared in the most prominent position—in the front rank, in the center, or even larger than the other artists. A typical advertisement from the 1917 Christmas season showed him hand in hand with Santa Claus himself, at the head of a procession of Red Seal artists. A widely published advertisement for Victor's annual record catalogue presented the three-hundred-plus-page volume open to the entry on Caruso, and in the catalogue's monthly supplements, recordings by Caruso were usually featured on the first page—even when the rest of the listing was strictly alphabetical. Through advertisements, catalogues, posters, and signs, Victor capitalized on every phase of Caruso's career: it heralded his arrival in 1903; lavished him with praise and vaunted his talents in the 1900s and 1910s; publicized his American boosterism during World War I; mourned his death in 1921; and basked in his recorded legacy in the 1920s and beyond. Although few acknowledged it at the time, Victor, in conjunction with the Gramophone Company, bore more responsibility than any other entities for making his name and reputation known. Victor emphasized to dealers in

1909, "There is no town or village in this country to-day where the name of Caruso isn't familiar; and why? Because Caruso is the greatest tenor the world has ever known? No; but rather because the Victor has spread his fame from one end of the country to the other—has made it known that Caruso is the greatest tenor."[13]

To underscore the link between the artists and the enterprise, Victor publicized its exclusive contracts with Caruso and other Red Seal performers, thereby transforming the agreements themselves into a form of symbolic capital. Printed catalogues frequently mentioned such agreements when describing an artist's records, and as befitted Caruso's prominence in the company's marketing, his contract received more coverage than any other. On the back cover of an instrument catalogue from 1908, a "Statement from Caruso" announced: "I wish to state to the people in all parts of the world who are interested in records of my voice, that I have not sung or made a record of any kind for anyone except the Victor Talking Machine Company of Camden, N.J., U.S.A. and [its affiliate] the Gramophone Company, Ltd., of London, England, since the year nineteen hundred and three (1903)."[14] On a basic level, the exclusivity clause in recording artists' contracts existed simply as a tool by which Victor and other companies protected their investment in individual performers, but publicizing such agreements transformed them into another component of the marketing system. In so doing, this practice showed that cultural production and commercial restriction were two sides of the same coin.

In the 1910s and '20s, Victor added another tactic to its efforts to solidify the association between leading artists and the phonograph: the company presented images of Red Seal artists directly and actively involved with the medium in some way—listening to phonographs, handling records, or inspecting records at the pressing plant. Such photos humanized an industrial process that might otherwise seem abstract and impersonal. In one catalogue, John McCormack examines what appears to be a freshly pressed record, and an accompanying article describes record production at Victor's Camden plant; other photos show artists posing next to phonographs or allegedly listening to their own records. Such images were a visual form of celebrity endorsement, and Victor encouraged dealers to purchase poster-size reproductions of these images to hang in their shops. These pictures showed

Caruso, Scotti and the Victrola (See page 17)

4.2 Enrico Caruso and the baritone Antonio Scotti listen to a phonograph. This is one of many images Victor circulated of Red Seal artists engaged with the medium. Other images showed artists inspecting the surface of records or touring the record-pressing facilities of the factory. *Voice of the Victor,* Feb. 1913, Rodgers & Hammerstein Archive of Recorded Sound, New York Public Library for the Performing Arts, Astor, Lenox and Tilden Foundations.

that artists' involvement with the company and with phonographs was active and deliberate, not incidental, that these artists knew and cared about not just the music but also the medium.[15]

Once the graphic motif of Red Sealers performing in consumers' parlors was well established, Victor began in the 1910s to promote informal, snapshot-style pictures of Red Seal artists in their own homes, suggesting visually that consumers had a kind of reciprocal relationship with them. Previously, the images in Victor's catalogues had consisted of studio portraits of artists, either in formal dress or in performance costume, but beginning around 1916, Victor's catalogue and promotional photographs increasingly showed Red Sealers involved in family life or leisure activities. (Such a visual style "will attract more attention through being informal snapshots," Victor told dealers.[16]) While formal posed portraits retained an important place in Victor's advertising repertoire, the informal photographs of Caruso and others added a new, more "personal" dimension to performers' public identities.[17]

Around the same time, Victor ran a series of advertisements showing a Victor disc record beside the image of a recording artist, such as Caruso, dressed as Rhadames in Verdi's *Aida*. With the legend "Both are Caruso," the text of the advertisement claimed, "The Victor Record of Caruso's voice is just as truly Caruso as Caruso himself. It actually *is* Caruso." Advancing a claim that the sound recording and the photograph were identical to the person, this advertisement obscured the distinction between a unique event and its mass-produced reproduction, and between a person and his recorded work.[18] Although such claims are unremarkable in advertising today, in the 1910s they conveyed an important contention about what sound recordings were and posited a new relation between representation and reality. If this was essentially a commercial argument, it was also more than that, and its effects were not limited to the economics of music.

Significantly, this and similar advertisements promoted more than the singer's "magnificent voice." In the advertising copy that followed, Victor promised that every one of its 103 recordings of Caruso offered consumers "not only his art, but his personality." The divergence from a musical culture based on sheet music could not have been clearer—it did not matter which composition was for sale; what Victor was advertising was the performance and the performer himself. To the extent that a recording did (or

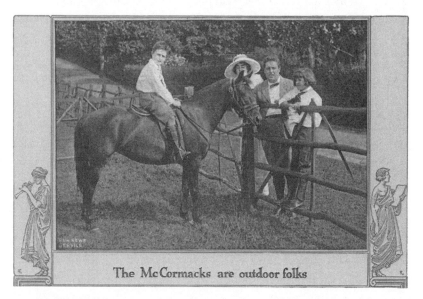

The McCormacks are outdoor folks

4.3 To give consumers the impression that they "knew" celebrity performers, in the 1910s Victor started to publish more informal pictures of them offstage, like this picture of tenor John McCormack and his family. (Note the informality of "folks" in the caption.) *New Victor Records,* Oct. 1918, Smithsonian Institution Libraries, Washington, D.C.

4.4 This is one of a series of advertisements claiming that Caruso and the other Red Seal artists and their recordings were one and the same thing. *Etude,* 1913, author's collection.

could) convey Caruso's "personality," it was even more remarkable for being made available to consumers through a performance for a machine. Crucial here was the concept of personality itself, one of the watchwords of the era, and references to Caruso's personality appeared frequently in all manner of advertisements, promotional material, and reportage. One newspaper article acclaimed Caruso's "bubbling personality and glorious voice"; another, an overview of Caruso's career, mentioned his "remarkable personality" in the article subheading.[19] In other cases, Victor applied the concept not to the performer but to the objects themselves. The introduction to a Victor record guide read, "This little book classifies the standard records, and talks about them briefly and non-technically—giving a *personality* to each one."[20] Indeed, this kind of commodity fetishization was central to twentieth-century consumer marketing on a mass scale.[21]

The notion of "personality"—as distinct from character—as it emerged in the early twentieth century connoted a distinct, confident individual identity, outwardly perceptible in comportment, dress, and elocution. Often defined as "the quality of being Somebody," the idea rested on being pleasing to others and had relatively little to do with existing rules or morals.[22] Such traits seemed perfectly suited to Caruso. He was charming and photogenic, mischievous and generous; he shrugged off his vices and peccadilloes and expected others to do so too; and he carried himself with extreme confidence, while displaying little of the stuffiness or self-importance that opera singers often exuded. For Caruso, as for other celebrity recording artists, his work as a performer did not cease to matter but was subsumed into something more complex, his celebrity. Newspapers tracked events in the life of the playful, debonair Caruso, not only his professional onstage endeavors but also the minutiae, private affairs, and foibles of his offstage life—and not merely in the music pages. One week it was the theft of his wife's jewelry, another it was the reaction of operagoers to Caruso's shaving off his moustache. In 1904, reports circulated about the new castle Caruso had purchased in Italy, which had once been owned by a friend of Dante's. In 1906 it was Caruso's firsthand account of the San Francisco earthquake: "Eet was most terr-r-r-r-ible whir-r-r-r. I can hear it still ringing in my ears, those ter-r-r-ible things, ze earthquakes." By 1910 the papers reported on blackmail and death threats against Caruso by the Italian organized crime group called the Black

Hand. In one sensational report, Caruso responded by defiantly purchasing a sword-cane, two pistols, and a bowie knife for self-protection. Another, however, reported: "Caruso Pays the Black Hand. Terrified, He Gives Up $2000." Other stories described Caruso's prodigious output as a caricaturist, his love of smoking, his fondness for American women, and his penchant for ventriloquism and other tricks.[23]

Of all the stories about Caruso the newspapers covered, however, the most notable was the one that appeared in 1906 after a policeman arrested Caruso for allegedly molesting a woman at the monkey house in the Central Park Zoo. Reports of the so-called Monkey House Incident and the ensuing trial —probably the first "celebrity" trial of the twentieth century—appeared on the front page of the New York newspapers for six weeks. The bizarre, sensational coverage included descriptions and diagrams of the coat Caruso was wearing at the zoo; accounts of slurs against Caruso's courthouse supporters (called "perverts and curs" by the prosecutor); and reports on the fate of the monkey before whose cage the incident allegedly occurred (Caruso's arrest triggered a deluge of visitors to the monkey house, and the attendant stress caused the monkey to become ill and within a short time to die). The complainant disappeared before the trial, and evidence emerged to suggest a police shakedown. In the end Caruso was found guilty and fined ten dollars.

Seen in broader perspective, the incident appears to mimic New York's other great scandal of 1906–1907—the murder by Harry Thaw of the prominent architect Stanford White over White's earlier affair with Thaw's wife Evelyn Nesbit, and the sensational trial that followed. With Caruso, the incident in question was not about murder or even adultery, but allegedly molesting a woman whose identity and even existence remained unconfirmed, in front of a monkey named Knocko. Harry Thaw was later found not guilty by reason of insanity, whereas Caruso was fined ten dollars. Yet before the Monkey House Incident disappeared from the papers, the coverage had encompassed issues of police bribery and intimidation; nativist hostility toward Italians; the risk to a woman's reputation resulting from her testifying at a harassment trial; and the unequal treatment before the law of a prominent performer—in other words, for all the frivolousness of the coverage, celebrity here had been a prism for a host of serious social issues.[24]

At the same time, it was telling how little Caruso's conviction mattered.

The real verdict came, in the end, not at the courthouse, but at the opera house, where Caruso, after great anticipation, made his season debut and was greeted primarily with rousing, indulgent applause. Under headlines such as "Caruso Triumphs before Opera Jury," newspapers reported widespread consensus on Caruso's popular vindication. It probably helped that Heinrich Conreid, the general manager of the Metropolitan Opera, circulated to the press a letter of support for Caruso signed by members of the troupe. Some of Caruso's fans knew, moreover, that the singer had been associated with rakish behavior before. One newspaper wrote in 1905, "Signor Caruso likes our American oysters. . . . And the American women! . . . Same as the oysters. Loves 'em." Another profile, from 1906, noted Caruso's playful penchant for chasing women, which included running around backstage at the Metropolitan Opera. "It is said that you kiss all the beautiful girls that let you!" the reporter said to Caruso. "'I kiss the homely ones, too,' he replied, 'to do penance.'" The lighthearted report continued, "He runs after Nordica, Fremstad, Marion Weed, at rehearsals, and behind the scenes at plays. He tries to kiss them, but they do not let him." These examples and Caruso's public exoneration after the Monkey House Incident suggest his supporters were ready to tolerate this kind of behavior from the otherwise august, fastidious Caruso. His Neapolitan upbringing and Mediterranean sensibility only enriched his public identity, thus anticipating the celebrity persona carved out in the 1920s by Rudolph Valentino, the quintessential Latin lover. Such behavior thus contributed to Caruso's celebrity in a way that it would not have for an African American singer, such as Roland Hayes or Paul Robeson a few years later, for whom the politics of notoriety worked quite differently.[25]

The Power of Voices

In the personality manuals that proliferated in the early twentieth century, the voice was invariably emphasized as an essential element of a strong personality, and few had a voice as impressive as Caruso's.[26] In a cacophonous age of mass urbanization, Caruso's voice rang out in all its power, pathos, and depth, as a testament to the achievement of human expression—to the capacity to make oneself heard, and not just superficially or fleetingly, but with all the resonance of love and pain and every other enduring human emotion that could be summoned up on the operatic stage. Of many published references to and reflections on Caruso, perhaps none evokes these values and their relation to his recordings as fully as does this reminiscence by the poet John Ciardi, the depth and power of whose words warrant quoting in full:

> When I was a kid my uncle used to have a tremendous collection of the scratchy old . . . Caruso recordings—and especially on rainy days, but all the time, I had a passion for Caruso. I heard him a couple of times "live," but I remember him best on scratchy recordings because my memory of that is longest. . . . But when you heard this voice you not only heard the song being sung, you suffered an expansion of your imagination—you discovered how well it was possible to sing these songs. Your very imagination was enlarged. You had a large sense of expectation. You couldn't have anticipated that these songs could have been sung so well. On two levels: the first place, you'd think, just in the animal quality of the singing. Caruso would hit a high note and you'd say this is as much as the human voice can do. You couldn't ask more of the human voice. And then he'd be beyond that. He'd exceed the expectation. But there's another thing. It took centuries to form the kind of consciousness that would sing these songs in this way. The kind of musical intelligence that touched the songs perfectly at every moment. We're enlarged by it. We have to hear those best voices. You have to open your imagination to Job asking his question, and when you've really heard that question ringing you know the difference between a great question and a lesser one. Then you know the size of a human decision.[27]

Such a voice was not merely an individual achievement, it was a collective historical one.

If the human voice had particular cultural resonance at this historical moment, it was served especially well by phonographic recordings of operatic arias. Such recordings were fragments of larger works, excerpts usually recorded for a single voice (generally with minimal accompaniment), disembedded from the theatrical ensemble, and detached from both the obligations and the privileges of social discourse and relations. More than any other kind of recording, and perhaps more than any other kind of aural experience, these recordings could convey the "grain" of the voice, the collision between the physicality of singing and the sound of the language, an effect heightened by the foreignness of that language for most listeners, which allowed or forced them to listen to the voice itself and let go of the meaning of its words. Such records created a semblance of real, bodily presence far beyond what images were capable of, an impression produced, if not by Caruso's unique soul, then by the way the sounds he uttered resounded in the muscles and bones of his own unique physical being. Yet this was never just a voice; it was a voice mediated by its technological reproduction. Just as a movie camera close-up altered the experience of seeing, by permitting and empowering viewers to scrutinize and savor visual detail, as they never could in a live, theatrical performance, sound recordings afforded the ability to listen over and over, to hear every note, breath, pause, inflection, coloration—the music and the sound, the voice and the body. This was the experience of listening simultaneously to Caruso's singing and to the technology itself, for the two could not be separated—here was the paradox of transcendent vocalization anchored in a mundane shellac disc, the human utterance inextricable from the surface noise of the needle in the grooves, the echo of the horn, the whirring and clicking of the machine.[28]

And here was Caruso, characterized in performance as "a manly singer" by the influential critic Henry Krehbiel of the *New York Tribune* and praised more over the years for his volume than for his tone (and certainly not his acting, which critics generally found mediocre). Yet most often, for most people, Caruso's voice was, indivisibly, a product of both man and machine that echoed deep into the expectations of listening, and ultimately conditioning the social experience of the live performance as well. This was suggested by an incident in 1908, recounted by the opera historian John Dizikes: the Metropolitan Opera company, on tour in Chicago, had been engaged to perform two operas on a double bill, one starring Caruso, the other starring the tenor Andreas Dippel. When Dippel was suffering from voice problems, Caruso offered to sing an offstage aria for him at the beginning of the opera. Unseen and unannounced, Caruso received only a polite, tepid response from the audience, yet the crowd later cheered him wildly during his designated performance. One way to interpret this episode is that Caruso's name and fame meant more to the audience than his singing. Another, though, is that those in attendance knew Caruso through their phonographs and were initially unaccustomed to hearing his voice in person. Either way, what people heard when they listened to Caruso was never something so simple as a strong and beautiful voice.[29]

Indeed, it was the combination of his charisma, his voice, and his critical reputation that underpinned Caruso's renown, although in some situations his voice did seem secondary. Telling in this respect is the recollection of Edward Bernays, a nephew of Sigmund Freud and pioneering public relations strategist, who to promote his fledgling PR firm decided to organize a widely publicized singing tour by Caruso around the United States in 1917. During his interactions with the singer, Bernays marveled at Caruso's astonishing personal magnetism. He later recalled, "His glamour affected me as it did others. I was talking to the sun god and the sun god by his light obliterated his surroundings. When we walked down Broadway together people forgot themselves and their interests for the moment and focused their attention on him."[30] Caruso evoked the reaction that movie stars do, Bernays noted—although in 1917 movie stars' celebrity was still purely visual; talking cinema was still a decade away.

On the tour, railroads ran special trains from outlying areas to enable the throngs to attend the performances, and Caruso's effect was the same everywhere. Although Bernays took credit for promoting the concerts, he also stood in awe of this man who "stepped out of the music page and was front-page news wherever he went and whatever he did." He also noted that Caruso's celebrity eclipsed his singing. Although Bernays did not cite Victor by name, his account registered the impact of its publicity: "I was impressed with the power an image has in affecting people; for the overwhelming majority of the people who reacted so spontaneously to Caruso had never heard him before. Some few may have listened to his recordings, but the attitudes of the mass had been formed by what they had read or heard about him." By year's end, the tour was over and Bernays, having been touched by Caruso's charisma and Victor's publicity, joined the government's pioneering wartime propaganda apparatus, the Committee on Public Information, where he made use of his experience on the Caruso tour and laid the groundwork for his highly influential postwar career.[31]

Paradoxically, after Victor's marketing and publicity work made such an impression on Bernays as he was starting out, the company then in the 1920s established a Bernays-style division called the Victor News Service. Its purpose was to feed stories and pictures of Victor artists to newspapers and magazines, *without* mention of the company name, in order to promote coverage of Victor artists as "news." Such work, the company explained to dealers, kept Victor's "great artists . . . before the public eye" in such a way that the newspaper or magazine editor did not have to "ignore his conscience in letting it into his columns, for it contains no reference to the relations of the artist with the Victor Company." And to assuage dealers who might have misgivings about such a strategy, Victor maintained that stories and photographs of Victor artists "are genuine *news,* not thinly disguised advertising" and insisted, "This is in no sense propaganda; leading figures in the musical world are as interesting as any to the newspaper public."[32]

Enrico Caruso was not a trademark of the Victor Company, but he did many of the things trademarks do, symbolizing a company's name, its products, its reputation. Yet Caruso stood for more besides, becoming over the years a metonym for the power and potential of the medium, the industry, and even music generally. If, however, Caruso could be likened to "a sun god," as Edward Bernays put it, whose "light obliterated his surroundings," it bears considering what the effect of his celebrity was, for Caruso's direct, demonstrable presence was limited. For all his stature, his recordings were not the records that most people listened to most of the time. At the same time, though, these recordings did have a real and lasting affective impact on the way people listened to recorded music. Years after the fact, his records were the ones people remembered, the ones that touched them most deeply, the ones that stretched their imaginations and filled the soundscape of their memories.

Caruso was not the only recording artist who moved listeners deeply, however. Recollections of his impact appear more frequently than for any other artist, but the stirring reminiscence of a woman from Pulaski, Virginia, from 1957, suggests that artists very different from Caruso could inspire the same kind of intense and enduring feelings. In the pages of *Hobbies* magazine, she recalled in precise detail her attendance at a concert of the Victor company's leading popular phonograph artists in 1917. "I still consider the night on which I heard those peerless performers sing and play to have been the greatest event of my life, and most of the details of the concert are as clear to me as if they had happened week before last," she wrote. Although generally forgotten today, the performers represented some of the most prolific popular music artists of Victor's Black Seal series, including Henry Burr, Arthur Collins, Billy Murray, Vess Ossman, and others. The concert of humorous songs, sentimental ballads, dancing, and skits took place in the Elks Theater. The front of the stage was lined with phonographs, furnished by the leading local dealers. "I thought about, talked about, and dreamed about that concert for months," the woman recalled. "There have been innumerable nights on which I have dreamed I am back in the old Elks Theater and waiting for the curtain to go up so I can hear another concert by the Record Makers. . . . I still consider that concert an even greater event in my life than my wedding day."[33]

Although her memory crystallized around a single event, the live performance, it was in relation to her deeply emotional experience with the phonograph at home that the concert took on its full meaning for her. All her family members "had individual preferences among the artists," and they all "regarded the leading phonograph stars of the day as personal friends, virtually members of our home."[34] Indeed, in a remark recalling A. J. Liebling's deification of Caruso, the writer described the phonograph as serving "almost as our family altar." This account is all the more remarkable in that the Black Seal artists to whom she felt so close never received the broad promotional backing that Red Sealers did, nor did they carry any of Red Seal's cultural capital.

The glare of Caruso's brilliant career also blinds us to how little there was to his persona beyond his celebrity. Reading between the lines of the many books about him, one is left with the impression that Caruso's life was surprisingly empty. The opera historian John Dizikes has written of the singer's performing career, "He was identified with no artistic movement or school, had no aesthetic ambitions, took no initiatives as de Reszke had done in the 1890s, [and] had no real concern with repertory, other than to be careful to avoid roles which did not suit his voice. . . . Conductors never complained about him." Onstage he often played the clown, but offstage he avoided parties and never sang or performed informally before friends, as, say, McCormack or Rachmaninoff often did. Instead, he enjoyed collecting coins and playing solitaire. He was warm, affable, and famously generous, yet he claimed very few close friends. He lived his entire adult life in hotels (he had a famous suite in New York's Knickerbocker Hotel), on the road, or at one of his walled villas in Italy. His widow stressed his simplicity: "His nature was not only uncomplicated; it was actually elemental. . . . He knew the taste of bread."[35]

As a model of modern celebrity Caruso enjoyed broad appeal across the social spectrum, his voice, personality, and renown never having a single, universal, or fixed meaning. In New York, for example, he was a touchstone for musical greatness among people as varied as African Americans in Harlem, socialites on the Upper East Side, and working-class immigrants downtown, but he symbolized something different in each of these environments and in others far beyond the city as well.[36] For the tenor Roland Hayes, born to a family of ex-slaves in 1887 on a poor farm in rural Georgia, Caruso was an inspiration. Hearing Caruso records when he was a teenager launched Hayes into a lifelong artistic pursuit and an internationally acclaimed career. For Italian immigrants on the Lower East Side Caruso was a *paisan*. They cheered him from the parterre in the Metropolitan Opera House, and at the time of the Monkey House Incident, they rallied to support him as one of their own. For New York socialists, he was a populist hero who, like them, hailed from humble origins. Martin Wolfson recalled, "We were an immigrant family of father and mother and eight of us children. . . . We worked ten and twelve hours a day and Saturdays. In factories. At night we went to the opera to hear Caruso, Galli Curci and Rosa Ponselle; et al. We sang opera all over the flat. We sang it at parties and on the third avenue el. We [had] a phonograph. Caruso all over the house." Far from the middle-brow pretension of Red Seal, Wolfson's poignant tribute showed the working class in solidarity with Caruso: "The factory worker—male and female—had to have his-her opera together with his-her union and his-her socialism. Caruso lived with the rich but he made his money with the proletariat."[37]

In the United States, Victor's two rivals reacted differently to the rising importance of celebrity in the music business. As in most things, Columbia followed Victor, in creating its own grand opera series and signing up and boosting the careers of a number of prominent performers. Like Victor, the rival company was also boosted by them in turn. Columbia had no Caruso—or Melba, McCormack, or Sembrich—but it had its share of respected artists and marketed them in much the same way as Victor did its Red Sealers. Meanwhile, Columbia's technology reflected Victor's growing dominance as well. At the turn of the century, Columbia manufactured and sold both cylinder and disc phonographs and records, but as Victor redefined the consumer market, Columbia became increasingly committed to the disc business, and it ended its cylinder production altogether in 1912.[38]

Victor's other rival, Thomas Edison's company, after pioneering the phonograph in the nineteenth century, limped along in the twentieth. In the 1910s, it introduced its own disc technology, the so-called Diamond Discs, a tacit admission of the company's defeat in the battle of technological formats. Edison himself was the biggest star his company had, and it was his face, not that of any recording artists, that appeared most frequently in the company's promotional materials. Indeed, Edison himself was another of the era's great celebrities—the Wizard of Menlo Park, genius inventor, adviser to industrialists and statesmen. As a businessman, however, his record was uneven. He understood how to market his inventions to large industrial clients much better than to individual consumers, and in the case of the phonograph, he believed that the marvel of the technology would sell itself. Eschewing the graphic enticements of his rivals' publications, Edison saw no need to include images in many of his catalogues. When pictures of the artists did appear, they were often grouped at the back rather than integrated into the listings.[39]

Indeed, many people did insist that Edison's technology sounded better than Victor's, especially after the introduction of his Blue Amberol cylinders in 1912, but technical superiority did not necessarily excite consumers the way celebrity artists did. In 1927, shortly before the Edison company collapsed, Edison's own vice president, Arthur Walsh, conceded the superiority of Victor's strategy: "Artists names was [sic] probably the best piece of sales promotion work for the Victor company that could have been put over." Reluctantly, Edison had begun to record some relatively big-name talent, but when it came to marketing, the company's own rhetoric reflected the degree to which Victor fixed the terms and conditions by which others would be

The GREAT ENTERTAINER

MR. EDISON has made his Phonograph so marvellously accurate that its reproduction of songs, stories and jokes has all the effect of a human entertainer, with the great advantage of being able to be turned on at will.

The amount of real enjoyment, entertainment, amusement and edification locked up in the wonderful Edison Phonograph and released by means of the ingenious Edison Gold-Moulded Records, is conclusive proof that Mr. Edison well deserves his title of "wizard."

If you are not now enjoying an Edison Phonograph, go today to the nearest dealer and hear it. If you want to know how and why a Phonograph can be made so agreeable, write today for a booklet about it.

If you own an Edison Phonograph, never forget that your Phonograph is new every time you get a new Record. Write today for the Complete Catalogue of Gold-Moulded Records, the Supplemental Catalogue and "The Phonogram" for March, published February 28th, which gives a little description of each new Record to be issued in March.

NATIONAL PHONOGRAPH COMPANY
12 Lakeside Avenue, Orange, N. J.

4.5 The image accompanying this 1907 advertisement published in *Collier's* suggests that it is Edison's phonograph, not the music, that these listeners find most impressive. Their dissimilar expressions seem a reaction to the wonder of the technology more than to the content of the recording, and their age links them to a generation of Americans accustomed to making things for themselves. Although the title of the advertisement points to the phonograph's use for entertainment, the text below keeps the emphasis on Edison and says nothing of the appeal of specific performers or recordings. Warshaw Collection of Business Americana–Phonographs, Archives Center, National Museum of American History, Behring Center, Smithsonian Institution.

judged. Hailing the availability of records by its new top opera singer, Riccardo Martin, the company's trade announcement read, "[He] has a remarkably fine tenor voice, but little inferior to the famous Caruso."[40]

Victor's successful fashioning and promotion of the Caruso phenomenon was another factor that distinguished the phonograph business from the player-piano business, with which it was interconnected in many ways. The player-piano business could and did advance marketing strategies based on music as cultural capital, as Victor did with Red Seal, but the player-piano business remained oriented toward compositions, not performers. Although the special reproducing player-pianos (which reproduced a recorded piano performance, not just preset notes, as did regular player-pianos) seem to be an exception to this, they constituted only the uppermost stratum of the industry. In 1923, for example, the peak year for player-piano production in the United States, fewer than 21,000 reproducing player-pianos were made, as compared with 177,000 regular player-pianos and 150,000 "straight," or nonplayer, pianos.[41] Today reproducing player-pianos are most often remembered for having recorded, as nothing else at the time could, piano performances by many of the era's leading composers and pianists (some of which have been reissued on CD in recent years). But these much-prized rolls were exceptional. Mostly, the catalogues of rolls for reproducing player-pianos were filled with dozens of names no one had heard of. The majority of these, it turned out, were pseudonyms, used by a small stable of staff pianists, who were given various aliases to suggest a broader and deeper pool of performers.[42]

Caruso died in 1921 at the age of forty-eight, mostly likely from peritonitis caused by a burst abscess. His name and voice have continued to reverberate, though; the echoes remain audible in everything from novels to movies to advertisements, and his recordings have cast a long shadow over all forms of musical culture. As recently as the year 2000, his recordings topped a *New York Times* list of the twenty-five most important events and achievements in twentieth-century *popular* music, and over the years his records have been reissued, repackaged, remixed, and re-recorded countless times. Recently the original recordings were even digitally stripped of their original thin-sounding accompaniments and re-recorded with a live modern symphony orchestra. A skeptical *New York Times* reviewer condemned the project as "woefully misbegotten" and wondered why the record company would not allow the "great recordings [to] speak for themselves, on their own terms."[43] The answer, of course, is that Caruso's recordings have never simply spoken for themselves and have always had an importance far greater than their musical value.

In the early twentieth century, Caruso embodied a great cultural shift taking place, as a result of which performers have attained an unprecedented level of social and cultural prominence. An exquisite performer, disciplined and professional, Caruso marked the extension of the nineteenth-century cult of the virtuoso into social relations in the age of mechanical reproduction. Part of a shared national culture, Caruso did not mean the same thing to everyone, but he stood as a common reference point, a symbol of greatness and possibility shared in the social imagination even of people who knew nothing of opera or who never heard his recordings.

Marketing had much to do with this nationally integrated experience, but so too did the sound and structure of the music technology. Where some artists faltered in the recording studio, Caruso thrived, the exemplar of a new era of performers capable of exploring the potential of human expression while staring into the black hole of the recording horn. Although the recorded discs that resulted were pressed in batches of many thousands, the relationship of performer to consumers was then constituted person by person. It was based on the twin elements of access—via inexpensive, widely available commodities—and repetition, which enabled hearers to listen to a single performance over and over. Both despite this technological mediation and because of it, countless anonymous listeners could cultivate relationships with performers that approximated real intimacy: knowing the rhythms of another human being's breath, registering the grain of another's voice in one's own body, and perhaps experiencing genuine feelings of exaltation or ecstasy. In some cases, this flood of emotion might burst forth most powerfully at a live performance, whether by Caruso or by the Black Seal singers in Pulaski, Virginia, but it issued from a reservoir of feeling collected in the home, the result of living with the voices of treasured performers, weaving them into the fabric of families and friendships, and hearing the captured moments of a single fleeting performance time and again.

↩ 5 ↪

Musical Properties

Appearing before a joint congressional committee in June 1906, John Philip Sousa began his testimony by rejecting a well-known claim by Alexander Fletcher, the Scottish politician and patriot. Fletcher, Sousa told the committee, "said that he cared not who made the laws of the land if he could write its songs. We composers of America take the other view. We are very anxious as to who makes the laws of this land." Given that Sousa powerfully symbolized confidence and assurance, it is particularly notable that he declared himself to be "anxious" about the legal situation. The March King was not alone in his anxiety, however: others throughout the music business were coming to realize as never before that the way in which music was defined and treated by the law had profound implications. Many of the issues that musicians and music entrepreneurs confronted had existed for some time but had sparked less concern before the twentieth century, when the stakes were relatively low. By the time Sousa and others in the music business descended on Congress, though, the substantial growth in the different sectors of the business exposed acute unresolved tensions.[1]

Alongside the rise of popular music, of new mechanical technologies, and of mass-marketed celebrity other, less visible changes were occurring in the political economy of music. Conflicting views about music as property threatened to halt the continued growth of the industry. In the same years, the legal foundations of American business were also shifting, and by establishing new property rights in music, the industry settled its most pressing conflicts, opened the way for future growth, and left one of its most influential legacies. As corporations grew in size and in economic and political power between the end of the Civil War and the start of the Great Depression, a fundamental legal restructuring took place in American business and society. In some cases, as with patents, the music industry benefited crucially from legal instruments it had had little hand in crafting. In other cases, as with copyrights, the music industry was a leader in effecting profound legal changes with major long-term implications, both within the world of music and far beyond it.

The music industry, never monolithic, encompassed various sectors by then, each of which sought to advance its own parochial concerns, even if the music itself rarely respected boundaries. As composition, performance, sound, and object, music functioned simultaneously in several different economies, and the needs of one did not always accord with those of the others. As the exploitation of music through live performance and mechanical reproduction became increasingly lucrative, the financial stakes increased and the push for expanded property rights became more and more systematic. The more the music industry filled the air with music, the more cognizant those in the business became of the commercial value of their products and the more jealously they sought to control who profited from them and under what conditions.

Copyright law—legal protection against unauthorized reproduction of creative works—was the central locus of conflict both within the industry and between the industry and other parties. In the American context, this body of law rested on the passage in the U.S. Constitution granting Congress the power "to promote the progress of science and useful arts, by securing for limited times to authors and inventors the exclusive right to their respective writings and discoveries" (art. I, sec. 8). Over time, lawmakers and jurists confronted a host of difficult questions about the meaning of this provision. Was its purpose to protect authors or to ensure the circulation of ideas? Who was entitled to protection as an author? What was a "limited" amount of time? Did a copy of "writings" include such things as phonograph records or player-piano rolls? Questions such as these were pivotal to establishing the economic foundation of the twentieth-century entertainment industries, of which the music industry emerged as a defining force. Certainly, book publishing, theater, photography, lithography, and cinema were also involved in testing, stretching, challenging, and redefining what Justice Joseph Story called in 1841 the metaphysics of copyright law, but perhaps no field was as active as music in connecting such metaphysics with the physics of commercial and social relations and with the ethics and poetics of the cultural environment.[2]

Music in the Age of Expanding Property Rights

Until after the Civil War, in American jurisprudence the prevailing, idealized conception of property was of a physical thing, such as land. In the last third of the nineteenth century, though, the courts moved definitively away from this "physicalist" conception of property, toward a more abstract definition of property as "a bundle of rights." When Justice Noah H. Swayne defined property in 1873 as "everything which has exchangeable value," his was a dissenting view on the bench and a minority view in American society at large. In the succeeding half century, however, concurrently with the growth of the music industry, legal scholars and jurists came to include under the definition of property such intangible claims as anticipated earnings and goodwill (that is, a firm's name and reputation). By 1922 Yale Law School's Arthur L. Corbin could look back at this transformation and conclude, "Our concept of property has shifted; incorporeal rights have become property. . . . 'Property' has ceased to describe any *res,* or object of sense, at all, and has become merely a bundle of legal relations—rights, powers, privileges, immunities." In the face of this abstraction, the philosopher Morris Cohen, in his article "Property and Sovereignty" (1927), offered a salutary reminder about the stakes for this conceptual shift: "Whatever technical definition of property we may prefer," he wrote, "we must recognize that a property right is a relation not between an owner and a thing, but between the owner and other individuals in reference to things."[3] This point was particularly pertinent when applied to music, which was a "thing" with no fixed, material form.

Meanwhile, this shift away from a "physicalist" conception of property reinforced the increasing level of abstraction within the law, and in numerous other aspects of American society. The growing futures markets, for example, traded in contracts for commodities the seller did not own and the buyer did not want, with a price to be determined at a future date. In the same years, the railroads, telegraph, and telephone transformed prevailing conceptions of time and space. And corporations, then expanding rapidly in size, complexity, and power, were declared "artificial persons" before the law. In other words, the growing disembodiment of business coincided with the phonograph's disembodiment of music making. Indeed, both these occurrences were part of the profound transformation in American political economy, from a system based on competition among small, proprietary business forms to one dominated by large, oligopolistic corporations favoring managed markets over the unpredictability of unfettered competition.[4]

In the music industry, nothing reflected this transition better than the contrast between the older, relatively competitive piano industry and the newer, oligopolistic phonograph business, which used a patent pool among the three leading phonograph manufacturers as a virtually insuperable weapon against would-be newcomers to the field. Rooted in the same constitutional clause as copyright, patent laws in the United States were originally devised as a novel means of encouraging invention and innovation by granting to a patentee a monopoly on the exploitation of the patent for a fixed number of years. By the mid-nineteenth century, however, patents were already becoming a tool not to stimulate ingenuity but to limit or stifle competition. Through agreements to share their patents, large firms both minimized costly conflicts of uncertain outcome and shored up their own position as industry giants. The first such patent pool was established in 1856 by the leading sewing machine manufacturers, an industry that had also influenced the music business in its sales and marketing strategies. By the 1890s, to avoid ongoing internecine conflict, Columbia and Edison arranged to cross-license each other's patents, and Columbia and Victor did the same in 1903 and 1907. The leading firms in the movie business tried the same thing in 1908 (their attempt was struck down by the Supreme Court in 1918), and in the 1920s, the same decade in which the U.S. Patent Office moved from the Department of the Interior to Herbert Hoover's Department of Commerce, a patent pool was also used to delimit the radio industry.[5]

In one important test of the power of patents to limit competition, the Supreme Court ruled in *Leeds & Catlin Company v. Victor Talking Machine Company* in 1909 that Victor's patented technology comprised the machine *and* the records, thus making it an infringement for another company to produce records playable on Victor phonographs.[6] Thus, through its legal grip on the form of musical production, Victor controlled the content as well. This was the cultural equivalent of the absolute authority that railroads initially claimed over both the physical rails and the means of conveyance—who and what traveled on its lines, and on what terms—and it was not until key phonograph patents expired in the second half of the 1910s that independent cultural producers—in this case, record companies that were not also phonograph manufacturers—could operate in the business with any kind of reliable legal foundation. Victor president Eldridge Johnson hailed the *Leeds & Catlin* decision and pointedly told dealers, *"There is no longer a great profit to be made for a small effort in the talking machine business. . . . It now requires large capital, large manufacturing plants and most of all a well-chosen and well-organized army of experts."*[7]

Notwithstanding the importance of patents to the legal structure of cultural production, copyright was the area of the law with the greatest bearing on the music industry. A relatively recent and unusual phenomenon, the rise of copyright law in the United States was consistent with the pattern of development in other industrial or industrializing nations from the eighteenth to the twentieth century. In ancient Greek, Chinese, Islamic, and Judeo-Christian writings, the expressive act was widely understood not as an individual achievement but as a divine gift, and for many centuries the right to make copies of a work did not fall to the individual creator but was controlled by the state, according to its particular prerogatives and interests. Such precepts began to change in the eighteenth century, however, with the growth of a middle-class reading public, major political challenges to the absolutist state, and the advent of a new, secular ideology of the origins of knowledge and creative expression. No longer did all thoughts and inspiration come from the heavens; they came from human beings, who had an interest, both individual and social, in the conditions in which works and ideas circulated.[8]

Since the eighteenth century, philosophical, legal, and political copyright debates have been structured by the tension between two opposing positions. On one side is the belief in a strong or absolute right to control the reproduction of creations of one's mind. This view is derived from John

Locke's philosophy of natural rights, beginning with his argument in the *Second Treatise* (1690) that a person's body is his own property, a fact that entitles him to the fruits of his labor. The contention that this should apply to labors of the mind, such as writing, was advanced in the eighteenth century by Edward Young in England, Denis Diderot in France, and Gotthold Lessing and Johann Gottlieb Fichte in Germany. On the other side is a concept of copyright grounded in social utility. A leading exponent of this perspective was Condorcet, who critiqued the idea of knowledge based on the Romantic ideal of individuality and instead posited the theory that all knowledge is produced socially. For Condorcet, knowledge might be a kind of property, but if so, it belongs to the realm of common property, in which everyone in a society has an equal claim, not private property, which is exclusive and individual. These two positions have been framed and articulated in various ways—for example, the legal scholar Paul Goldstein presents copyright law as representing a tug-of-war between the "optimists," who wish to extend the property rights of knowledge producers, and the "pessimists," who wish to limit those rights, on the strength of the public's right to access—but the essence of the debate has remained constant. Indeed, England's Statute of Anne (1710), the Copyright Act of 1790 in the United States, the French copyright law of 1793, and the corresponding laws in Germany before and after unification all represent attempts to balance these two interests.[9]

On the basis of the precedent set by the English case of *Donaldson v. Becket* (1774), this balance has most often been struck through entitling an author to a "limited property right" in his or her work, meaning exclusive control over publication for a fixed period of time, although the meaning of "limited" has varied considerably in different times and places. It is notable, however, that the concept of authors' property right in their writing, which first appeared in the English Statute of Anne, was advanced initially not by authors themselves but by the Stationers' Company, which seized on the natural-rights argument as a strategy to protect its publishing interests.[10] As the cult of the individual Romantic genius grew in the eighteenth and nineteenth century, it came to serve as the keystone for arguments in favor of more restrictive laws protecting individual creation, notwithstanding the fact that it has most often been publishers—in the United States and elsewhere—who have pushed hardest for stronger statutory protections.

Although music was not mentioned explicitly in the first U.S. copyright law, in 1790, its congressional drafters had already begun to expand the constitutional protection of "authors" and their "writings" by explicitly protecting not only books against unauthorized reproduction, but also charts and maps. In practice, the law did protect some musical works that were published as books and filed as such with the copyright office.[11] Music was included explicitly for the first time in the revised copyright law of 1831, by which time there had been a considerable growth in the publication of sheet music in the United States. At that time, it was not yet clear, as it would be later, how inherently problematic it was to make traditional literary authorship the basis for a property right in music or other kinds of cultural production. Above and beyond thorny questions about the creative autonomy of a writer of poetry or novels or essays, the notion of autonomy was even more complex when applied to areas such as theater or music making. Each of these was a live and social form of cultural production, which might not exist in a single definitive version. Indeed, its very existence and success as a creative work depended not just on an originary composer but also on those who executed the work, including both the director (theatrical or musical) and performers. This complicated the Lockean notion of a natural right to the fruits of one's labor, for here a singular, unified model of labor and production did not necessarily apply: What of the value created by the virtuoso performance? What of the value created by a celebrity performer? Despite the poor fit between the musical and literary cases, it was exactly this author-centered literary model of copyright which the legal structure of music-making would come to reinforce.

Except in cases of piracy, which was not a serious problem in the United States, as it was in England and on the Continent, before the late nineteenth century copyright was not a major issue in the music business. Other legal issues, like bankruptcy law, tended to have greater bearing on the music trade. One reason for the relative unimportance of copyright was that in the early years of the United States lawmakers and publishers favored relatively weak copyright laws, leaning more toward broad public availability in the philosophical tug-of-war between the social utility of access and the protection of natural rights. In a pattern typical of developing nations, this tendency included a refusal to honor foreign copyrights, as the country relied heavily on cultural products imported from Europe. (In the twentieth century, China, Egypt, and many other nations likewise resisted recognition of foreign copyrights.) This situation had begun to change by the late nineteenth century, when the volume and value of American products reached a level at which it became advantageous for publishers and lawmakers to seek stronger protections for copyrighted material. Thus, copyright owners in the United States came to be protected internationally through a long list of presidential proclamations, bilateral treaties, and multilateral international conventions (though until 1989 it spurned the widely supported Berne Convention agreement of 1886). Indeed, this pulled the United States more or less into line with the advanced industrial nations of Europe, which were also moving toward a more restrictive, property rights–based philosophy of copyright in the late nineteenth century.[12]

Starting in the late nineteenth century, as the legal conception of property was becoming more abstract, property law came to absorb matters that had not fallen strictly within its purview earlier. This tendency was particularly clear in the case of copyright and patents, which politicians and lawyers a century earlier had discussed more in the language of monopoly than of property.[13] Today, copyright and patents belong to the legal category of *intellectual property* (along with trademarks, trade secrets, and a few other legal subcategories), but this term was essentially unknown in American jurisprudence until recently. Although a U.S. circuit court mentioned "intellectual property" once in 1845 and a decision by the Supreme Court in 1873 quoted a letter in which the phrase appeared, it did not appear again in a decision by the high court until 1949. (Even today, the Copyleft movement and other radical critics of current intellectual property rights have questioned the legitimacy of treating issues subsumed under this phrase as a subset of those pertaining to tangible property.)[14]

Moreover, although technological developments (photography, phonographs, cinema, and so on) raised new questions about copyright, these developments alone did not produce the expansion of copyright. The court could just as well have rejected the extension of protection to new media, and in many early cases it did. When George Washington signed the first U.S. copyright law in 1790, that act was explicitly designated "an Act for the encouragement of learning," but by the time of the landmark case of *Bleistein v.*

Donaldson (1903), the Supreme Court had turned away from the social enrichment aspect of copyright protection and reframed it as a protection based on private property. This case concerned the unauthorized reproduction of advertising posters for a circus, and the court found the pirated copies to be an infringement of the copyright to which the producer of the poster was entitled. The important distinction in the ruling was the court's rejection of artistic quality as a factor determining eligibility for copyright, although that consideration had been the basis for extending copyright protection to photographs in 1884. The court expanded the law to cover works that were produced deliberately or primarily for commercial purposes. Writing for the majority, Oliver Wendell Holmes maintained that it was not the place of jurists to be art critics, and if the posters "command[ed] the interest of any public," they must have some value—commercial, educational, or aesthetic. "The taste of any public is not to be treated with contempt," Holmes wrote. "That these pictures had their worth and their success is sufficiently shown by the desire to reproduce them without regard to the plaintiffs' rights." Thus, couching his opinion in self-effacing, democratic language, Holmes opened the door to protecting a wider and wider pool of ideas and works as private property.[15]

This was an apposite decision for an era when the line between art and advertising was becoming increasingly blurred, but it increased the burden on the antiquated statutory copyright law. Its procedures for registering and renewing copyrights were Byzantine and inflexible, and the law was inadequate to deal with phonograph records, player-piano rolls, or moving pictures, not to mention the growing economy of entertainment and leisure—vaudeville, musical theater, dance halls, as well as dime novels and mass-circulation illustrated magazines—all of which used copyrighted works as a matter of course. In 1905 the distinguished Register of Copyrights Thorvald Solberg published *Copyright in Congress, 1789–1904,* a book detailing the woeful inadequacy of the existing law to protect "valuable literary and artistic property rights." Then, in December of that year, President Theodore Roosevelt amplified on Solberg's complaint in an address before Congress, calling for "a complete revision" to the copyright law, which he categorized as ill suited for "modern reproductive processes," difficult for the courts to interpret, and imposing "hardships" on copyright holders that did nothing to serve or protect the public interest. From this call followed more than three years of agitation, lobbying, scheming, and debate, leading ultimately to a new law. On his final day in office, Roosevelt signed into law the Copyright Act of 1909, the statutory foundation of American copyright until 1976.[16]

Property Rights in Music Redefined

Before passage of the bill was secured, numerous drafts of it were the subject of long and labored hearings and debates. Music publishers had a leading role in writing the initial draft of the bill, and in hundreds of hours of congressional testimony, by far the greatest number of witnesses to appear from any single field came from the music industry—nearly the number of witnesses from all other fields (book publishing, photography, libraries, and so on) combined. The push for copyright reform was in large part a by-product of huge growth within the music industry. The value of products in the music section in the U.S. Census of Manufactures increased by 58 percent from 1899 to 1904, and the value of goods produced by the music printing and publishing business alone increased by 69 percent during the same interval.[17] Growing sheet music sales notwithstanding, music publishers objected to the exploitation of their copyrighted material for others' economic gain. The law at that time protected them against the production and sale of unauthorized printed copies of their work, but it was silent about the use of their material by, say, a manufacturer of piano rolls or phonograph records. The closest the law came was an 1897 amendment to the copyright code that prohibited unauthorized public performances of copyrighted works. This provision, however, did not address the niceties of mechanical reproduction, contained no enforcement mechanism, and had little practical impact.[18] Conceived and written with printed works in mind, statutory law granted publishers a monopoly over reprinting the musical notation and lyrics of a composition, therefore, but it did not address music as an aural phenomenon whose economic value varied according to how, where, and to what end it was played.

In the traditional, tangible, written sense, *copying* was not so much the issue as was others' commercial *use* of copyrighted material. This use was manifest in two different domains, performance-based and machine-based, of which the latter was the more prominent concern. Mechanical reproduction of music was growing at a stunning rate; the value of the products of the phonograph industry, for example, increased from $2.2 million in 1899 to $10.2 million in 1904 and showed no signs of abating.[19] Although a huge amount of the material appearing on piano rolls and phonograph records was not protected by copyright—including traditional or folk songs, various forms of European art music, humorous monologues and political and historical speeches, and songs whose copyrights had lapsed or expired—manufacturers' catalogues contained much copyrighted material as well. Beyond mechanical reproduction, though, by the early twentieth century various kinds of live commercial musical performances had been increasing for several decades. From high-society ballrooms to working-class dance halls, music was a prominent feature of "going out" in the expanding urban commercial culture. Whereas the reliance on skilled laborers was declining in many forms of industrial production, the demand for the skilled labor of musicians was growing, and copyrighted music constituted a large proportion of the music they played.[20]

Publishers looked at the surging business in mechanical reproduction and live performance and claimed that their copyrights were being infringed. It struck some contemporaries as contradictory, however, for publishers to make such claims. For one thing, rather than undermining the economic value of copyrighted material, wide distribution often enhanced it; the copyright in a song widely sung was much more valuable than the copyright in a song no one knew or liked.[21] For another thing, only a fine line separated publishers' desire to gain exposure for their material from their anxiety that someone might expropriate it. Publishers condemned uncompensated forms of reproduction and performance, but their complex plugging operations were promoting songs in many of the same ways—and at great expense to the publishers. Indeed, the phonograph manufacturers had used copyrighted material since the 1890s, but publishers showed no concern earlier, when the stakes in the phonograph industry were negligible. As far as the publishers were concerned, of course, the difference was between unregulated and regulated distribution and between someone else's profits and their own. Even if the revenues of publishers as a group were increasing, they objected to their musical products' being systematically used as raw material in other increasingly profitable businesses.

5.1 In the late nineteenth and early twentieth centuries, people could hear live music in a greater number and variety of locales than ever before. Here, elegant patrons at Willow Grove outside Philadelphia listen to the Sousa Band. Brown Brothers, Sterling, Pa.

On the other side of the copyright divide, theater owners, band and orchestra leaders, musicians, and manufacturers of piano rolls and phonograph records rejected publishers' claims. For those who stood accused of infringement, the situation looked quite different. They claimed that they did compensate publishers for the use of their material—when they purchased the sheet music or score. They also contended they had a right to do what they wished with published music they purchased, just as individual consumers did. More formally, in court, piano roll manufacturers argued that they were not producing "copies" of any copyrighted material in the strict legal sense, because the perforated holes in a piano roll were illegible to humans. Phonograph manufacturers made this argument too, in contending that their discs were not "copies" because no person could read and identify a piece of music from its imprint in the shellac grooves. They also claimed that their phonographic reproductions did not hurt but rather helped sheet music sales, an assertion that in some instances was no doubt true. A profound struggle, then, was taking shape over the nature of music as property, waged by the music publishers against those who used their works as part of new and growing forms of commercial musical exploitation.

In June and December of 1906 and March of 1908, the Joint Congressional Committee on Patents held hearings about proposed changes to the United States copyright code, at which dozens of witnesses from the music industry appeared.[22] These included celebrities like Sousa and Herbert, lawyers for industry trade groups, and unaffiliated, independent inventors. Nominally, Herbert had a dual identity as a composer and a performer, speaking as both president of an ad hoc group called the Authors' and Composers' Copyright League of America and a representative of the American Federation of Musicians, but in practice his remarks did not address the effects of copyright reform on professional musicians, nor did any other witnesses testify on their behalf. What the hearings did explore, however, was numerous other aspects of the idea of extending copyright protection on musical works —such as whether copyright holders had a moral right to protection against unauthorized public performance or mechanical reproduction; whether the protection of such rights was constitutional (that is, in accordance with the meaning of "author" and "writing" before the law); and what the economic implications would be for the music industry of a statutory royalty applied to the mechanical reproduction of copyrighted material. Nathan Burkan, the attorney for the Music Publishers' Association (MPA), for example, testified about the legal precedents for expanding the definition of "writings" protected under the Constitution. In strong opposition to copyright reform, the Columbia Phonograph Company's S. T. Cameron denied its constitutionality and likened the idea of phonograph companies' paying a royalty on records to Sousa's having to pay a royalty on the patented instruments played by the members of his band. On behalf of the Victor Talking Machine Company, Horace Pettit took a position that was at once more moderate and more radical than Columbia's. He testified that Victor did not in theory oppose the payment of a royalty but preferred an expanded property right that would protect sound recordings as well—"the characteristic manner in which [the sound] is uttered," regardless of whether the thing uttered was copyrighted or not.[23]

The most forceful arguments by supporters of copyright reform employed the language of natural rights, of the property right of authors in the products of their labor, and this tended to obscure that it was the big publishers, not authors or composers, who spearheaded the campaign. J. L. Tindale, for example, a publisher and member of the MPA executive committee, argued that composers had a moral claim over mechanical reproduction of their work. Generally, publishers did not speak of their own interests, but rather positioned themselves as representatives of composers, with the implication that the interests of the two groups were identical. "This is a new form of property that the composer has found, which has dropped into his lap," Tindale maintained, "and that he reserves to himself." Two exceptional composers who did appear and who argued forcefully for stronger protection were Victor Herbert and John Philip Sousa. They were closely aligned with the publishing business, however, and as artists who had achieved extraordinary commercial success, they did not necessarily express the interests and priorities of rank-and-file composers. The hearings were based on an initial reform bill that grew out of a series of conferences with music publishers, to which other representatives of the music industry were not invited, and after a systematic review of the congressional committee's memoranda and correspondence, F. W. Hedgeland, an inventor of musical instruments, testified that he had "failed to find a single, solitary letter from any one composer petitioning or asking for protection under a measure of this kind."[24] Although proponents of reform extolled the virtues of individual creativity, it was all but incidental in the push for a new law. To grasp the reasons, it is important to remember that copyright does not protect ideas, but protects only the *expression* of ideas—a book can be copyrighted, but a plot cannot—and that neither the music industry nor the existing copyright law had creative innovation as its goal. Indeed, the publishers of Tin Pan Alley fought publicly alongside several distinctive and unusually successful composers for expanded copyright protection, but as a business Tin Pan Alley was dependent not on originality but on formula and standardization.

To strengthen their hand, publishers worked vigorously both within and beyond Washington to line up support for a reform bill in Congress. In an example of unabashed lobbying chutzpah, Isidore Witmark tried to marshal the support of the five or six thousand aspiring songwriters whose works his firm had *rejected* in recent years, by sending to each one a letter suggesting that his or her song might have been accepted for publication if not for the phonograph and piano roll businesses, whose reckless and opportunistic exploitation of others' music—free of charge—handicapped publishers' growth and ability to acquire new songs. He urged the songwriters to write their elected representatives to demand a revision of the copyright law.[25]

Around the same time, Sousa published an article titled "The Menace of Mechanical Music," which is often cited as one of the signature statements of the period on the cultural ramifications of mechanical reproduction. The article had two sections. In the often-quoted first section, Sousa established his principled opposition to machine-assisted music making and warned that its proliferation was supplanting amateur musicianship, was causing "the national throat" to atrophy, and was undermining widely held musical and civic values. But Sousa's underlying concern was not cultural as much as financial, and in the second half of the article, he railed against phonograph companies' failure to pay composers a royalty for use of their works. Here was Sousa's real motivation, for Sousa was hardly an avowed opponent of the phonograph industry. His band had been probably the most widely recorded ensemble of the 1890s, and for several years his endorsements appeared in Victor Talking Machine Company catalogues. When he testified before Congress in support of the bill, he was forced to concede the flimsiness of his putatively principled stance:

> *Senator Reed Smoot:* If you were protected in your productions and received a royalty from the talking machines, would that lessen the use of the talking machine any and strengthen the use of the voice and the brass band and the home choir, and so on?
>
> *Mr. Sousa:* I do not think so. . . .
>
> *Sen. Smoot:* Then, it is simply a question of your receiving the royalty that you think you are entitled to?
>
> *Mr. Sousa:* Yes, sir.

His opposition to the phonograph vanished after the copyright law eventually passed, granting a royalty to composers and publishers for mechanical reproductions of their work. By the 1920s Sousa was crediting the phonograph for contributing to the nation's thriving musical culture.[26]

Given the nature of these issues, one might readily assume that the political factions simply pitted the music publishers against the manufacturers of piano rolls and phonograph records, but the surprising reality was more complex. In the course of the hearings, it was revealed that the Aeolian Company, the leading manufacturer of player-pianos (and rolls), had in 1902 signed contracts with the members of the American Music Publishers Association, which comprised all but two of the nation's biggest firms, granting Aeolian the exclusive right to issue piano rolls of the publishers' works if the law declared that producing unauthorized piano rolls and phonograph records was in fact an infringement of copyright. The agreement also shielded Aeolian from liability for royalties up to such time. Aeolian even committed to testing the copyright infringement principle in the courts, which, if they decided *against* the manufacturers of piano rolls, would have handed to Aeolian a thirty-five year monopoly on the catalogues of nearly every leading publisher in the country. It was more or less a win-win proposition for Aeolian: either the courts affirmed that Aeolian (and other piano roll manufacturers) could continue to use copyrighted musical material for free, or it overturned that precedent and allowed Aeolian to wipe out its competition.

Through a legal campaign spearheaded by Charles Evans Hughes, one of the leading lawyers in the country (later U.S. secretary of state and Chief Justice of the Supreme Court), a test case advanced through the judiciary. That case was *White-Smith v. Apollo,* which the Supreme Court agreed to hear at the same time that copyright reform was being debated in Congress. In 1908 the high court ruled that piano rolls did not constitute copyright infringement, because they did not fall within the constitutional meaning of "writings." The law had long since included musical composers as "authors," so that was not an issue. The sticking point was whether a piano roll could be a "writing" if no human could read it, and the court held that it could not— that piano rolls were "performances," not "copies." The ruling struck many contemporaries as profoundly unsatisfying, even if it was legally sound. As

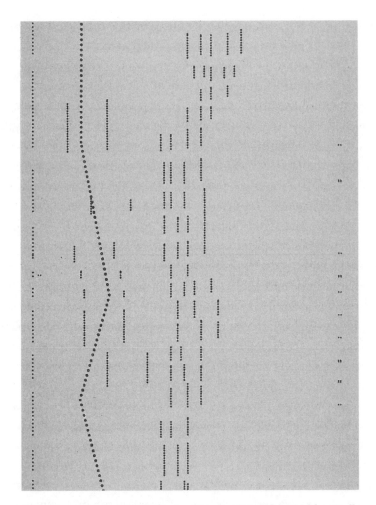

5.2 Pictured here is a detail of a player-piano roll. In *White-Smith v. Apollo* (1908), the Supreme Court ruled that under copyright law such perforations were not "writings." Author's collection.

Justice Holmes expressed it in his concurring opinion, the decision seemed to follow the letter of the law at the expense of its deeper intention, and he bemoaned the outdated copyright statute that made such a decision necessary.[27]

Passed the following year, the epochal Copyright Act of 1909 fixed the course of American musical copyright law for most of the twentieth century. The provisions directly related to music, appearing primarily in the first section, affirmed older claims and opened up big new ones. It reserved to the copyright holder the right to authorize mechanical reproduction of his or her work and required that manufacturers of mechanical copies pay a two-cent royalty for every copy made—what has come to be known in the law as a copyright holder's "mechanical right." To subvert the kind of monopoly that the Aeolian Company was maneuvering to create, however, the law also stipulated that once a copyright holder permitted the mechanical reproduction of a work, any other firm could also make mechanical copies, as long as it paid the royalty. This "compulsory license"—obligating copyright holders to license their material for use—is the legal basis for "cover" songs: once a composition is recorded, it is fair game for anyone else at the same rate. The composer still received the royalty, but after the first sale, he or she had no control over who made subsequent reproductions. The other landmark provision was to expand copyright to include control over "public performance for profit," which was the subject of much less comment at the time but would in coming years be the basis for a valuable new "performing right." Numerous other sections of the law also broadened the value of music as property, in part by extending the copyright term to twenty-eight years, renewable for another twenty-eight, and increasing the penalties for infringement. Although a few composers and publishers grumbled about terms of the final bill—some wanted a higher rate, and many criticized the compulsory license—they rejoiced at the passage of the law. Leo Feist singled out the attorney Nathan Burkan and the publisher Isidore Witmark for special commendation. The new law "will increase the revenue of the music publishers to a wonderful extent," F. A. Mills said contentedly.[28]

One thing that did not change, however, was the legal understanding of sound. Although the law now identified piano rolls and phonograph records as "copies" of copyrighted music within the meaning of the law, it did not make the sounds themselves the object of copyright. Piano rolls and phonograph records were copies, according to the law, to the extent that they were analogous to a written score, like a kind of sheet music that only machines could read. The music of piano rolls and phonograph records was inscribed into law not as sound but as "text," albeit text beyond legibility for humans. To register the copyright in a work, one had to submit some kind of written score. It could be vague and it could, hypothetically, be based on a recording, but the notes, not the sounds, were what the copyright protected. Indeed, it would not be until many decades later that the U.S. Copyright Office came to accept sound recordings for registration, and not until the 1971 amendment to the Copyright Act that the law extended protection to sound itself.[29]

Shortcomings aside, the law did redress many of the serious points of confusion and ambiguity in the earlier law—by simplifying registration procedures, for example, and clarifying the extent to which works eligible for copyright in the United States had to be produced there—and it marked a new era in copyright through its dramatic assertion of a new kind of property right, the mechanical right. At the same time, the law affected music in other, more subtle ways as well. It defined and privileged musical "authorship" in a way that gave increased power to publishers and composers—and not only in relation to manufacturers of records and rolls but also to all others in the field of musical culture.[30] Fetishizing the composer and the composition, copyright law reaffirmed and materially strengthened the value of music as property, not as process.

In the broad field of cultural production, music making encompasses many elements and involves many people, including not just composers and performers but also copyists and arrangers, instrument makers and audience members, managers and booking agents, critics and editors and educators. Within the province of law, though, music was something else altogether, something composed and fixed—not a relation or a dynamic process, but a product, stopped in its tracks. It mattered little that this definition flew in the face of the experience and knowledge of publishers, phonograph manufacturers, and especially consumers: that the performer, the performance, the sound, and the social context mattered enormously in the valuation of a musical work. Among other things, the careers of Caruso, Al Jolson, and others signaled how performers increasingly invested songs with commercial value as much as composers did, and sometimes more. The law, therefore, protected only one dimension of the creative labor of music making. If the purpose of the law was truly to protect works of the imagination or offer incentives for those whose originality created something of economic value, then it left much to be desired.

Defining music as product, not process, the law put economic before social considerations. It favored a kind of creative work that could be fixed and captured, the antithesis of cultural production based on musical improvisation—or what some jazz musicians would later call spontaneous composition—which was predicated on dynamic interaction, both among performers and between performers and audiences. It also stood in fundamental opposition to a musical model based on tradition and repetition. In many rural "folk" cultures the idea that one version of a musical work is definitive would fly in the face of the social character of the music. In such a setting, value derives from creative reuse—a matter of *copy rites,* not copyrights.[31]

Notwithstanding the exclusive ideology strengthening the treatment of copyright as a kind of private property, the committing of ideas to paper, not their originality, mattered in the eyes of the law. By the 1920s, countless ad hoc versions of blues and folk songs, cobbled together from an amorphous pool of shared phrases, verses, and musical figures, were being recorded, transcribed, titled, and deposited in the copyright office. Indeed, by this time the renowned jurist Learned Hand had already acknowledged that originality was not a master that copyright was capable of serving. In 1916 he abandoned it as a definitive qualification for copyright when he took into account the close similarities that could exist between two works of art, such as paintings or photographs of the same subject. The same principle of close resemblance obtained for maps, charts, or directories, in which the element of novelty might be minimal. "No one doubts that two directories, independently made, are each entitled to copyright, regardless of their similarity," he wrote in his influential 1924 decision, *Fred Fisher v. Dillingham.* "Each being the result of individual work, the second will be protected, quite regardless of its lack of novelty." Dramatic works raised still other problems with the metaphysics of copyright, and these problems applied to music as well in some instances. Given that plays were continually modified and adapted for different theatrical productions, when was the proper time to deposit a play for copyright? What was its definitive moment or version? Deposited too soon, and one risked protecting a work substantially different from the one that would be presented to the public; deposited too late, and one risked exposing the work to copying or theft. Together, issues such as these suggest how mismatched were artistic practice and the social relation of art to the static, formal, rationalized administration of copyright law, and how awkward was their interaction.[32]

The idea of granting rights holders protection against unauthorized "public performance for profit" generated much less discussion during the congressional hearings than did debates over mechanical reproduction, but the inclusion of the provision in the final law had major long-term consequences. Of course, in some cases publishers and composers welcomed having their works performed publicly, but in others they sought commercial control over their works, in order to receive compensation for their use. The 1909 law established, for the first time, a statutory foundation for this claim, including fines and penalties for noncompliance. How the claim would be enforced, however, was much less clear.

Just as manufacturers of phonograph records and piano rolls did, impresarios, bandleaders, and performers usually rebuffed publishers' demands for compensation and often claimed that public performance helped, rather than hindered, sheet music sales, an assertion some merchants supported. As those on the performance side of the equation knew, however, many musical compositions that were extremely popular when played by an orchestra sold very few individual copies. Music for dining and for dancing contributed increasingly to leisure activities and amusement, and publishers looked on as other establishments systematically profited from such performance songs, as the industry called them.

Then, in October 1913, a small group of publishers and songwriters met at Luchow's restaurant in New York to form a trade organization to police copyright holders' so-called performing right. In 1911 the French performing rights society the Société des Auteurs, Compositeurs, et Editeurs de Musique (SACEM), established in 1851, had opened an office in New York to collect fees for music written by French copyright holders that was performed in the United States. Two years later, the idea for a similar American organization emerged from a conversation between composer Raymond Hubbell, George Maxwell, who was the U.S. representative of the Italian publisher Ricordi, and lawyer Nathan Burkan, who had worked on behalf of the publishers to shepherd the 1909 copyright law through Congress. Virtually all the European nations had established performing rights societies similar to SACEM by this time (Italy in 1882, Austria in 1897, Spain in 1901, and Germany in 1903). The exception was England, whose copyright history closely paralleled that of the United States. There, the Copyright Act of 1911, the counterpart of the 1909 act in the United States, especially with regard to music, led to the organization of England's own Performing Rights Society (PRS) in 1914. The initial organizational meeting to form an American group comparable to SACEM was not promising; out of the thirty-six publishers and composers invited, only nine, owing to bad weather and bad prospects, attended—Hubbell, Maxwell, and Burkan, plus Victor Herbert, Glenn MacDonough (the librettist for many of Herbert's works), Jay Witmark, and the composers Gustave Kerker, Silvio Hein, and Louis A. Hirsch.[33]

This inauspicious beginning gave no hint of the future formidable strength of their organization, which they called the American Society of Composers, Authors, and Publishers (ASCAP). Membership was broken down into classes from AA to D, with AA being the highest, on the basis of seniority, catalogue size, sheet music sales, and number of hits. Its board of directors was split evenly between publishers and songwriters, and the songwriters were split evenly between composers and lyricists. Unlike SACEM, which sought to collect a fee based on each performance of a member's work, the aim of ASCAP was to license its members' works en masse to subscriber organizations (hotels, restaurants, and so on) and at the end of year, after covering its operating costs, to divide its revenues among its members (split equally between composers and publishers), prorated according to class. Many of the leading Tin Pan Alley publishers and writers signed on quickly (including the Witmarks, Harry Von Tilzer, Irving Berlin, and Jerome Kern), and within a few years, a number of the leading African American songwriters also belonged—Harry T. Burleigh, James Weldon Johnson, J. Rosamond Johnson, Will Marion Cook, R. C. McPherson, and Will H. Tyers. Voting rights in the organization were weighted by membership class as well, a manifestly undemocratic arrangement that chafed some members but which was consistent with the underlying nature of the society. As Oscar Hammerstein II put it some years later, "ASCAP is a group of property owners. . . . This is not a group of federated states, or a nation or a commune. . . . This is not the United States; it is more like United States Steel."[34]

Establishing a performing-rights organization was one thing, but making it functional was another. By the end of its first year, eighty-five hotels in New York had agreed to license ASCAP's music for a fee of five to fifteen dollars a month each, but many organizations scoffed at the idea. To test its legal claim, two of the society's most eminent composers, with legal and financial support from the society, then pushed test cases into the courts. In the first, John Philip Sousa, through his publisher John Church & Co., sued New York's Vanderbilt Hotel over a rendition of his "From Maine to Oregon" performed without permission in its dining room. Although Sousa's suit triumphed in district court, the court of appeals rejected his claim. In that decision, the court held that customers came for the food, not the music, a ruling that discounted Sousa's assertion that the hotel's use of his music was "performance for profit."[35]

In the second case, Nathan Burkan brought a suit on Victor Herbert's behalf against the famed Shanley's Restaurant in Times Square for unlicensed performance of Herbert's "Sweethearts." In May 1915 Learned Hand ruled against Herbert in the district court. He explained in his ruling that, again, people went to Shanley's for the food, not the music. Hand's judgment was upheld in the court of appeals, but in January 1917 the U.S. Supreme Court, weighing both the Sousa and Herbert cases, reversed the lower courts' rulings and established the legal doctrine of performing rights. Affirming the protection the law afforded against unauthorized performance for profit, Oliver Wendell Holmes wrote in his well-known decision, "If the rights under the copyright are infringed only by a performance where money is taken at the door, they are very imperfectly protected. . . . The defendants' performances are not eleemosynary. They are part of a total for which the public pays. . . . It is true that the music is not the sole object, but neither is the food, which probably could be got cheaper elsewhere. . . . If music did not pay, it would be given up. If it pays, it pays out of the public's pocket.

5.3 When ASCAP wanted to test the doctrine of "performance right" in court, it made use of well-known plaintiffs to bring suits against high-profile defendants. The parties in the definitive case were Victor Herbert and Shanley's Restaurant. Picture Collection, Branch Libraries, New York Public Library, Astor, Lenox and Tilden Foundations.

Whether it pays or not, the purpose of employing it is profit, and that is enough." In this landmark ruling, Holmes's commonsense reasoning also revealed one way in which the music business was implicated in the rise of American consumer culture broadly. What restaurateurs and other managers of commercial spaces appreciated was that music helped create a more pleasurable, aesthetically appealing aural environment, with potentially profitable implications. If people enjoyed the music they heard, consciously or not, the presence of the music contributed to their sensory experience of the space. Music may not have been the prevailing factor when they chose one restaurant over another, decided to linger a little longer at a café, or elected to go to the movies instead of for a walk, but it was not an inconsequential one either.[36]

5.4 A phalanx of copyright warriors prepares for battle (picture taken at Pennsylvania Station, New York, in 1924): from left, Victor Herbert (with hand in pocket), John Philip Sousa, Irving Berlin, Harry Von Tilzer, and William Jerome. In back, between Von Tilzer and Jerome, is Nathan Burkan, the attorney who led the publishers' fight in Congress that led up to the Copyright Act of 1909; he helped form ASCAP in 1914. The men were on their way to Washington, D.C., to testify against the Dill bill, which would have allowed radio stations to play copyrighted music without compensating the copyright holders. The bill was defeated. Courtesy of Edward Samuels and Herbert Jacoby.

This was a definitive moment for ASCAP. Its victory attracted to the organization many who had been skeptical earlier. In the coming years, ASCAP would prevail in several other crucial showdowns as well. In the 1920s, radio presented ASCAP with its next big challenge: protesting against radio stations' unlicensed use of its members' copyrighted material. As it had with Shanley's, ASCAP pursued a carefully chosen test case, in this instance against WOR, the radio station operated by the Bamberger Department Store in Newark, New Jersey. As in all ASCAP's legal actions, the case was filed in the name of one of its members, in this instance M. Witmark and Sons, rather than in the name of ASCAP itself, lest the organization appear before the court as a kind of publishers' and composers' trust. Closely following Holmes's *Shanley* decision, the district court of New Jersey found in 1923 that commercial broadcast radio was another form of "performance for profit" and thus handed ASCAP another major triumph. In the same years, ASCAP also prevailed in securing licensing agreements with the vaudeville and movie houses, and in staving off the first of several antitrust suits by the Department of Justice.[37]

Given how farsighted many leaders in the phonograph industry were, especially those linked with the Victor Talking Machine Company, it is surprising that they were slower to grasp the financial potential, not just the liability, inherent in the rights established by the 1909 law. The man who changed this for the industry was Ralph Peer, who organized some groundbreaking recording sessions of Southern music, including the first recordings of Fiddlin' John Carson, the Carter Family, and Jimmy Rodgers, that reverberated throughout the industry and beyond in the late 1920s. Peer understood that every record that came out had in it a lucrative "mechanical right" to exploit, and in 1926, when he went to work for Victor as a producer, he negotiated for the company to sign over to him all the copyrights of the recordings whose sessions he organized, in lieu of receiving any salary. Victor, believing Peer foolish to negotiate such a deal, gladly agreed, but Peer knew what he was doing. In the second quarter of 1928 alone, he earned close to $250,000. Concerned that Victor would get wise to the amount of money he was taking in, he then set up several publishing companies for cover, which by the 1930s and '40s had expanded into a multimillion-dollar international publishing empire.[38]

As the showdown over property rights receded, it left behind some of the most important unintended consequences of the rise of the music industry. According to the industry's new prerogatives, music was something fixed, not just in durable objects like phonograph records and player-piano rolls, but in concept. This understanding put the power of the state behind a particular definition of "making" music, which in turn expanded the rights enjoyed by publishers and composers, though their interests and gains were not identical, and imposed restrictions on music as a kind of common property—something shared, dynamic, mutable. This system has been favorable to some kinds of music, but others, like the folk ballads "John Henry" and "Stagger Lee," written and rewritten a thousand times, given new words, melodies, and meanings, or the compositions of Charles Ives, which he adapted and reworked over and over, showed how other music defied a single definitive iteration.[39]

The Copyright Law of 1909 and Holmes's 1917 *Shanley* decision redefined the essential nature of music publishing, by transforming the publisher from primarily a seller of sheet music to primarily a manager of copyrights, which could be exploited in a number of ways. This transition occurred because new technologies and changing social practices altered how music functioned—and could function—commercially. The unique properties of music—it was ephemeral, invisible, portable, reproducible, and capable of assuming many different forms (live performance, mechanical reproduction, sheet music or published score)—dictated that publishers had to remain ever vigilant, for fear of some unauthorized use of their property. As explained by Leonard Feist, the son of Tin Pan Alley pioneer Leo Feist and himself an important publisher, "A song publisher never entirely ends his function on any one song, for wherever there is a possibility of another performance, another recording, a use in films, or any other use, the popular song publishing process goes on." Indeed, printed music is now a relatively negligible factor in the business, but music publishing organized around protecting and administering copyrights persists as an extremely important component of the culture industries. Today, with most of its licensing through radio, television and movies (and increasingly cell phones and video games), revenues of ASCAP and the two other leading music licensing organizations in the United States, BMI and the much smaller SESAC (Society of European Stage Authors and Composers), exceed $1 billion. Or as the title of a recent *New York Times* article put it, "Music's Hottest Star: The Publisher."[40]

If the American legal system and the phonograph business needed several years to understand how copyright law applied to something as ethereal as music, to the publishers it was a direct and personal affair. The "dean of the publishers," Max Dreyfus, mentor to Jerome Kern and George Gershwin and publisher of a huge swath of what has become the American songbook, conveyed this notion in an extreme way. According to composer Richard Rodgers, Dreyfus claimed that having no children of his own, he treated his copyrights as his offspring, caring for them, nurturing them. When another songwriter mentioned that at least Dreyfus would not ever suffer as a mutual friend had whose son had died in a car accident, Dreyfus replied, "Yes, but I have songs that go into public domain."[41]

6

Perfect Pitch

At a banquet in April 1923, the vice president of the United States, Calvin Coolidge, stood before a group of A-list musical and political dignitaries and waxed eloquent on music and nation. As "the art especially representative of democracy," music deserved to be "recognized as an important national asset," for "our response to music" and "love of freedom" were both expressions of the "strength of our ideals." The event occasioning Coolidge's remarks was the centennial celebration of the first piano made by the pioneering Jonas Chickering, whose revolutionary iron-framed instruments later launched a new era in the history of the piano. Coolidge had served as honorary chair of the organizing committee for the event, which had warranted a congratulatory telegram from President Harding himself, and not surprisingly, the piano came in for particular tribute. "Jonas Chickering . . . ministered to a national desire, [in giving] the people additional power to rise above the contemplation of material things to the contemplation of spiritual things. . . . We cannot imagine a model New England home without the family Bible on the table and the family piano in the corner." The effects of such an instrument were both individual and collective. Not only had "the young of many generations made their first acquaintance with the infinite mysteries of art through accidental pilgrimages over the black and white ivories," he explained, "[but] for a hundred years, [Chickering's] work has had an effect on the political and military life of the nation," which the Great War had recently shown in new ways—in trenches, in military hospitals, on the home front. Jonas Chickering, he said in closing, had done more than bring "the broadening and humanizing spirit of a great art within the reach of all humanity." Chickering had "strengthened the bonds of our common brotherhood, giving us a new security and increased the power of the people to rule."[1]

Filled with lofty, celebratory rhetoric, the speech hewed mostly to familiar themes, embellished with a few contemporary accents. The most notable feature of the address, in fact, was its provenance. It went unmentioned at the time that the promotions staff of the American Piano Company, a trust that had acquired Chickering & Sons in 1908, had penned virtually the entire address. Nor was this fact mentioned following Coolidge's ascent to the presidency, after which newspaper and magazine articles reprised his remarks, as did music advertisements during National Music Week, a widely observed annual event concocted by a trade group called the Music Industries Chamber of Commerce (MICC). The speech by Coolidge belonged to a period of close cooperation between government and business and of massive corporate consolidation, both within and beyond the music industry, which by this time incorporated the business of pianos and that of player-pianos as a single, integrated entity. Not only did the American Piano Company (or Ampico) control more than a dozen piano makers, it also manufactured and marketed one of the leading player-pianos on the market. Meanwhile, the phonograph business, already in the hands of a very few firms, was increasingly dominated by the Victor Talking Machine Company, by then the single most important firm in the music industry as a whole. In 1921 Victor produced 54 percent of the 596,000 phonographs made in the United States (compared with 221,000 pianos made the same year), and by the time of Coolidge's address, it had enjoyed more than two decades of breathtaking growth. The number of records Victor sold, for example, increased on average *20* percent *annually* from 1902 to 1923.[2]

Notwithstanding the growth of music as a national industry, however, in the decades before and after World War I, the commercial revolution in music was also increasingly localized, and aggregate national statistics can hide the neighborhood-level transformation taking place in cities and towns all over the country. This localized transformation was the result of two movements within the industry. The first was commercial and took the form of professionalizing musical salesmanship and standardizing the appearance and practices of retail stores. The second was ideological and involved embedding the music business in institutions of public and civic life—school, community, and nation. The Victor company pioneered both movements, attempting to influence every aspect of retail salesmanship and, through its so-called Education Department, to use schools to expand the company's current and future markets. During World War I and its aftermath, the ideological power of music grew, and the music industry adapted new and influential means of exploiting an idea of music as intrinsic to community and nation. Outside the music industry, numerous debates took shape around such issues as the character of music in a consumer economy, its relative capacity to provide entertainment or uplift, and the social effects of mechanical reproduction. Yet if critics, educators, professional performers, and consumers disagreed over these issues, the industry was content to leave them conspicuously unresolved, for the greater the tensions and contradictions were in contemporary musical culture, the more deep-seated music was in the practices and discourses of modern life.

The Local Face of the Victor

In the early twentieth century, the phonograph business, the precocious upstart of the music industry, had demonstrated the effectiveness of national print advertising and "high-class" musical recordings in stimulating consumer interest in its products, but these alone did not animate local markets. As R. G. Chappell of Galesburg, Illinois, a merchant with decades of experience, put it in 1917, "I have never heard of a store handling only nationally advertised lines succeeding without doing a liberal amount of advertising themselves, locally." In his case, he reported, simply adding Victor goods to his wares generated very little business. Sales in Victor merchandise took off only when he established a special Victor department, canvassed the area for prospective customers, and began a prodigious local advertising campaign. "National advertising," he explained, "did not bring customers into our store to buy the Victor products."[3]

To complement the magazine spreads and opera records, the phonograph companies could have enhanced their direct contact with consumers by operating their own retail stores, as a group of music publishers attempted to do, with only limited success. Instead, with only a fraction of the capital investment and probably far greater effect, the phonograph manufacturers used their influence on existing merchants to reshape the way the music business worked on a local, personal level—that is, to encourage the kind of initiatives taken by R. G. Chappell. Manufacturers could undertake centralized programs from their headquarters, but retailers were the ones who encountered consumers in person, mounted the window displays they walked by, placed advertisements on their streetcars and in their neighborhood circulars, and answered their questions and remembered their names and tastes when they returned to buy a few new records. Thus, through an organized program of training and professionalizing retail representatives, phonograph manufacturers set out to transform not just *what* merchants sold but also *how*.

In shaping the music business on the local level, phonograph manufacturers faced several challenges. One was the diversity of the retailers they had relationships with and were trying to motivate. In large and medium-sized cities, the most important phonograph retailers were department stores; in smaller cities and towns, retailers could be music shops or furniture dealerships; in rural areas, a market initially dominated by Thomas Edison, frequently a general dry goods merchant whose wares ranged from fishing tackle to bassinets also sold phonographs. Many of these dealers, hardly the go-getting students of salesmanship that manufacturers would have wished, viewed their occupation in a relatively conservative, unsophisticated way. In its success motivating these dealers and transforming music retailing, the Victor company did more than take advantage of the high quality of its products. It cultivated complex relationships with dealers, grounded simultaneously in opportunity and obligation, partnership and subservience.

The underlying goal was to strengthen its ties to effective, cooperative dealers and to eliminate the others. It effected that aim through a push-and-pull combination of inducements and threats. At the same time, Victor undertook to teach its retailers about all aspects of salesmanship, from professional letter-writing to window displays. Its main instrument of instruction was the *Voice of the Victor*, a monthly (or for a time bimonthly) trade magazine for dealers, which Victor began publishing in 1906 and which by 1916 was mailed to more than six thousand dealerships across the country.[4] In its pages, merchants found all manner of musical, technical, and commercial information, along with a steady diet of motivational or inspirational editorials and regular reminders about the vigorous bond linking each individual dealer to the Victor corporation as a whole. Occasionally an article appealed to dealers' vanity or social aspirations—for example, through references to the "dignity and prestige" that Victrolas added to a dealer's shop. More often, though, the *Voice* promoted a cooperative or collaborative connection with dealers. A typical article from 1910 appealed to them this way: "You are just as vitally interested in Victor success as we are.... Let's all work together for still greater business. We will do our part by constantly improving the Victor and Victor Records, and by the best and biggest advertising campaign in our history. Will you boost from your end?" Another article maintained, "'The Voice of the Victor' is *your* paper as well as ours." Elsewhere stress fell on the modern idea of corporate "organization": "Wherever there is success there is bound to be found Organization—an army of individuals all working for a common cause, striving by concerted effort and action to accomplish a specific end—success. The Victor is such an Organization."[5]

The *Voice of the Victor* was a sophisticated tool designed to standardize and professionalize Victor's retail sales force. One component of this program was training for retail agents in the precepts of managerial efficiency, for example, on instituting record-keeping systems for inventory, factory orders, and individual sales. A second was training dealers and their employees in modern methods of salesmanship. Not only did the *Voice* reprint articles from specialized advertising and marketing trade journals such as *Advertising Age* and *Modern Methods,* but it also showered dealers with series, features, and editorials on rationalized techniques of selling in general. Alongside such columns as Some Pointers on Salesmanship, Hints for the Salesman, and Sales Ideas for Victor Dealers, dealers read profiles of "master salesmen" and briefs about how and why to "standardize [sales] arguments." Other articles, such as "How to Handle a Difficult Customer," "Help in Closing the Sale," and "Handling the Undecided Customer," introduced dealers to the practices of customer relations.[6] Whereas records by prestigious artists like Caruso were said to have brought about a "democratization" of culture, the *Voice* fostered the obverse—the "aristocratization" of consumers—that is, the treatment of customers in a solicitous, deferential manner. (The vestiges of this approach persist today in the form of "customer service" desks and the greeting "How may I help you?") In this vein, Victor instructed dealers in the commercial value of fine stationery and personal courtesy, including remembering customers' names. One article, "Always Apply the Personal Touch," for example, taught dealers that "people like to have their name singled out. . . . Playing upon this amusing human weakness is profitable and perfectly ethical."[7]

Through the *Voice,* Victor also influenced the commercial and aesthetic design of the retail environment. Articles, many accompanied by photographs, frequently mentioned or described the interiors of exemplary shops. More important, though, the *Voice* devoted particular and assiduous attention to shop windows, a major element in the sophisticated apparatus of modern retailing. In a typical article from 1910, Victor tried to break down into simple, practical guidelines its recommendations for window display: (a) it should be attractive and not overcrowded; (b) it should tell a story and do so in a "simple and convincing manner"; and (c) dealers should never let a window display become dusty or stale. Even with advice, however, many dealers showed little talent for the niceties and nuances of window display. Thus, to assist dealers, Victor established a special Window Display Service, under the direction of Ellis Hansen, a designer whose displays had won awards from the trade journal *Merchants Record and Show Window.* The service sold display wares, such as pedestals, and display templates, known as Victor Ready-Made Window Displays. Together, these promoted a more standardized quality of displays across the country, as well as constituting a small amount of additional income for Victor.[8]

Victor encouraged dealers to project their influence beyond their retail spaces and out into the community by means of aggressive and persistent local advertising. The company offered dealers electrotypes, streetcar cards, outdoor electric signs, and lantern slides—sometimes free, sometimes at a cost—as well as personalized suggestions on the best ways to use various media.[9] In the series Good Advertisements Made Better, for example, the Victor advertising department critiqued dealers' advertisements, showing them before and after improvements, and explaining the nature and effect of the changes. The *Voice* expounded on the general benefits of advertising in such

Window Display From Now and Until After the Holidays is Indispensable

The Dealer Who Won't Try to Make His Windows Attractive at This Season Might Just as Well Board Them Up and Sell the Space to the Billposter

WE have presented enough window display arguments during the past eighteen months to almost convince a "dead one" that this up-to-date form of advertising would prove the salvation of a "bankrupted business," but in the face of the great success of Victor Ready-Made Window Displays, our order sheets show us that there are thousands of Victor Dealers who won't even give window display a chance to show its value.

Victor Windows are windows that sell Victors and Victor Records, and their small cost enables even the smallest Dealer to take advantage of the original ideas of this biggest and best department of its kind in the world.

Every large Distributor has with us a standing order for every window, and some of the great big Distributors have on order as many as fifty of each window, and they are as enthusiastic as they can be on the selling qualities of these windows that many of you Dealers let pass you without a thought.

You might neglect your window eleven months in the year without realizing your loss, but any Dealer who lets the Christmas holidays get by without making the one big effort to stop the passerby, who is searching every window for his holiday purchases, is certainly "asleep at his post."

For Christmas we are preparing a window display that will almost stop a 90-horse-power automobile, but our standing orders have grown so big, we are compelled to ask you to place your order for a Christmas display with your Distributor at once. It will cost you less than $5, but it will be the best investment you ever made and will make your store the attraction of your street.

In the meantime, order Window No. 19 (Verdi Window), just as soon as you receive notice that it is ready.

NO.18-BAND WINDOW

NO.21-PEACOCK WINDOW

NO.19-VERDI WINDOW

A Few Window Pointers

Your windows are the least expensive form of advertising you can do and yet they are of untold value to you when properly dressed.

They are mirrors into which the public are gazing for a reflection of your business. You must see that they do you justice.

If your windows are crowded and unattractive, if they do not offer a pleasing invitation to enter your store, you have lost the opportunity of making a first favorable impression, which means so much to you.

You should be just as careful of the appearance of your window displays as you are of your store and salespeople. You must not let your window displays get dusty and stale. Keep your windows clean, for dirty windows shut out trade as well as light.

Let your window have an individuality. Do not display different kinds of goods at one time. Always make your display tell your story in a simple and convincing manner.

6.1 Articles about window displays were among the regular features in the *Voice of the Victor*. Rodgers & Hammerstein Archive of Recorded Sound, New York Public Library for the Performing Arts, Astor, Lenox and Tilden Foundations.

articles as "Advertising—the Foundation of Success," "How to Get More from Your Advertising," and "Repetition in Advertising: Why It Pays to 'Keep Everlastingly at It.'" These pieces linked Victor's success to its aggressive advertising and urged dealers to synchronize their local campaigns with Victor's national ones.[10]

As was true of many large businesses of the era, one of the principal functions of sales personnel was to explain products to prospective customers or clients. For companies selling particularly complex goods, such as machine tools or insurance, sales depended heavily on the ability to explain the intricacies and subtleties of a product. Phonographs fit into this pattern in a peculiar way, because phonograph merchants had to be knowledgeable and articulate not just about technical and mechanical matters, but also about music. Lest dealers lose sight of the phonograph's most powerful enticement, articles such as "Are You Selling Music or Mechanisms?" reminded dealers repeatedly that the phonograph was "a musical instrument"—not a toy, not furniture, not a mechanical curiosity. Meanwhile, an endless stream of articles plied dealers with all kinds of musical information, from music trivia to technical explanations of acoustics. In a single month, for example, a regular feature called "Musical Gossip—which Will Be of Interest to Your Customers" included musical aphorisms ("The oldest music is new to the man who never heard it"); some pithy nonmusical sayings by Ralph Waldo Emerson, Henry Ward Beecher, and Abraham Lincoln; and an explanation of the problems in recording pipe organ music and the way they had been addressed on a recent Victor recording. The *Voice* also featured regular interviews with recording artists and accounts of notable recording sessions, all of which allowed dealers to project an air of musical expertise and an insider's knowledge in their interactions with customers.[11]

More broadly, the *Voice* stressed Victor's aim to develop long-term customers for records, not one-time phonograph buyers. Over the years this message proved one of the most constant to appear in the pages of the *Voice*, whose editors maintained that the demand for machines was limited but the demand for records was elastic and could be "greatly stimulated by . . . the Dealer." Thus, the point conveyed to dealers was that a "silent Victrola" had not "been properly sold," and that "every owner of a Victor should buy records every month in the year." Such purchases should be viewed as part of the dealer's balance sheet, the company maintained. On one side, "every new Victor owner should be an additional dividend paying asset"; on the other, each phonograph owner who no longer bought records meant an actual loss—a loss for which merchants themselves were responsible: "Any time you let a Victor owner stop buying records, you are sacrificing a part of your income, which should be just as fixed and regular as the interest on U.S. Government bonds." Among many suggestions for avoiding this outcome was an early but aggressive form of data mining: the *Voice* urged dealers to compile lists of local Victrola owners and watch what they bought. Then, "the minute you find their record purchases falling off, pay them a personal visit and find out exactly why they are not buying records."[12]

Encouraging listeners' record-buying habits dovetailed with a growing system of consumer credit. Because most phonograph purchases were financed on an installment plan, dealers already had an ongoing relationship with their customers. Dave Kapp, for example, recalled how his father, a phonograph salesman in the early part of the century, brought new records to people's homes and gave demonstrations of them when he went around to collect payments. Such selling plans, the *Voice* told dealers, were "the quickest way of . . . securing an immediate demand for records." This attempt to cultivate record buying is even more important in light of the phonograph industry's impact as a leading promoter of consumer financing generally, which marked a dramatic change in the relations between people and goods. Until the mid-1800s, most people tried to avoid incurring debt, but this attitude began to change in the latter half of the nineteenth century, especially when it came to the purchase of sewing machines, pianos, and furniture. Phonograph manufacturers, both in the United States and in England, were leaders in expanding the use of credit in the twentieth century. Columbia reported "a great amount of installment business transacted in New York" in 1904 and welcomed this as "a radical departure from the old-time methods of doing business." When Victor published a booklet in 1907 called *How to Sell Victors on Installments,* the company reported more than two thousand requests for copies.[13] According to most estimates, 80 to 90 percent of phonographs were purchased "on time," and by the late 1920s, phonographs accounted for 5 percent of the national consumer debt. (Automobiles made up more than 50 percent.)[14]

As for records, many in the industry believed that consumers were profoundly ignorant and that they craved guidance from sales personnel, yet good salesmanship dictated that dealers defer to the consumers' untutored impulses—and then channel them toward some generically "respectable" cultural investment. "Find the one piece of music that means more to your prospect than any other and the deal will be made then and there," one article advised. "*Let him choose the first record you play;* in fact, *make* him choose it."[15] Once customers bought, or were committed to buying, an instrument, dealers were to urge them to think not just of acquiring individual recordings but of amassing a record library, which customers could see as a testament to their cultivation and good taste and dealers could exploit as a stimulus to future purchases: "Impress on every customer the idea that each new record bought is an addition to his 'library of music.' Get him interested in forming a 'collection' of records. . . . Once started on this basis he has a fixed object in view—to make his collection as complete as possible . . . and . . . prides himself on his selections." Furthermore, dealers were to encourage the acquisition of records in a range of musical styles, as befitting a "library," in order to maximize the customer's long-term interest. Within any category, however, the emphasis remained on cultivating demand. Dealers were encouraged to favor records to which customers responded quickly and to steer clear of more challenging pieces or music for which a listener's enthusiasm might wane after repeated auditions: "You must give them music that will induce a longing for more of the same class, rather than the kind that commences to jar them after about the fifteenth or twentieth playing." If the dealer successfully executed this strategy, he might reap "a regular devotee of the Victor"— that ideal customer who went "along steadily and indefinitely adding record after record to his musical library."[16]

Beyond such specific tactics and subjects, however, the *Voice* echoed a set of deeper ideals, the optimistic religious outlook of "mind cure," whose sunny worldview and commitment to positive thinking reverberated through the dominant business culture. Although the various mind cure groups— Christian Scientists, theosophists, acolytes of New Thought, and others— varied in their specific beliefs, they shared a roseate faith that through will, conviction, and hope it was possible to create a terrestrial paradise in the here and now. The groups themselves advanced no particular politics, but their ideas attracted the support of numerous business leaders, advertisers, and economists, who promoted a commitment to happiness and self-fulfillment as a guiding social and economic virtue. Thus, while mind cure penetrated popular culture in books like Eleanor Porter's *Pollyanna* and L. Frank Baum's *Wonderful Wizard of Oz* and informed the influential consumerist planning of the economist Simon Patten, the cheerful optimism of mind cure entered the workplace through such instruments as the *Voice of the Victor.*[17] "Wake up and give yourself a chance," one article urged dealers, and another told them, "Your business is what you make it." Another month the watchword might be "The fact that people come to you to buy Victors, Victrolas, and Victor Records only shows what can be done if YOU go after them" or "Be enthusiastic. It pays."[18]

Such boosterism may sound naive or platitudinous today, but in the years before World War I it was on the cutting edge of business-speak, representative of the broad psychological tendency in both advertising and management. Indeed, Victor's pursuit of such a strategy deeply impressed Frank Holman, a writer for *Printers' Ink,* a leading trade magazine of the advertising industry, who marveled at the way that Victor (and another, unrelated company) had begun applying the precepts of New Thought to motivating dealers. "Some might call it psychology, some ginger, and perhaps a few impertinence," wrote Holman, "But at least two of the ablest and most extensive advertisers are using the method, and evidently with success." Struck by the phonograph company's unabashed promotion of the power of positive thinking, he quoted directly from a recent communiqué to dealers (most likely from the *Voice of the Victor*):

> Think Victrolas and you will sell them.
> The whole secret is in your own mental attitude.
> If you are a Victor dealer and not enthusiastic over the Victrola your mind is not in the right attitude. Your eyes are not wide open. You are not thinking high enough.

Holman acknowledged that this might not be mind cure as such, but "if [it] is not 'New Thought' or 'Christian Science,'" he argued, "it verges closely to it."[19]

Dealers may have taken the *Voice*'s prescriptions with a grain of salt, and some may have resisted Victor's corporate boosterism. Most, however, realized that it was in their interest as businessmen to take Victor's advice seriously, for Victor came to them with expertise, prestige, capital, and vision. Meanwhile, complementing the positive encouragement Victor offered to dealers was the intimation of discipline and obligation. The company's most basic tool for this was its contract with dealers, which enjoined them to adhere to Victor's pricing schedule and to uphold certain professional standards, conditions that Eldridge Johnson vigorously defended as an extension of his right to control his patents. When Victor found that its dealers had violated these terms, it published their names in the trade press, suspended or canceled their contracts, and barred its other dealers from doing business with them. Because sales grew so steadily in the 1900s and 1910s, many dealers willingly accepted and in fact valued Victor's compulsory pricing. In the 1910s the company provided "an exclusivity and a protection for the phonograph record dealer, and he used to cherish it," recalled Milt Gabler, later the owner of New York's famed Commodore Record Shop. At the same time, the *Voice* condemned opponents of the pricing system in articles such as "Who Suffers Most from Price Cutting? YOU Do!" and "'Price maintenance'—a Bad Name! Should Be 'Standardization of Fair Prices.'"[20]

Those most likely to resist the price maintenance system were department stores and other large retailers, which sought to increase profits by selling more merchandise on smaller margins. When the Fair Department Store in Chicago sued Victor over its restrictive policies, Victor mounted a vigorous legal defense, and its success before the U.S. Court of Appeals in 1903 stood as an important precedent in commercial law generally. In subsequent years, Victor became one of the leading proponents in the country of price regulation, while opposition to such anticompetitive practices continued to grow. When legislative action threatened the structure of Victor's licensing and pricing plans, the company was quick to mobilize its dealers. In "How Much Will It Cost to Send a Telegram?" Victor exhorted distributors, dealers, clerks, and others to send telegrams to Congress opposing proposed changes in the laws governing the right to set prices. Victor also benefited from the strategizing of its crack legal department, which at various times retained such eminent counsel as Charles Evans Hughes, who had also worked for the Aeolian Company, and Elihu Root. By the mid-1910s, however, the legal climate began to change. Congressional hearings in 1917 on the effects of retail price maintenance focused heavily on Victor, and later that year, in a

6.2 The representatives of Victor's Traveling Department, who were dispatched all over the country, combined the roles of consultant and corporate spy. *Voice of the Victor*, Sept. 1914, Rodgers & Hammerstein Archive of Recorded Sound, New York Public Library for the

suit brought against Victor by Macy's, the Supreme Court struck down the compulsory pricing plan as an illegal restraint of trade.[21]

This outcome brought to an end an antitrust suit under preparation at the Department of Justice, whose investigators found that Victor had used "bribery, threats, coercion, oppression, and intimidation" to keep its distributors and dealers in line. Instrumental in maintaining discipline was Victor's so-called Traveling Department. Established in 1913, the department had responsibility both for monitoring dealer compliance with pricing and other policies and for assisting dealers with techniques for sales and shop management. Part spy, part consultant, and part quality-control supervisor, the Traveling Department representative embodied the mixture of discipline and support the company brought to bear in its relations with dealers. On the one hand, like earlier salesmen of brand-name goods, the twenty-five or so employees of the Traveling Department distributed advertising and helped local merchants manage their stores more professionally in a wide variety of ways, by advising them on store appearance, window display, advertising, business methods, personnel training, stocking of a wide assortment of merchandise, and marketing techniques using the telephone and the mails. They also gave demonstrations and explained to dealers the subtle design differences in the new phonograph models released each year. On the other hand, if the Traveling Department agent found that a dealer was not "giving satisfactory representation" to Victor, he alerted the distributor and recommended an appropriate response. The *Voice* contributed to the effort to police dealers by publishing bimonthly suspension lists, instructing distributors not to service aberrant dealers and shaming those dealers before the trade.[22]

Music, Education, Community

In 1911, two years before Victor launched the Traveling Department, Frances Elliott Clark, the first director of the Victor Talking Machine Company's newly established Education Department, addressed the annual convention of Victor dealers. A veteran music educator steeped in the philosophy of Lowell Mason, who championed the importance of music for children's moral, physical, and intellectual development, Clark stood before the retailers and urged them to place phonographs in schools for the good of civil society. "Our schools are the most precious possession of the commonwealth," Clark told her audience, "and the education of the young, for citizenship, the most important function of the State." Education should provide every student, "no matter what his station," with the necessary resources "to take his place in the community," and music was an indispensable part of that education. The training of children had undergone a beneficial revolution in the previous decade, but the recent emphasis on practical skills threatened to push out the cultivation of invaluable old virtues. Indeed, Clark maintained, in inculcating "a love of the beautiful" and stimulating the imagination and the emotions, music was second only to reading and elocution for training "helpful" members of a community. To this end, Victor "offer[ed] a perfect solution . . . the highest class of music, classified and arranged to fit right into the schools at every point."[23]

Victor's initiative to promote phonograph use in schools accorded with the movement to include music in school curricula at all levels, which had been building for three-quarters of a century. Only in the previous few decades had major American universities established the first chairs in music (Harvard and the University of Pennsylvania in 1875, Yale in 1894, and Columbia in 1896); meanwhile, the movement to introduce music into schools at the lower levels had found a strong champion in G. Stanley Hall, the leading behavioral psychologist of the age, and another in his student John Dewey.[24] Against this backdrop, the Education Department was conceived as a new, third prong of Victor's overall marketing strategy, along with the company's extensive advertising and distinguished Red Seal catalogue. This department, explained Victor's general manager, Louis F. Geissler, represented the company's fervent belief in the "value of the influence of the Victor in the Public Schools." The *Voice* stressed this great commercial potential: "In taking a place among the other departments of the Victor Company, its entire force and energy will be exerted with the one idea of opening up this gigantic avenue of business to Victor Dealers."[25]

Extending arguments that had long linked music and cultural advancement, this view cast dealers who placed Victor phonographs in schools as performing a kind of moral and civic duty. "You are the great army of musical educators," the *Voice* told dealers, "and owe it to yourself to foster the love of music." At the same time, however, the education program was unapologetically opportunistic and commercial. "Do you realize the advertising value of the child?" one article began. "Children are everywhere, and how they do talk!" The industry trade journal *Talking Machine World* recognized this potential as well: "'Once a customer always a customer.' Why not bring your product to the attention of the children in a way that they can understand and [that] pleases them?" This article went on to suggest holding short musical programs for children or setting aside a children's corner in the store.[26]

Schools, it was noted, offered a triple benefit to dealers: schools constituted a large market in themselves, they used children to reach their parents, and they trained children to be lifelong phonograph consumers. To penetrate this market, the Education Department at the outset mailed more than two million of pieces of promotional literature to schools and sent thousands of letters to school supervisors and superintendents. Dealers, meanwhile, were urged to "get after school boards," or better, to target teachers directly.[27] If teachers believe in the educational use of the phonograph, "they will in some way manage to make it possible . . . to place Victor in the school." To facilitate this placement, Victor created a wide range of products for the educational market. These included not only diverse musical record packages and books, such as *What We Hear in Music* and *Music Appreciation for Little Children,* but also English-language instruction records for foreigners, foreign-language instruction records for English speakers, recitations from American and English literature, and special phonograph models for school use. Meanwhile, Victor published advertisements showing phonographs in use in physical education programs, roller-skating activities, penmanship instruction, dance or typewriting classes, and so on. Ultimately, both Clark and the *Voice* claimed, phonograph use in schools would also expand home markets through the offices of children, who would "give [their parents] no peace until they buy this and that record that is heard in school."[28]

To assist dealers further, Victor offered detailed guidelines on how to establish a local Education Department. Dealers were encouraged to set aside retail space for this purpose, to label the Education Department visibly, to adorn it with pictures of phonographs in schools (preferably local ones), and to maintain it for school-related business ("except of course in the Christmas rush, etc."). Dealers were also to be mindful to reserve some area in their shops that would be friendly to children, where dealers could schedule demonstrations and music programs. The instructions for outreach included creating a file card system to track each school in the area, drawing multi-colored maps to chart the stages of outreach to different schools, targeting school board members, music supervisors, and librarians, and cultivating friendships with principals and purchasing directors. The dealer was urged to establish a presence at a school, once it did acquire a phonograph, and to visit at regular intervals with a fresh supply of records. "Become known in the schools as the 'Victor man.' Have the children know where your store is. They will bring their parents to it." Indeed, dealers were told, installation of a school phonograph marked the beginning, not the end, of this commercial market: "You have only put your hand on the knob of the door, which, if opened, will admit you to a volume of home prospects."[29]

By 1914 almost eighteen hundred cities and towns around the United States were using Victor phonographs in their schools, with the Northeast and the Midwest accounting for the greatest concentration of the machines. Four years later, in 1918, the total number had jumped to nearly seven thousand cities and towns nationwide, and four years after that the number climbed to over ten thousand. According to the *Voice,* in 1922 22.7 million schoolchildren were using Victors in three hundred thousand public schools, and those included all kinds of schools in all parts of the country. With these numbers, the *Voice* asked dealers, how could they "afford *not* to" pursue educational programs in schools, "for the *advertising* value alone"? Even poor rural schools could usually afford a phonograph and a few records. If the school itself could not afford the expense, the school district could buy it, or else the members of the school community could take up a special collection.[30]

Victor's program to market to schools was even more significant in light of its broad influence. Columbia started its own education department in 1913. Ampico, Aeolian, and other leading player-piano firms likewise established education departments, modeled on Victor's. An Ampico sales manual called *How to Sell the Ampico to Schools* brought out some familiar themes. School sales, it explained, (1) were a means of reaching the parents of pupils; (2) helped cultivate future customers; (3) legitimated the player-piano, by "establish[ing] definite acceptance of [the] Ampico as a factor in music education (making it desirable in homes where there are children)";

and (4) building prestige, which would enhance other sales. To advance this strategy, one of its architects later recalled, the company sought "to install the Ampico in leading colleges and conservatories, secure testimonials from their presidents and music teachers, and then use their names in national advertising."[31]

On the eve of the United States' entry into World War I, Victor had already achieved a remarkable level of success at establishing the phonograph as a feature of the sound and structure of the educational experience in thousands of the nation's schools. In wartime Frances Clark's notion of a connection between music and the state took on new meanings, far beyond the use of phonographs in school. By 1919 the industry was boasting that the phonograph promoted both democracy and Americanization.[32] Indeed, once the United States declared war, the phonograph, and music generally, were linked not just with the civic aims of education but also with the military aims of the nation. Every sector of the music industry contributed to the war effort, and every sector benefited commercially. As a result, World War I became a watershed period for the music industry, one that amplified its cultural as well as its economic status.

The connection between music and war was not in itself new; the two have been connected at least as long as people have been beating drums. But during World War I the part music played in the prosecution of war and in wartime culture changed. The music industry's capacity *as* an industry was brought to bear on the war movement. Tin Pan Alley, for example, which excelled at factory production of catchy, often topical songs, easily turned out dozens of popular patriotic compositions. Recognizing the lucrative potential of this market, the publisher Leo Feist paid $25,000 on the spot, it was said, for the martial strains of George M. Cohan's "Over There." Among phonograph companies, large parts of their manufacturing operations were converted to war production: detonator cases and shell assemblies were made in the metal shops, and rifle stocks and wooden airplane wings in the cabinet departments. Victor's factory at Camden also produced more than fifty sets of wings for the navy's NC-4 "flying boats," which were designed to bomb U-boats, though the war concluded before the aircraft were put into use. Elsewhere, phonograph music was used to reduce the monotony of

6.3 The music industry contributed to the war effort in numerous ways, among others by encouraging the purchase of war bonds. Rodgers & Hammerstein Archive of Recorded Sound, New York Public Library for the Performing Arts, Astor, Lenox and Tilden Foundations.

work in munitions factories and to boost productivity among Red Cross workers sewing or winding bandages.[33]

The industry also actively supported fund-raising efforts and recruitment. Victor, for example, pressured distributors and dealers to buy war bonds, and it was not uncommon for leading recording artists to perform at fund-raisers. For many of the foreign-born artists, such events also served as opportunities to demonstrate their loyalty to the United States. Enrico Caruso, for instance, raised a reported $21 million by singing at wartime benefits, converted all of his prewar securities into U.S. government bonds, invested all his wartime income in Liberty bonds, and donated huge sums of money to the American Red Cross and the Allied relief organizations. Other artists contributed their talents (and shored up their bona fides) as well, such as the Russian-born violinist Mischa Elman, who performed at a Red Cross benefit that raised $35,000.[34]

The music of World War I differed from that of previous conflicts in that the products of the music industry were used in direct support for the military—and not just by the United States. Tin Pan Alley publishers sent sheet music gratis to soldiers, and American phonograph companies prepared foreign-language instruction kits, such as "'First Aid' French for Soldiers," which contained three language instruction records and a twenty-four-page phrase book, all packed in a durable waterproof case.[35] Meanwhile, phonographs and even player-pianos earned a status as a kind of war matériel: all the belligerent powers sent phonographs to their troops to alleviate the monotony and demoralizing stalemate of trench warfare.[36] The recording engineer Fred Gaisberg recalled that "popular patriotic songs were recorded and distributed by the thousands" and "the military authorities of both sides . . . looked upon [the phonograph] as a vital necessity"; and the chair of Harvard University's music department even claimed that the salutary effect that music had on morale and moral character made it as important to the troops as ammunition. Musical support for the troops also came from women's groups, which advocated the collection of phonographs, records, and needles for American training camps, in the hope that wholesome musical entertainment would keep the soldiers from visits to prostitutes and other disreputable behavior.[37] Concurrently, a national committee of prominent musicians, singers, and writers established the National Phonograph Records Recruiting

6.4 During World War I many claimed that music, because of its effect on morale, had become a kind of war matériel. Here, soldiers of the 344th Infantry, Company E, at Camp Grant in Rockford, Illinois, gather for some singing around a piano. DN-0068967, *Chicago Daily News* negatives collection, Chicago Historical Society.

Corps to determine what records were in greatest demand among soldiers and then to collect, pack, and ship those records to the troops.[38] At the same time, a Canadian nurse noted in a letter home the effect of phonograph music on convalescents: "We have a phonograph with a rasping voice that plays from morning to night. The soldiers love it; the poor things are so used to noise that they don't seem happy without it."[39] Another, more novel use of the phonograph was the recording of spoken-word records in Czech, Hungarian, and other languages that urged soldiers to abandon their fight, which were played back across the trenches to encourage desertions.[40]

"The man who disparages music as a luxury and non-essential is do-

MUSIC AND MUNITIONS SIDE BY SIDE IN WAR

The Proximity of the Phonograph to the Rifle in the Above Picture Indicates Just About How Closely Music and Munitions Are Related in the Present War. The Scene Was Taken in Van Cortlandt Park, New York, and Shows a Victrola Entertaining Some of the Members of the Seventy-first New York Regiment

6.5 Members of the Seventy-first New York Regiment listen to a portable phonograph in Van Cortlandt Park, New York. *Music Trades,* Sept. 29, 1917, Music Division, New York Public Library for the Performing Arts, Astor, Lenox and Tilden Foundations.

ing the nation an injury," President Woodrow Wilson declared. "Music now more than ever before, is a national need. There is no better way to express patriotism than through music." This view was, however, neither self-evident nor universal. In 1916 the newly established MICC, which was led by the piano industry, fought to convince the War Industries Board of the "absolute indispensability" of the music trades to the war effort. So too did the leaders of the phonograph business, but when the War Revenue Act was passed, musical merchandise—from pianos to phonographs to music boxes—was classified as a "semiluxury," and manufacturers were forced to accept a 5 percent excise tax on their goods, which was more than on chewing gum or soap (3 percent) but less than sporting goods or cameras (10 percent). The tax remained in effect after the war, although the industry continually pressed for its repeal. By then, however, business leaders were in a stronger position than ever to argue music was a necessity of daily life, and they secured an exemption for all musical products in the Revenue Act of 1921.[41]

Patriotic music accounted for part of wartime demand, but desire for many styles of music soared. Two factors contributing to musical activity in the home were the federal fuel administrator's mandate that theaters had to be dark one night a week, and the 10 percent tax imposed on all concert and theater tickets. Meanwhile, in light of wartime calls for public and private thrift, the *Talking Machine World* repeated that music was a necessity of daily life and urged dealers to distinguish themselves from purveyors of more dispensable goods. In order to offset the "campaign against so-called luxuries," dealers had two obligations: "One is to fight the false economy propaganda, and the other is to advertise talking machines as never before." Despite limited production of Victrolas due to government rationing of raw materials, in 1916 and 1917 Victor enjoyed its highest record and instrument sales to date, and at the end of the war, distributors had back orders for as many as five million records.[42]

When hostilities ceased, Victor stood in a stronger position than ever, and by 1919 advertisements were proudly calling attention to Victor's patriotic wartime service. After the shortage of records set the stage for a postwar boom, in 1921 Victor sold the most records of any year in the company's history to date: it sold more than 54 million discs worldwide.[43] It was more than just Victor, though; the entire American phonograph industry had mushroomed during the war years, in part owing to the expiration of crucial patents that had earlier blocked newcomers from entering the field. According to the U.S. Census of Manufactures, the number of firms producing phonograph-related products jumped from 18 in 1914 to 166 in 1919, with a corresponding increase in the value of their products from $27.1 million to $158.5 million.[44]

This growth in the phonograph industry reflected the dramatic expansion of music across the soundscape during the war and in the early '20s. Most remarkable of all on the home front was the surge in organized musical activ-

ity at the local level in many parts of the country, especially public singing events called community sings. These gatherings had started before the
war but were popularized nationally by group singing organized in military
camps to boost morale, which then spread to soldiers' hometowns. The community music movement continued after the war through the late 1920s. Its
leaders organized festivals and compiled songbooks, and it grew to encompass a variety of musical groups, ranging from mandolin clubs to choirs. In
the postwar period public concerts also enjoyed broad support across the
country, while at the same time the "industrial music" movement led to the
organizing of music groups in workplaces, particularly those with a large
number of female employees, such as Marshall Field and Bell Telephone.
Probably no firm did more to promote music, however, than the H. J. Heinz
Company in Pittsburgh, which blended corporate paternalism with a German commitment to music. Not only were Heinz's six hundred women employees serenaded with piano music in the lunchroom, they also enjoyed
a variety of programs in the company's great auditorium, which, according to
a company historian, had its own "musical director, 1500 opera-type seats, a
gallery with two proscenium boxes, 2000 incandescent bulbs, a pipe organ,
a Pianola, a Steinway Concert Grand Piano, an Edison Stereo-Projecting
Kinetoscope, and a large dome with artistically designed stained glass."
Middle-class women's music clubs constituted another example of musical
activity at the local level. By 1919 more than six hundred such clubs, com-
prising more than two hundred thousand members, were hosting recitals,
organizing concert series, and sponsoring music education in schools.[45]

Another form of community musical activity was the "music memory contests" in which children competed to identify musical compositions from a
predefined list of recordings. The putative goal of such events, first established in 1916, was to cultivate children's musical knowledge, but as was true
of phonograph use in schools, this aim was not easily separated from the
commercial motivations of many of its backers. As Frances Clark, the head of
Victor's Education Department, told dealers, the most effective way to set up
a contest was for the school supervisor to appear to be the "king pin of the
whole idea," buttressed by women's music clubs in the area. Although it was
the dealer's responsibility to set the process in motion, he had to remain "in
the background. The contests must not seem to be commercial." By 1926

1,400 cities in the United States were holding music memory contests, often organized and financed by department stores or music dealers. Many of the contests were held in conjunction with an industry-sponsored annual event called National Music Week that involved the simultaneous promotion—commercial and cultural—of music in as many ways as possible. In New York in 1920, for example, promotion involved sermons, bell-ringing, and music programs in five hundred churches, extensive music programs in the public schools, and concerts or community sings associated with large businesses, including Macy's, Wanamaker's, Bonwit Teller, *McCall's Magazine,* Edison Lamp Works, and others. The programs also featured a recital at Carnegie Hall by the pianists Arthur Rubinstein and Leo Ornstein, punctuated by on-stage player-piano demonstrations, along with a large commercial exposition, the National Music Show, at the Grand Central Palace, featuring three floors of music displays and demonstrations, including personal appearances by phonograph recording artists.[46]

In the early decades of the twentieth century, music became a visible and audible part of civic life, promoted by the industry but belonging to the national culture at all levels. With considerable justification, Victor was happy to claim much of the credit for this development. "Victor dealers are not in business for their health," an editorial on the cover of the *Voice* ran, "but *do they realize* that no other business exerts so profound an influence upon the life and spiritual well-being of the nation?" Nowhere was the connection between music and nation as clear as in the White House, where the presence of music had been growing for some time. Although it had always had some music, not until Theodore Roosevelt occupied the White House did a president hold regular musical programs there. When William Howard Taft was president, he often listened to music on a phonograph, including recordings of "Alexander's Ragtime Band" and of Caruso, whom he adored; and Woodrow and Edith Wilson enjoyed an electric player-piano and a Victrola, to whose strains the president sometimes danced. Warren Harding, whose wife was a conservatory-trained musician, had a fondness for vaudeville, musical comedy, and concert bands, and Calvin Coolidge invited Al Jolson to the White House to help launch the president's reelection campaign in 1924. Thus, by 1931, when Herbert Hoover signed the act making "The Star-Spangled Banner" the official national anthem, the nation's first residence had for three decades mirrored the growing prominence music had attained, in all its forms and styles, throughout American society.[47]

Through the intense localism of phonograph use in schools, community sings, music weeks, and memory contests, the music industry enjoyed an unprecedented popularity and visibility in the 1910s and 1920s. The surge in enthusiasm for music making, however, hid a shift in the balance of power taking place within the music industry itself. Never again would piano production in the United States reach the levels it had in 1910, and of the pianos produced, player-pianos outnumbered manual pianos from 1919 to 1925, after which the piano business as a whole fell into major decline. As the consumer-centered culture of the twentieth century displaced the producer-centered one of the nineteenth, it made perfect sense for Calvin Coolidge to declare, "We need good listeners even more than good performers."[48]

The widespread popularity of player-pianos would not outlast the 1920s, but the importance of the phonograph, and especially of the Victor company, in the business and culture of music continued to grow. Indeed, in the years following World War I, which had caused major disruptions in the global phonograph business, Victor's efforts to build community-based markets in the United States coincided with a sweeping effort to increase its holdings overseas. In 1920 it bought outright a 50 percent stake in the Gramophone Company, its erstwhile affiliate, followed by numerous other international acquisitions. These marked an important counterpoint to the community-level activity in the same years and presaged the increased internationalization of the industry by the end of the 1920s.[49] All the while, the music industry in the United States cemented its commercial and ideological connections to community and state. Certainly, not every music dealer assimilated the professionalized practices promoted by the *Voice of the Victor* and other trade publications and some merchants probably scoffed at the idea that they were foot soldiers in the "army of musical educators." In thousands of cities and towns all over the country, however, countless dealers saw that it was to their advantage to adopt at least some of the new sales methods. Through these merchants, manufacturers projected their influence into the local communities where people lived, shopped, worked, and went to school. In these spaces, in war and peace, the sounds of music filled people's lives in new ways, and the music industry became a neighborhood institution.

7

The Black Swan

In an article on corporate mergers in the music industry a few years ago, the *New York Times* music critic Jon Pareles observed this paradox: the larger the major music companies grew, the more invisible they seemed. With their tremendous economic and cultural influence, they forced small, independent producers from radio airwaves and retail shelves, and as they did so their impersonal corporate structures became the norm, making other models of musical culture increasingly scarce. Even though smaller companies often retained a sense of human identity, Pareles wrote, "no sane music fan thinks, 'Gosh, I want that album because it's on Reprise Records, not Columbia.'" The result was that the administrative needs and commercial goals of the largest music corporations were naturalized. There was nothing to throw the priorities and policies of the large corporations into relief. Thus, unrivaled and unchallenged, they escaped notice and slipped into the unremarkable background of everyday reality.[1]

In the 1910s and '20s the music industry as a whole likewise achieved a certain invisibility. Its stars and its advertising notwithstanding, what did consumers know about how the music business worked? The process of becoming invisible did not come about naturally or automatically; it was actively created. It grew out of the production of commodities particularly well suited to becoming fetishes, as Marx referred to them—that is, objects that took on a quasi-magical power by obscuring the social and economic relations intrinsic to their production. Indeed, this was not merely an attribute of phonograph records and piano rolls; it was their raison d'être. As music-producing objects, their very purpose was disembodiment: the sundering of body and voice in the case of phonograph recordings, the substitution of a mechanical algorithm for physical and mental labor in the case of piano rolls. This division was reinforced by the material characteristics of the objects themselves, which bore few traces of the production process: sheet music covers featured the names of the performers who popularized a song much more prominently than those of the songwriters or publishers; phonograph records usually came in generic paper sleeves at that time, without pictures or liner notes (these developed much later), and with title, performer, and composer indicated only in small letters on the paper label affixed to the disc; and piano rolls came in long, thin boxes, most often brown or black, with only a paper label glued to the end and a few lines on the roll itself to distinguish it from any other. At *most,* therefore, a consumer held in her or his hands a fragment of information about the producer of the *music* but not of the *object,* and even less, of course, about the general production process—for instance, who decided what compositions would be published and which performers would make recordings, and on the basis of what factors?

On another level, invisibility or the intent to mislead was central to the music industry's promotional strategies. The motivation behind the "prestigious" Red Seal Record series, Victor's internal documents explicitly stated, was advertising, not consumer edification. Ampico instructed its dealers to cultivate educational markets but to hide the dealers' commercial involvement. In Tin Pan Alley, the sentimental lightheartedness of the songs masked the deliberate, calculated way they were crafted and promoted. In some instances, the industry even used this obfuscation as a selling point in its print advertising, best symbolized by Victor's ubiquitous trademark dog and the Gulbransen player-piano's widely publicized baby—two uncomprehending subjects beguiled by the technology of music commodities, neither having even the remote possibility of understanding them.

A radical attempt to confront, challenge, and disrupt the invisibility of the modern music industry did occur during its developmental period, however; this initiative came in the form of the first major black-owned record company, Black Swan Records, which was launched in 1921. Led by a former protégé of W. E. B. Du Bois, Harry H. Pace, the Black Swan venture strove to create a new kind of music company and in the process revealed how questions such as who made records, under what circumstances, and toward what ends made a difference in the distribution of power in society. Given that the success (that is to say, profitability) of the music industry up to that time had depended on obscuring just such issues, Pace and the other musicians, activists, and entrepreneurs who contributed to the Black Swan experiment sought explicitly to reconnect issues of production and consumption, thus in a sense defetishizing the music and fashioning it instead into an instrument of social and economic justice.

In both sound and structure, Black Swan had as its goal to bridge the political economy of race and the moral economy of music. Those involved in the company knew from experience that the music industry did not exist independently of the racial politics of the society in which it functioned. For institutions possessing the cultural and economic power that the music industry had by the postwar years, there could be no neutrality on "the race question." Whatever success or failure such institutions experienced bore the imprint of the ways that race was created and recreated in the economics and culture of daily life. These included not only notions of what race *looked* like but ideas about what it *sounded* like too. When derisive coon songs sold well, Tin Pan Alley had an interest in writing the catchiest coon songs it could and having them performed, heard, and sung again as widely as possible. Conversely, if African American chamber musicians disturbed widely held ideas about African Americans' cultural and moral inferiority, then people who had an investment in a social and economic order resting on such beliefs had an interest in denying or avoiding the musicians' work. Although such interests were not always definitive in shaping how the industry operated—for then as now, the market offered incentives for occasional exceptions—this dynamic underpinned the industry and shaped its development far more often than not. Ultimately, the Black Swan experiment lasted only a few years, but in both its rise and its fall, it revealed the possibilities and limitations of realizing social and political change through music and markets. The short history of this one small company says a great deal about the music industry generally and its relations with society at large.

Racial Uplift and the Politics of Cultural Production

As the American music industries grew in size and prestige in the early twentieth century, sheet music, piano rolls, and phonograph records established music as an essential component of the growing consumer economy and of national mass culture. By the end of World War I, the U.S. music industries produced goods worth more than $335 million, and never before had these industries exerted such cultural authority or financial influence in American life.[2] The music industries, however, were not an equal opportunity employer. Despite the disarming charm and popularity of the singer-comedian Bert Williams, the broad acclaim for the bandleader James Reese Europe, and the nation's widespread (though not universal) embrace of ragtime, African Americans found their opportunities in the music industries tightly restricted. While phonograph manufacturers appealed to immigrant groups by issuing thousands of titles in dozens of foreign languages and working hard to cultivate consumers in immigrant or "ethnic" communities, they all but refused to issue records by African Americans and disregarded African American consumers. In the instances where African Americans did make records, the recordings were generally limited to comedy or novelty styles, the effect of which was to establish coon songs and minstrelsy as the industry's dominant (and increasingly influential) paradigm of African American culture. A few records by James Reese Europe—who was the musical accompanist for the dance pioneers Vernon and Irene Castle and for the armed forces' famed "Harlem Hellfighters" regiment—and by the concert vocalist Carroll Clark marked only minor exceptions to this pattern and did nothing to alter the industry's low valuation of African American talent, its reluctance to depict African Americans as performers of so-called quality music, or its general pattern of marginalizing or excluding African American musicians.[3]

When the United States entered World War I, many African Americans lent their support only reluctantly, in the hope that they could leverage the fight for democracy abroad to effect a renewed commitment to democracy at home after the war's end. This heightened sense of entitlement, in combination with the bloody race riots of 1919, radicalized large numbers of African Americans. African Americans' political assertiveness took many forms around the country, but black Americans shared, as the *Chicago Defender* put it, "new thoughts, new ideas, new aspirations" as the postwar years unfolded.[4]

It was in this environment that the bright, charismatic businessman named Harry H. Pace launched the first major black-owned record company. Conceived as an enterprise to produce a broad range of music *by* and *for* African Americans, the company that became known as Black Swan Records was an audacious didactic project designed to harness the combined power of music and business in the cause of racial uplift and the fight for social justice. A small African American–owned company called Broome Records, established in 1919, may have awakened Pace to the possibility of such an undertaking.[5] Musically speaking, Pace sought to issue all kinds of records—not just blues, ragtime, and comic records, but also opera, spirituals, and classical music—the combined effect of which would challenge stereotypes about African Americans, promote African Americans' cultural development, and refute racist arguments about African American barbarism. At the same time, the company would be a model of economic development, inspiring and instructing African Americans in capital accumulation and the potential for economic self-determination.[6]

Black Swan Records, then, was a radical experiment in the political economy of African American culture, in the guise of musical entertainment and small-business development. The company's discrete but connected priorities—music and business—were at once practical and symbolic, designed to effect real change in the condition of African Americans in the United States. Black Swan's musical goals, emphasizing diversity and quality, would uplift and empower African Americans, as well as challenging (white) public opinion about African Americans' attributes and capabilities. The company's business aims brought together competing strands of African American political activism around their shared support for black economic self-determination. Closely though unofficially aligned with the National Association for the Advancement of Colored People (NAACP), Black Swan also benefited from the direct support and guidance of Du Bois, who invested the project with heavyweight political credibility. This record company was about more than selling records, and the one-two punch of its cultural and economic agendas made its brief history an important, revealing milestone in the African American political struggles of the twentieth century. By the time the company collapsed in the mid-1920s, however, the potential for achieving racial uplift through the commercial music industries was down for the count.

Despite the political, ideological, and programmatic diversity among African American leaders, they were unified in their support for black-owned business development—a common commitment that gave Black Swan a broad political foundation on which to build. Although support for African American business development is sometimes associated more narrowly with the political leadership of Booker T. Washington and his National Negro Business League (NNBL), Washington's pioneering business network actually grew out of an idea hatched by Du Bois at a Tuskegee conference, The Negro in Business, in 1899, and Du Bois remained a consistent champion of black business development in succeeding years, even as he focused greater attention on African American civil rights.[7] Washington's death in 1915 and the effects of World War I changed the political landscape dramatically, but by the time Black Swan was established, support among African American leaders for economic development was as strong as ever. Most notably, the political vacuum left by Washington's death was filled largely by the Jamaican-born Marcus Garvey, whose Universal Negro Improvement Association (UNIA) upheld business development as one of its fundamental goals.[8]

Meanwhile, images of African Americans and ideas about African American music had been central to the nation's musical entertainment since the rise of minstrelsy in the mid-nineteenth century. By the turn of the twentieth century, the popularity of coon songs and ragtime placed African Americans at the center of American musical culture. But African Americans themselves exercised little control over the terms of their employment or the kinds of music they could produce professionally, and by the late 1910s they were even being displaced as the primary interpreters of musical styles they had originated.[9] Despite the commercial success of numerous African American songwriters, New York had only one significant music-publishing company run by African Americans before the late 1910s, and its nominal success may have depended on consumers' ignorance of its African American ownership. At best, then, the professional opportunities open to African Americans were extremely restricted (for example, to performing in blackface comedy), while at worst, as in the rapidly growing phonograph business, African Americans were excluded almost completely from musical culture.[10]

In his landmark book *The Souls of Black Folk* (1903), Du Bois asserted that the end of the Negro's striving was "to be a co-worker in the kingdom of culture." But how could African Americans become such co-workers when the established culture producers did not welcome their labor? As early as 1916, the *Chicago Defender* had encouraged its readers to write to phonograph companies to demand releases by Negro artists, but the companies were either indifferent or overtly hostile to the idea. A series of events, however, broke this impasse in the phonograph industry. A number of lawsuits and court decisions, along with the expiration of patents, loosened the stranglehold that Victor, Columbia, and Edison had on the phonograph business, thus making it possible for the first time for new, "independent" record companies to enter the market. At the same time, after years of African American pressure on phonograph companies, one of the new labels, OKeh Records, issued two records by an African American vaudeville singer, Mamie Smith. These historic recordings from 1920 were the result of a dogged campaign by the African American songwriter and publisher Perry Bradford, who recalled that he had "walked out two pairs of shoes" and faced "many insults and wise-cracking" recording engineers before securing an agreement with OKeh's Fred Hager. Indeed, Hager had allegedly received letters threatening a boycott of OKeh products if he had "any truck with colored girls in the recording field," but Bradford convinced Hager to take a chance on Mamie Smith. When the two records appeared, in February and August 1920, they sold phenomenally well among African Americans and heralded the possibility of a new era of African American music.[11]

These distinct but overlapping movements in business, race politics, and music were more than the backdrop of the founding of Black Swan. They were also written in a complex way into Harry Pace's own biography. When he began to organize the company in late 1920, he brought years of experience and an array of talents as a teacher, banker, insurance executive, political organizer, songwriter, and music publisher, and this breadth and depth directly informed his expectations and aspirations.[12] Born the son of a blacksmith in rural Covington, Georgia, in 1884, the ambitious and energetic Pace

7.1 Harry Pace brought his past experience in music, business, and political activism to Black Swan Records. *Crusader,* Feb. 1921, General Research and Reference Division, Schomburg Center for Research in Black Culture, New York Public Library, Astor, Lenox and Tilden Foundations.

enrolled at Atlanta University, where he fell under the tutelage of W. E. B. Du Bois. After graduating as valedictorian of his class in 1903, Pace accepted Du Bois's offer to become the business manager of Du Bois's new journal of African American ideas and culture. That magazine, which was based in Memphis, became the groundbreaking *Moon Illustrated Weekly,* the main precursor to the *Crisis,* the NAACP organ that served as Du Bois's main outlet from 1910 to 1934. The *Moon* also initiated Pace into the business of cultural politics.

When inadequate funding forced the *Moon* to cease publication after eight months or so, Pace pursued ventures in education, in politics, and in the bedrock industries of African American business: banking and insurance.[13] After two years of teaching Latin and Greek at the Lincoln Institute in Missouri, he returned to Memphis in 1912, secured a position at the black-owned Solvent Savings Bank, and became active in Republican politics. Through this work, he developed relationships with many of Memphis's most important African American leaders, and these connections soon led Pace to Atlanta, where he worked for six years as secretary-treasurer of what was probably the most prominent and respected black-owned business of the era, the multimillion-dollar Standard Life Insurance Company. Meanwhile, his political involvement deepened when he and several other employees established Atlanta's first chapter of the NAACP—a particularly notable event in a period when most black-owned businesses, especially in the South, were closely aligned with Booker T. Washington and Washington's more oblique approach to political activism. (Pace served as the Atlanta chapter's first president; the position of secretary was filled by a young man Pace had recently hired named Walter White, who later became the NAACP's national executive secretary.)

Remarkably, however, these events represented only one side of Pace's activities during this period. At the same time that he was working at the Solvent Savings Bank in Memphis and then at Standard Life in Atlanta, he was involved in a music-publishing partnership with Beale Street's favorite son, W. C. Handy, the self-proclaimed "father of the blues," who pioneered written arrangements of and formal publication of blues music. Pace had penned some "first rate song lyrics," Handy later remembered, and, together, the two men composed and published several successful songs. In addition, they established their own publishing firm, the groundbreaking Pace & Handy Publishing Company, of which Pace served as president. In 1918 Pace convinced Handy to move their growing business to New York, where, despite continued commercial success, they also confronted repeated indignities from, as Handy, who was normally quite even-tempered when voicing his opinions, put it, "the beast of racial prejudice." Pace was to recall, "I ran up against a color line that was very severe" when the firm relocated to New York.[14]

In Handy's recollection, one recording manager refused to record a Pace & Handy blues number performed by a white singer, and another refused to issue records of songs published by Pace & Handy because he did not want the black publishers to earn royalties from the phonograph company's records. Meanwhile, like Perry Bradford, Handy and Pace were also trying to secure recording dates for African American singers. Handy wrote, "In every case the managers quickly turned thumbs down. 'Their voices were not suitable.' 'Their diction was different from white girls.' 'They couldn't possibly fill the bill.'" When Pace tried to persuade phonograph companies to record African Americans performing nonblues material, he was told that white prejudice made it commercially impossible; company representatives, he reported, claimed "it would ruin their business to have a colored person making records of high class music."[15]

Pace and Handy, therefore, were extremely attuned to the racial politics of production and consumption in the music business. Indeed, when they published the songs on Mamie Smith's first record, their advertisement urged consumers to use their purchasing power to send a message to record companies: "Lovers of music everywhere, and those who desire to help in any advance of the Race should be sure to buy this record as encouragement to the manufacturers for their liberal policy and to encourage other manufacturers who may not believe that the Race will buy records sung by its own singers."[16] This style of activist advertising foreshadowed the methods Pace later used to promote Black Swan. Indeed, a short time later Pace split with his partner to start the record company that combined his commitment to black-owned business and his belief in the social importance of music. All Pace's professional experiences to this point—his relationship with Du Bois, the personal contacts he developed in Atlanta, Memphis, and New York, his business experience in banking and insurance, and his music business experience with Handy—thus converged and came to bear on his new venture.

The purpose of the record company as a means of achieving racial uplift was clear from the outset. To some contemporaries, the name Black Swan itself would have echoed that of the Black Star shipping line that Marcus Garvey was then organizing as the base of his economic program. In fact, however, Pace took the name of his company, at Du Bois's suggestion, from the stage name of the most accomplished African American concert singer of the nineteenth century, Elizabeth Taylor Greenfield (ca. 1824–1876).[17] Even though many people probably missed the allusion—Taylor's career had ended almost half a century earlier—it symbolized Black Swan's special commitment to music of "the better sort" and the widely held belief that the best music cultivated moral and spiritual growth.

In many iterations, the idea that music could both ennoble and unite people rested exclusively on the great works of European concert music, but musical uplift could encompass a unique African American musical tradition as well.[18] *Dwight's Journal of Music,* the standard-bearer of high musical culture in nineteenth-century America, published some of the first accounts of the singing of slave spirituals—alongside its orthodox celebrations of Mozart and Beethoven. Du Bois, moreover, had structured *The Souls of Black Folk* in a way that emphasized this counterpoint of European and African American culture: the epigraphs to each chapter juxtaposed a literary excerpt—usually of European poetry—with a musical transcription of a strain of African American music—generally a slave spiritual. He then devoted the final chapter in the book to the transcendent, redemptive power of African American spirituals.[19]

Particularly important for African Americans, however, was the dual character of musical uplift—its orientation both toward other African Americans and toward the rest of society at large. The Music School Settlement for Colored People, for example, which included Du Bois on its board of directors, fostered music education as a means both of achieving personal edification and of breaking down social barriers. It was founded in Harlem in 1911 by David Mannes, the concertmaster of the New York Symphony Society and an instructor at the Music School Settlement on New York's Lower East Side (and the son-in-law of Walter Damrosch). Unlike most other settlement projects involving music, this one had a specifically racial agenda, for Mannes believed that "through music, which is a universal language, the Negro and the white man can be brought to have a mutual understanding."[20]

The school was greatly aided by several annual benefit concerts organized by James Reese Europe, whose outstanding music and career linked African American popular music with order and respectability. By the time of his early death in 1919, Europe had combined musical talent, organizational deftness, and social respectability in a manner that made him the incarnation of racial uplift through music. In "Jazzing Away Prejudice," the *Chicago De-*

fender wrote, "The most prejudiced enemy of our Race could not sit through an evening with Europe without coming away with a changed viewpoint. For he is compelled in spite of himself to see us in a new light. . . . Europe and his band are worth much more to our Race than a thousand speeches from so-called Race orators and uplifters."[21] The statement exemplified the outward dimension of uplift—its active, self-conscious projection of African American dignity, creativity, and control.

Harry Pace pushed this idea further: in his view, the shaping of public opinion was an actual prerequisite for effecting meaningful change for African Americans. In a 1921 speech, "Public Opinion and the Negro"—which predated Walter Lippmann's landmark book *Public Opinion* by several months—Pace argued, "Unless we take hold vigorously of this matter of creating and shaping Public Opinion itself, all other efforts we may put forth in any line will be useless so far as our status among the races of the world is concerned." The speech did not refer explicitly to music or to Black Swan, but coming as it did in the middle of Black Swan's first year, it may be taken as an expression of Pace's broad strategy at the time. He did not naively believe that bad public relations alone caused racial violence or other problems—"The Problem of the Races in this country is Economic," he asserted flatly—but control of public opinion was a powerful tool in confronting difficult social issues. Distilling his ideas, Pace explained that there were two ways to regard public opinion, one passive and retrograde, the other active and full of promise: "One [way] is to think of it as it already exists, to deplore it if it happens to be unfavorable, to watch it run its course, and to take the consequences if it does not react favorably to you. The other way is the present day idea which we as a people are just beginning to learn, and that is to anticipate Public Opinion and to help mould it and shape it so as to be sure that it does react the way we want."[22]

Du Bois apparently concurred, for he used his position at the *Crisis* to issue a veiled multipart endorsement of Black Swan. In February 1921 he published an editorial, "Phonograph Records," which condemned the restricted opportunities open to African American performers because of white demand for "'comic darky songs' but nothing else." With a supportive Negro audience already in place, he argued, "we must now develop a business organization to preserve and record our best voices." Such an effort would "reveal the best music, not only of [the Negro] race but of all races and ages." He ended by stating, "We are pleased to learn that such a company is now forming with adequate capital and skilled management of guaranteed integrity." Then, one month later, Du Bois published a profile of Elizabeth Taylor Greenfield, which ended with another appeal to support the new record company (and which called attention the company's allusive name). Like Black Swan itself, these articles represented a belief in the convergence of art and business for the purposes of racial progress. Du Bois forcefully articulated his position on the politics of art and public opinion a few years later in an address before the national conference of the NAACP. After acknowledging that some members might question how art pertained to the political gathering, he offered a strong defense of the political relevance of art, concluding with this statement: "I do not doubt that the ultimate art coming from black folk is going to be just as beautiful, and beautiful largely in the same ways, as the art that comes from white folk, or yellow, or red; but the point today is that until the art of the black folk compels recognition they will not be rated as human. And when through art they compel recognition then let the world discover if it will that their art is as new as it is old and as old as new."[23]

Culture and Capital

In organizing the record company, Pace tapped into a rich vein of African American talent and experience. He assembled a board of directors (which was itself unusual for a small phonograph company) whose membership included a wide range of business and professional leaders. The most notable board member, however, was Du Bois, whose eminence and personal connections were an invaluable asset to the company and whose ideas about culture and activism informed the enterprise in a great many ways.[24] In addition, Pace brought to Black Swan several outstanding employees from the publishing company he had founded with W. C. Handy. These included Fletcher Henderson, soon to be one of the leading bandleaders of the 1920s and '30s, who was enlisted as the phonograph company's recording manager, and William Grant Still, later an eminent composer, who became Black Swan's in-house arranger. Most of the company's financing came from or through its board of directors, although when Bert Williams died in 1922, Pace reported that the comedian, too, had invested heavily in the company—and had pledged to make records for it when he completed his contract with Columbia.[25]

Public reaction to the announcement of the new company cut in two directions. On the one hand, from African Americans there came an outpouring of support: enthusiastic articles on the company appeared in a wide range of periodicals, and Pace received many letters from well-wishers and people requesting commissions as sales agents. On the other hand, some music industry personnel proved overtly hostile to this African American initiative and tried to intimidate Pace, to prevent him from continuing. Pace & Handy received threats of a boycott of its publications, which forced Pace to sever all ties with the publishing firm. Then, according to Handy, his songs were indeed boycotted by people who falsely believed that he had some formal connection with the record company. Opposition continued after Black Swan became operational; most disturbing of all, in September 1922 a bomb was found in a coal shipment bound for the furnace in the company's manufacturing facilities.[26]

Such hostility notwithstanding, Black Swan issued its first title in May 1921. Symbolically, Pace chose for that record the sentimental, inspirational song "At Dawning," backed with "Thank God for a Garden," sung by the concert vocalist and pianist Revella Hughes. Hughes, who had at her command a repertoire of both popular and "serious" music, was a prominent activist for Marcus Garvey and performed regularly at Garveyite functions ranging from the annual UNIA convention to informal weeknight gatherings at Liberty Hall on 135th Street in Harlem. Although Black Swan was certainly not a Garveyite business and Pace later had a bitter falling out with Garvey, this first entry in Black Swan's catalogue of recordings reflected the affinity that non-Garveyites like Pace felt for the Garvey movement at that time.[27]

Following "At Dawning," Black Swan by and large made good on its promise to issue "music of the better sort" recorded by African Americans. Black Swan's second record consisted of two ballads by the concert vocalist Carroll Clark, one of the only African Americans to have recorded "serious" music before that time. He made his first discs for Columbia in 1908, but tellingly that company had refused to publish photographs of Clark in association with anything other than popular music.[28] In all, Black Swan recorded and issued at least forty-five sides of "serious" music, both sacred and secular, performed by African Americans, for whom almost no other recording opportunities then existed. As a whole, the "serious" component of Black Swan's output laid claim to a broad swath of musical territory, including African American spirituals, arias by Giuseppe Verdi and Charles Gounod, Christmas carols, the first recording of a work by the composer R. Nathaniel Dett, and the first recorded performance of "Lift Ev'ry Voice and Sing," the so-called Negro national anthem.

The point of Black Swan's issuing recordings of serious music, noted one early article, was not to depreciate "the commercial value of comic songs, 'blues' and ragtime songs," but to supplement those styles with "every type of race music, including sacred and spiritual songs, the popular music of the day, and the high-class ballads and operatic selections." In short, commerce and art were understood to be discrete but interdependent domains. As the reference to the "commercial value" of popular music anticipated, however, Black Swan came to depend overwhelmingly on its blues, jazz, and other popular recordings for revenue. In the end, all its best-selling records were blues records; and jazz, blues, popular songs, and dance music made up two-thirds of its total releases.[29] (Blues, in this context, referred exclusively to the style now usually referred to as classic or vaudeville blues, meaning blues performed by individual singers, usually women, accompanied by a piano or a small syncopated band. Recordings of male-oriented "down-home" or "country" blues were still several years away.[30])

As a means of maximizing available capital, Black Swan adopted an informal system of triage. Singer Ethel Waters recalled in her autobiography that when she first entered the company in 1921, she had a lengthy discussion with Pace and Henderson about "whether [she] should sing popular or 'cultural' numbers." In the end, the two men decided she would sing popular blues material and agreed to pay Waters the sizable sum of one hundred dollars for two songs. (She was then performing for thirty-five dollars a week plus tips.) Underlying this exchange between Waters and Henderson and Pace were uncomfortable class tensions. Waters recalled, "Remember those class distinctions in Harlem, which had its Park Avenue crowd, a middle

class, and its Tenth Avenue. That was me, then, low-down Tenth Avenue."³¹
The fact that Waters did not fit the recognized social profile for a singer
of "cultural" songs may well have influenced where the men placed her in
the company's recording roster, regardless of the fact that she, like Revella
Hughes and most other musicians, had a repertoire encompassing a variety
of styles.

Whatever the explanation, Waters proved a good investment for Black
Swan: her first record—featuring "Down Home Blues" and "Oh, Daddy"—
became so enormously popular that it reversed the company's economic fortunes. Pace exaggerated when he claimed later that it sold half a million copies in six months, but the record did sell briskly and, as Waters noted, was
popular among both black and white audiences. By the end of 1921 Black
Swan had turned a small profit of $3,100 on revenues of over $104,000, and
with a genuine hit on the market, Pace signed Waters to an exclusive one-year
contract. By the spring of 1922, after twelve months in business, the company may have sold as many as four hundred thousand records.³²

If it was hardly the centerpiece of Black Swan's musical uplift project,
blues—or at least a certain respectable strain of blues—was not entirely at
odds with it either. Voicing widespread concern in the postwar years over the
"respectability" of African American culture, a Black Swan advertisement in
the *Chicago Defender* maintained that Ethel Waters had "changed the style of
Blues singing overnight, and brought a finer interpretation of this work. She
dignified the Blues." Although many African Americans scorned the blues as
profane, lower-class, or culturally backward, Black Swan's promotion of the
blues reflects how it had become to a certain degree fashionable and even respectable. On Friday, January 20, 1922, Harlem held its first widely publicized blues contest, at the Manhattan Casino. The event featured the famed
ragtime songwriter Noble Sissle acting as master of ceremonies and opened
with a performance by Will Vodery's sixty-seven-piece regimental band. The
audience included Governor Nathan L. Miller, the former alderman and future mayor Fiorello La Guardia, the social dance pioneer Irene Castle Tremaine, Dorothy Caruso (Enrico Caruso's widow), and the socialite Mrs. Oliver Harriman. Each of the four contestants entered in an elegant satin gown
and performed with musical accompaniment by "the father of stride piano,"
James P. Johnson. The competition was decided by audience applause,

which declared the newcomer Trixie Smith the evening's champion. As a result, Black Swan signed Smith to a recording contract several days later, and by February the company had released Smith's first two sides, "Desperate Blues," written by Alex Rogers and James P. Johnson, and the contest winner she had written herself, "Trixie's Blues." When Black Swan's monthly quarter-page advertisement in the trade journal *Talking Machine World* appeared, it boasted, "We Announce that we have ready for delivery the first recordings by Trixie Smith Winner of the NATIONAL Blues Singing Contest Held at Manhattan Casino, New York (The Winner's Cup was presented by Mrs. Irene Castle)."[33]

To promote both the blues and the company by other means, Black Swan also organized a remarkable music and vaudeville tour by a troupe it called the Black Swan Troubadours, which included singing, dancing, and comic skits. Headlined by Ethel Waters and led musically by Fletcher Henderson, the tour lasted from fall 1921—little more than a year after Mamie Smith's breakthrough recordings—until July 1922. It began in Washington, D.C., traveled through Philadelphia, Baltimore, Pittsburgh, and cities in West Virginia, Ohio, and Kentucky, then Saint Louis and Indianapolis, before arriving in Chicago at the end of January 1922. From Pittsburgh on, the tour was managed by Lester Walton, whose multifaceted career also included important work as a journalist, theater manager, and civil rights activist.[34] At the end of the Chicago stint, the management announced the troupe would next depart on an extended tour of the South. Four musicians refused to go and quit the ensemble, but Ethel Waters stuck with it. Despite the hostility that the band would face in the South, the *Defender* reported, Waters "felt it her duty to make sacrifices in order that members of her Race might hear her sing a style of music which is a product of the Southland." In short, the tour itself was also cast as a means toward racial uplift. In the following months, the group traveled through Tennessee, Arkansas, Oklahoma, Texas, Louisiana, Alabama, and North and South Carolina, before returning north for the tour's finale.[35]

On the road, the troupe encountered some unpleasant circumstances, but it also achieved pathbreaking success. In Paris, Texas, where a lynching had taken place shortly before the group's arrival, the Troubadours still received a warm welcome, and both black and white dancers attended and enjoyed their performance. In another town, according to the Black Swan singer Alberta Hunter, who was not on the tour, a young black boy was lynched after he "talked back to a white man," and when the Troubadours arrived, the boy's corpse was thrown into the lobby of the theater where the group was to perform. Later on the tour, however, the *New Orleans Daily Item* arranged for the troupe to perform on the radio when they passed though Louisiana—perhaps the first radio performance anywhere by African American musicians. The radio concert, the *Savannah (Georgia) Tribune* reported, was heard in five states and in Mexico.[36]

This vigorous promotion of popular music, however, could not resolve the politics of class conflict inscribed in Black Swan's musical program. On the one hand, blues was commercially and culturally valuable, and as a former songwriter and popular-music publisher, Pace himself had deep roots in popular music. On the other hand, no matter what style of music the company was producing, the recordings were oriented toward middle-class standards of dignity, refinement, and self-restraint—standards that lay at the core of the idea of uplift. In religious music, for example, Black Swan favored formal arrangements of concert spirituals over syncopated gospel music, which was at that time still associated with the Pentecostal movement, or the "holiness" and "sanctified" churches frequented by poorer, less-educated African Americans. Indeed, for all Black Swan's stated ambition to be inclusive, the company appears not to have been comfortable with certain strains of working-class African American culture—particularly those which diverged from the norms of refinement and respectability. Before Bessie Smith recorded for Columbia Records and became one of the most important and commercially successful singers of the 1920s, for example, she auditioned for Black Swan. Her style was coarse and boisterous—"blacker," according to the racial taxonomy of the period—quite unlike the lighter, more lyrical singing of most other Black Swan singers. When she stopped abruptly in the middle of her first test recording and said, "Hold on, let me spit," she thrust herself outside the "respectable" model of musicianship that Black Swan endorsed, and the company declined to add her to its roster. At the other end of the blues spectrum was the singer and actress Isabelle Washington, whom Black Swan did record; her quasi-bluesy renditions of popular songs sounded "white," that is, her mannered warble conformed to stereotypes about white singers' thin, controlled, trained voices, by contrast with the muscular, rough-hewn singing style ascribed to African Americans.[37]

A few Black Swan numbers, with titles such as "He May Be Your Man (But He Comes to See Me Sometimes)" and "My Man Rocks Me (with One Steady Roll)," were more explicitly risqué, but musically the company's recordings celebrated polish more than passion. In this respect, Fletcher Henderson, for all his talents, was criticized for being refined to a fault. Ethel Waters, for example, bristled under Henderson's efforts to keep the music from getting too "hot." "Fletcher, though a fine arranger and a brilliant band leader, leans more to the classical side," Waters recalled. "I kept having arguments with [him because he] wouldn't give me what I call 'the damn-it-to-hell bass,' that chump-chump stuff that real jazz needs." Clarinetist Garvin Bushell added that Henderson left little room for improvisation on the recordings, almost everything being played in strict accordance with his arrangements. Contrasting Henderson's style with that of Bessie Smith, whose voice was once likened to "a flamethrower licking out across the room," the historian David Levering Lewis has written, "Instead of a flamethrower, Fletcher Henderson held a torch. It dazzled and warmed but it did not leave audiences blind and scorched."[38]

In other words, Pace and company enjoyed the blues only to the extent that it did not conflict with the overall project of uplift. While they deeply esteemed "popular music" in many forms, they also remained committed to middle-class ideals of refinement and self-control. Before the National Association of Negro Musicians (NANM), a group that favored classical-music education for African Americans, Pace explained that his company was "dedicated to racial service along a new line." His speech depicted Black Swan's endorsement of popular music as a strategic, temporary concession that would lead ultimately to a higher cultural end. He explained: "We have had to give the people what many of them wanted to get them to buy what we wanted them to want." Such a disavowal of popular music may have been somewhat disingenuous, given Pace's extensive involvement in it, but cultivating a taste for "high" musical culture was central to Black Swan's musical mission. He concluded his speech, "I believe that we [Negroes] want every kind of music other people want and it behooves some of us to undertake the job of elevating the musical taste of the race. . . . Black Swan Records are trying to do their part."[39] The conflict within Black Swan, however, demonstrated how ill-defined and contested the category of "popular music" actually was. For all Pace's avowed commitment to catholicity in Black Swan's recording program, not to mention his experience as a writer and publisher of "popular" songs, thriving musical currents existed that he could not hear, elements of working-class African American life that conflicted with "respectable" middle-class values. Infused with both pathos and pleasure, the candid sexual politics of Ma Rainey and Bessie Smith, for example, not only deviated from polite middle-class norms but did so insouciantly, vibrantly, and at times defiantly. In the end, it required more conventional record companies, indifferent to African American cultural politics, to record their music.[40]

Although Pace struggled to balance Black Swan's social, economic, and cultural agendas, he maintained constant pressure on all of them. To an African American business group, he promoted his ideas about economic self-determination. At an Eastertime music celebration at Garvey's Liberty Hall he was welcomed as a featured speaker.[41] Pace worked to expand the business and to stabilize it, and he paid close attention to the potential of advertisements to communicate Black Swan's multifaceted character to a broad, mass-media audience. Many advertisements featured this tongue-in-cheek slogan: "The only genuine colored record. Others are only passing for colored." Thus, in a few artful words, Black Swan promoted a cultural politics of race pride and, in playing on the notion of racial passing, mocked the superficiality of the emerging commercial interests of white-owned record companies.

As an aggressive businessman, Pace tried to make Black Swan records available wherever people might acquire them. Beyond retail phonograph shops, Pace also found sales outlets in drug stores, furniture dealers, newsstands, barber shops, beauty shops, pool halls, and even speakeasies—anyplace, in other words, that conducted business with a heavily African American clientele—and this did not include Black Swan's sizable mail-order sales.[42] In addition, one Black Swan advertisement in *Talking Machine World* suggests that Pace made some attempts at "forward" integration of the company, into wholesale. On a list of ten jobbers distributing Black Swan records regionally, three had names that hint at a possible affiliation: Black Swan Sales Company of Boston, Pace Phonograph Corporation of Virginia, and Black Swan Music Company of Pittsburgh. (Unfortunately, no other information on this last component of Pace's activities appears to have survived.) Elsewhere, advertisements for a Black Swan Swanola phonograph indicated an attempt at "horizontal" integration of the business, into machine sales.[43]

Indeed, in the expanding consumer culture, print advertising was one of the most powerful tools at Pace's disposal to promote his program of musical and commercial uplift. Appearing in the trade press, black newspapers, and black political periodicals, Black Swan's advertisements varied widely and served different purposes. In *Talking Machine World*, Black Swan advertisements (usually a quarter page) appeared every month from August 1921 through October 1922, each advertisement highlighting one or several new records in the catalogue, almost always blues. In this industry-wide organ, the Black Swan advertisements corroborate Ethel Waters's comment that her records appealed to both black and white audiences. Similar in content were the newspaper advertisements that Black Swan placed in the entertainment pages of the nation's many African American newspapers, where they appeared adjacent to advertisements for theatrical productions, sheet music, other record companies, and sundry cosmetic products. Usually these advertisements focused on new releases and aimed to keep the label in the public eye, sometimes through bold, eye-catching pronouncements, such as "The Best BLUES SINGER in America is ETHEL WATERS" or "Every Time You Buy a Black Swan Record You Buy the Only Record Made by Colored People."[44]

Such straightforward advertising was not to be taken for granted. Over the course of the 1920s, many of Black Swan's rivals at least occasionally used advertising that revealed an underlying contempt for African American artists and consumers. Racist caricatures appeared in advertisements for both black and white artists, and some record catalogues included text in Negro "dialect," such as a "race records" catalogue issued by OKeh around 1924 that declared: "Every smilin', teasin' brownskin gal in dis book of Greatest Blues has jes got it natchely, the dawggone Blues." Indeed, when advertisements showed blues fans in urbane, well-appointed environments, they were

7.2 This advertisement, showing two blackface-style characters being pursued by a policeman, while an unhappy woman looks on, ran in 1924 in the *Chicago Defender,* the nation's most widely read African American newspaper. Advertisements such as this one stood in marked contrast to advertisements for Black Swan, which promoted both the company's music and its mission as a black-owned enterprise. *Chicago Defender,* Oct. 25, 1924, author's collection.

often depicted as white or of indeterminate appearance (seen only in shadow or silhouette, for example), and record companies' discomfort with images of urban black respectability may have been a factor in their focusing more resources, in the late 1920s and '30s, on rural, down-home blues.[45]

In light of the hostility of this environment, it is especially notable that Black Swan also advertised regularly in the radical black press, frequently featuring some kind of polemical statement that invoked Black Swan's social mission. In magazines such as the *Crisis* and Chandler Owen and A. Philip Randolph's socialist monthly, the *Messenger,* Black Swan's full-page advertisements often looked beyond artists and record releases. Instead, the advertisements exhorted readers to patronize black-owned businesses and to support Black Swan's effort to create an autonomous alternative to white-owned record companies. Suggesting that Black Swan was on the front lines in the struggle for the social and economic betterment of the "race," these advertisements recast support for Black Swan as a matter of political solidarity.

When rival labels began to issue increasing numbers of records by African American musicians, for example, one Black Swan advertisement charged that a few white-owned record companies had established "a Jim Crow annex" in their businesses and that they were dumping on the market records by "a few short-sighted colored people" in order to wipe out companies such as Black Swan. A more contentious advertisement challenged readers who paid lip service to the idea of black-owned business but who, "in private," patronized white-owned companies. Other advertisements focused squarely on the political economy of musical uplift. The most notable of these appeared in the *Crisis* in the January 1923 issue and ran for six straight months in the *Messenger.* "Colored People Don't Want Classic Music!" its headline read, and it continued:

So our Dealers write us. "Give 'Em Blues and Jazz. That's all we can sell."

We Believe the Dealer is Wrong. But unless we furnish him with What he has Demand for, he will not handle our Goods.

If you, the person reading this advertisement, earnestly want to Do Something for Negro Music, Go to your Record Dealer and ask for the

Better Class of Records by Colored Artists. If there is a Demand he will
keep Them. Try this list of the Better Class.

There followed a list of records that included music sung by Antoinette
Garnes, the only African American member of the Chicago Grand Opera
Company, and two leaders of the classically oriented National Association of
Negro Musicians, the soprano Florence Cole-Talbert and the violinist Kemper Harreld.[46] Another advertisement, under the headline "Caruso's Voice,"
commended the Victor Talking Machine Company for having preserved the
voice of the great tenor (who had just died) but criticized "the white companies [for] preserving only the type of Negro voice that sings comics [*sic*]
and rag-time." Further down, the text invited readers to compare Caruso's
recording of one song, "For All Eternity," with a recording of the same song
by Black Swan's Carroll Clark.

More than simply trying to sell records, these advertisements urged readers to understand the connection between cultural achievement and market
relations. They positioned Black Swan not as an alternative force to consumer culture, at odds with the rest of society, but rather as a progressive
force within it. By buying these classical records, argued one of the advertisements, "you will Encourage Us to make more and more of this kind," by
shaping what dealers would stock. In his speech before the NANM, conversely, Pace had analyzed the implications that weak classical music sales
could have. He explained, "If through lack of patronage for our higher class
numbers we are compelled to discontinue that phase of activities and record
only 'blues' and 'ragtime' the public critics and the white companies will join
in a chorus of 'I told you so' and the dictum will go forth that the Negroes
will not buy good music and the chance of our artist ever recording his voice
for any white organization will fade into the realm of chances lost and not
to be regained." Earlier in the century, activists against child labor had pioneered consumer campaigns to shape conditions of production. Now, in a
different context, Black Swan was attempting something similar by linking
consumer buying habits with the reality of cultural production.[47]

Seen in historical perspective, the complete integration of the different
components of the project—business leadership, musical uplift, and popular

"Colored People Don't Want Classic Music!"

So our Dealers write.us. "Give 'Em Blues and Jazz. That's all we can sell".

We Believe the Dealer is Wrong. But unless we furnish him with What he has Demand for, he will not handle our Goods.

If you—the person reading this advertisement—earnestly want to Do Something for Negro Music, Go to your Record Dealer and ask for the Better Class of Records by Colored Artists. If there is a Demand he will keep Them. Try this list of the Better Class. Buy one or all of them:

$1.00 7101—Caro Nome (Rigoletto), Antoinette Garnes, Soprano.

1.00 7102—Ah Fors'E'Lui (Traviata), Antoinette Garnes, Soprano.

1.00 7103—The Bell Song (Lakme), Florence Cole Talbert, Soprano.

1.00 7104—The Kiss (Il Bacio), Florence Cole Talbert, Soprano.

60004 (Autumn Leaves, Piano Solo, Donald Heywood.
75c (Operatic Dream.

60005 (Swanee River, Violin Solo, Kemper Harreld.
75c (Souvenir.

2001 (At Dawning, Revella Hughes, Soprano.
75c (Thank God for a Garden.

2015 (The Rosary, Marianna Johnson, Contralto.
75c (Sorter Miss You.

2013 (Since You Went Away, J. Arthur Gaines, Tenor.
75c (Who Knows.

You will enjoy these and you will Encourage Us to make more and more of this kind of A Record.

We have a special Proposition for Music Teachers. Write for it.

Agents Wanted In Every Community.

Black Swan Phonograph Company, Inc.

HARRY H. PACE, Pres.

2289 Seventh Avenue   New York, N. Y.

Mention THE CRISIS

7.3 Black Swan promoted its political program in regular advertisements in the black radical press, especially in the *Crisis,* the monthly journal of the NAACP. This advertisement urging readers to think about—and act on—the link between cultural achievement and market relations appeared in January 1923 in the *Crisis* and ran for six straight months in the *Messenger,* the socialist journal edited by A. Philip Randolph and Chandler Owen. Author's collection.

entertainment—is striking. In May 1923 in the *Crisis,* Black Swan advertised a record of two comic monologues by Charles Winter Wood, "Honey You Sho' Looks Bad" and "When De Co'n Pone's Hot." Lest this type of humor strike a sour note with the "high class" crowd, the description of the record

CARUSO'S VOICE

Will live as long as there are men to hear it. The original plates are imperishable.

The Victor Company made Phonograph Records of his voice on millions of Records. What a loss the world would have sustained but for Phonograph Records!

Is there not some Negro Singer or Musician whose Voice You Feel Should also be Preserved?

The Phonograph Records made by white companies are preserving only the type of Negro voice that sings comics and rag-time.

BLACK SWAN RECORDS

Made by a Company owned and controlled by Colored People are trying to do for Negro Voices and Negro Musicians what white companies do for their people.

If every Colored Phonograph Owner bought as many BLACK SWAN RECORDS as he buys of other kinds he would make possible a reproduction of Negro Music and Voices similar to Caruso's. In addition you will find that BLACK SWAN RECORDS are as good as any Record made!

COMPARE THEM

For the sake of comparison play on your machine Caruso's Victor record No. 8333 of "For All Eternity." Then with the same kind of needle and at the same speed play Carroll Clark's BLACK SWAN RECORD, No. 2002, of the same song.

We will leave the verdict to you. Try it. There is a delightful surprise awaiting YOU.

YOU will then want to hear Harry Delmore, Revella Hughes, Arthur Gaines and Marrianna Johnson, all high-class, exclusive BLACK SWAN Artists.

YOU can buy Our Records from YOUR Regular Phonograph Dealer. Ask Him? If not, send us his name.

PACE PHONOGRAPH CORPORATION
257 W. 138th Street   New York, N. Y.

Mention THE CRISIS.

7.4 This advertisement alludes directly to the impact of the Victor Company and Caruso in shaping the phonograph market. The eye-catching headline "Caruso's Voice" tries to turn the tenor's broad appeal to Black Swan's advantage and urges consumers to support a company that would cultivate comparable talent. *Crisis,* Sept. 1921, author's collection.

noted that Wood was financial secretary of the Tuskegee Institute, as well as an expert elocutionist, exemplifying "a rare combination of business and artistic ability." The notice also indicated, again, the breadth of Black Swan's political base. Although some African American leaders may not have approved of Negro dialect humor, few could question the uplift credentials of the top financial officer of Booker T. Washington's flagship.[48]

At the same time, however, Black Swan was pulled in different directions by its dedication to race business, its promotion of cultural uplift, and its need to respond to changes in the musical marketplace. Although tensions between Black Swan's goals and the exigencies of the market had existed from the beginning, Pace initially succeeded in keeping them in check. Then, in 1922 and 1923, three factors upset this delicate balance: (1) poorly timed capital investment, (2) the growing popularity of blues and jazz, and (3) the introduction of radio. These factors revealed latent contradictions between the different strands of Black Swan's mission, and ultimately these contributed to the company's demise.

The first problem lay in ill-timed capital expansion. In the wake of the enormous success of Ethel Waters's first record, the company moved out of its basement office in Pace's Strivers' Row apartment and purchased its own building on Seventh Avenue, just south of 135th Street. Within only a few months, Black Swan had grown to fifteen people, including an eight-man orchestra and seven office employees, plus an additional seven district managers in larger cities around the country. The company was shipping a reported twenty-five hundred records a day to dealers and agents throughout the United States, and to the Philippines and West Indies as well. Then, in the spring of 1922, to reduce nagging uncertainty about recording and manufacturing facilities, Harry Pace purchased the Olympic Disc Record Corporation, a recently bankrupted record company and pressing plant in Long Island City, New York. With a recording studio, pressing plant, and printing press (for labels and sleeves), Black Swan could cut marginal costs and stabilize production. It would be a model of economic self-sufficiency, and the new facilities could even generate additional income by doing contract work for other companies.[49]

The *Chicago Defender*, lauding the acquisition, noted proudly that Olympic's erstwhile owner, the Remington Phonograph Corporation, had been founded by a scion of one of America's great manufacturing families, re-nowned makers of rifles and sewing machines. Significantly, however, this large investment also put a strain on the capital available for other vital needs, such as promotions and artist development, and even required a public stock issue to stabilize the company's capital base. Meanwhile, other musical and economic developments put additional pressure on Black Swan's resources, and the company's high level of activity obscured the more important issue of profitability. "We went into the factory purchase just at the wrong time," Pace later recalled, "but who could tell that it was the wrong time, at the rate we were making and selling merchandise then[?]"[50]

One factor that made the timing so poor was the surge in popularity of blues and jazz records. Across the market, both the quality and the quantity of blues and jazz records soared from 1922 to 1924. Following the promi-nent success of Black Swan, OKeh, and several other early labels, a host of new companies jumped into the field, including Columbia, Aeolian, Ajax, Gennett, Brunswick, and Victor. In the second half of 1922 Black Swan re-corded as many African American blues artists as all the other labels com-bined, but within six months Black Swan's artists were outnumbered almost four to one.[51]

What was more, some of the decade's most popular and influential stars made their recording debuts on other labels at this time, including Bessie Smith, Ma Rainey, Louis Armstrong (in King Oliver's band), and Jelly Roll Morton.[52] Since Black Swan preferred to maintain a safe distance from these "hotter," more rough-edged artists, their huge popularity made it more diffi-cult for Black Swan to promote its program of musical uplift and increased the economic power of Black Swan's rivals. The vexing paradox was that Black Swan was to some extent victimized by its own success. As one of its *Crisis* advertisements reminded readers, Black Swan's initial strong sales en-couraged other companies to produce records targeting African American consumers, sometimes by remaking the very same songs that had attracted people to Black Swan.[53] Moreover, given their deeper pockets and bigger advertising budgets, these companies could easily woo away Black Swan's blues singers with higher-paying contracts.

The third factor precipitating Black Swan's demise was the introduction of radio, which took the entire phonograph business by storm. In January

THE CRISIS ADVERTISER   91

Passing for Colored

Has become popular since we established **Black Swan Records** as the only genuine Colored Records, sung by Colored Artists and made by a Colored Company.

At least three white concerns are now catering to Negro buyers and advertising in Negro newspapers who never did so previously.

One Company issues a catalog and calls its Record "the new Race Record". In other words it is attempting to "Pass for Colored".

"The World Do Move!"

Don't be deceived. We Repeat: The Only **Genuine** Colored Record is

 BLACK SWAN

Buy them regularly from your Agent and Dealers.

We have some exceptionally good records of recent issue and they are better and better.

Every kind of Record from Blues to Grand Opera.

Send for Complete Catalog.

Agents Wanted In Every Community.

Black Swan Phonograph Company, Inc.

Harry H. Pace, Pres.

2289 Seventh Ave.   New York, N. Y.

Mention THE CRISIS

7.5 Consumers and African American newspapers benefited from the increasing number of companies producing records of interest to African Americans. For Black Swan the increase led to incursions into the market the company had cultivated. This 1922 advertisement mocks Black Swan's rivals for trying to "pass for colored." *Crisis*, Dec. 1922, author's collection.

1922 the *New York Times* reported optimistic projections for the growing phonograph industry, but half a year later the *Times* reported a sharp drop in sales—by 15 percent in some places, and more in others—as compared with the same time a year earlier. As this reversal continued over the following two years, the popularity of radio emerged as the clearest explanation. Although radio programming was not yet standardized and was still erratic in many areas, the popularity of the technology was becoming increasingly clear. Initially markets for the phonograph and the radio stimulated each other; both were part of a broader cultural expansion in commercial entertainment. By 1924, however, the rapidly expanding public investment in radio equipment —$60 million in 1922, $136 million in 1923, and $358 million in 1924— had become serious competition for the phonograph industry. The industry leader, the Victor Talking Machine Company, for example, saw its sales of records drop by more than 50 percent from 1921 to 1925. Making matters worse for Black Swan, the advent of radio coincided with the purchase of expensive custom-made record presses for the Long Island City factory. "Before [the machines] were up and running, radio broadcasting broke and this spelled doom for us," Pace later recalled. "Immediately dealers began to cancel orders that they had placed, records were returned unaccepted, [and] many record stores became radio stores."[54]

Indeed, Black Swan's problems were emblematic of those affecting the entire industry. This was evident in an emotional letter that Pace wrote to the board of directors after the company's fate was sealed:

> Does it mean anything to you to know that Columbia went bankrupt, that Pathé [Frères] did also, that the Aeolian Company sold its magnificent building on 42nd Street to the Schulte Cigar Stores, and practically gave away its record business to the Brunswick Company, whose chief business is the making of pool tables? Does it indicate anything that when we began business there were 24 record making concerns and today there are only seven? . . . How could we survive with a meager capital of about $40,000 and a limited market when concerns with millions . . . either died or were mortally wounded?[55]

The problem of radio, however, symbolized deeper conflicts between music and market, and the strain radio placed on the industry exposed the fundamental illogic of approaching music through racial categories. Indeed, the intense economic pressures under which Black Swan was operating pushed the company to take a step completely at odds with its stated musical mission—namely, to reissue records by *white* artists whose identities were hidden behind generic pseudonyms in Black Swan's ostensibly all-black catalogue. The white stage singer Aileen Stanley became "Mamie Jones," while Lindsay McPhail's Jazz Band appeared as Fred Smith's Society Orchestra. Amazingly, different groups might be given the same pseudonym, as with Black Swan's releases of the "Laurel Dance Orchestra," which was really either the Tivoli Dance Orchestra or the Wallace Downey Dance Orchestra, depending on the recording. This practice began as early as November 1921 and increased considerably after the purchase of the factory in Long Island City, which provided a ready supply of free material from the bankrupted Olympic label.[56] In the end, approximately a third of the titles in Black Swan's catalogue—including both vocal and instrumental records— were reissues of records made by white musicians for other companies.

On the one hand, it was not uncommon for small record companies to issue discs—sometimes under pseudonyms, sometimes not—that other companies had recorded. On the other hand, other companies did not, of course, repeatedly insist that they employed "colored singers and musicians exclusively." However disingenuous the company's "all-black" claims were, the promotion of records by white performers was an attempt to keep the cash-starved company in business. Acknowledging publicly that Black Swan was issuing records by white performers would have been tantamount to conceding that the Black Swan project as a whole was untenable. Indeed, all evidence suggests that Pace considered sales of recordings by white artists a temporary measure, necessary only until the record company was on stable fiscal ground.[57]

Paradoxically, this deception also served as a demonstration of the contingent, extrinsic character of racial categories in music—which had been one of Black Swan's basic goals. What is most striking about Black Swan's marketing sleight of hand is that people apparently did not detect anything amiss; there were no indignant editorials, no boycotts, no letters of protest. This silence suggests that people either did not care or could not perceive any difference. Racial difference was not audible; rather, it was artificially and arbitrarily assigned. In this way, Black Swan's high-minded program of musical uplift and its desperate, deceptive reissuing of recordings by white musicians were less at odds than they appeared, for both demonstrated the speciousness of racial boundaries in music. By rejecting musical categories based on race, Black Swan showed that racial distinctions were neither natural nor fixed. Likewise, the fact that records by black and white performers could be interchanged without anyone's noticing proved how unstable music categories based on race actually were.

Black Swan issued its last records in the summer of 1923, and its last advertisements appeared around the same time.[58] The company that had sought to be a lodestar, a strong guiding light, was instead a flare in the night sky shining brightly for a moment but burning out soon after it had gone up. Its short flight notwithstanding, the company did however accomplish many of its stated goals, even if only temporarily. It issued 180-odd recordings, sold hundreds of thousands of discs, and distributed its products around the country and abroad. Moreover, it was particularly notable that Black Swan was a manufacturer, for among African Americans, control of manufacturing capital was especially rare.[59] Musically, the company's program was a definite, if qualified, success as well. Black Swan launched the recording careers of such important artists as Fletcher Henderson, Ethel Waters, Trixie Smith, and Alberta Hunter, and it issued records by many musicians who in all likelihood would not have had other opportunities to record.[60]

The company's records reached some unlikely destinations as well. To the west, a Hollywood society hostess boasted that her parties were improved by her Black Swan record collection. To the east, Black Swan records left a strong impression on the French composer Darius Milhaud, who wrote in his memoirs that he "never wearied of playing, over and over, . . . Black Swan records I had purchased in a little shop in Harlem." The avant-garde composer Edgard Varèse was so impressed by Black Swan records that he wrote to the company to ask whether any young African American composers would be interested in studying with him—an invitation seized on by the arranger William Grant Still, who then studied with Varèse from 1923 to 1925 and went on to become, in Leopold Stokowski's words, "one of our greatest American composers."[61]

Given the constraints on political and economic opportunity, music represented one of the only media through which African Americans could confront the barriers to social and economic equality. Yet to an important extent, Black Swan's focus on a racialized niche market undermined the possibility of its succeeding. Once bigger white-owned companies saw the success of Black Swan's advertisements and marketing, it was relatively easy for them to create their own better-financed models of race marketing, which were not based on programs of economic or cultural uplift for African Americans. Even as this chain reaction undid Black Swan's market standing, however, it at least had some rewards for African American musicians (even if those effects were generally limited to blues and jazz musicians) and for black newspapers, which benefited from the large advertisements taken out by the white-owned companies.

In May 1924 Pace announced that another firm, the New York Recording Company, would begin to lease the Black Swan catalogue and would reissue it through its own label, Paramount Records, in exchange for a fixed monthly fee. Pace claimed that it was the best deal he could arrange under the circumstances, but some contemporaries, such as the activist Chandler Owen, condemned the deal, likening it to a "merger" between the lion and the lamb that had lain down together, only to have the lamb wind up in the lion's belly. That the analogy exaggerated Paramount's strength in the phonograph industry—it was no lion by comparison with Columbia or Victor— was beside the point. Pace countered that he would have sold out to a black-owned company if another one had existed in the business, and that he had maintained the integrity of the Black Swan project by retaining ownership of the master recordings and leasing them out, rather than selling them outright. What he refused to concede, though, was that without the capital to produce and market records, ownership of those masters amounted to quite little. In fact, the arrangement with Paramount lasted little more than a year, and despite Pace's hopes of reviving Black Swan, nothing ever happened.[62]

As the exchange between Pace and Owen suggests, Black Swan's problems as a race business went beyond individual decisions; they reflected the predicament of black-owned business generally in the 1920s. In the final chapter of *Black Manhattan* (1930), James Weldon Johnson (whose brother-in-law, John Nail, sat on Black Swan's board of directors) concluded that race-based business was essentially impracticable: "It is idle to expect the Negro in Harlem or anywhere else to build business in general upon a strictly racial foundation or to develop it to any considerable proportions strictly within the limits of the patronage, credit, and financial resources of the race." More acidly, in *Blues People,* LeRoi Jones (Amiri Baraka) condemned the whole Black Swan experiment as "one of the . . . most cruelly absurd situations to develop because of the growth and influence of a definable black middle class in America."[63] It was relatively easy and inexpensive for other firms in the phonograph business to expand the exploitation of African American musicians, and they did so in the form of ghettoized "race records" series. By the late 1920s virtually every record company had established a specialized "race" catalogue, and this classification remained an ordinary component of the business until it was renamed "rhythm and blues" in the 1940s.

Black Swan had been further handicapped by the contradictions and competing priorities of the uplift project. The concept of uplift embraced numerous goals and agendas, and these sometimes worked at cross-purposes, compromising the potential for uplift to succeed.[64] On the one hand, Black Swan was committed to propagating a gospel of serious music, while on the other, it sought to record and promote as wide a variety of music by African Americans as possible. At the same time, for the sake of liberating cultural production from the shackles of race and for the sake of promoting "race business," Black Swan strove to be a model of economic self-reliance, but this end heightened the company's focus and dependence on its most commercially successful music, which in this case was usually blues and popular music. Each of these three goals implied a different direction for Black Swan's musical development, and the company's inability to reconcile conflicting priorities eliminated any possibility of overcoming the challenges facing an undercapitalized firm in an increasingly competitive market.

In the study of epistemology, the black swan is a metaphor for the problem of inductive knowledge, that is, the derivation of general conclusions about the world from specific examples or experiences. As David Hume framed the problem, could one really conclude that all swans were white simply because one had never seen a black one?[65] (Indeed, such swans were later discovered in Australia.) Black Swan Records posed a similar challenge to knowledge based on appearances, by offering counterinstances of African American manufacturing, commercial development, and musical diversity. Its successes, short-lived as they were, complicated the music industry's pat rhetoric about the "democracy" of musical culture. A comparison of Black Swan with the Victor Talking Machine Company sets in relief how radically appearance and reality diverged in the music industry at large. Victor promoted music education because of its commercial value, but Black Swan, which also placed special emphasis on "serious music," attempted to make uplift through music real. Victor had a huge, wide-ranging catalogue of recordings because it stood to gain financially from that breadth of choice at relatively little cost; Black Swan tried to demonstrate the stakes in a program of real creative diversity, albeit without ever resolving its discomfort with working-class culture. Victor's Eldridge Johnson showed little interest in music; Harry Pace knew and was committed to music as well as to business.

More than any other leader in the music industry, Harry Pace understood that record companies made culture in the broadest sense. Their recordings, their advertisements, the performances of their artists—all these affected the field of social relations and the distribution of power in society. In a critical, self-conscious, and imperfect way, Pace grappled with the core issues in the relation between music and power: how the field of music was defined, who did the defining, and what the stakes were. The meaning of music, he understood, depended not just on what was recorded but also which messages were associated with those recordings, how those messages were communicated to consumers, and how the recordings functioned in the market. From the point of view of those who made the music, not the records, however, the empowerment made possible by the music business came with restrictions as well. Black Swan's greatest star, Ethel Waters, benefited greatly from the exposure she received because of her recordings, but she had to accept someone else's deciding whether she would record blues or "cultural" numbers (the idea that she might have done both does not appear to have been considered). Although Pace was committed to challenging some structures of cultural power, there was never any question that Black Swan was the ultimate arbiter of what she recorded and which recordings were issued.

In the years following Black Swan's collapse, attempts at racial uplift through music or art took many forms, but none was as multilayered or grounded in issues of material production as Pace's company. Instead, such programs tended to be oriented toward composition or performance, based on an implicit belief in the autonomous power of art to change how people thought and acted.[66] Harry Pace was never so credulous, for he understood that influencing material conditions depended on controlling material resources. The Black Swan project, however, showed that reconciling the lofty and the mundane was much more complex than even Pace had anticipated. Black Swan's burden was to chart a course between elite culture and popular culture, between the colorblindness of music and the racism of the music business, between ideologically based enterprise and the impinging realities of capitalist markets. The hazards of such a course were evident; the way to navigate safe passage was not.

8

The Musical Soundscape of Modernity

At the onset of the Great Depression, the sound of daily life in the United States, and other industrialized nations as well, differed greatly from what it had been half a century earlier. In many cases it was louder, but the change amounted to more than just an increase in volume. Indeed, the modern soundscape was produced by an ongoing tension between the forces that made sounds—such as industrial machinery, automobile traffic, and crowds on city streets—and countervailing forces trying to manage sounds or keep them in check, including noise abatement movements and the emerging science and business of architectural acoustics. Music belonged to both camps, as part of the proliferation of modern sounds and the drive to control them. Never before had so many forms of music been audible in so many environments, and never had the economic value of music been so extensively and meticulously cultivated.[1]

To champions of this sonic dialectic, the new musical soundscape rang out as a symbol of cultural democracy, but embrace of the new order was not universal. One of its sharpest critics was the composer and educator Daniel Gregory Mason, who perceived it not as a "golden age of music," as some contemporaries did, but rather as an era of cheapness and superficiality. In "The Depreciation of Music," an essay published in 1929, Mason inveighed against the ways in which the ideology of industrial production had penetrated and degraded musical culture and shackled it to the logic of the market, which stripped music of its potential as a means of transcendent human expression. "Our fundamental error," Mason wrote, "seems to have been the too uncritical assumption that the methods of quantity production by machinery, with their conveniences of reduction of overhead, standardization of product, ease of marketing, and the rest, could be applied with equal success to our far more important spiritual interests, such as art." Indeed, Mason, once a leading proponent of the music appreciation movement, now felt thoroughly dispirited by its results. "Why not stop leading unthirsty horses to water? They only muddy it."[2]

In some ways, these are the words of a fusty Brahmin whose conservative music was enjoying much less acclaim at the end of the Jazz Age than the daring, dynamic work of his modernist contemporaries. As a grandson of Lowell Mason, the founder of the movement to teach music in American public schools, and a nephew of two cofounders of Mason & Hamlin, the venerable piano manufacturer, Daniel Mason was a scion of the nineteenth-century musical establishment, a Harvard-educated WASP who wrote unapologetically conventional works, derived from the traditions of European art music. In contrast, his more celebrated coevals were concentrated in New York and steeped in jazz; they were by and large Jews or immigrants.[3]

Mason's observation about the pervasive influence of business and mechanization was widely borne out, however. Augustus Zanzig, for example, the author of *Music in American Life* (1932), took pride in the businesslike methods used in preparing his glowing overview of amateur musical activity in the United States. "Our study has resembled those economic surveys frequently undertaken by government and commercial organizations, [in that it is based on] an estimate of our resources, the wealth derived through development of them, and the possibilities for further development."[4] Moreover, Mason's critique appeared as the drive toward business and mechanization was coming to a head. After decades of development, the new musical order reached the end of its formative period in a wave of corporate mergers. By the years of Great Depression, the cultural and economic repercussions of the new musical order were clearly evident. Musical culture, both as expressive behavior and aesthetic works and as a component in the material and psychic relationships that constitute society, now functioned in ways that would have been unrecognizable half a century earlier. Through electrical loudspeakers, sound now reached and enveloped people as never before, and through multimedia conglomerates music was a crucial, permanent part of the apparatus of entertainment and communications.

Beyond Mason's aesthetic judgments, therefore, his commentary touched on the great paradox of musical soundscape of modernity. That is, the genuine democratization of audiences developed in tandem with the increasingly centralized, highly managed structure of cultural production. On the one hand, the new order allowed countless people to hear, feel, and be touched by a broad range of music, on a vast, unprecedented scale. On the other, this expansion depended on a restricted system of production based more and more on large-scale capital investment and a high degree of technical and musical expertise.[5]

Hearing and Listening in the Machine Age

Reactions to the changing relationship between music and machines fell along a broad spectrum. At one end were the boosters, who viewed player-pianos and phonographs as a vehicle for positive social change, especially for uplifting the collective taste of the masses or serving as a bulwark against the socially corrosive effects of popular music. Ernest Newman, among the most eminent music critics of the early twentieth century, championed the player-piano and the phonograph as great instruments of musical uplift, as did the prominent critic and composer Deems Taylor. As Taylor put it, "the player-piano must be taken seriously. . . . [It] is bound to exert a tremendous influence upon the musical taste of the American people during the next generation; an influence which, if intelligently directed, cannot fail to raise the level of that taste." His words echoed those of an earlier critic, Carroll Brent Chilton, who had welcomed the player-piano as a "serious and permanent musical instrument" capable of repelling the aesthetic assault of popular song.[6]

Among other proponents of the integration of music and machines were men such as Henry C. Lomb, an engineer and music industry representative. Coming from a different angle, he professed an engineer's faith in the uplifting power of industrial standardization. Lomb, writing in 1928 in the *Annals of the American Academy of Political and Social Science*, defended standardization as a means of bringing the benefits of music to more people more efficiently. Musical pitch could be standardized, he reasoned, so why not the striking of musical notes as well, which could be accomplished by mechanical playing? Still more radical in their claims were composers and critics who saw phonographs and player-pianos as liberating composers by offering them the chance to communicate directly with listeners, thus bypassing the interpretive mediation (or interference) by performers. H. H. Stuckenschmidt, writing in Germany, and Rudhyar D. Chennevière and Frederick H. Martens, writing in the United States, emphasized this great potential artistic benefit of mechanical music. Stuckenschmidt, for example, welcomed an idealistic, posthuman musical age: "The resistance of sentimentalists will not be able to impede the development of music. The role of the interpreter belongs to the past."[7]

At the other end of the spectrum of critical opinion stood the purists or "humanists," in whose eyes machine-made sounds were absolutely and intrinsically incompatible with the nature of music as art. As Arthur Whiting put it in the *Yale Review* in 1919, "the presentation of music depends for its effect on the gamble in human fallibility"—a quality that machines were deliberately designed to eliminate. This was the position of Daniel Gregory Mason, as well, who found in mechanized music the crux of the problem of commercialized art. "The fundamental and ineradicable defect of music from the machine [is that] its standardized, wholesale, impersonal quality [violates] the essential uniqueness, particularity, and personal reference of all vital artistic expressions," Mason wrote. "Commerce can appeal to everybody, but it is the essence of art that it has to appeal to somebody, and to somebody who can get something from it only if he reacts to it, meets it halfway, with his own responses and from his own point of view."[8]

Between the boosters and the purists, a range of other contemporaries viewed mechanical music not necessarily as a means to a musical utopia but as something that, within limits, could have salutary effects. As the narrator of *Tono-Bungay*, H. G. Wells's 1908 novel, said of the player-piano, it might be a "musical gorilla, with fingers all of one length, [but it has] a sort of soul. . . . It's all the world of music to me." To some of these optimists, the player-piano and phonograph could not be expected to produce "real art," but they might convey a pleasant, if limited, ersatz art. In *The Player-Piano: How and Why* (1914), P. J. Meahl argued that although the instrument would not turn a tired businessman into an artist, it was still enjoyable. In another view, a writer for the magazine the *Musician* believed the phonograph could be an important aid to vocal instruction, provided that students did not become overly imitative in their practice. Other writers found the machines perfectly suitable for popular music but inadequate for more complex musical forms. "I am devoted to that pianola," the writer William Saroyan noted about his baby grand player-piano, in a letter to novelist William Gaddis, "but only to the razzle dazzle style of rolls. . . . Some of these pieces have definite greatness. The 'serious' rolls stink of course."[9]

Perhaps the most interesting "optimistic" reaction came from modernist composers and critics, however, who found in automatic music machines new creative possibilities. From 1917 until around 1930, Igor Stravinsky composed or arranged numerous works for both regular and reproducing player-pianos, in cooperation with Pleyel in Paris and the Aeolian Company in London, as well as several other composers engaged in similar experiments and explorations. Without abandoning conventional composition and instrumentation, Stravinsky viewed the player-piano, he explained, as "a means of making legitimate music in a new way." Choosing a metaphor from the visual arts to defend this work, he wrote: "The results I seek are those of the lithograph or fine etching, in which the artist has completed his work upon the original plate. It is the work of his own hands. Only the process of multiplication of the lithograph or etching is mechanical." Thus, decades before the landmark compositions by Conlon Nancarrow in the 1950s, '60s, and '70s, Stravinsky, Paul Hindemith, George Antheil, and others had written works either partially or exclusively for player-piano. As the composer Ernst Toch pointedly explained, the object of such work was to supplement, not displace, other modes of music: "Just as I do not want to spend my days and nights in water, since I am a human being, not a fish, but nonetheless partake of the quite incomparable enjoyment of a sporadic dip, so the 'coolness' of mechanical music is not meant to replace the 'heat' of the usual, but exist beside it as something special, unique."[10] In the early 1920s László Moholy-Nagy imagined the phonograph as a new creative element in musical composition; Kurt Weill included a phonograph recording in his "Tango-Angèle" (1927); and both Hindemith and Toch experimented with the phonograph as a means of sonic manipulation, prefiguring by several years John Cage's better-known composition for phonographs, *Imaginary Landscape No. 1* (1939).[11]

On both sides of the Atlantic, composers swept away the conventional musical wisdom and posited a new relation between music, machines, and the modern industrial soundscape. In 1913 the Italian Futurist Luigi Russolo published a manifesto, *The Art of Noises,* calling for instruments that would create a music based on the whirring, throbbing, clanging noises of modern industrial life. He proceeded to invent such instruments, which he called *intonarumori,* and he hoped to patent and market them. The Futurists' aesthetic project was, however, derailed by World War I, during which all Russolo's instruments were destroyed. A few years later in Paris and then New York, the American George Antheil premiered his *Ballet Mécanique,* whose score included not just player-pianos but also a siren and an airplane propeller. Meanwhile, in an interview with the *New York Morning Telegraph* in 1916, the French composer Edgard Varèse, who had moved to New York the year before, also called for the invention of new musical instruments and used sirens in his *Amériques* (1921) and *Hyperprism* (1923). These composers, along with Henry Cowell and a few others, called many eduring musical pieties into question; together, they challenged some of the fundamental dichotomies on which musical culture was structured—music versus noise, human versus machine, the urban soundscape versus the rarefied atmosphere of the concert hall.[12]

In the spectrum of critical opinion about mechanization in the musical soundscape, some views remained rooted deeply in the musical past and others reached excitedly into the future. At different moments and in various circumstances, one view or another commanded greater attention, but generally no single position predominated. Indeed, the diversity of opinion on the subject probably benefited the music industry considerably, more than would have been the case if any single view, even that of the boosters (whose ideas most closely accorded with the industry's marketing rhetoric), had prevailed. Still, the difference of opinion would have been of little importance had the technologies not been widely adopted. Debate was one thing; social consequences were another. What really mattered—what really animated these discussions—was how extensively music machines entered the warp and weft of people's actual daily lives.

In *Towards a New Architecture* (1923), the modernist manifesto by Le Corbusier, the iconoclastic architect defined the home as "a machine for living in." Among the appliances that should furnish the ideal dwelling, he

GEORGE ANTHEIL

A prophet of machinery and music from Trenton, N. J., and Paris, France, presenting his Ballet Mecanique and other discoveries at Carnegie Hall to-morrow evening.

8.1 This drawing published in the *New York Sun* in 1927 previewed the Carnegie Hall premiere of George Antheil's *Ballet Mécanique,* whose instrumentation included numerous player-pianos and an airplane propeller. Courtesy of the Estate of George Antheil.

listed phonographs, player-pianos, and radios, whose conveyance of disembodied music, he imagined, would offer a favorable alternative to live performance. Not only would they "give you exact interpretations of first-rate music," he wrote sardonically, but "you [could] avoid catching cold in the concert hall, and the frenzy of the virtuoso."[13] In a house with real inhabitants, however, the sonic transformation of the home could produce cacophonous effects as suggested by a 1924 cartoon by Rube Goldberg. In it, a hapless everyman walks through his house in search of a quiet place to relax, but in each room he is besieged by the clamor of modern life, issuing from a player-piano, a phonograph, a radio, a telephone, and so on. In the last panel, the man finally finds rest—in a cemetery, atop a seventeenth-century tombstone. Peace and quiet are thus no longer to be attained among the living, and aural assault is an ineluctable condition of modern existence. This narrative does more than reflect Goldberg's heightened awareness of changes in the aural environment; it also shows the effect of such changes on people not directly or actively involved with the new technologies. The most significant aspect of the cartoon, though, may be how unremarkable the cacophony now seems: with one or two substitutions (a television for the player-piano, for example) this cartoon depicts a soundscape virtually indistinguishable from our own. Indeed, Goldberg was bearing witness to the moment when our own modern sound world came into being.

As early as 1909, E. M. Forster had anticipated some of the most contentious aspects of the musical mechanization of society in "The Machine Stops" (1909), a short story depicting a machine-dominated subterranean dystopia, where music is available everywhere via "music-tubes" and the experience of life on the earth's surface is captured and preserved through phonograph recordings and movies. Although music and sound factor into the story in numerous ways, Forster suggests in a subtle way that the underlying function of music in this society is to provide diversion. At a point when the protagonist Vashti becomes flustered and is trying not to think about the faltering of the "machine," the unseen computerlike mechanism that regulates all aspects of people's lives, she blurts out, "Let us talk about music," in a desperate bid to distract herself and her companion. Even more telling, however, is the continuous noise—a low murmur—apart from which modern society did not function. This constant sound was an example of what the

8.2 The cacophony of the modern domestic soundscape beset Rube Goldberg's everyman (1924). Bancroft Library, University of California, Berkeley.

sound ecologist R. Murray Schafer would later term the keynote of a sound-scape. When the machine experiences a catastrophic malfunction, Vashti and others are altogether undone by the disintegration of their aural environment: "Then she broke down, for with the cessation of activity came an un-expected terror—silence. She had never known silence, and the coming of it nearly killed her—it did kill many thousands of people outright. Ever since her birth she had been surrounded by the steady hum. It was to the ear what artificial air was to the lungs." Through the use of sound and silence, music and machines, Forster shows the mutually constitutive relationship between the structural organization of society, the environment, and the "nature" of human experience.[14]

If Rube Goldberg and E. M. Forster were able to suggest something about the character of the changes that had taken place, data on phonograph and radio ownership give an idea of the scope of such changes. Robert S. Lynd and Helen Merrell Lynd, in their classic study *Middletown,* noted the findings from a study of thirty-six cities: 59 percent of the homes surveyed had a phonograph, 51 percent a piano, 1 percent an organ, and 11 percent other musical instruments. Not surprisingly, in a detailed study of Muncie, Illinois (Middletown), the Lynds found the percentage of ownership highest in middle- and upper-income homes, but more than 23 percent of working-class homes also reported owning a phonograph.[15] As for radio ownership, it was still relatively sparse when the Lynds conducted their survey in 1924, but it grew rapidly, if unevenly, in the coming years. By 1930, 40 percent of households in the United States reported owning a radio, and substantially higher percentages did in urban areas, especially in the Northeast and Midwest. In the South, where many rural households lacked electricity, radio ownership spread more slowly, but families were often eager to acquire hand-cranked phonographs. According to a 1930 survey by the sociologist Charles S. Johnson of the poor, rural African American residents of Macon City, Alabama, more than 50 percent of households had no indoor plumbing but 12 percent of households reported owning a phonograph.

William Faulkner's novel *As I Lay Dying* (1929), although it offers few clues about the *rate* of phonograph ownership in the South, gives some idea of the phonograph's powerful, captivating influence. The book traces the arduous journey of a poor family into town to bury the wife and mother. The eldest son, Cash, meanwhile, has an ulterior motive for the trip: to buy a phonograph. Circumstances prevent him from doing so, but as the story ends, he and the family come together around a phonograph to listen to records purchased through a mail-order catalogue. Not only does the phonograph exercise a peculiar hold on Cash's imagination, but Faulkner's blank assertion that Cash enjoyed the "music" and "records" leaves the impression that the particular type of music playing on the phonograph did not really matter. As these sounds waft through the novel's final paragraphs, they mark a counterpoint to the first third of the book, in which the insistent keynote of the soundscape was the sound of Cash's manual labor, as he built his mother's coffin.[16]

The creation of the musical soundscape was more than an indoor, domestic phenomenon. In urban areas, where the majority of the population of the United States lived by 1920, music proliferated not just in concert and dance halls, vaudeville, and musical theater, where it could be expected, but also in restaurants, department stores, hotels, and cafés, and in public spaces such as schools and parks. Building on the nineteenth-century movement to stage public concerts to promote civic health and enrichment, the organization of concerts in public parks thrived in the 1920s. The Music Industries Chamber of Commerce worked with individual municipalities to capitalize on the recent boom in such events: during the war even medium-sized cities were organizing more than a hundred concerts annually.[17] Meanwhile, the sounds of barrel pianos, song pluggers, and street musicians made street life more musical, and private commercial establishments used music to try to attract business from the street. Movie houses, for example, often kept their doors open, so that the music from within would serve as a form of promotion and enticement to passersby. (Five-and-dimes and other merchants sometimes used the same tactic.[18]) One film critic claimed he had been fired from his job as a piano player at the best theater in Saint Louis because his playing was not adequately audible from outside. Many of the public elements of the musical soundscape were well established in the 1910s, but in the mid- and late 1920s, with the rise of wireless radio and the advent of the electrical loudspeaker, the aural environment grew louder and more musical still.

The development of radio in this period echoed many of the themes already associated with the rise of the phonograph and in some ways embodied its logical extension. The commercial development of radio began in earnest in 1922, although as had been true of the phonograph in 1901, this had been preceded by several decades of critical foundation-building. The radio was a direct offshoot of experiments conducted by Guglielmo Marconi in developing the wireless telegraph, part of the general proliferation of technical innovations fostered by World War I, especially under the auspices of the United States Navy, AT&T, and General Electric. By the postwar years, thanks to solid military and corporate backing, a substantial infrastructure for a mass consumer-based industry was solidly in place.[19]

The growth of radio resembled that of the phonograph in many ways. Not only did it involve a complex relation between the equipment and the sounds it conveyed, but radio also experienced a war between rival formats (wired versus wireless), critical design changes, and a growing orientation toward musical content. Radio had its origins in point-to-point communication, but in the mid-1920s the focus of its commercial development shifted to broadcasting—transmitting to many receivers at once. Driving this change initially was the goal of selling radio hardware. In the words of David Sarnoff, then vice president of the Radio Corporation of America (RCA), a subsidiary of General Electric owned jointly with AT&T and Westinghouse in 1924, "We broadcast primarily so that those who purchase [RCA radios] may have something to feed those receiving instruments with." Meanwhile, to make radio sets more acceptable additions to the home (and to women), the design of receivers was simplified to hide the unwieldy wires and complicated control mechanisms inside. Moreover, in the mid-1920s, electrified loudspeakers, which often resembled the morning glory–shaped horns of the early phonographs, replaced the ear tubes on which earlier listeners had had to rely. Radios could now project their sound into an entire room or through several rooms, and this modification made possible the fuller integration of the sound of radio into people's active lives.[20]

Nothing made radio an inherently musical medium, but as Victor had discovered with the phonograph, music was extremely effective at building an audience. By 1926, in a survey of leading radio stations all over the country, forty-nine out of fifty broadcasters reported that music was their most popular kind of programming.[21] Yet to musically sensitive ears, the rising tide of radio was gradually inundating the soundscape. One person who found the

8.3 Early radio listening required the use of headsets. Here, girls listen to the radio in San Francisco's Chinatown in 1922. Bettmann/CORBIS.

growing omnipresence of radio overwhelming was Daniel Gregory Mason. Was there, he wondered, "any escape for the musically-timid from the street-corner loudspeaker?" The English composer and conductor Constant Lambert, writing a few years later, made clear that this musical surfeit was not limited to the United States. In his widely read *Music Ho! A Study of Music in Decline,* Lambert linked the musical situation and the economic depression, both of which he saw as a problem of "overproduction": "Never has there been so much food and so much starvation, and . . . never has there been so

8.4 The Hollywood actress Helen Lynch listens to a radio whose loud-speaker resembles the morning glory design of early phonographs. Bettmann/CORBIS.

much music-making and so little musical experience of a vital order. Since the advent of the gramophone, and more particularly the wireless, music of a sort is everywhere and at every time. . . . The loud speaker is little short of a public menace." Indeed, in a 1929 *Washington Post* survey about noise concerns, readers ranked radio loudspeakers first.[22]

On the surface, the disapproval of Mason and Lambert can seem like the grumbling of the dyspeptic old guard, but their critiques illuminate how music was changing the social and economic order. If the ideology of consumption and consumer goods, and the attendant effects on social relations, were far more pervasive in American and English life by the 1920s than they had been a generation earlier, music made the extent and meaning of this change visible and audible. In *Middletown* the Lynds reported a decline in singing and participatory music making in adult social settings from the 1890s to the 1920s, while the popularity of ready-made entertainments soared. At the same time, Carl Van Vechten chafed at the way the limited schedules of concert orchestras prevented music lovers in New York from "hearing what you want when you want it." Expressing a new form of consumer entitlement, he complained, "A man of temperament . . . would like to order his music as he orders his library or his veal kidneys." Indeed, the value placed on music and other consumer goods marked an essential difference between the generations. "The old folks put every dollar they can wring from a reluctant environment into real property or the banks," George Jean Nathan and H. L. Mencken wrote in *The American Credo* (1920), "[but] the young folks put their inheritance into phonographs, Fords, boiled shirts, yellow shoes, cuckoo clocks, lithographs of the current mountebanks, oil stock, [and] automatic pianos."[23]

As music became more extensively linked to consumption, the definition of musicality itself changed. Earlier, it had referred to the skill and talent of composers and performers. In the new musical order, it signaled only a general affinity for or openness to music, especially "good" music. "If one loves to listen to good music, one *is* musical," as a prominent music advocate put it in 1917.[24] This expanded concept of musicality lay at the heart of the "music appreciation" movement that blossomed in the years surrounding World War I. Music educators and critics overwhelmingly endorsed the greater support for music education and performance, yet they diverged over music appreciation and its heavy reliance on mechanical music makers. J. Lawrence Erb, writing in the *Musical Quarterly*, declared that the phonograph, player-piano, and radio "opened wide vistas to millions of persons whose inadequate technical music education had hitherto made an intimate knowledge of good music impossible." Skeptics, however, raised doubts about the form and efficacy of the instruction these offered, as well as concern about the production of inert listeners. The *New York Times* sounded ambivalent: "Grand opera is administered to the children in five-minute doses at their morning gatherings." More overt criticism focused on listeners' passivity, which even some supporters of music appreciation reluctantly acknowledged, or held that most listeners remained ignorant and easily impressed by superficial flourishes. To most audience members, a concert was an experience of "sensuous enjoyment," completely devoid of aesthetic comprehension, Constantin Von Sternberg wrote. "Their applause may nevertheless be perfectly sincere, but in the overwhelming majority of cases it is addressed exclusively to the interplay of colors on the orchestral palette, to the chirography of the message, while the design of the piece . . . remains entirely unperceived."[25]

As many people saw it, therefore, one irony of the growing presence of music, in both formal settings like schools and informal ones like cafés, was a new culture of degraded listening that came with it. Although the classicist-cum-music-critic Isaac Goldberg was not altogether hostile to popular music, he believed that "the song of to-day is machine-made, machine-played, machine-heard."[26] For Theodor Adorno, who wrote extensively about music and society, nonlistening was conditioned by the form of commercial popular music itself. In "On the Fetish-Character in Music and the Regression of Listening," written only a few years after Lambert's book, Adorno argued that in addition to a host of external social and cultural factors, the musical organization of popular song acculturated auditors not to listen. Because of the formulaic, predictable nature of such music, he contended, listeners as a rule knew exactly how a song went—both musically and lyrically—even the first time they heard it.[27] For Adorno, the structure of European "art" music, whatever its other flaws, both demanded and rewarded active, informed listening, whereas popular music did not, because its form and content were essentially self-evident.

As Adorno and others recognized, however, the problem of nonlistening did not stem from musical form alone but was rooted in the social conditions in which people heard music. As Lambert characterized the situation in England, "it would not matter so much were the music bad music, but, as the B.B.C. can boast with some satisfaction, most of it is good. We board buses to the strains of Beethoven and drink our beer to the accompaniment of Bach." The affront, as these commentators saw it, was to the integrity of the listening experience. "How can any artistic experience have value," Mason asked, "in which the audience . . . may turn off at any moment the performance . . . or turn it on at any moment as not quite successfully ignored background for conversation?" Adorno asked much the same question in his withering critique "The Radio Symphony." So too, years earlier, had French composer Erik Satie, himself a consummate modernist and devotee of popular music. Indeed, even before the advent of radio, in 1920 Satie presented the first performances of what he called *musique d'ameublement,* or "furnishing music," the first works composed deliberately as background music (and precursor of today's "ambient" music). For Satie, this was a half-serious, half-mischievous sally into the culture of nonlistening, which had appeared in France in much the same form as it had in the United States and England. In presenting it as music to be talked over, Satie mocked the consumerist predilection for incidental music to accompany other activities. Audiences did not know what to make of this candid offering, however. At the premiere of this work, during the intermission of a play by Max Jacob at a Parisian art gallery, Satie was said to have been confounded when audience members remained in their seats and listened more or less attentively; the composer urged them to resume talking. According to some sources, he implored people, "Whatever you do, don't listen!" At the same time, however, the *musique d'ameublement* was more than just playful. Tongue in cheek or not, Satie was also presenting a strategy for preserving active or serious listening. By designating some music as not warranting or requiring deliberate attention, he sought to differentiate it from other music that did.[28]

Around the same time, between 1920 and 1922, Thomas Edison was underwriting a series of studies on the psychological effects of music, conducted by Walter Van Dyke Bingham of the Carnegie Institute of Technology, who promised Edison valuable data on the psychological benefits of music that Edison could use in his marketing. If fully realized, such research could enable Edison to stimulate desire for his products, or as Bingham put it, the results of the research might "be useful . . . in bringing the public to . . . want these emotional effects of music which Mr. Edison [had] made accessible to them." Although Edison himself appears to have been quite skeptical, his vice president William Maxwell and others backed Bingham enthusiastically. In the end, however, Bingham's research yielded little useful information for Edison, who eventually denied Bingham continued funding. Still, as market research on the psychic effects of music—such as what music would be most effective to calm a woman's nerves after a hectic day of shopping—these experiments marked a growing attentiveness being paid to the differ-

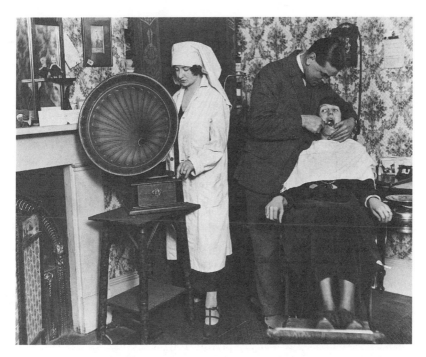

8.5 Walter Van Dyke Bingham's clinical experiments yielded no substantial conclusions about the mood-altering effects of music, but he was not the only one who showed an interest in this subject in the 1920s. This 1922 photo shows a nurse operating a phonograph while a dentist extracts a patient's tooth. Hulton-Deutsch Collection/CORBIS.

ence between hearing and listening. The research centered on the deliberate use of sound to achieve a particular emotional or behavioral effect, rather than as something to be listened to and appreciated as music. (Bingham, meanwhile, went on to become an important industrial psychologist and designer of aptitude tests widely used in American schools from the 1930s through the 1950s.)[29]

Perhaps the most systematic attempts to build a culture of nonlistening, though, took form in the growing use of music in the workplace. This initiative, having begun with numerous isolated instances during World War I, expanded through the music-in-industry movement in the late 1910s and 1920s and found its most ambitious and sophisticated expression in the development of Muzak in the 1930s. During the war, fragmentary accounts had surfaced of increased productivity or enhanced morale among workers when a phonograph was introduced into the workplace, and in the postwar period there was a revival of interest in the behavioral effects of music. In 1880 Johann Dogiel had found that music could affect blood pressure, pulse rate, and breathing. In the 1920s researchers returned to the question of the physiological effects of music, by which time their work dovetailed with the increased attention to music in the fields of behavioral and industrial psychology.[30] According to some studies, workers engaged in tasks requiring a high degree of repetition reported that they experienced less fatigue when music was playing while they worked. In the same years, with the emergence of the "music-in-industry" movement, many large workplaces began to sponsor vocal and instrumental music groups. Although their activities differed from the systematic introduction of music on the shop floor, they represented another sign of the growing interest in the relationship between music and work. Some uses of music in the workplace were aimed at reducing turnover, others at boosting output; all sought to use music to advance specific material and emotional outcomes.[31]

In some respects the integration of music and work was not new at all. Indeed, it has a history as long and varied as that of human labor itself: people have sung songs as they brought in the harvest, spun wool, and laid railroad tracks. Nevertheless, Wired Music, the venture started by George Owens Squier in the 1920s and renamed Muzak in the 1930s, marked a radical break with all preceding work music. Muzak, which the company described as "functional music," consisted of original recordings of well-known compositions that were programmed centrally and distributed via a wired network to subscribing businesses. Beginning in 1936 under Squier's successor Waddill Catchings, each Muzak recording was assigned a "stimulus code," based on rhythm, tempo, and other characteristics, so that programming could be tailored to compensate for the fluctuating human rhythms of the work day. When energy levels sag, play something with a little pep. When work is cooking along, play something a little smoother. The hallmark of this work music was not just its reliance on technology but its character as extrinsic to the work. Traditional work songs came from workers, and the music grew out of or in response to the rhythm of their labors. Muzak was piped in from the outside and bore no relation to the work itself. Conversely, from the point of view of employers or the Muzak programmer, the music itself was beside the point: the *impression* left by the music was the thing that mattered. The goal was to provide music that would affect people without distracting them. In the 1950s a former Muzak vice president explained the company's product in words that apply equally well to earlier use of phonographs and radios in workplaces: Muzak is "non-entertainment," he said, intended for people "to hear, not listen to."[32]

The Birth of the Culture Industries

Paradoxically, in the 1920s, as music in workplaces increased, work for musicians was contracting. During the early development of both cinema and radio, live musicians were in high demand, but this suffered a sharp reversal by the late 1920s. Although initially the two industries had no formal connection with the organized music business, cinema and radio both underwent a radical reconfiguration in the late '20s, which resulted in both cases in the forging of a permanent link with the music industry and a dramatic contraction in the demand for live professional musicians. Seen as a whole, these seismic changes altered the fundamental structure of the entertainment industries.

In the mid-1920s the phonograph and the movies formed the two most influential sectors in the popular entertainment industries, but they had had no direct connection with each other up to that time, despite their having developed along similar paths. Indeed, the similarities between them were striking. In the 1890s, before the phonograph became an accoutrement of the parlor and before the advent of dedicated movie houses, both sound recording and cinema had roots in penny arcades and fairs. The businesses surrounding both media weathered protracted patent disputes, intermittent antitrust suits, and broad accusations of debasing popular taste or corrupting youth. And both came to be dominated by giant corporations.[33]

Although the phonograph and the movies followed parallel, rather than intersecting, paths, cinema was certainly not unmusical. Contrary to the mythology about the "silent" era of cinema, the social experience of movies always involved music and sound in important ways. Live musicians provided an aural accompaniment to the images on screen, of course, but their music also functioned as a means of keeping noisy crowds relatively quiet, of drowning out the sound of loud projectors, and of enticing potential movie-goers in from the streets outside. Often a solo pianist or organist supplied the accompaniment, but quite a few different configurations of musicians were common. Not many halls offered musical spectacles comparable to that of New York's Capitol Theatre with its eighty-piece orchestra, or the Roxy, whose orchestra numbered more than a hundred players (circa 1927), but every theater featured music of some kind, usually six or seven nights a week.[34] Music, performed not only during the movie but as a rule before and after too, functioned as a distinct component of the cinematic spectacle. Given that the performers, or at least the conductor, had to be able to see the screen, musicians were a visible presence as well as an audible one. Although the necessity of providing live music saddled theaters with a substantial expense, theater owners generally understood it as a cost of doing business—and one not to be skimped on. Music accounted for 40 percent of the attendance at good movies, the Theater Exhibitors' Chamber of Commerce reported in 1921, and 95 percent of the attendance at bad ones. By 1926 approximately twenty-two thousand musicians were working in movie houses in the United States, and performers from their ranks made up a fifth of the membership of the American Federation of Musicians (AFM).[35]

At the outset, it was the musicians or bandleaders who decided what music was best suited to accompany a film, often under the influence of local audiences. Studios and theater owners valued this music because it enhanced the attraction of cinema, but they resented their reliance on the live performers. Consequently, challenges to the musicians' autonomy began in the 1910s—although they initially had little effect. In the mid-1910s, film companies began to send out "cue sheets" with their films, designating specifically what music should be played, and when, by the local performers, and eventually all the studios built up large music departments, with a complement of full- and part-time musicians, arrangers, and copyists who worked out the music for each film. In most cases, the music consisted not of original compositions but of bits and pieces of popular songs, well-known classical pieces, and easy-to-execute sound effects. Cue sheets marked the industry's attempt to standardize and centralize film music, but film studios had only limited power to enforce their musical prescriptions. In practice, many musicians and bandleaders would pick and choose what they wanted from the "official" score, or disregard it altogether. Meanwhile, the first signs of mechanized automation were appearing in the form of "photoplayers," special automatic pianos and organs for movie houses. These machines, however, were expensive (priced from one thousand to five thousand dollars), mechanically unreliable, and musically inflexible, in comparison to live performers, and thus did relatively little to reduce the importance of live musicians.[36]

In 1926 Warner Brothers introduced its new Vitaphone technology, which could effectively provide sound to accompany the moving images on-screen, an idea that filmmakers had experimented with off and on for more than two decades. Developed in conjunction with Western Electric, the manufacturing subsidiary of AT&T, this technology electrically recorded sounds that were then played back on a phonograph-type disc, which was precisely synchronized with the film's visual elements. The premiere of the sound-on-disc system took place on August 6, 1926, at the Warner Theater on Broadway in New York, in conjunction with a series of short films and a feature-length action film, *Don Juan,* starring John Barrymore. (One of the shorts, it is worth noting, featured the Metropolitan Opera's Giovanni Martinelli singing "Vesti la Giubba," from Leoncavallo's *I Pagliacci,* among the best-known roles and arias of the late Enrico Caruso.) In 1927 the studio released *The Jazz Singer* for distribution around the country. A more fitting film for this turning point in the American entertainment business could hardly be imagined. In the film, Jakie Rabinowitz, New York–born son of observant Jewish immigrants, aspires to become a singing star of the stage under the name Jack Robin. Played by Al Jolson, vaudeville's biggest star and Tin Pan Alley's most powerful hit maker, Jakie/Jack is torn between the Old World and the New World, between his father's wish for him to become a cantor and his own wish to be a professional entertainer. Although the title refers to jazz, the film's operative musical aesthetic is vaudeville and Tin Pan Alley through and through. Performing in blackface, Jakie moves from one world to the other performing "My Mammy," his signature song, which at once epitomizes his maternal adulation, one of Tin Pan Alley's most persistent themes, and celebrates the deep roots of the popular music business in the tropes of minstrelsy.

The plot comes to a head when Jakie is forced to choose between his big professional break and abiding by the wish of his ailing father that Jakie sing the Yom Kippur service in his stead. Faced with the contest between the sacred music of the religious service and Broadway performance, Jakie withdraws from the commercial domain; but as luck would have it, he gets his break in the end just the same. Not only does the film resolve Jakie's anxieties about his move into popular entertainment; it also, by using both conventional title cards and synchronized sound, bridges the old and new eras of film technology. "Wait a minute. You ain't heard nothing yet," Jolson says after finishing his first musical number, speaking at once to an on-screen audience and to the live movie audience in theaters.[37] The success of the film and its sound technology quickly pressured other studios into developing their own sound techniques, and by 1932, only 2 percent of movie theaters lacked the equipment to present films with sound. In another telling parallel between the phonograph and cinema, Warner Brothers, like Victor before it, was in the weakest competitive position of the companies in the mix. At the time the Warners pursued their risky commercial venture, their company was the smallest of the major film studios; it thus had the least to lose and the most to gain—much as the Victor Talking Machine Company had a quarter of a century earlier, when it had gambled so heavily on advertising and on developing its prestigious Red Seal recording catalogue.[38]

In the case of movies, though, the transformation was even quicker and more conspicuous: it ended the era when cinema and the organized music industry occupied separate worlds. *The Jazz Singer* initiated not just the age of "talkies" but also that of the Hollywood musical. How better to exploit the new sound technology, the studio moguls reasoned, than through music? In order to systematize the production of musical content for the films, the Hollywood studios went on to conduct a wholesale buyout of the songwriting and publishing firms of Tin Pan Alley, nearly all of which relocated to Southern California in the late 1920s and early '30s. Warner Brothers, for example, bought eleven publishing firms through its newly established Music Publishing Holding Corporation, beginning with M. Witmark and Sons in November 1928, a purchase followed in 1929 by that of T. B. Harms, De Sylva, Brown & Henderson, and Jerome H. Remick & Co. Other acquisitions included those of the firms of Leo Feist and Carl Fischer by RCA/RKO; Robbins by MGM; and Red Star Publishing Company by Fox. One result of this tidal wave of takeovers was that in their role as publishers, the movie studios soon came to dominate ASCAP as well, so that by 1935, Warner Brothers, Metro-Goldwyn-Mayer, Paramount, and Twentieth Century Fox controlled more than half the music that ASCAP licensed. In the 1930s Hollywood's importance as an engine of musical production increased in another domain as well; while Europe was descending into chaos, the American film studios became a leading employer of modernist and avant-garde émigré composers.[39]

Audiences loved the new talking—and often singing—movies, but this "sound revolution" in cinema had a devastating effect on professional musicians, which was made all the worse by the effects of the Depression. In 1926 approximately twenty-two thousand musicians were employed by movie theaters in the United States. By 1930 that number had dropped to fourteen thousand, and four years later it had plummeted to forty-one hundred. Thereafter, music for cinema was not produced locally but rather was issued centrally from Hollywood, where it was controlled by the film studios and the small cadre of composers, arrangers, and performers they employed. Although all musicians working in theaters were deeply affected, the transition to sound film had particular reverberations along the lines of race and gender. Many theaters had employed women as pianists or organists, and in African American neighborhoods, movie theaters were an important source of work for African American musicians. In this sense, the centralization of musical labor in Hollywood eliminated jobs formerly held by women and African Americans, and did so at exactly the time—during the Depression —when they had the greatest difficulty in finding other work. For theater owners, installation of the equipment necessary to play the new sound films represented a sizable initial investment, but it could provide substantial financial savings on labor costs. It delivered to owners perhaps an even greater dividend, however, by eliminating their reliance on workers who sometimes failed to show up for work or went out on strike for higher wages.[40]

The rise and rapid transformation of broadcast radio both paralleled and complemented the growth of cinema in the 1920s. Cinema was descended from photography, developed in the mid-nineteenth century; radio grew out of the development of telegraphy, which emerged in the mid-nineteenth century as well. Spectators of early cinema looked individually through the eyepieces of free-standing, hand-cranked "kinetoscopes"; early radio users listened through individual headsets. Later, moviegoers watched moving images projected on a screen, and radio listeners listened through loudspeakers; that is, both audiences adapted to a shared social experience. And just as cinema stimulated demand for live professional musicians but then underwent a period of dramatic consolidation in the late 1920s, so it was too with radio.

From the early years of radio, the transmission of music represented an ideal form of broadcasting. For one thing, radio realized longstanding fantasies about bringing music and sound into the home from afar. In his utopian *New Atlantis* (1627), Francis Bacon had envisioned a world in which "we have [the] means to convey sounds in trunks and pipes, in strange lines and distances." Edward Bellamy developed this vision further in *Looking Backward* (1888), in which citizens of the future listened to concerts in the home by means of telephone lines. E. M. Forster imagined a similar kind of musical transmission in "The Machine Stops," and the inventor Thaddeus Cahill attempted to actualize these ideas through a complex musical technology he called the telharmonium, a short-lived venture around 1906–1908, widely reported on at the time.[41] For broadcasters, meanwhile, music had a strong practical appeal. The earliest musical programs were established by local broadcasters who needed programming to fill their airtime and consequently opened their studios to a wide range of both amateur and professional musicians. Such haphazard programming had the virtue of spontaneity but the risk of inconsistency, and when it became technologically possible in the mid-1920s to broadcast remote transmissions live, station managers quickly began to devise shows around live performances by local professional orchestras at concert halls and dance halls. Indeed, the popularity of these shows enabled many AFM locals across the country to negotiate for improved wages and working conditions.

Beginning in 1926, the same year that Warner Brothers first demonstrated sound-on-disc film technology, radio experienced its own form of centralization and standardization in the form of networks, which reversed the high demand for local professional performances. In 1926 the Radio Corporation of America (RCA) purchased a powerful New York radio station, WEAF,

8.6 Given that programmers needed to fill airtime, music by both amateurs and professionals was an important element of radio broadcasting from the outset. Here, two women perform in the cramped quarters of Pittsburgh radio station KYW in the early 1920s. Bettmann/CORBIS.

and established a subsidiary called the National Broadcasting Corporation (NBC), through which it then began to transmit commercial programming from WEAF to affiliated broadcasters around the country. Through this pioneering network, NBC offered national advertisers unprecedented access to local radio stations, which received payments of thirty to fifty dollars for each program broadcast. This scheme brought in revenues of some $7 million for NBC in 1927. It was followed almost immediately by the company's establishment of a second network, centered around another New York station, WJZ, and the establishment of another network by an upstart rival to NBC, the Columbia Broadcasting System. (With rumors circulating about a merger between Victor and RCA, the Columbia Phonograph Company entered briefly into a partnership with the entrepreneur Arthur Judson to start the CBS network. Columbia soon dropped out, the Paley family of Philadelphia came in, but the Columbia name stuck.) By 1931 NBC claimed seventy-six affiliated stations in its web, CBS claimed ninety-five, and each company posted profit of more than $2.3 million. All this growth had a devastating effect on the demand for local performers. Programming through the national networks introduced elevated standards of professionalism that many amateurs and local professionals could not match, and from that time on, musical programming on radio stations around the country increasingly radiated outward from the large urban centers.[42]

For those in the music industry proper, radio prompted reactions ranging from suspicion to alarm. Quickest to adapt were the music publishers, who negotiated a system for radio stations to license ASCAP-administered works, which allayed the publishers' most serious concerns.[43] Indeed, publishers also saw that radio could, as many broadcasters had claimed, boost sales in other media (phonograph records, piano rolls, sheet music), and radio soon became publishers' primary channel for plugging new songs. Publishers not only worked to get their material performed by live orchestras but also hosted their own radio shows, during which they gave demonstrations of the latest numbers. When the music industry faced a dramatic contraction in the early years of the Depression, conflict between ASCAP and the broadcasters flared up again, but the main bone of contention was the schedule of licensing rates. The issue of whether or not radio could be profitable for publishers had long since vanished.[44]

Although leaders of the phonograph business projected an optimistic outlook about radio, they faced a more complicated situation. In 1923 *Talking Machine World* emphasized the possibility that phonograph dealers could benefit from the popularity of radio, rather than suffer from it, and in February 1924 the *Voice of the Victor* suggested to dealers that they might organize sales promotions to coincide with performances on local radio stations. Privately, however, many people in the industry were worried. In late 1924 Victor suffered disappointing sales during the Christmas season for the first time in the company's history, and increasingly, commentators in the phonograph business saw radio as one among numerous intense rivals. *The Voice of the Victor* noted the next summer, "Amusements have tremendously increased in both number and variety" since World War I, including radio, movies, theater, and automobiles (which had been declining in price). "None of them figured nearly so largely ten, five—even two, years ago," and the result was "a grand fight for a share of the amusement dollar."[45] Not only was the radio industry an extremely aggressive advertiser, as the phonograph business was, but radio programming came free to consumers after the purchase of a receiver, whereas phonograph owners who wanted new music had to buy new records.

The problem facing the phonograph business was not just commercial but aural as well.[46] Because radio technology condensed sound with an electrical microphone and amplified it with an electrical loudspeaker, radio generally sounded louder and clearer than phonographs, whose acoustic technology had changed very little in a quarter century. Thomas Edison's company did very little to respond, and its fortunes grew worse and worse. On November 1, 1929, a few days after the stock market crash, the company started by the man who had invented the phonograph more than half a century earlier announced that it would cease producing phonographs and records. Columbia and Victor, on the other hand, both licensed an electrical recording process developed by Western Electric, a subsidiary of AT&T, and in 1925 began preparations to unveil new lines of phonographs and recordings. (Brunswick-Balke-Collender, a furniture company that had emerged as a legitimate competitor in the phonograph field, did not license the technology but was at work on its own process of electrical amplification.) At the forefront of this commercial push was Victor, which launched the biggest advertising campaign in the company's history, at a cost of more than $5 million—first to sell off as much of its old stock as possible and then, in the fall, to build interest in its new lines. The company created print advertisements, street banners, and window displays; it staged sneak previews for celebrities, politicians, and other VIPs; and it arranged for dealers to give demonstrations in their stores, at meetings of the Rotary, Kiwanis, and Lions clubs, and for church groups, sewing circles, and other social gatherings. In November, with tremendous fanfare, the company introduced nineteen models of phonograph, priced from $17.50 to $1,000, that could play its new "orthophonic" recordings, and it came out with twenty-four more models the next year, including the first to incorporate electrical amplification.

Victor's strategy had two other components on the level of product design, in addition to the introduction of the orthophonic recordings, and these further symbolized the reconciliation of sound recording and radio and the integration of music technology into the rhythms of everyday life. First, starting in 1926 Victor began to sell combination units it called Victrola-Radiolas, which integrated RCA radios with its phonograph. Other companies had begun to market combination units earlier, but Victrola-Radiolas represented a union of the leaders in the two fields. Second, after insisting for many years that its phonographs were their own instruments, entitled to their own distinct design, Victor introduced several new "flat-top" models, which concealed the phonograph equipment inside. Thus, like the mechanical counterpart of Erik Satie's "furnishing music," modern sound technology was made to blend in seamlessly to the physical environment.

If changes in Victor's product design constituted one aspect of the integration of the technologies of the music business into daily life, then the dizzying "mergermania" that overtook the international phonograph industry in the second half of the 1920s marked a parallel kind of integration. In 1926, worn out from three decades in the phonograph business and facing health problems, Eldridge Johnson sold the Victor Talking Machine Company to the New York investment bankers Speyer & Company and J. & W. Seligman, in what was reported to be the single largest business deal in the music industry up to that time: Johnson, the majority shareholder, was paid more than $23 million and other shareholders split an additional $7 million.[47] Meanwhile, the company continued to grow. From 1926 through 1928, Victor absorbed its largest independent distributors, based in New York, Baltimore, Chicago, Dallas, San Francisco, and Seattle, and in 1927–28, it expanded its international holdings by acquiring the Victor Talking Machine Company of Canada (in which it had owned a controlling interest since 1924), the Victor Talking Machine Company of Japan, Ltd., the Victor Talking Machine Company of Brazil, and the Victor Talking Machine Company of Chile. Then, consummating the marriage between the radio and the phonograph and launching a new era of integrated multimedia conglomerates, RCA acquired Victor in 1929.[48]

Meanwhile, the frenzy of mergers and acquisitions also touched Victor's lifelong European affiliate, the Gramophone Company, and Columbia, Victor's principal American rival. These transactions highlighted both the complex transnationalism of the industry by the end of this formative period and the disproportionate presence of Americans. In England in 1931, Electrical and Musical Instruments Ltd., or EMI, was created by a merger of the Gramophone Company (of which RCA Victor owned 50 percent), the Columbia Graphophone Company (of which J. P. Morgan then owned 80 percent), and several other companies. As for Columbia, which had fallen into receivership in 1923, it was acquired in 1925 by the Columbia Graphophone Company of Great Britain, owned by the American-born Louis Sterling, who had taken over the English branch of the American firm in 1909. Then, because of antitrust concerns raised by the EMI merger, Sterling was forced to sell off the American Columbia, to the Grigsby-Grunow Company, manufacturer of radios and refrigerators in the United States. Three years later, Grigsby-Grunow sold Columbia to the American Record Corporation (ARC), a conglomerate of small record companies formed in 1929, which was owned by the Consolidated Film Industries. Finally, in 1938 ARC sold Columbia to its namesake, the Columbia Broadcasting System, where it stayed until 1988, when CBS sold it to Sony.[49]

In the end, the complex details of these changes in ownership matter less than what they reveal about the interplay among music, sound, and the matrix of modern social and material relations. Indeed, this multinational, multimedia consolidation threw into relief the impact of the U.S. music industry on the modern musical soundscape around the world. The reaching across international borders was not remarkable in and of itself, because the music business in the United States was never uniquely, independently American, although it took shape within specific national conditions. The growing internationalization of the business signified that the United States was no longer a cultural colony of Europe, a net importer of culture, as it had been in many respects in the nineteenth century. In some cases, as with the influence of African American music on European musical modernism, the change could be seen as a reversal in direction of influence. More important, though, was the opening up of dynamic, transnational flows of industrial, financial, and cultural capital, which created a truly international political economy of culture—with a heavy American accent. This transformation had been manifest in the opening of a Steinway & Sons piano factory in Hamburg in 1880; the establishment in 1898 of the first Continental disc phonograph company (Deutsche Grammophon), initiated by Emile Berliner, an American who hailed originally from Hanover; the assembling of the Red

Seal records catalogue jointly by Victor and the Gramophone Company in the early twentieth century, as well as in the recording (both in the United States and abroad) of thousands of foreign-language ("ethnic") records to sell to American immigrants and to use as the basis for establishing markets outside the United States. This increase in transnational circulation was visible in the signing of international copyright agreements by all the major industrial nations, as well. Although exports never made up more than 6 percent of Victor's total sales, this still comprised many millions of records and phonographs. (Or, to put it differently, this relatively low percentage says more about the enormous market in the United States than about the insignificance of the market abroad.)[50]

Moreover, once music fused with cinema and radio, the substantial distinction between the music business and other entertainment industries ceased to exist. Indeed, here was the capstone in the architecture of the soundscape of consumer capitalism. In terms of technology, radio transmitted sounds of the present, phonographs preserved sounds that had passed, and all the entertainment industries sought to shape sounds of the future. On the rational, emotional, and sensory levels, their sounds reverberated in spaces public and private and affected experiences both individual and social. As an integrated unit, the "culture industry" was no longer divisible along lines of medium or culture. The economic and cultural value of music could not be evaluated apart from the imbrication of music in copyright, sound-recording technology, radio, and movies—and vice versa. In the end, some music thrived in these new circumstances, and other music suffered. No music was left unaffected. And this fact makes a difference in the way we understand the meaning and value of culture—including the capacity of creative, expressive forms to enlighten, comfort, and inspire individual minds and to forge personal, social, and political bonds. To claim that this corporate integration matters is not to romanticize the discreteness of the individual arts or to fetishize their autonomy in relation to one another, but rather to call attention to the fact that it was interlocking corporate ownership, not intellectual or aesthetic affinity, that bound them together.

Today the tapered morning glory–shaped phonograph horns of the early twentieth century are icons of nostalgia, but at the time they epitomized something decidedly modern. Each of these was a horn of plenty, a cornucopia of aural pleasure, from which issued a whole world of sound. Yet the new age of aural abundance was not a democracy in any real sense. Although even humble consumers could partake of breathtaking performances by some of the world's most esteemed artists, shopping and listening were not voting. If music-loving consumers enjoyed an unprecedented freedom to choose from among a vast range of goods, they were not equally free to start their own phonograph companies or radio stations. To do so required large amounts of capital, technical and legal expertise, and the ability to overcome the concerted efforts of those dominating the industry to minimize competition, either by undermining newcomers or by absorbing them. Unless listeners could transmit radio messages as well as receive them, Bertolt Brecht argued in 1932, radio was only a tool of distribution, not one of communication, and his logic applied to the phonograph as well. Nor were relations within the industry democratic. Executives and managers had far greater control over the music industry's output than did the artists they hired; and ASCAP, the performing rights organization, refused membership to most blues and hillbilly artists. Indeed, as an organization ASCAP was resolutely undemocratic, its bylaws assigning voting rights according to a composer's sales.[51] The new musical culture was not a meritocracy, either. Music publishers worked doggedly to influence which sounds audiences heard, whether by cutting a performance artist in on a royalty, buying a round of drinks for a band, or making cash payments to the program director of a radio station. As for record companies, opera became their signature product not because they believed in its cultural or aesthetic superiority but because it recorded well and helped sell phonographs.

The ideas, practices, and institutions of the music business did not foreclose the possibility of meaningful cultural experience, but they did ensure that the way that most people thought about music and integrated it into their lives would be forever changed. At the same time, the new cultural order was never static or homogenous, and the growing concentration of power in the culture industry did not mean that that it was experienced by everyone in the same way. The establishment of the modern culture industry signaled the emergence of a new prevailing cultural matrix, but consolidation was neither permanent nor stable. Older, precommercial cultural strains persisted;

newer, sometimes oppositional, forms emerged. The dominant culture remained in continual negotiation with both.

The new musical order thus was paradoxical in numerous ways. Broadened access came with increased centralization. Intensified localism came with growing internationalization. And beyond these, a more subtle transformation was taking place as well. As the corporate producers of music grew larger and more complex, the music and voices they produced sounded increasingly intimate. Beginning in the mid-1920s, dramatic improvements in microphone technology and electrical recording and transmission enabled phonographs and radio to convey sounds that would previously have been lost in surface noise or static. Before 1925, making a good recording of a song required a singer with a stentorian, resonant voice, deftly directed into the cone-shaped recording horn. With the advent of condenser and ribbon microphones, however, relaxed, conversational voices recorded just as well. Al Jolson sounded as if he were singing *at* you, one critic recalled, but Bing Crosby sounded as if he were singing *to* you. When radio stations broadcast Franklin Roosevelt's Fireside Chats beginning in 1933, the president's voice had an air of familiarity and closeness, and only because of changes in the sonic properties of radio could he effectively disavow the impersonal voice of authority. He addressed listeners as "my friends," and many took him at his word.[52] Indeed, Roosevelt was the first president whose voice was widely known, and he showed as well as anyone how the world could seem smaller and more personal through sound.

Epilogue

In 1996 the conceptual artists Vitaly Komar and Alex Melamid and the musician-composer Dave Soldier conducted a survey of people's tastes in music, and on the basis of the musical elements that found greatest favor or disfavor with respondents, Soldier and a collaborator wrote and recorded two compositions. The first, "The Most Wanted Song," is a love song performed by a small ensemble, with male and female vocals in a rock and rhythm-and-blues style, of moderate duration, tempo, range of pitch, and volume. According to a straight analysis of their data, they explained, this recording would be "liked" by 72 percent of listeners, with a standard deviation of 12 percent. The other, "The Most Unwanted Song," combines the musical elements respondents liked the least. Lasting more than twenty minutes, it careens wildly between loud and soft volume, high and low pitches, and fast and slow tempos. The piece is performed by a large ensemble, and its instrumentation features the most unpopular instruments (bagpipes, accordion, tuba, banjo, and flute), along with an operatic soprano vocalist singing and rapping atonal music, political slogans, advertising jingles, and "elevator" music, supported by a group of children singing holiday songs.[1]

The symmetrical pairing of the "most wanted" and "most unwanted" songs gives the project its structure, but it is the most disliked elements that infuse the project with real meaning. With its blend of popular elements, "The Most Wanted Song" scarcely distinguishes itself from other songs commonly heard on "lite" popular music radio stations around the country—that is, songs produced without irony, whose aim is to appeal to as wide a market as possible, the same principle expounded by Tin Pan Alley veterans Charles K. Harris and Harry Von Tilzer in their songwriting how-to books a century earlier. In contrast, the impact (and humor) of the project lie in "The Most Unwanted Song" combining so many unfavorable elements, the dismal and diffuse periphery in relation to the concentrated popularity of the core. "The Most Wanted Song" closely mimics how the music business actually works; "The Most Unwanted Song" parodies music making based not on the unique imperatives of creative expression but on impersonal, aggregate data. The title of the project, *The People's Choice Music,* underscores how problematic the definition of "popular" music really is.

In a world in which music assumes so many forms in so many kinds of spaces, *The People's Choice Music* implicitly raises additional questions about the aural environment we live in: Who makes the music around us and why? What circumstances lead it to enter our ears in a given time and place? Of all the possible sounds in the universe, why these sounds? Because music is intensely personal, such questions can easily go unformulated, unasked. Each of us has a unique, sui generis relationship with music—we all have our own favorites, our own memories; for many of us our musical attachments help define who we are. Such personal, individual connections, however, can obscure fundamental questions about the musical culture that we share—its origins, its functions, its effects. To articulate these issues, though, is to acknowledge music as a social construction, and therefore a historical one. Our knowledge and understanding of music is always inductive, based on specific examples. Music does not exist in the abstract; to think of music in general is to have in mind some music in particular—which means music created in and for specific historical conditions.

The achievement of the modern music industry was to increase the amount and variety of music people experienced, but at the same time, it introduced new forms of social and economic power. Indeed, the rise of the music industry resulted in what has been the monumental paradox of modern musical culture: the simultaneous expansion of audiences and the access to musical works, on the one hand, and the growing power of heavily capitalized corporations and declining involvement in the relations of production, on the other.[2] Consumers relished the greater range of choices, but insofar as musical activity was linked to consumption, the boundaries of music came to depend increasingly on what the industry decided to market. That is, the range of music in most people's daily experiences was set, by and large, by the industry, within which commercial values took precedence over aesthetic values; in whose interest it was to avoid challenges to the prevailing social order; and whose growing dominance made alternative models of cultural production increasingly scarce. When short, chorus-oriented songs were easier to sell, longer narrative ballads became outmoded and rare. When the value of publishing rights made new songs more lucrative than old ones, the industry promoted a system of continual novelty and steered performers away from traditional material. When the industry was hostile to African Americans, racist caricatures were commonplace and black musicians struggled to find good work.

The musical culture that had taken shape in the United States by the 1930s was never monolithic, its impact never totalizing or static. Indeed, residual precommercial elements persisted both alongside and within the dominant culture. The present never completely buried the past or foreclosed the expressive possibilities of the future. Old songs continued to be sung, especially in remote or rural areas, whose residents were less likely to have been touched by vaudeville, movies, and other modern entertainments. Wherever people learned to play musical instruments or sang improvised songs, however, they reaffirmed a connection to a musical culture beyond the one defined by the music industry. Amateur and informal music making did not disappear altogether, nor are they ever likely to do so. Meanwhile, some older elements persisted even within the recording industry, albeit at its edges. In the 1920s and 1930s companies began to make recordings of old-time fiddlers, banjo pickers, and other rural performers whose repertoire reached back to the nineteenth century and earlier. Such recordings were inexpensive to make and to issue, and their performers extracted little in the way of recording fees or royalties. Through these musicians, however, ancient ballads of the type collected, analyzed, and enumerated by Francis Child and his followers, which were the antithesis of commercial music, crept into the margins of the music industry. These records, made for a niche market, were not hits, but they did not subsequently disappear, either. Indeed, many of them resurfaced in *The Anthology of American Folk Music,* the influential six-LP, eighty-four-song collection issued by Folkways Records in 1952. The collection was compiled and richly annotated by the eccentric polymath Harry Smith, who provocatively identified these atavistic songs as "folk" music, although the recordings had been made and distributed under the auspices of the commercial music industry. In the folk music revival of the 1950s and 1960s, *The Anthology* functioned as both an inspiration and a resource, and through Bob Dylan and others it came to reverberate through rock music as well. More recently, the 1997 reissue of *The Anthology* enjoyed unexpected commercial and critical acclaim. As sales mounted to more than half a million copies, *The Anthology* cast the spell of its archaic songs anew over the most recent generation of artists and listeners.[3]

The dominant culture also always contained certain emergent elements defined in opposition to the status quo. These sensitive, creative impulses expressed feelings and ideas that the rest of the society could not, or anticipated needs that society in general was as yet unaware that it had. By contrast with the music business, which was busy embedding music in objects, pioneering composers such as Charles Ives, Henry Cowell, and later John Cage (Cowell's student) were stretching the concept of music itself. Distanced from the orthodoxy of the machine, they sought to elicit new effects from old instruments (for example, the strumming of the piano's internal strings in Cowell's *Aeolian Harp*), and each in his own manner promoted a music that had listened to the world in new ways. Meanwhile, such musicians as Jelly Roll Morton and Louis Armstrong made jazz a fertile idiom for musical experimentation, and by the late 1920s Duke Ellington was beginning to reimagine the whole palette of American music.

Apart from the pull of the past and the thrust toward the future, the defining of the horizon of musical expectations for most people had contradictory effects. On the most basic level, the proliferation of music offered sustenance, and people took pleasure from it. Even Theodor Adorno acknowledged the deep human value of music in pubs and cafés. "Background music is an acoustic light source [for patrons]," he wrote in 1934, "it lights them up. . . . When café music falls silent, it sounds as if a miserly waiter is turning off a couple of electric light bulbs." Adorno was referring specifically to live music, but recordings had real, salutary effects, too. With the rise of recorded music, listening to records emerged as a new and valuable dimension of people's lives. Those who listened to records together sometimes forged deep affective bonds. Notwithstanding caricatures of listeners' abject passivity, such listeners talked about what they heard, shared feelings with one another, and used music in myriad creative, meaningful, and even subversive ways.[4] Yet even as mechanical reproduction of music brought much into people's lives, its popularity had the concomitant effect of pushing out live music. When it did, it sacrificed music making as a means of forging dynamic social bonds, both among musicians and between musicians and audiences. Live musicians could interact with audiences, and vice versa, both groups of participants contributing to the musical event, in real time. With mechanical reproduction, the music on a record existed not as a dynamic process but literally as a product—an outcome. Musically, its results were guaranteed. It could thrill, but it would not surprise, at least after a few auditions. Although the artistic achievement remained intact, it sacrificed what one critic called "the gamble in human fallibility." Playing a record, you know the tenor is going to hit the high C every time.[5]

Based on large amounts of corporate capital and a high degree of technical knowledge, mechanical reproduction had other effects as well, particularly in flattening the differences among disparate kinds of music and between music and other commodities. In magazines and department stores alike, phonograph companies ranked among the nation's leading manufacturers of consumer goods. Notwithstanding slight variations in packaging (such as the red labels of Victor's Red Seal discs), the records looked the same, played about the same length of time (two to four minutes), and were purchased in the same places. The recordings also resembled one another sonically, for no matter what the instrumentation or style of music, the prevailing technology gave all records a similar timbre and limited them to a narrow range of dynamics and frequencies. Indeed, this standardization was audible in the basic elements of popular song as well. No matter how the genres shifted over time (from coon songs to show tunes to rock and roll, and so on), popular songs followed an enduring template according to which the songs were musically simple, chorus-oriented, and about three minutes in length.

Radio altered the musical field in some respects, but overall it reinforced the flattening effect, rather than reversing it. In the commercial economy of radio, broadcasters made money by selling their audience to advertisers. The larger the audience was, the greater its value. The corollary to this principle was the underlying goal of commercial broadcasting: not just to attract listeners but to keep them tuned regularly. To build a stable listenership, broadcasters sought a high degree of standardization, while avoiding total predictability, which might alienate listeners. In other words, to attract the largest audiences possible, broadcasters promoted music and other programs that had wide, mainstream appeal and that kept surprises to a minimum, so that listeners would tune in, confident they knew what was coming. Meanwhile, in order for the most delicate and most thunderous musical passages to be audible on radio, it had to render both at moderate volume, and although radio initially offered sound superior to that of phonographs, radio too had a range of dynamics and frequencies much narrower than what the human ear was accustomed to perceiving. For all its appeal, then, radio funneled sound into a relatively limited channel: no one would have mistaken the sound of a radio broadcast for that of a live performance.

As for content, the offerings of the music industry were vast and impressive, but they were not universal. Indeed, the impact of the music industry, as it attained increasing prominence in the cultural landscape, was evident not only in the goods it made available, but also in the musical forms it discarded or excluded. The success of the chorus-oriented song, for example, led the industry to deemphasize longer, more story-oriented songs, which sometimes functioned as valuable repositories of historical memory. Thus, workers' songs sometimes served as the only historical record of labor struggles of the past or as counterhistories to the accounts entered into the official historical records. One labor group that held particularly deep convictions about music and its power beyond the music business was the Industrial Workers of the World (IWW). Established in 1905, the year before the introduction of the enclosed-horn Victrola, the IWW issued a well-known thirty-eight-song collection called *The Little Red Song Book* with each union card, and these songs helped the IWW overcome the linguistic barriers that separated laborers of dozens of different nationalities. When the IWW mobilized textile workers in Lawrence, Massachusetts, in 1912, for example, music helped unite the strikers, who came together in song at meetings, at rallies, and in the street. Remarkably, in 1931 Columbia did issue one commercial record by the labor firebrand Aunt Molly Jackson (née Mary Magdalene Garland), a spiritual heir to the IWW; but this record, "Kentucky Miner's Wife," gives little idea of her rich and extensive repertoire, from which the Library of Congress eventually recorded more than 150 songs.[6]

Many labor songs were based on hymns or other forms of religious song, which, in turn, had their own peculiar associations with the music business. Christmas songs, hymns, and gospel quartets meshed easily with the music business, and some labels issued recordings of abbreviated sermons as well. To proponents of religious recordings, the music industry was simply another conduit for God's word, but critics charged that forcing religious music to conform to the musical idioms and commercial channels of the music business subverted the music's underlying message—the glorification of spiritual values that transcended the market. At the same time, some devotional music was never compatible with the new musical order, especially music that did not fit easily into a three-minute recording.

The limits of the industry's recordings aside, the phonograph companies did document and preserve a rich body of vernacular American music, both sacred and secular, although this achievement had nothing to do with the goals of the industry. Recordings that sold well stayed in print; those which did not were deleted from the catalogue. Companies made an exception for records with particular prestige value, like Victor's Red Seals, whose cachet the company used above all as advertising, but with most other recordings, availability depended primarily on the market. Over the years, however, smaller record companies, independent of the multinational giants, have frequently appeared to challenge the industry's leading producers over music they have neglected or allowed to languish. Black Swan Records, the first major black-owned record company, was one such intervention, an attempt to record all styles of music made by African Americans, not merely the blues, jazz, and popular numbers that were widely validated by the market. In the 1930s jazz aficionados established labels to reissue prized recordings that the industry had let fall out of print. In subsequent decades, such small labels have—either by issuing new recordings from beyond the margins of the mainstream industry or by reissuing older recordings—managed to check the large companies' power to decide what recorded musical culture would and would not include. Perhaps no one rejected the major companies' one-dimensional economic filter as clearly as Moses Asch, whose Folkways Records, established in the 1940s, issued everything from Native American folk songs to underwater recordings of fish. Dedicated to the accumulation of an encyclopedic library of recorded sound, not large profits, Asch kept all his records in print. As he was fond of saying, "You don't take the letter 'J' out of the dictionary because it's used less than the letter 'S.'"[7]

For most in the music industry, however, music represented a lucrative, if unusual, commodity. Unlike other commodities, such as wheat or cotton, music exists simultaneously in fundamentally different forms—as sound, as object, as performance, as composition. These are intricately interrelated, but each also has its own dynamics, its own economy. If the aesthetic and acoustic qualities of Caruso's voice boosted the industry, so too did the patent and copyright laws underpinning the redefinition of music as a protected form of property. Indeed, the multidimensional character of music made it a particularly effective component of the new consumer economy. It could be associated with a wide range of values, from duty and respectability to fantasy and pleasure, and could hover easily in the space between the rational, disciplined order of industrial production and the more emotional domain of consumer enchantment. With its capacity to entice, delight, and move people, music was in the world of consumer goods but not of it. No matter how strictly ordered the production of songs or phonograph records was, music was first and foremost something that people felt, aurally, physically, and emotionally. Whatever people *thought* about the music they heard followed later.

At the same time, more than the culture of music was transformed by the music industry. The culture beyond music—that is, outside its traditional boundaries—was, too. Just as the grand sweep of the Industrial Revolution affected all of society, not just people employed in industrial occupations, the commercial revolution in music ensured that all aspects of music resonated in a new way. The mutable and multivalent character of music, as sound above all, also made it possible to assimilate it easily into nonmusical spaces and activities—at school and home, work and leisure, war and peace. As the brief history of Black Swan Records showed, sound could be a means of both contesting and reinforcing social divisions. As the 1909 copyright battle demonstrated, it could also be a tool in the expansion of property rights.

In the form of sound the social and geographical reach of the music industry extended into the furthest corners of American life. In the 1930s the folklorists John and Alan Lomax went in search of Americans unchanged by the new commercialized musical culture. One of the few places in the United States they found them was among the inmates serving long sentences in remote prisons in the South—people who were literally removed from the rest of society. And even among *them,* the Lomaxes found many modern influences.[8]

The shock to the consumer economy of the Great Depression triggered a period of critical reckoning for the music business, during which it suffered some devastating reversals and completed the displacement of the piano from the center of American musical life. From 1927 to 1932 the sale of records dropped from 104 million to 6 million, the production of phonographs from 987,000 instruments to 40,000. Meanwhile, production of "straight" pianos (as opposed to player-pianos) dropped from 137,000 in 1925 to fewer than 49,000 in 1931, and, most dramatically, production of player-pianos dropped from 169,000 to as few as 2,700 in the same years, a precipitous decline from which this once-successful sector of the industry never recovered.[9] More remarkable than the setbacks the industry suffered, however, was its persistence and expansion. As the consumer economy crumbled in the 1930s, the commercial precepts of the music industry only became more entrenched. Whereas sales to individual consumers of pianos, player-pianos, and stand-alone phonographs declined sharply during the Depression, Hollywood musicals, radios, and the proliferation of jukeboxes sustained and reinforced the place of the music industry in American life.

In succeeding decades, the music industry would confront new challenges. These ranged from wartime supply shortages and the professional musicians' strike in the 1940s to the payola scandal in the 1950s, the British Invasion in the 1960s, and the do-it-yourself ethos of punk and hip-hop in the 1970s, which attested to the inadequacy of the consumption-oriented cultural model to satisfy everyone's musical needs. None of these removed music from the center of American consumer culture, however. The music industry had a formidable capacity to assimilate musical challenges from the outside, as it had done with jazz and race records in the 1920s, and the development of new technologies (including long-playing records, 45 rpm "singles," and cheap, portable transistor radios) helped ensure that music remained audible for all kinds of consumers. Nevertheless, the way people thought about recording did change. With increasingly inventive techniques and technologies, the mimetic character of sound recording—the notion of documenting a live, aural event—was overshadowed by sound recording as an artificial creation. In a pure sense, recordings had always been artificial creations, but never before had the artifice been so conspicuous. By the 1960s nothing symbolized this shift more than the decision by musicians as dissimilar as Glenn Gould and the Beatles to abandon live performance in favor of the manipulation and control of magnetic tape and multi-track recording.

Looking back from the vantage point of the early twenty-first century, it is easy to see that in recent years the ground has been shifting, most notably in the erosion of the music industry's monopoly on the means of production. Beginning with the introduction of inexpensive four-track tape recorders and dramatically expanding with digitization, the Internet, and other computer technologies, the power to make, reproduce, and distribute high-quality sound recordings has ceased to reside exclusively with institutions possessing sizable capital and technical resources. The line between producer and consumer blurs when anyone with a high-speed Internet connection can download free digital editing software such as Audacity, broadcast over his or her own Internet "radio" station, and exchange files, copyrighted or otherwise, through decentralized peer-to-peer distribution networks. Many radical technologists have embraced these and similar developments as harbingers of a democratic utopia in which user-driven alternatives to the corporate, commercial model of cultural production and distribution can thrive. These developments, however, although they mark the start of a new era, do not yet herald a new order. The major music companies have been failing to keep pace with the winds of change, but they are far from defunct. The Recording Industry Association of America (RIAA) remains a powerful lobbying agent in Washington, as the Digital Millennium Copyright Act of 1998 demonstrated. No matter how much file traders and free-information activists would welcome the fall of the ancien régime, the existing structure of copyright law will not be reversed or undone easily, and as long as that law remains on the books, the power of the state stands behind its enforcement. Much depends on the outcome of these challenges. The underlying concern is not just the circulation of goods and information but also the circulation of ideas and feelings and the cultivation of human relationships that are not governed by the market. Indeed, these challenges raise issues about property and access, creativity and control, memory and inspiration—issues that help define the meaning of music itself.

On the south side of Union Square in New York City, there stands a phantasmagorical emporium called the Virgin Megastore, one of the largest retail establishments in this part of the city. On the cusp of a new musical era, such spaces are becoming increasingly rare. Inside its doors, amusement is for sale, in the form of DVDs, books, glossy magazines—and in the café, soft drinks. The greatest emphasis, of course, is on sound—on the selling of hundreds of thousands of musical recordings in styles too numerous to count. As you drift up and down the aisles, your ears are filled with music from the in-house sound system, invisible overhead, and when the bass is strong enough, you not only hear the music, you feel it penetrate your body. Surrounding you are countless recordings whose origins span the globe and stretch through time, reaching back sixty, seventy, eighty years, or more. The regular rhythms in your ears and the standardized packaging at your fingertips blur the breathtaking diversity represented in these recordings; in this environment they converge, and the recordings become interchangeable. Where everything from field recordings to electronic studio trickery is on offer, from pop nuggets to the Ring Cycle, sound recordings are the lowest common denominator of human culture. Here, Britney Spears, Balkan funeral marches, postcolonial Afrobeat, Indian ragas, and the London Philharmonic are all available for $17.98 each. Selling musical recordings is only one of this store's functions. Another is simply to advertise the Virgin brand, the symbol of a multimedia commercial conglomerate that currently includes an airline, a healthcare company, cell phones, and a line of cola drinks. It all started with music, though: a small record company and music publishing company in England founded in the 1970s.

A few doors to the west of the Virgin Megastore, just across Fourteenth Street, the music publishing firm of M. Witmark and Sons opened its first offices outside the family home across town in Hell's Kitchen in 1888. At that time, Union Square was the principal entertainment district in the city, and it was abuzz with sounds. These included everything from opera at the Academy of Music to piano concerts at Steinway Hall to vaudeville at Keith and Albee's Union Square Theater. Strains of "serious" European music commingled with musical theater and the boisterous homegrown influence of minstrel shows from the Bowery. The commercial success of the music industry grew by balancing these elements, interweaving them, playing them off one another, and marketing them in ingenious ways. Over the years, M. Witmark and Sons and other publishers migrated up Broadway to Twenty-eighth Street and Times Square and then eventually to Hollywood and beyond. Their musical world reimagined the relation between making sounds and hearing them, between sense and cents. Their songs reverberate still.

To hear selected recordings discussed in the book, go to **davidsuisman.net.**

ABBREVIATIONS IN NOTES

NOTES

ACKNOWLEDGMENTS

INDEX

Abbreviations in Notes

MT	*Music Trades*
MTR	*Music Trade Review*
NYT	*New York Times*
TMW	*Talking Machine World*
VoV	*Voice of the Victor*

CCHS-VTM	Victor Talking Machine Company files, Camden County Historical Society, Camden, N.J.
CU-OHROC	Oral History Research Office Collection, Columbia University
EMI	EMI Archives, Hayes, Middlesex, England
EMI-ERJ	Eldridge Reeves Johnson personal files, EMI Archives, Hayes, Middlesex, England
HAG-ALD	B. L. Aldridge files, Radio Corporation of America Collection, RCA Victor Division, Hagley Museum and Library, Wilmington, Del.
HAG-PEN	Nicholas Pensiero files, Radio Corporation of America Collection, RCA Victor Division, Hagley Museum and Library, Wilmington, Del.
HAG-TR	Trade literature collection, Hagley Museum and Library, Wilmington, Del.
LC-HVT	Von Tilzer/Gumm Collection, Library of Congress, Washington, D.C.
NMAH-ATLC	Alphabetical Trade Literature Collection, National Museum of American History, Smithsonian Institution, Washington, D.C.

NMAH-NTLC   Numerical Trade Literature Collection, National Museum of
                 American History, Washington, D.C.
NMAH-WAR   Warshaw Collection of Business Americana, Archives Center,
                 National Museum of American History, Washington, D.C.
NYPL-IGP   Isaac Goldberg Papers, Manuscripts and Archives Section, New
                 York Public Library
NYPL-JTH   John Tasker Howard Papers, Music Division, New York Public
                 Library
NYPL-LFP   Leo Feist Papers, Music Division, New York Public Library
NYPL-LOCKE105   Robinson Locke Scrapbook, no. 105, Theater Division,
                 Performing Arts Library, New York Public Library
NYPL-LOCKE106   Robinson Locke Scrapbook, no. 106, Theater Division,
                 Performing Arts Library, New York Public Library
TAE   Thomas E. Jeffrey et al., eds., *Thomas A. Edison Papers: A
                 Selective Microform Edition,* part 4, *1899–1910* (Bethesda,
                 Md., 1999)
UMD-FEC   Frances Elliott Clark Papers, Michelle Smith Performing Arts
                 Library, University of Maryland, College Park, Md.
UMD-HC-IPA   International Piano Archives, Howe Collection, University of
                 Maryland, College Park, Md.
UMD-HC-MMI   Mechanical Musical Instruments, series: General Information,
                 subseries: Miscellaneous, Howe Collection, Michelle Smith
                 Performing Arts Library, University of Maryland, College Park,
                 Md.
WEBD   *The Papers of W. E. B. Du Bois* (Sanford, N.C., 1980), microform
                 edition
WUSTL-WG   William Gaddis Papers, Washington University in Saint Louis,
                 Saint Louis, Mo.

Notes

Prologue

1. This account is drawn from Isidore Witmark and Isaac Goldberg, *From Ragtime to Swingtime: The Story of the House of Witmark* (New York, 1939), 1–79, 148, 429; and Julius Witmark, Jr., "Reminiscences of Julius Witmark" [1958–59], CU-OHROC. The first of these works, based on Isidore Witmark's recollections, also drew heavily on the unpublished memoirs of Julius Witmark, who died in 1929.

2. In 1885 a suit brought by the Society for the Prevention of Cruelty to Children threatened to curtail Julius's performing career, but the suit was defeated and the attendant publicity actually proved to be a windfall. Witmark and Goldberg, *From Ragtime to Swingtime,* 52.

3. Emile Berliner, *The Gramophone: Etching the Human Voice* (n.p., 1888), online at *Emile Berliner and the Birth of the Recording Industry,* memory.loc.gov/ammem/ berlhtml/berlhome.html, accessed June 4, 2008.

4. See Thomas A. Edison, "The Phonograph and Its Future," *North American Review* 126 (May–June 1878): 527–536.

5. For an interesting example of this use of the phonograph, see *Debate '08: Taft and Bryan Campaign on the Edison Phonograph,* compact disc (Archeophone Records, ARCH 1008, 2008).

6. Berliner, *The Gramophone,* 19–20. Edison did mention recording speeches by political figures, but only as a form of preservation.

7. John Blacking, *How Musical Is Man?* (Seattle, 1973); Bruno Nettl, "Music," *Grove Music Online,* ed. L. Macy, www.grovemusic.com, accessed June 5, 2008. On the various functions music serves across cultures, see Alan P. Merriam, *The Anthropology of Music* (Evanston, Ill., 1964), 223–227.

8. David S. Reynolds, *Walt Whitman's America: A Cultural Biography* (New York, 1995), 176.

9. Walt Whitman, *Leaves of Grass: The Deathbed Edition* (1892; New York, 1992), 9.

10. Jean-Christophe Agnew has made the point that consumer culture generally, not just music, now constitutes the "air we breathe." See his "Coming Up for Air: Consumer Culture in Historical Perspective," in *Consumption and the World of Goods,* ed. John Brewer and Ray Porter (London, 1993), 19–39.

11. On music in hospitals, see, for example, Daniel J. Wakin, "While in Surgery, Do You Prefer Abba or Verdi?" *NYT,* June 10, 2006. On ring tones, see Sasha Frere-Jones, "Ring Tones," *New Yorker,* Mar. 7, 2005. On "Happy Birthday," see "Profitable Happy Birthday," *Times (London),* Aug. 5, 2000, 6; Robert Brauneis, "Copyright and the World's Most Popular Song," GWU Legal Studies Research Paper no. 1111624, available online at http://ssrn.com/abstract=1111624 (accessed Nov. 12, 2008). See also Justice Stephen Breyer's dissent in *Eldred v. Ashcroft,* the Supreme Court's ruling on the twenty-year extension of the term of copyright, provided for in the Sonny Bono Copyright Term Extension Act of 1998; *Eldred v. Ashcroft* 537 U.S. 186 (2003).

12. Keith Hart, "On Commoditization," in *From Craft to Industry: The Ethnography of Proto-Industrial Cloth Production,* ed. Esther Goody (Cambridge, 1982); Timothy D. Taylor, "The Commodification of Music at the Dawn of the Era of 'Mechanical Music,'" *Ethnomusicology* 51 (Spring–Summer 2007), 281–305; Arjun Appadurai, "Introduction: Commodities and the Politics of Value," in *The Social Life of Things: Commodities in Cultural Perspective,* ed. Arjun Appadurai (Cambridge, 1986), 3–63; and Igor Kopytoff, "The Cultural Biography of Things: Commoditization as Process," ibid., 64–91.

13. My thinking about these dynamic and complementary concepts of culture was aided by Raymond Williams, *The Long Revolution* (New York, 1961), 41–47; and Williams, *Politics and Letters: Interviews with New Left Review* (London, 1979), 133–174.

14. Simon Frith, "The Industrialization of Music," in *Music for Pleasure: Essays in the Sociology of Pop* (New York, 1988), 11–23.

15. William Leach, *Land of Desire: Merchants, Power and the Rise of a New American Culture* (New York, 1993).

16. *VoV* 2 (May 1907): 4 (emphasis in the original).

17. Babson Bros., *Edison Phonograph Distributors* (Chicago, [1907]), HAG-TR.

18. Isaac Goldberg, *Tin Pan Alley: A Chronicle of American Popular Music* (1930; New York, 1961), 211.

19. Jean Aberbach, "Reminiscences of Jean Aberbach" [1958–59], p. 13, CU-OHROC.

20. Williams, *The Long Revolution,* 48–71; Raymond Williams, *Marxism and Literature* (Oxford, 1977), 128–135. See also James H. Johnson, *Listening in Paris: A Cultural History* (Berkeley, 1995).

21. In a study of history textbooks, George H. Roeder noted historians' general inattention to the sensory dimensions of historical experience. Roeder, "Coming to Our

Senses," *Journal of American History* 81 (Dec. 1994): 1112–1122. In the past few years, however, a range of scholars have begun to turn their ears toward the past. Some of the most suggestive of these works include Jonathan Sterne, *The Audible Past: The Cultural Origins of Sound Reproduction* (Durham, N.C., 2003); Emily Thompson, *The Soundscape of Modernity: Architectural Acoustics and the Culture of Listening in America, 1900–1933* (Cambridge, Mass., 2002); John Picker, *Victorian Soundscapes* (New York, 2003); Bruce R. Smith, *The Acoustic World of Early Modern England: Attending to the O Factor* (Chicago, 1999); Leigh Eric Schmidt, *Hearing Things: Religion, Illusion, and the American Enlightenment* (Cambridge, Mass., 2000); Lisa Gitelman, *Scripts, Grooves, and Writing Machines: Representing Technology in the Edison Era* (Stanford, 1999); Derek Vaillant, *Sounds of Reform: Progressivism and Music in Chicago, 1873–1935* (Chapel Hill, N.C., 2003).

22. Robert Jütte, *A History of the Senses: From Antiquity to Cyberspace* (Cambridge, 2004); Anthony Synnott, "Puzzling over the Senses: From Plato to Marx," in *The Varieties of Sensory Experience: A Sourcebook in the Anthropology of the Senses*, ed. David Howes (Toronto, 1991), 61–76. Jacques Attali, *Noise: The Political Economy of Music* (1977; Minneapolis, 1985).

23. Lucien Febvre, *The Problem of Unbelief in the Sixteenth Century: The Religion of Rabelais*, trans. Beatrice Gottlieb (1942; Cambridge, Mass., 1982), 423–436.

24. Quoted in Synnott, "Puzzling over the Senses," 73–74.

25. Edmund Gurney, *The Power of Sound* (1880; New York, 1966), 1.

26. Walter Benjamin, "The Work of Art in the Age of Its Technological Reproducibility" (3rd version), trans. Edmund Jephcott and Harry Zohn, in *Selected Writings*, vol. 4, *1938–1940*, eds. Howard Eiland and Michael W. Jennings (Cambridge, Mass., 2003), 255; and Benjamin, *Charles Baudelaire: A Lyric Poet in the Era of High Capitalism*, quoted in Jonathan Crary, *Techniques of the Observer: On Vision and Modernity in the Nineteenth Century* (Cambridge, Mass., 1990), 112.

27. Nathaniel Hawthorne, *The American Notebooks*, quoted in Leo Marx, *Machine in the Garden: Technology and the Pastoral Ideal in America* (London, 1964), 11–16.

28. The concept of the soundscape was first developed by R. Murray Schafer in *The Tuning of the World* (New York, 1977), repr. as *The Soundscape: Our Sonic Environment and the Tuning of the World* (Rochester, Vt., 1993). A helpful introduction to thinking about the senses historically can be found in Alain Corbin, "A History and Anthropology of the Senses," in *Time, Desire, and Horror: Towards a History of the Senses* (Cambridge, 1995), 181–195.

29. On "rough music," which also existed in Italy as *scampanate* and in Germany as *Katzenmusik, Haberfeld-treiben*, or *Thierjagen*, see E. P. Thompson, "Rough Music," *Annales* 20 (1972): 295–312; Thompson, "Rough Music Reconsidered," *Folklore* 103 (1992): 3–26; Natalie Zemon Davis, *Society and Culture in Early Modern France;* Mary Russo and David Warner, "Rough Music, Futurism, and Postpunk Industrial Noise Bands," *Discourse* 10 (1987–88): 55–79; Mark McKnight, "Charivaris, Cowbellions, and

Sheet Iron Bands: Nineteenth-Century Rough Music in New Orleans," *American Music* 23 (Winter 2005): 407–425. Other works considering the preindustrial relation between sound and power include Shane White and Graham White, *The Sounds of Slavery: Discovering African American History through Songs, Sermons, and Speech* (Boston, 2005); and Mark M. Smith, *Listening to Nineteenth-Century America* (Chapel Hill, 2001). On preindustrial sound and sensory experience generally, see Richard Cullen Rath, *How Early America Sounded* (Ithaca, N.Y., 2003); Peter Charles Hoffer, *Sensory Worlds in Early America* (Baltimore, 2003); Jean-Pierre Gutton, *Bruits et sons dans notre histoire* (Paris, 2000).

30. Alain Corbin, *Village Bells: Sound and Meaning in the Nineteenth-Century French Countryside* (New York, 1998).

31. On the contemporary use of both sounds and smells by hotel designers, see Susan Stellin, "Eau de Hotel," *NYT*, Sept. 11, 2007.

32. Smith, *The Acoustic World of Early Modern England*, 10; Walter Ong, *The Presence of the Word: Some Prolegomena for Cultural and Religious History* (New Haven, Conn., 1967), 17–110; Martin Jay, "Scopic Regimes of Modernity," in *Vision and Visuality*, ed. Hal Foster (New York, 1988); Jonathan Crary, *Techniques of the Observer: On Vision and Modernity in the Nineteenth Century* (Cambridge, Mass., 1990).

33. Theodor Adorno and Hanns Eisler, "The Politics of Hearing," in *Audio Culture: Readings in Modern Music*, ed. Christoph Cox and Daniel Warner (New York, 2004), 74.

34. I do not mean to imply that musical reception and behavior are historically unimportant. On the contrary, they have been used to illuminate important complexities in the changing field of social relations, from the sexually liberating experience of social dancing for young, working-class women to the effect of foreign-language records on homesick immigrants. See, for instance, Kathy Peiss, *Cheap Amusements: Working Women and Leisure in Turn-of-the-Century New York* (Philadelphia, 1986); and Lizabeth Cohen, "Encountering Mass Culture at the Grassroots: The Experience of Chicago Workers in the 1920s," in *Consumer Society in American History: A Reader*, ed. Lawrence B. Glickman (Ithaca, N.Y., 1999).

35. William Leach follows a similar focus on creation, as opposed to reception, in *Land of Desire*. See esp. xiii–xv.

36. "Musicians do not make records" paraphrases Roger Chartier, *The Order of Books: Readers, Authors, and Libraries in Europe between the Fourteenth and Eighteenth Centuries*, trans. Lydia G. Cochrane (Stanford, Calif., 1994), 10.

37. Stephen Siwek, *Copyright Industries in the U.S. Economy* (n.p., 2006), 5, 9, available online at www.iipa.com (accessed Nov. 12, 2008). Siwek is an economist who has been issuing reports on copyright industries since 1990. The "core" copyright industries are defined as those industries whose primary purpose is to create and sell copyrighted products.

38. *Fifteenth Census of the United States: 1930* (Washington, D.C., 1931), 1342–

1343; *Statistical History of the United States* (Stamford, Conn., [1976]), 417; *Biennial Census of Manufactures: 1933* (Washington, D.C., 1936); Pekka Gronow, "The Record Industry: The Growth of a Mass Medium," in *Popular Music (Yearbook)*, ed. Richard Middleton and David Horn (Cambridge, 1983), 60; Craig Roell, *Piano in America, 1890–1940* (Chapel Hill, N.C., 1989).

1. When Songs Became a Business

1. Herzen quoted in Isaiah Berlin, "My Intellectual Path," in *The First and the Last* (New York, 1999), 46. The term *popular song* acquired its modern meaning at the end of the nineteenth century.

2. Frédéric Louis Ritter, *Music in America* (New York, 1890), 421.

3. Dale Cockrell, "Nineteenth-Century Popular Music," in *The Cambridge History of American Music,* ed. David Nicholls (Cambridge, 1998), 161–169; Dave Laing, "A Voice without a Face: Popular Music and the Phonograph in the 1890s," *Popular Music* 10 (1991): 1–9.

4. Elise K. Kirk, *Musical Highlights from the White House* (Malabar, Fla., 1992), 82; Craig H. Roell, *The Piano in America, 1890–1940* (Chapel Hill, N.C., 1989); Booker T. Washington, *Up From Slavery* (New York, 1901), 113; *Leavenworth Herald* quoted in Lynn Abbott and Doug Seroff, "'They Cert'ly Sound Good to Me': Sheet Music, Southern Vaudeville, and the Commercial Ascendancy of the Blues," *American Music* 14 (Winter 1996): 404.

5. Joseph Horowitz, *Classical Music in America: A History of Its Rise and Fall* (New York, 2005); Lawrence W. Levine, *Highbrow, Lowbrow: The Emergence of Cultural Hierarchy in America* (Cambridge, Mass., 1988).

6. Harry Thurston Peck, "Migration of Popular Songs," *Bookman* 2 (September 1895): 97. Peck disagreed with this common view of popular songs.

7. Harry Von Tilzer, introduction to Edward Michael Wickes, *Writing the Popular Song* (Springfield, Mass., 1916), xv–xvi; "Business with Music Publishers," *MTR* 38 (May 14, 1904): 43.

8. For the sake of simplicity, I will sometimes use *Tin Pan Alley* anachronistically, to refer to the business as it took shape in the 1880s and 1890s as well.

9. Hazel Meyer, *The Gold in Tin Pan Alley* (Philadelphia, 1958), 39–40; Harry Von Tilzer, "Mr. Tin Pan Alley, Himself," 1942, pp. 1–2, box 1, folder 13, LC-HVT.

10. This description is based on Theodore Dreiser, "Whence the Song," *Harper's Weekly,* Dec. 8, 1900, 1066; and Maurice A. Richmond to Isaac Goldberg, Aug. 9, 1930, box 1, NYPL-IGP.

11. Thorstein Veblen, *The Theory of Business Enterprise* (New York, 1910), 1–65, quotation on 51; Von Tilzer, introduction to *Writing the Popular Song,* xv; Charles K. Harris, *After the Ball: Forty Years of Melody—An Autobiography* (New York, 1926), 361.

12. David Ewen, *All the Years of American Popular Music* (Englewood Cliffs, N.J.,

1977), 101; Charles Hamm, *Yesterdays: Popular Song in America* (New York, 1979), 260.

13. Dena J. Epstein, introduction to *Board of Music Trade, Complete Catalogue of Sheet Music and Musical Works, 1870* (New York, 1973), xxiii. See also Hamm, *Yesterdays*, 265, 284.

14. Charles Hamm, "Popular Music," in *The New Grove Dictionary of American Music*, ed. H. Wiley Hitchcock and Stanley Sadie (London, 1986), 3:593. On nineteenth-century sheet music sales, see Epstein, introduction to *Board of Music Trade*, x.

15. Based on figures in Hamm, *Yesterdays*, 483–484. On Foster, see also Ewen, *All the Years of American Popular Music*, 41–46; John Tasker Howard, "Stephen Foster and His Publishers," *Musical Quarterly* 20 (January 1934): 77–95; Ken Emerson, *Doo Dah! Stephen Foster and the Rise of American Popular Culture* (New York, 1997).

16. Hamm, *Yesterdays*, 264; Von Tilzer, "Mr. Tin Pan Alley, Himself," 13.

17. "The Growth of Music Publishing," *MTR* (June 1904): 39.

18. Reginald De Koven, "Music-Halls and Popular Songs," *Cosmopolitan*, Sept. 1897, 531. See also MacDonald Smith Moore, *Yankee Blues: Musical Culture and American Identity* (Bloomington, Ind., 1985); and Barbara Tischler, *An American Music: The Search for an American Musical Identity* (New York, 1986).

19. Epstein, introduction to *Board of Music Trade*, xv–xx; Russell Sanjek, *American Popular Music and Its Business: The First Four Hundred Years*, vol. 2, *1790–1909* (New York, 1988), 357–361.

20. Von Tilzer, "Mr. Tin Pan Alley, Himself," 11; Von Tilzer, introduction to *Writing the Popular Song*, xx.

21. Frank Presbrey, *The History and Development of Advertising* (Garden City, N.Y., 1929); Frank Luther Mott, *A History of American Magazines*, 5 vols. (Cambridge, Mass., 1938–1968); Daniel Boorstin, *The Americans: The Democratic Experience* (New York, 1973), 137–139.

22. Goldberg, *Tin Pan Alley*, 103–104; Ewen, *All the Years of American Popular Music*, 101–102; Isidore Witmark and Isaac Goldberg, *From Ragtime to Swingtime: The Story of the House of Witmark* (New York, 1939), 61–62. Generally, the use of illustrated sheet music covers was restricted to popular music, and "serious" music had simpler, nonpictorial cover design. See Jean M. Bonin, *American Life in Our Piano Benches: The Art of Sheet Music* (Madison, Wisc., 1985), 3.

23. Witmark and Goldberg, *From Ragtime to Swingtime*, 63, 60, 63, 98–99; Hamm, *Yesterdays*, 288. On royalty ballads, see E. D. Mackerness, *A Social History of English Music* (London, 1964), 231.

24. Harris, *After the Ball*, 15, 27.

25. W. L. Hubbard, *History of American Music* (New York, 1908), 85; Ernest Jarrold, "The Makers of Our Popular Songs," *Munsey's Magazine*, June 1895, 292.

26. Charles K. Harris, *How to Write a Popular Song* (New York, 1906), 2, 6, 12–13; Harris, *After the Ball*, 40.

27. Harris, *After the Ball*, 36, 78, quotation on 36; Harris, *How to Write a Popular Song*, 2; Goldberg, *Tin Pan Alley*, 206; "Made Popular by Songs," *MTR* 19 (Sept. 8, 1894): 11; Gilbert Tompkins, "Making of a Popular Song," *Munsey's Magazine*, Aug. 1902, 747.

28. Harris, *After the Ball*, 86–87; Tompkins, "Making of a Popular Song," 747. On Sousa, see Neil Harris, "John Philip Sousa and the Culture of Reassurance," in *Cultural Excursions: Marketing Appetites and Cultural Tastes in Modern America* (Chicago, 1990), 198–232.

29. Hamm, *Yesterdays*, 286; Witmark and Goldberg, *From Ragtime to Swingtime*, 114.

30. Goldberg, *Tin Pan Alley*, 108–109; D. G. Arnoth, "At the 'Popular' Music Publishers," *Outlook*, May 1920, 179. See also, for example, "How the Jewish Song Trust Makes You Sing," *Dearborn Independent*, Aug. 13, 1921, reprinted in *The International Jew: The World's Foremost Problem* (Dearborn, Mich., 1920). For an example of the more sanguine view of Jews in Tin Pan Alley, see Kenneth Aaron Kanter, *The Jewish Contribution to American Popular Music, 1830–1940* (New York, 1982).

31. Witmark and Goldberg, *From Ragtime to Swingtime*, 28; "Harry Von Tilzer's Wife Dies," *Variety*, Oct. 1, 1930.

32. Ben Yagoda, "Lullaby of Tin Pan Alley," *American Heritage*, Oct.–Nov. 1983, 90.

33. Berndt Ostendorf, "'The Diluted Second Generation': German-Americans in Music, 1870–1920," in *German Workers' Culture in the United States, 1850 to 1920*, ed. Hartmut Keil (Washington, D.C., 1988), 261–287; Joseph Horowitz, *Wagner Nights: An American History* (Berkeley, Calif., 1994), 4–5; Jon Newsom and H. Wiley Hitchcock, "Sonneck, Oscar G. T.," *Grove Music Online*, ed. L. Macy, www.grovemusic.com, accessed June 5, 2008.

34. Ostendorf, "'The Diluted Second Generation,'" 283–284; Neil Gabler, *An Empire of Their Own: How the Jews Invented Hollywood* (New York, 1988).

35. Many of these patterns are noted in Edward Pessen, "The Great Songwriters of Tin Pan Alley's Golden Age: A Social, Occupational, and Aesthetic Inquiry," *American Music 3* (Summer 1985): 180–197. Pessen's quantitative analysis should be approached skeptically, however, because his analytical categories are based only on subjective aesthetic judgments.

36. Witmark and Goldberg, *From Ragtime to Swingtime*, 112.

37. Harris was born in Poughkeepsie, New York, but grew up in Michigan and Wisconsin; Von Tilzer was born in Detroit and raised in Indianapolis; Dresser was born in Terre Haute.

38. Witmark and Goldberg, *From Ragtime to Swingtime*, 280. See also Frank Dumont, *Witmark Amateur Minstrel Guide and Burnt Cork Encyclopedia* (London, 1899).

39. Jeffrey Melnick, *A Right to Sing the Blues: African Americans, Jews, and American Popular Song* (Cambridge, Mass., 1999), 33. Rogin quoted ibid.

40. James H. Dormon, "Shaping the Popular Image of Post-Reconstruction American Blacks: The 'Coon Song' Phenomenon of the Gilded Age," *American Quarterly* 40 (December 1988): 450–471.

41. David A. Jasen and Gene Jones, *Spreadin' Rhythm Around: Black Popular Songwriters, 1880–1930* (New York, 1998), 32.

42. Melnick, *A Right to Sing the Blues,* 33.

43. Witmark and Goldberg, *From Ragtime to Swingtime,* 197.

44. Dreiser, "Whence the Song," 1066; Ewen, *All the Years of American Popular Music,* 158.

45. Wayne D. Shirley, "The House of Melody: A List of Publications of the Gotham-Attucks Music Company at the Library of Congress," *Black Perspective in Music* 15 (Spring 1987): 79–112; Thomas Bauman, "Enterprise and Identity: Black Music, Theater, and Print Culture in Turn-of-the-Century Chicago," in *Music and the Cultures of Print,* ed. Kate Van Orden (New York, 2000), 201–235; W. C. Handy, *Father of the Blues: An Autobiography,* ed. Arna Bontemps (1941; New York, n.d.), 108; and Jasen and Jones, *Spreadin' Rhythm Around,* 58, 119–132. At least one black-owned publisher predated Gotham-Attucks, but it does not appear to have left a substantial mark. This was a firm established in 1903 in Chicago by N. Clark Smith and J. Berni Barbour. See Eileen Southern, *Music of Black Americans: A History,* 3rd ed. (New York, 1997), 308.

46. Berndt Ostendorf, "The Musical World of Doctorow's *Ragtime,*" *American Quarterly* 43 (1991): 584–591; Matthew Mooney, "An 'Invasion of Vulgarity': American Popular Music and Modernity in Print Media Discourse," *Americana: The Journal of American Popular Culture* 3 (Spring 2004); Bauman, "Enterprise and Identity," 219. On ragtime at the Saint Louis World's Fair, see clipping from *St. Louis Globe Democrat,* Jan. 23, 1904, in Louisiana Purchase Exposition—Music folder, information files, Missouri Historical Society, Saint Louis. On the condemnation of ragtime by the Ohio Federation of Colored Women's Clubs, see *Wisconsin Weekly Advocate,* Jan. 4, 1902, quoted in Bauman, "Enterprise and Identity," 217.

47. Rudi Blesh and Harriet Janis, *They All Played Ragtime: The True Story of an American Music* (London, 1958), 239.

48. Charles Hamm, "Alexander and His Band," *American Music* 14 (Spring 1996): 65–102.

49. Georg Lukács, "Reification and the Consciousness of the Proletariat," in *History and Class Consciousness: Studies in Marxist Dialectics* (Cambridge, Mass., 1968), 83–110.

50. "How Popular Song Factories Manufacture a Hit," *NYT,* Sept. 18, 1910; Walter Bishop, "Reminiscences of Walter Bishop," Sept. 1958, p. 23, CU-OHROC; Goldberg, *Tin Pan Alley,* 100.

51. Louis Bernstein, "Reminiscences of Louis Bernstein," 1958, p. 3, CU-OHROC.

52. Jay Gorney, "Reminiscences of Jay Gorney," 1958, p. 10, CU-OHROC.

53. Edward B. Marks and Abbot J. Liebling, *They All Sang: From Tony Pastor to Rudy Vallee* (New York, 1935), 25–26. See also "The Professional Copy a Menace," *MTR* 43 (Nov. 24, 1906): 52.

54. S. N. Behrman, "Profiles: Accoucheur," *New Yorker*, Feb. 6, 1932, 20. Behrman is here paraphrasing John Golden, the songwriter.

55. Goldberg, *Tin Pan Alley*, 11.

56. Ibid., 201–202.

57. Hamm, *Yesterdays*, 289–290; Tompkins, "Making of a Popular Song," 746; Wickes, *Writing the Popular Song*, 2. Composers, it might be noted, ranked slightly higher than lyricists.

58. Hubbard, *History of American Music*, 83; Jack Yellen, "Reminiscences of Jack Yellen" [1958–59], p. 29, CU-OHROC; Behrman, "Profiles: Accoucheur," 20–24; and Yagoda, "Lullaby of Tin Pan Alley," 88–95.

59. "Fortune in a Popular Song," *Literary Digest*, 53 (July 1, 1916): 30, 33.

60. *MT* 35 (Feb. 1, 1908): 44; Philip Robert Dillon, "Princely Profits from Single Songs," *Scrap Book* 4 (Aug. 1907), 181–189. A copy of the latter can be found in subject file "Songs, Popular—U.S.," Music Division, New York Public Library.

61. For a casual, nonsystematic view of songwriting, see Edgar Leslie, "Reminiscences of Edgar Leslie," 1959, p. 1068, CU-OHROC; Irving Caesar, "Reminiscences of Irving Caesar" [1958–59], p. 9, CU-OHROC; Harris, *After the Ball.*

62. L. Wolfe Gilbert, *Without Rhyme or Reason* (New York, 1956), 13; Bernstein, "Reminiscences," 14; Marks and Liebling, *They All Sang*, 39; Von Tilzer, Introduction to *Writing the Popular Song*, xix.

63. Richard Severo, "Irving Caesar, Lyricist of Timeless Hits Like 'Tea for Two,' Dies at 101," *NYT*, Dec. 18, 1996.

64. Adolph Olman, "Reminiscences of Adolph Olman" [1958–59], pp. 4, 27, CU-OHROC; Bernstein, "Reminiscences," 14; Arthur Somers Roche, "The Gentle Art of Song-Writing," *Harper's Weekly*, Jan. 1, 1910, 31.

65. Frank Ward O'Malley, "Irving Berlin Gives Nine Rules for Writing Popular Songs," *American Magazine*, Oct. 1920, 242. Emphasis in the original.

66. On women and consumer marketing, see Charles McGovern, "Consumption and Citizenship in the United States, 1900–1940," in *Getting and Spending: European and American Consumer Societies in the Twentieth Century*, ed. Susan Strasser, Charles McGovern, and Matthias Judt (Cambridge, 1998), 45; and Andreas Huyssen, "Mass Culture as Woman: Modernism's Other," in *Studies in Entertainment: Critical Approaches to Mass Culture*, ed. Tania Modleski (Bloomington, Ind., 1986), 188–207.

67. Goldberg, *Tin Pan Alley*, 98; Von Tilzer, introduction to *Writing the Popular Song*, xv. Jasen and Jones, *Spreadin' Rhythm Around*, 18, also suggests that women were assumed to be the consumers of sheet music.

68. "Our $600,000,000 Music Bill," *Literary Digest*, June 1913, 1426–1427.

69. Marks and Liebling, *They All Sang*, 73.

70. Jean V. Lenox, "The Woman as a Song Writer," *MTR* 46 (Sept. 12, 1908): 29.

71. Irving Berlin, "'Love-Interest' as a Commodity," *Green Book Magazine*, Apr. 1916, 695.

72. Yagoda, "Lullaby of Tin Pan Alley," 92.

73. A copy of "The Fatal Night of the Ball," published by Pioneer Publishing, can be found in the Music Division of the Library of Congress.

74. Meyer, *The Gold in Tin Pan Alley*, 38. Harry Von Tilzer claimed that the purpose of the newspaper in the piano strings was actually to make the piano sound more like a banjo, not to muffle the volume. See Harris, *After the Ball*, 214; Marks and Liebling, *They All Sang*, 74; and Harry Von Tilzer, "Mr. Tin Pan Alley, Himself," 1–2.

75. Bert Williams, "The Comic Side of Trouble," in *Speech and Power*, ed. Gerald Early (Hopewell, N.J., 1993), 2:5.

76. David Paul Nord, "An Economic Perspective on Formula in Popular Culture," *Journal of American Culture* 3 (Spring 1980): 17–31, esp. 23–24. On dime novels, see Michael Denning, *Mechanic Accents: Dime Novels and Working-Class Culture in America*, rev. ed. (London, 1998).

77. Philip Scranton, *Endless Novelty: Specialty Production and American Industrialization, 1865–1925* (Princeton, N.J., 1997).

78. Harris, *How to Write a Popular Song*; F. B. Haviland, *How to Write a Popular Song* (New York, 1910); Samuel Henry Speck, *The Song Writer's Guide: A Treatise on How Popular Songs Are Written and Made Popular* (Detroit, 1910); E. M. Wickes and Richard H. Gerard, *Popular Songs: How to Write and Where to Sell* (New York, 1913); *Hints to Songwriters and Composers* (Washington, D.C., 1914); Marks-Goldsmith, *Successful Songwriting* (Washington, D.C., 1914); Wickes, *Writing the Popular Song*; Harry J. Lincoln, *How to Write and Make a Success Publishing Music* (Cincinnati, 1919); Abel Green, *Inside Stuff on How to Write Popular Songs* (New York, 1927); Edward Michael Wickes, *The Song Writer's Guide* (New York, 1931).

79. Lincoln, *How to Write and Make a Success Publishing Music*, 10. See also Wickes, *Writing the Popular Song*, ix–xiii. The disregard for originality apparently also applied to the how-to books themselves, for Lincoln plagiarizes whole passages from Wickes, *Writing the Popular Song*.

80. Harris, *How to Write a Popular Song*, 31.

81. Lincoln, *How to Write and Make a Success Publishing Music*, 10–12.

82. Harris, *How to Write a Popular Song*, 14; Wickes, *Writing the Popular Song*, 45.

83. Goldberg, *Tin Pan Alley*, 8. Jean Aberbach also explained, "In most cases, we have to get [our message] across in the first eight bars. That is also the reason why the title is so vitally important." Jean Aberbach, "Reminiscences of Jean Aberbach" [1958–59], p. 5, CU-OHROC.

84. Harris, *How to Write a Popular Song*, 14–17. See also Wickes, *Writing the Popular Song*, 79.

85. Goldberg, *Tin Pan Alley*, 228; Harris, *How to Write a Popular Song*, 16–7; Hamm, *Yesterdays*, esp. 255, 291–294, 358–361, Whiteman quoted on 359.

86. Karl Hagstrom Miller, "Segregating Sound: Folklore, Phonographs, and the Transformation of Southern Music, 1888–1935" (Ph.D. diss., New York University, 2002), chap. 3; D. K. Wilgus, *Anglo-American Folksong Scholarship since 1898* (New Brunswick, N.J., 1959).

87. James Porter, "Child, Francis James," *Grove Music Online*, ed. L. Macy, www. grovemusic.com, accessed June 5, 2008.

88. William Arms Fisher, "The Greatest Musical Fraud in History," *Etude* (Jan. 1923): 19. See also Fisher, "Song Sharks and Their Victims," Music Teachers National Association, *Proceedings* 16 (1922): 118–120; Wickes, *Writing the Popular Song*, 156–161; Frank H. Grey, "What It Means to 'Put Over' a Popular Song," *Etude* (Mar. 1925): 165–166. A full history of song sharking has yet to be written, but when it is, it may well benefit from the large amount of sheet music published by song sharks on deposit in the Copyright Division of the Library of Congress. I am indebted to Wayne Shirley of the Music Division of the Library of Congress for calling my attention to the importance of the song-sharking business and for taking me on a tour of the sheet music section of the Copyright Division.

89. Theodor Adorno and Max Horkheimer used the term *culture industry* in their famous essay "The Culture Industry: Enlightenment as Mass Deception" because they found the same problem with *mass media* and other terms—that is, they could suggest initiative by the masses. See Theodor Adorno, "Culture Industry Reconsidered," *New German Critique* 6 (Fall 1975): 12–19.

90. Fred Mierisch, "In Tin Pan Alley," *NYT*, Feb. 23, 1923; Robert Haven Schauffler, *The Musical Amateur* (Boston, 1911), 221–222.

91. Gilbert Seldes, quoted in Nord, "An Economic Perspective on Formula," 24; Nicholas Johnson, quoted ibid., 32n38.

92. David Lacy, "The Economics of Publishing, or, Adam Smith and Literature," *Daedalus* 92, no. 1 (1963): 42–62.

93. "How Popular Song Factories Manufacture a Hit," *NYT*, Sept. 18, 1910.

94. "Leo Feist," *Variety*, June 25, 1930; "Edward Marks," *NYT*, Dec. 18, 1945. The Roosevelt administration later asked Marks to serve on the president's committees of the Council for Fair Trade Practices and the Council for Financial Aid to Small Enterprises.

95. "Notable Developments in the Music Publishing Field during 1907," *MT* 34 (Dec. 7, 1907): 109.

96. Ben Singer, *Melodrama and Modernity: Early Sensational Cinema and Its Contexts* (New York, 2001).

97. The following analysis of "Alexander's Ragtime Band" draws on Robert Dawidoff, "The Kind of Person You Have to Sound Like to Sing 'Alexander's Ragtime Band,'" in *Making History Matter* (Philadelphia, 2000), esp. 118, 121–122; Charles Hamm, "Genre, Performance and Ideology in the Early Songs of Irving Berlin," *Popular Music*

13 (1994): 143–150; Hamm, *Irving Berlin: Songs from the Melting Pot: The Formative Years, 1907–1914* (New York, 1997); Richard Crawford, *America's Musical Life: A History* (New York, 2001), 546–551; Laurence Bergreen, *As Thousands Cheer: The Life of Irving Berlin* (New York, 1990), 33.

2. Making Hits

1. Henry T. Finck, "What Gives a Popular Song Its Vogue?" *Lippincott's Monthly,* Feb. 1900, 298, 299.

2. "The Case against Popular Song," *Musical America,* June 8, 1912, 13.

3. See also, for example, Elise Fellows White, "Music Versus Materialism," *Musical Quarterly* 8 (1922): 42; William E. Walter, "The Industry of Music-Making," *Atlantic Monthly,* Jan. 1908, 91–96.

4. Gilbert Tompkins, "Making of a Popular Song," *Munsey's Magazine,* Aug. 1902, 746.

5. After studying songbooks and published song sheets (broadsides), Paul Charosh has argued that historians have erred in characterizing "hits" as a by-product of Tin Pan Alley. I would argue, however, that Charosh confuses hits with large sales, without considering where hits came from and how they functioned. See his "Studying Nineteenth-Century Popular Song," *American Music* 15 (Winter 1997): 459–492.

6. Isaac Goldberg, *Tin Pan Alley: A Chronicle of American Popular Music* (1930; New York, 1961), 103.

7. Edward B. Marks and Abbot J. Liebling, *They All Sang: From Tony Pastor to Rudy Vallee* (New York, 1935), 3, 22.

8. Nicholas E. Tawa, *Sweet Songs for Gentle Americans: The Parlor Song in America, 1790–1860* (Bowling Green, Ohio, 1980), 104; Jean M. Bonin, *American Life in Our Piano Benches: The Art of Sheet Music* (Madison, Wisc., 1985), 3.

9. Neil Harris, *Humbug: The Art of P. T. Barnum* (Chicago, 1973).

10. Arnold Shaw, "The Vocabulary of Tin Pan Alley Explained," *Notes* 3 (1949–50): 47.

11. Maurice A. Richmond to Isaac Goldberg, Aug. 9, 1930, NYPL-IGP; Irving Berlin to Leo Feist, July 23, 1976, box 1, folder 3, NYPL-LFP.

12. Theodore Dreiser, "Birth and Growth of a Popular Song," *Metropolitan Magazine,* Nov. 1898, 499, 501.

13. Jean Aberbach, "Reminiscences of Jean Aberbach," 1958–59, p. 3, CU-OHROC.

14. Ira Gershwin to Isaac Goldberg, n.d., box 1, folder "Garfield-Godoy," IGP-NYPL; Ray Walker, "Veteran Songplugger Recalls Glamor of Early Tin Pan Alley Era," *Variety,* Jan. 2, 1952, 227, 246.

15. Cary Morgan, "Reminiscences of Cary Morgan," 1958, p. 18, CU-OHROC;

Harry Ruby, "Reminiscences of Harry Ruby," 1959, p. 2012, CU-OHROC; Hazel Meyer, *The Gold in Tin Pan Alley* (Philadelphia, 1958), 56–57.

16. Ben Yagoda, "Lullaby of Tin Pan Alley," *American Heritage* 34, no. 6 (1983), 92; Robert Miller, "Reminiscences of Robert Miller," 1958, pp. 16–17, CU-OHROC.

17. Goldberg, *Tin Pan Alley,* 208.

18. Adolph Olman, "Reminiscences of Adolph Olman," 1957, pp. 12–13, CU-OHROC.

19. David Ewen, *All the Years of American Popular Music* (Englewood Cliffs, N.J., 1977), 154; Kerry Segrave, *Payola in the Music Industry: A History, 1880–1991* (Jefferson, N.C., 1994), 11; Meyer, *The Gold in Tin Pan Alley,* 56.

20. Lew Brown, Robert King, and Ray Henderson, "Ain't My Baby Grand?" Shapiro, Bernstein & Co. (New York, 1925).

21. Miller, "Reminiscences," 1; Olman, "Reminiscences," 12; Goldberg, *Tin Pan Alley,* 208; Marks and Liebling, *They All Sang,* 154; Segrave, *Payola,* 13; Richard Abel, "That Most American of Attractions, the Illustrated Song," in *The Sounds of Early Cinema,* ed. Richard Abel and Rick Altman (Bloomington, Ind., 2001), 143–155.

22. Marks and Liebling, *They All Sang,* 17; Meyer, *The Gold in Tin Pan Alley,* 53–54; Charles K. Harris, *How to Write a Popular Song* (New York, 1906), 7; E. M. Wickes and Richard H. Gerard, *Popular Songs: How to Write and Where to Sell* (New York, 1913), 25–26; Charles K. Harris, *After the Ball: Forty Years of Melody, an Autobiography* (New York, 1926), 176–182, quotation on 181; Goldberg, *Tin Pan Alley,* 128–129; Rick Altman, *Silent Film Sound* (New York, 2004).

23. Wickes and Gerard, *Popular Songs,* 25–26.

24. E. M. Wickes, *Writing the Popular Song* (Springfield, Mass., 1916), 162; Marks and Liebling, *They All Sang,* 147.

25. Harris, *After the Ball,* 20. On claques, see, for instance, Jay Robert G. Teran, "The New York Opera Audience, 1825–1974" (Ph.D., New York University, 1974), 168.

26. David Ewen, *American Popular Songs: From the Revolutionary War to the Present* (New York, 1966), 352; Brooks McNamara, *Step Right Up* (Jackson, Miss., 1995); Lisa Gitelman, "Reading Music, Reading Records, Reading Race: Musical Copyright and the U.S. Copyright Act of 1909," *Musical Quarterly* 81 (Summer 1997): 273–274; Kenneth Aaron Kanter, *The Jewish Contribution to American Popular Music, 1830–1940* (New York, 1982), 31.

27. Reprinted in "The Song Claque Nuisance," *MTR* 42, no. 11 (Mar. 17, 1906): 46.

28. Charles Hamm, *Yesterdays: Popular Song in America* (New York, 1979), 379; Ewen, *All the Years of American Popular Music,* 173; Kanter, *The Jewish Contribution to American Popular Music,* 38. On dinner clubs, dancing, and the growing number of venues for popular music, see Lewis Erenberg, *Steppin' Out: New York Nightlife and the Transformation of American Culture, 1890–1930* (Chicago, 1981).

29. Marks, *They All Sang*, 154. On wages, difficult work, and pluggers' attitudes about their work, see Olman, "Reminiscences," 9–10; Ruby, "Reminiscences," 2012; Morgan, "Reminiscences," 1–2, 18; and Miller, "Reminiscences," 1.

30. Samuel B. Charters and Leonard Kunstadt, *Jazz: A History of the New York Scene* (1962; New York, 1981), 15; Marks and Liebling, *They All Sang*, 18.

31. Louis Bernstein, "Reminiscences of Louis Bernstein," 1958, pp. 9–10, CU-OHROC; Marks and Liebling, *They All Sang*, 4.

32. Hardin quoted in Nat Shapiro and Nat Hentoff, eds., *Hear Me Talkin' to Ya: The Story of Jazz as Told by the Men Who Made It* (1955; New York, 1966), 91–92.

33. Dreiser, "Birth and Growth of a Popular Song," 502; J. H. Girdner, "The Plague of City Noises," *North American Review* (Sept. 1896): 296, 300.

34. Susan Smulyan, *Selling Radio: The Commercialization of American Broadcasting, 1920–1934* (Washington, D.C., 1994), 125–153.

35. Isidore Witmark and Isaac Goldberg, *From Ragtime to Swingtime: The Story of the House of Witmark* (New York, 1939), 363–364; Meyer, *The Gold in Tin Pan Alley*, 58–59.

36. "Leo Feist as Press Agent," *MTR* 47 (Sept. 12, 1908): 41; "About Interesting People," ibid., 37; Segrave, *Payola in the Music Industry*, 10; [undated profile of Leo Feist], typescript, n.d., box 2, folder 23, NYPL-LFP.

37. Linda L. Tyler, "'Commerce and Poetry Hand in Hand': Music in American Department Stores," *Journal of the American Musicological Society* 45 (Spring 1992): 75–120, esp. 78–82, 87, 95–96, and 99. On department stores, see William Leach, *Land of Desire: Merchants, Power and the Rise of a New American Culture* (New York, 1993); Leach, "Transformations in a Culture of Consumption: Women and Department Stores, 1890–1925," *Journal of American History* 71 (September 1984): 319–342.

38. Tyler, "'Commerce and Poetry Hand in Hand,'" 83.

39. Russell quoted in "Furnishing Music in a Department Store," *MT* 44 (Dec. 14, 1912): 23.

40. "Ninety-four Housewives Tell Why They Buy" *System* 28 (1915): 485, quoted in Tyler, "'Commerce and Poetry Hand in Hand,'" 94.

41. Harris, *After the Ball*, 37–38; Marks and Liebling, *They All Sang*, 61–67, quotation on 67; Ewen, *All the Years of American Popular Music*, 178.

42. The discussion of vaudeville circuits in this paragraph and the two succeeding paragraphs draws on Robert W. Snyder, "The Vaudeville Circuit: A Prehistory of the Mass Audience," in *Audiencemaking: How the Media Create the Audience*, ed. James S. Ettema and D. Charles Whitney (Thousand Oaks, Calif., 1994), 215–231; and Marks and Liebling, *They All Sang*, 128–134.

43. Olman, "Reminiscences," 11; Julius Witmark, Jr., "Reminiscences of Julius Witmark," 1958, p. 2, CU-OHROC; Ewen, *All the Years of American Popular Music*, 178–179.

44. Snyder, "The Vaudeville Circuit," 218; Ewen, *All the Years of American Popular Music*, 179.

45. Marks and Liebling, *They All Sang,* 129.

46. Ibid., 129–130; Herbert Marks, "Reminiscences of Herbert Hilliard Marks," 1957, p. 28, CU-OHROC; Rocco Vocco, "Reminiscences of Rocco Vocco," 1959, p. 2047, CU-OHROC; Bernstein, "Reminiscences," 13.

47. Miller, "Reminiscences," 12.

48. Jay Gorney, "Reminiscences of Jay Gorney," 1958, pp. 12–13, CU-OHROC.

49. Caesar quoted in Robert Kimball and Alfred Simon, *The Gershwins,* cited in Hamm, *Yesterdays,* 346. Harris, *After the Ball,* 214; Segrave, *Payola in the Music Industry,* 8, 11; Joseph Meyer, "Reminiscences of Joseph Meyer," 1958, p. 10, CU-OHROC; Goldberg, *Tin Pan Alley,* 204.

50. Jack Yellen, "Reminiscences of Jack Yellen," 1958, p. 28, CU-OHROC; Fulton Oursler to Isaac Goldberg, May 22, 1930, box 1, NYPL-IGP; Goldberg, *Tin Pan Alley,* 203–204; Harris, *After the Ball,* 214; Segrave, *Payola,* 12–13; Vocco, "Reminiscences of Rocco Vocco," p. 2072; Shaw, "The Vocabulary of Tin Pan Alley Explained," 41.

51. Harris, *After the Ball,* 78; Marks and Liebling, *They All Sang,* 134–135; Segrave, *Payola,* vii, 1, 12–16; Von Tilzer, "Mr. Tin Pan Alley, Himself," 132.

52. Snyder, "The Vaudeville Circuit," 221, 227–228.

53. *MTR* 39 (Nov. 5, 1904): 47; *MT* 34 (Oct. 19, 1907): 47; *MT* 36 (Dec. 5, 1908): 111; Von Tilzer, "Mr. Tin Pan Alley, Himself," 101–104.

54. *MTR* 44 (May 11, 1907): 44; *MTR* 44 (Apr. 13, 1907): 44; *MTR* 44 (Apr. 27, 1907): 48; Russell Sanjek, *American Popular Music and Its Business: The First Four Hundred Years,* vol. 2, *1790–1909* (New York, 1988), 414. The publishers involved in the American Music Stores were Isidore Witmark, Charles K. Harris, Fred B. Haviland, Leo Feist, and F. A. Mills. Those involved in the United Music Stores included Maurice Shapiro, Helf & Hager, Louis Dreyfus, and Francis, Day, & Hunter.

55. *MTR* 45 (Sept. 28, 1907): 49. The unnamed publisher was probably Charles K. Harris.

56. Another factor was the erosion of the legality of the joint venture. In August 1907 the Supreme Court decided that a combination of book publishers intent on blocking Macy's discounting of their books was guilty of illegal restraint of trade. See Sanjek, *American Popular Music and Its Business,* 2:419.

57. *MTR* 45 (Sept. 28, 1907): 49; *MTR* 48 (Nov. 2, 1907): 47–48; *MTR* 49 (Sept. 18, 1909): 3. See also publisher John Stark's circular, sent out to retailers, quoted in Rudi Blesh and Harriet Janis, *They All Played Ragtime: The True Story of an American Music* (London, 1958), 240–241.

58. Marks and Liebling, *They All Sang,* 154; Irving Berlin, "'Love-Interest' as a Commodity," *Green Book Magazine,* Apr. 1916, 698.

59. Irving Berlin, "The Popular Song," ibid., 695.

60. "The Growth of Music Publishing," *MTR,* special issue, *World's Fair Number* (June 1904): 39; Arthur D. Pratt, "The Diary of a Popular Song," *Puck,* Sept. 13, 1905, 6–8; Tompkins, "Making of a Popular Song," 748; Goldberg, *Tin Pan Alley,* 219.

61. J. Peter Burkholder, "Ives, Charles," *Grove Music Online,* ed. L. Macy, www .grovemusic.com, accessed June 5, 2008; Daniel Albright, ed., *Modernism and Music* (Chicago, 2004), 154–162; Richard Crawford, *America's Musical Life: A History* (New York, 2001), 495–523.

62. On the interconnection of consumption and national identity, see Charles McGovern, *Sold American: Consumption and Citizenship, 1890–1945* (Chapel Hill, N.C., 2006); Lizabeth Cohen, *A Consumer's Republic: The Politics of Mass Consumption in Postwar America* (New York, 2003).

3. Music without Musicians

1. Clarence Flynn, "The Sound-Reproducing Machine as a Music Teacher," *Etude* (Dec. 1919): 789; "The Democracy of Music Achieved by Invention," *Current Literature* 42 (June 1907): 670; Robert Haven Schauffler, "Mission of Mechanical Music," *Century* 89 (Dec. 1914): 298; Carroll Brent Chilton, "A Musical Caliban," *Independent* Apr. 11, 1907, 841. The final *Etude* quotation appeared in *VoV* 2 (May 1907): 10.

2. Quoted in Dave Laing, "A Voice without a Face: Popular Music and the Phonograph in the 1890s," *Popular Music* 10 (1991): 3–4.

3. On the phenomenological and ontological dimensions of the phonograph, see Friedrich A. Kittler, *Gramophone, Film, Typewriter,* trans. Geoffrey Winthrop-Young (Stanford, Calif., 1999); Douglas Kahn, "Track Organology," *October* 55 (Winter 1990): 67–78; Lisa Gitelman, *Scripts, Grooves, and Writing Machines: Representing Technology in the Edison Era* (Stanford, Calif., 1999); Eric W. Rothenbuhler and John Durham Peters, "Defining Phonography: An Experiment in Theory," *Musical Quarterly* 81 (Summer 1997): 242–264; Michael Chanan, *Repeated Takes: A Short History of Recording and Its Effects on Music* (New York, 1995); Chanan, *Musica Practica: The Social Practice of Western Music from Gregorian Chant to Postmodernism* (London, 1994); and Evan Eisenberg, *The Recording Angel: The Experience of Music from Aristotle to Zappa* (New York, 1987). On time in objects, see Jacques Attali, *Noise: The Political Economy of Music,* trans. Brian Massumi (1977; Minneapolis, 1985).

4. *Biennial Census of Manufactures: 1925* (Washington, 1928), 1066, 1082. In 1923 197,000 player-pianos were produced, whose combined value was $61.8 million; in the same year 997,000 phonographs were manufactured, valued at $57 million.

5. Arthur W. J. G. Ord-Hume, *Barrel Organ: The Story of the Mechanical Organ and Its Repair* (South Brunswick, N.J., 1978); Arthur W. J. G. Ord-Hume, *Musical Box: A History and Collector's Guide* (London, 1980); Cynthia A. Hoover, *Music Machines— American Style: A Catalogue of the Exhibition* (Washington, D.C., 1971); Thomas B. Holmes, "Music Machines," in *International Encyclopedia of Communications* (New York, 1989), 3:111.

6. On the history of automata, see Thomas L. Hankins and Robert J. Silverman,

Instruments and the Imagination (Princeton, N.J., 1995); and Gaby Wood, *Edison's Eve: A Magical History of the Quest for Mechanical Life* (New York, 2002). On the phonograph's roots in work on the telegraph and telephone, see, for example, Andre Millard, *America on Record: A History of Recorded Sound* (Cambridge, 1995), 17–36.

7. Harvey Roehl, *Player-piano Treasury: The Scrapbook History of the Mechanical Piano in America,* 2nd ed. (Vestal, N.Y.), 51; *Biennial Census of Manufactures: 1925,* 1066.

8. Leon Forrest Douglass, "Memoirs of Leon Forrest Douglass (Condensed)," series 2, box 2, folders 50–53, HAG-ALD; B. L. Aldridge, "Confidential History," pp. 35 and 41, series 1, box 1, HAG-ALD. See also *VoV* 5 (July 1910), 2.

9. Dick Hebdige, "Object as Image: The Italian Scooter Cycle," in *The Consumer Society Reader,* ed. Martyn Lee (n.p., 2000), 142–143. Barthes quoted ibid.

10. Wolfgang Schivelbusch, *The Railway Journey: The Industrialization of Time and Space in the 19th Century* (Berkeley, 1986), ch. 2.

11. David Nasaw, *Going Out: The Rise and Fall of Public Amusements* (New York, 1993), 120–134; Q. David Bowers, *Put Another Nickel In: A History of Coin-Operated Pianos and Orchestrions* (Vestal, N.Y., 1966), 81, 95; Roehl, *Player-piano Treasury,* 101–150. On dealers at picnics and parades, see *VoV* 8 (Oct. 1913): 17. On phonographs in public, see *MT* 36 (Dec. 5, 1908): 105.

12. Q. David Bowers, *Encyclopedia of Automatic Musical Instruments* (Vestal, N.Y., 1972), 309, 739.

13. Alfred Dolge, *Pianos and Their Makers* (Covina, Calif., 1911), 1:328–333, quotation on 329.

14. Ibid., 1:330–331, quotation on 330; Aeolian Company, *The Aeolian Company, Aeolians, Aeolian Orchestrelles, Aeolian Pipe-Organs, and the Pianolas* (New York, 1901), HAG-TR.

15. Dolge, *Pianos and Their Makers,* 1:332; ibid. (Covina, Calif., 1913), 2:33–34; Richard K. Lieberman, *Steinway and Sons* (New Haven, Conn., 1995), 127.

16. "Knabe Player-piano Style J," advertisement, *New York Tribune,* Mar. 26, 1916.

17. Aeolian Company, *Catalogue of the Aeolian,* trade cat., n.d., p. 9, UMD-HC-MMI.

18. Harold Vincent Milligan, "The Music in Your Home," *Woman's Home Companion,* Apr. 1920, 36; Alvin Langdon Coburn, "The Pianola as Means of Personal Expression," *Sackbut* (London) 1, no. 2 (1920). A copy of the latter can be found in box 122, folder 428, WUSTL-WG.

19. See Arthur Whiting, "The Mechanical Player," *Yale Review* 8 (July 1919): 828–835; "Music Ex Machina," *Atlantic Monthly,* Nov. 1913, 714–716; "Piano-Players, Human and Mechanical," *Literary Digest* (June 1913), 1376; Gustav Kobbé, *The Pianolist: A Guide for Pianola Players* (New York, 1907); Frederick Kitchener, "Popular Music and Its Popularity," *The Player Monthly,* no. 1 (1910); Brent Chilton, "A Musical

Caliban," 838–844; Edwin Evans, "Pianola Music," *Musical Times* 62 (Nov. 1, 1921): 761–764; Harry Drake, *The Player-piano Explained* (London, 1922).

20. Adam Carroll, interview by Nelson Barden, 1969, ed. Richard J. Howe, Ampico files, UMD-HC-IPA; Angelico Valerio, interview by Nelson Barden, 1969, ed. Richard J. Howe, Ampico files, UMD-HC-IPA.

21. *Biennial Census of Manufactures: 1921* (Washington, D.C., 1924), 1153; *Biennial Census of Manufactures: 1925,* 1066; *Biennial Census of Manufactures: 1931* (Washington, D.C., 1935), 1128–1136.

22. United States Bureau of the Census, *Census Reports,* vol. 10, *Manufactures: Part IV Special Reports on Selected Industries* (Washington, D.C., 1902), 182, 185.

23. *New Victor Records,* May 1916.

24. "Notebook of General Operating and Sales Statistics," box 1, folder 16, HAG-ALD; Aldridge, "Confidential History," 6–8; Peter Martland, "A Business History of the Gramophone Company Ltd., 1897–1918" (Ph.D. diss., Cambridge University, 1992), 48–56; E. R. Fenimore Johnson, *His Master's Voice Was Eldridge R. Johnson* (Milford, Del., 1974), 54–55.

25. On Johnson's willingness to sell the business, see Eldridge Reeves Johnson to Elsie Reeves Johnson, 1900, black box "Victor Talking Machine Co., 1895–1900," folder 1900, EMI.

26. Marsha Siefert, "The Audience at Home: The Early Recording Industry and the Marketing of Musical Taste," in *Audiencemaking: How the Media Create the Audience,* ed. James S. Ettema and D. Charles Whitney (Thousand Oaks, Calif., 1994), 186–214; Siefert, "Aesthetics, Technology, and the Capitalization of Culture: How the Talking Machine Became a Musical Instrument," *Science in Context* 8, no. 2 (1995): 417–449. On cultural capital, see Pierre Bourdieu, *Distinction: A Social Critique of the Judgment of Taste,* trans. Richard Nice (Cambridge, Mass., 1984).

27. Agreement between Eldridge R. Johnson and the Gramophone and Typewriter Ltd., signed Sept. 4, 1901, black box "Victor Talking Machine Co.—Agreements," EMI. This agreement was renewed and expanded in 1904 and 1907. Copies of these agreements can be found ibid.

28. Roland Gelatt, *The Fabulous Phonograph, 1877–1977,* 2nd ed. (New York, 1977), 116, 121; F. W. Gaisberg, *The Music Goes Round* (New York, 1942); Jerrold Northrop Moore, *Sound Revolutions: A Biography of Fred Gaisberg, Founding Father of Commercial Sound Recording* (London, 1999).

29. Gaisberg, *The Music Goes Round,* 30.

30. Moore, *Sound Revolutions,* 61–62.

31. According to another source, the idea of charging more for records by eminent performers came from Chaliapin himself. Jacques Lowe Russell Miller and Roger Boar, *The Incredible Music Machine,* quoted in Siefert, "Aesthetics, Technology, and the Capitalization of Culture," 436.

32. See also Gelatt, *The Fabulous Phonograph,* 112–113.

33. Ibid., 117; Jack L. Caidin, "Caruso Recordings: A Discography," in *Enrico Caruso: His Life and Death,* ed. Dorothy Caruso (New York, 1945), 289; S. P. Martland, "Caruso's First Recordings: Myth and Reality," *ARSC Journal* 25, no. 2 (1994): 192–201.

34. Consolidated Talking Machine Company, *Improved Gramophone, Manufactured Exclusively by Eldridge Reeves Johnson* [trade catalogue, ca. 1901], box 1, "Victor Miscellany" folder, HAG-PEN.

35. Lawrence W. Levine, *Highbrow, Lowbrow: The Emergence of Cultural Hierarchy in America* (Cambridge, Mass., 1988), 85–104; John Dizikes, *Opera in America: A Cultural History* (New Haven, Conn., 1993); Richard Crawford, *The American Musical Landscape* (Berkeley, Calif., 1993), 87; John Freund, "Italians at the Opera," *Musical America* (Nov. 27, 1909); Jay R. G. Teran, "The New York Opera Audience, 1825–1974" (Ph.D. diss., New York University, 1974); Luciano J. Iorizzo and Salvatore Mondello, *The Italian-Americans* (New York, 1971), 91; John Rosselli, "The Opera Business and the Italian Immigrant Community in Latin America, 1820–1930," *Past and Present* 127 (May 1990): 155–182; "Sympathy Vote in St. Louis," *NYT,* Nov. 29, 1906, 2.

36. Gaisberg, *The Music Goes Round,* 83; [*Philadelphia*] *Evening Bulletin,* Dec. 11, 1933, box 1, folder "Sooy Memoirs—Correspondence," HAG-PEN.

37. F. W. Gaisberg, "Notes from My Diary: Enrico Caruso," *Gramophone* (Jan. 1944): 117.

38. Gaisberg, *The Music Goes Round,* 85, 181; Martland, "A Business History of the Gramophone Company Ltd.," 365. See also the detailed description of the recording process in Raymond Sooy, "Memoir," HAG-PEN.

39. Gaisberg, "Notes from My Diary," 117; Sooy, "Memoir"; *Courier Post,* Dec. 20, 1938, box 1, folder "Sooy Memoirs—Correspondence," HAG-PEN.

40. Quoted in Gelatt, *The Fabulous Phonograph,* 120.

41. *Victor Talking Machine New Records* (Aug. 1904), HAG-TR; *Victor Records* (1908), HAG-TR.

42. On the policing of cultural fields, see Pierre Bourdieu, "The Field of Cultural Production, or: The Economic World Reversed," in *The Field of Cultural Production: Essays on Art and Literature* (New York, 1993), 29–73.

43. Joseph Horowitz, *Wagner Nights: An American History* (Berkeley, 1994).

44. Victor Talking Machine Company, *The Victor,* 1911, HAG-TR; Victor Talking Machine Company, *Red Seal Ten-Inch Records by the Greatest Artists of the Musical World,* 1903, NMAH-NTLC; *TMW* 1 (Feb. 15, 1905): 15.

45. On the politics of culture, see Levine, *Highbrow, Lowbrow,* 83–242; Raymond Williams, *Culture and Society, 1780–1950* (New York, 1958); Terry Eagleton, *The Idea of Culture* (Oxford, 2000); John Storey, *Inventing Popular Culture* (Oxford, 2003).

46. Walter Benjamin, "The Work of Art in the Age of Mechanical Reproduction," in *Illuminations,* ed. Hannah Arendt (New York, 1969), 217–251.

47. Walter J. Ong, *The Presence of the Word: Some Prolegomena for Cultural and Religious History* (New Haven, Conn., 1967).

48. Allan Sekula, "On the Invention of Photographic Meaning," *Artforum* 13 (Jan. 1975): 39.

49. According to phonograph historian Raymond Wile, neither the Gramophone Company nor Victor was the first company to issue records with red paper labels, but no other producer had created a series around the color of paper labels or used them as a special seal of approval. See Siefert, "Aesthetics, Technology, and the Capitalization of Culture," 437n20.

50. On this kind of antieconomy, see Bourdieu, "The Field of Cultural Production," 39–40.

51. Leon Douglass to dealers, Mar. 9, 1903, "Victor Miscellany," box 1, HAG-PEN; Eldridge R. Johnson to Gramophone Company, Oct. 13, 1904, black box "Victor Talking Machine Co., 1895–1900," folder 1904, EMI; *VoV* 4 (Jan. 1909): 5.

52. *TMW,* Jan. 15, 1905, 3.

53. Frank L. Dyer to C. H. Wilson, May 16, 1908, reel 216, *TAE;* Studs Terkel, *And They All Sang: Adventures of an Eclectic Disc Jockey* (New York, 2005), xvii.

54. For a closer analysis of Victor's advertising, see David Suisman, "The Sound of Money: Music, Machines, and Markets, 1890–1925" (Ph.D. diss., Columbia University, 2002), 155–196.

55. Frank Presbrey, *The History and Development of Advertising* (Garden City, N.Y., 1929), 404–405; James D. Norris, *Advertising and the Transformation of American Society, 1865–1920* (New York, 1990), 74; Siefert, "Aesthetics, Technology, and the Capitalization of Culture," 432.

56. Aldridge, "Confidential History," 33–34, 57; Gelatt, *The Fabulous Phonograph,* 69, 142; Presbrey, *The History and Development of Advertising,* 405.

57. Eldridge R. Johnson to Gramophone Company, Jan. 27, 1903, black box "Victor Talking Machine Co., 1895–1900," folder 1903, EMI.

58. Stephen R. Fox, *The Mirror Makers: A History of American Advertising and Its Creators* (Urbana, Ill., 1997), 129–130; Craig H. Roell, *The Piano in America, 1890–1940* (Chapel Hill, N.C., 1989), 175–177; Elsie S. Hebert, "Raymond Rubicam," in *The Ad Men and Women: A Biographical Dictionary of Advertising,* ed. Edd Applegate (Westport, Conn., 1994), 287–288. On N. W. Ayer & Son's influence on modern advertising practice, see John Vivian, "Francis Wayland Ayer," in *The Ad Men and Women,* 1–13; N. W. Ayer & Son, *Forty Years of Advertising* (Boston, 1909), 17–19.

59. Aldridge, "Confidential History," 33–34, 38.

60. Daniel Pope, *The Making of Modern Advertising* (New York, 1983), 43–45; *Philadelphia Ledger,* Dec. 9, 1924, 26, quoted in *VoV* 20 (Jan. 1925): 17.

61. *VoV* 11 (Feb. 1916): 26.

62. Reprinted in *VoV* 2 (May 1907): 8.

63. *Victor Records 1925* (Camden, N.J., 1925), HAG-TR. On economies of scope, see Alfred D. Chandler, Jr., *Scale and Scope: The Dynamics of Industrial Capitalism* (Cambridge, Mass., 1990).

64. For more interpretive readings of Nipper, see Siefert, "The Audience at Home," 197; Michael Taussig, *Mimesis and Alterity: A Particular History of the Senses* (New York, 1993); William Howland Kenney, *Recorded Music in American Life: The Phonograph and Popular Memory* (New York, 1999), 55; Eisenberg, *The Recording Angel*, 63–64; John Picker, *Victorian Soundscapes* (New York, 2003), 142–145. On fidelity, see also Emily Thompson, "Machines, Music, and the Quest for Fidelity: Marketing the Edison Phonograph in America, 1877–1925," in *Musical Quarterly* 79 (Spring 1995): 131–171.

65. Leonard Petts, comp., *The Story of "Nipper" and the "His Master's Voice" Picture Painted by Francis Barraud* (Bournemouth, Eng., 1973); "Early Company History," box 3, folder 47, HAG-ALD; Oliver Berliner to Robert W. Wythes, June 25, 1971, folder "Victor Talking Machine—Misc. Papers," CCHS; Martland, "A Business History of the Gramophone Company Ltd.," 192–200. The breathtaking scope of Nipper's many iterations can be gleaned from the 1022-page *Collectors Guide to "His Master's Voice" Nipper Souvenirs*, comp. Ruth Edge and Leonard Petts (Reading, Eng., 1997). The Nipper trademark had been registered in the United States by Berliner, who transferred the rights to Johnson, but the latter did not begin to use the trademark until after the rights were reaffirmed in the 1901 agreement with the Gramophone Company.

66. Edgar Hutto, Jr., "Emile Berliner, Eldridge Johnson, and the Victor Talking Machine Company," *Journal of the Audio Engineering Society* 25 (Oct. 1977): 669; Lisa Gitelman, *Always Already New: Media, History, and the Data of Culture* (Cambridge, Mass., 2006), 80–81.

67. "How a Man with an Idea Made Millions in Twelve Years," *NYT*, Aug. 28, 1910; Ulysses "Jim" Walsh, "Early Victor Photographs [*sic*] and Catalogs, Parts III," *Hobbies*, Mar. 1968, 37; "Early Company History," HAG-ALD; Martland, "A Business History of the Gramophone Company Ltd.," 246–250; Gelatt, *The Fabulous Phonograph*, 108.

68. "Use the Victor Trade-Mark," *VoV* 11 (Nov. 1916): 203. Emphasis in the original.

69. *VoV* 19 (Aug. 1924): 8.

70. Frank Andrews, "'His Master's Voice': The Discovery of the Photograph Showing the Original Painting," in *The Story of "Nipper" and the "His Master's Voice" Picture Painted by Francis Barraud*, 4.

71. Nasaw, *Going Out*, 125.

72. *The Phonograph and How to Use It* (New York, 1900). On Edison's ideas from the 1870s, see Thomas A. Edison, "The Phonograph and Its Future," *North American Review* 126 (May–June 1878): 527–536.

73. Picker, *Victorian Soundscapes*, 126–133; Arthur Conan Doyle, "The Mazarin Stone" (1921), in *The Complete Sherlock Holmes*, vol. 2 (New York, 2003); Agatha Chris-

tie, *The Murder of Roger Ackroyd* (London, 1926); Leonard C. McChesney (hereafter LCM) to Frank L. Dyer, Aug. 25, 1908, reel 216, *TAE.* Picker notes that the phonograph also figured in Conan Doyle's "The Voice of Science."

74. On Edison's marketing to the "masses," see LCM to William E. Gilmore, Feb. 21, 1907 [1908], reel 216, *TAE;* LCM to Thomas A. Edison, Dec. 9, 1907, ibid.; LCM to William E. Gilmore, Aug. 25, 1908, ibid.

75. "Record Unit Sales, Domestic and Export, 1901–45," in vertical file "Hit Records, Etc.," Victor Talking Machine Co. files, CCHS.

76. *TMW,* Oct. 15, 1905, quoted in Gelatt, *The Fabulous Phonograph,* 141–142; "Record Unit Sales, Domestic and Export, 1901–45," CCHS; Gramophone Company [William Barry Owen?] to Eldridge R. Johnson, Nov. 1904, black box "Victor Talking Machine Co., 1895–1900," folder 1904, EMI. On the Red Seal School, see Aldridge, "Confidential History," 63.

77. Joan Shelley Rubin, *The Making of Middlebrow Culture* (Chapel Hill, N.C., 1992); Janice A. Radway, *A Feeling for Books: The Book-of-the-Month Club, Literary Taste, and Middle-Class Desire* (Chapel Hill, N.C., 1997).

78. Gitelman, *Always Already New,* 68–69, 76. On democracy and consumer goods, see Charles McGovern, *Sold American: Consumption and Citizenship, 1890–1945* (Chapel Hill, N.C., 2006); Eric Foner, *The Story of American Freedom* (New York, 1998), 147–151; Daniel Boorstin, *The Americans: The Democratic Experience* (New York, 1973); Richard Tedlow, *New and Improved: The Story of Mass Marketing in America* (Boston, 1996), 16.

79. Fenimore Johnson to B. L. Aldridge, May 13, 1958, HAG-ALD; Eldridge R. Johnson to Gramophone & Typewriter Company, July 17, 1907, subject file Enrico Caruso, Recorded Sound Reference Center, Library of Congress; Mary Molek, *Guide to Eldridge Reeves Johnson: News Stories, 1927–1945* (n.p., 1973), in box 1, folder RCA-VTM Biography Eldridge Johnson, HAG-ALD; *NYT,* Nov. 15, 1945.

4. The Traffic in Voices

1. A. J. Liebling, *Between Meals: An Appetite for Paris* (1959; New York, 1986), 44. The critic Alfred Kazin recalled a remarkably similar experience in his own childhood in New York. Caruso, he recalled, "inspired in my father and mother such helpless, intimidated adoration that I came to think of what was always humbly referred to as *his golden voice* as the invocation of a god. . . . Caruso . . . seemed to me the echo of some outrageously pagan voice at the roof of the world." Alfred Kazin, *A Walker in the City* (New York, 1951), 63–64.

2. Studs Terkel, *And They All Sang: Adventures of an Eclectic Disc Jockey* (New York, 2005), xviii; *Musical America,* Nov. 20, 1909, in NYPL-LOCKE106; "Mouse Risks Life to Hear Caruso Sing," *Boston Traveler,* Aug. 31, 1909, ibid.

3. *A Night at the Opera,* dir. Sam Wood, 1935; Eric Hobsbawm, "The Caruso of

Jazz," in *Uncommon People: Resistance, Rebellion, and Jazz* (New York, 1998); Eddie Cantor, "'Greatest Voice I Ever Heard,'" [unidentified newspaper clipping], Jan. 9, 1963, Caruso clippings file, Theater Division, New York Public Library; *Fitzcarraldo,* dir. Werner Herzog, 1982. Other examples include Charles Dodge, *Any Resemblance Is Purely Coincidental* (New Albion Records, 1994, NA O43 CD); and Barbara Paul, *A Cadenza for Caruso* (New York, 1984).

4. The first Edison quotation is from Raymond R. Wile, comp., *Edison Disc Artists and Records, 1910–1929,* 2nd ed., ed. Ronald Dethlefson (Brooklyn, N.Y., 1990), 87 (emphasis in the original); the second is from Leonard DeGraff, "Confronting the Mass Market: Thomas Edison and the Entertainment Phonograph," *Business and Economic History* 24, no. 1 (1995): 93.

5. See Richard Schickel, *Intimate Strangers: The Culture of Celebrity* (Garden City, N.Y., 1985), 29–30.

6. Edward L. Bernays, *Biography of an Idea: Memoirs of Public Relations Counsel* (New York, 1965), 138.

7. Thomas E. Dow, Jr., "An Analysis of Weber's Work on Charisma," *British Journal of Sociology* 29 (Mar. 1978): 83–84.

8. Dana Gooly, "Franz Liszt: The Virtuoso as Strategist," in *The Musician as Entrepreneur, 1700–1914: Managers, Charlatans, and Idealists,* ed. William Weber (Bloomington, Ind., 2004), 145–161; Neil Harris, *Humbug: The Art of P. T. Barnum* (Chicago, 1973); Harris, "John Philip Sousa and the Culture of Reassurance," in *Cultural Excursions: Marketing Appetites and Cultural Tastes in Modern America* (Chicago, 1990), 198–232; Leo Braudy, *The Frenzy of Renown: Fame and Its History* (New York, 1986), 499–504.

9. *VoV* 19 (July 1924).

10. *VoV* 5 (Mar.–Apr. 1910): 4 (emphasis in the original).

11. Figures for Caruso's income come from Victor Talking Machine Company to Alfred Seligsberg, Jan. 27, 1917, and other documents in Caruso income tax file, New York Metropolitan Opera, and from C. G. Child to Gramophone Company, June 6, 1919, subject file "Enrico Caruso (Peter Martland Materials)," Recorded Sound Division, Library of Congress. Geraldine Farrar, probably the second-highest-paid Victor artist, was guaranteed $17,000 a year. On Caruso's wealth, see *Toledo News Bee,* July 8, 1909, in NYPL-LOCKE106. See also *Atlanta Journal,* Feb. 28, 1909, ibid., and *Boston Herald,* Oct. 9, 1909, ibid. The estimate of $3 million comes from B. L. Aldridge, "Confidential History," p. 35, series 1, box 1, HAG-ALD. See, for royalty rates, ibid., 36, and Enrico Caruso, recording contract, 1906, in subject file "Enrico Caruso," Recorded Sound Division, Library of Congress.

12. *VoV* 2 (May 1907): 6; Victor Talking Machine Company, *Red Seal Ten-Inch Records by the Greatest Artists of the Musical World* (n.p., 1903), NMAH-NTLC; Aldridge, "Confidential History," 33–34. See also Mark Katz, "Making America More Musical through the Phonograph, 1900–1930," *American Music* 16 (Winter 1998): 455–457.

On the transformation of advertising in this era, see T. J. Jackson Lears, "From Salvation to Self-Realization: Advertising and the Therapeutic Roots of the Consumer Culture, 1880–1930," in *The Culture of Consumption: Critical Essays in American History, 1880–1980,* ed. T. J. Jackson Lears and Richard Wightman Fox (New York, 1983), 3–38; and Roland Marchand, *Advertising the American Dream: Making Way for Modernity, 1920–1940* (Berkeley, Calif., 1985).

13. "Why You Should Be a Victor Dealer," *VoV* 4 (May 1909): 3. A copy of the Christmas advertisement can be found in box 458C, DeVincent Collection of Illustrated American Sheet Music, National Museum of American History.

14. Victor Talking Machine Company, *The Victor* (Camden, N.J., 1908), HAG-TR.

15. See *VoV* 8 (Feb. 1913): cover; *VoV* 8 (Apr. 1913): cover; Victor Talking Machine Company, *The Victor,* in HAG-TR; and *New Victor Records,* June 1914; *New Victor Records,* Sept. 1919; *New Victor Records,* May 1921 (available in NMAH-ATLC). Undated samples of the posters can be found in NMAH-NTLC.

16. "Victor News Service Spreads Artist Publicity," *VoV* 19 (July 1924).

17. *VoV* 12 (Aug. 1917): 155; "Victor News Service Spreads Artist Publicity."

18. See also "Which Is Which?" advertisement featuring Caruso, May 1908, series "Phonographs," box 1, folder 34, NMAH-WAR.

19. *Philadelphia Inquirer,* July 28, 1914, in Alma Gluck Collection, box 6 (scrapbook, 1914–15), Performing Arts Division, Library of Congress; *Atlanta Journal,* Feb. 28, 1909, in NYPL-LOCKE106. See also "The Deathless Voice," *NYT,* Aug. 14, 1921.

20. Albert E. Wier, comp., *The Victor Rapid Record Selector* (New York, 1916). Emphasis in the original.

21. William Leiss, Stephen Kline, and Sut Jhally, *Social Communication in Advertising: Persons, Products and Images of Well-Being,* 2nd ed. (London, 1990).

22. Warren I. Susman, "'Personality' and the Making of Twentieth-Century Culture," in *Culture as History: The Transformation of American Society in the Twentieth Century* (New York, 1984), 271–285. For a critique of Susman's analysis of personality, see Andrew R. Heinze, "*Schizophrenia Americana:* Aliens, Alienists and the 'Personality Shift' of Twentieth-Century Culture," *American Quarterly* 55 (June 2003): 227–256. The etymological development of the word *personality* underscores its link with public performance. It comes from the Latin *persona,* meaning a stage mask or, later, a character in a play. Between the seventeenth century and the nineteenth, this usage gave way to its modern meaning designating a specific or unique quality, comparable to individuality. In the twentieth century, traces of the original meaning resurfaced in the emphasis on strong or lively personalities, particularly in reference to celebrities, who were often stage performers. Meanwhile, the multiple meanings of *personality*—a mask, a role, an individual identity—intersected at this time in the works of Sigmund Freud and other psychoanalytical theorists. Raymond Williams, *Keywords: A Vocabulary of Culture and Society,* rev. ed. (New York, 1983), 232–235; Stuart Ewen, *PR! A Social History of Spin* (New York, 1996), 131–145.

23. *NYT,* Dec. 4, 1904; *New York American,* Apr. 25, 1906, in NYPL-LOCKE105; *New York Sun,* Mar. 5, 1910, in NYLP-LOCKE106; *Los Angeles Examiner,* Mar. 24, 1910, ibid.; *New York Sun,* May 16, 1910, ibid. See also "Caruso in Role of Practical Joker" (source unidentified), July 1906, and similar articles in NYPL-LOCKE105 and NYPL-LOCKE106.

24. *NYT,* Dec. 8, 1906; *NYT,* July 4, 1907; *NYT,* Nov. 17, 1906. For a complete account, see David Suisman, "Welcome to the Monkey House: Enrico Caruso and the First Celebrity Trial of the Twentieth Century," *Believer* 2 (June 2004): 15–20.

25. *New York Globe,* Nov. 9, 1905, in NYPL-LOCKE105; *New York American,* Jan. 10, 1906, ibid. On Valentino, see Gaylyn Studlar, *This Mad Masquerade: Stardom and Masculinity in the Jazz Age* (New York, 1996), 150–198. On the politics of black masculinity, see Gail Bederman, *Manliness and Civilization: A Cultural History of Gender and Race in the United States, 1880–1917* (Chicago, 1995); Hazel V. Carby, *Race Men* (Cambridge, Mass., 1998).

26. Susman, "'Personality' and the Making of Twentieth-Century Culture," 280.

27. John Ciardi quoted in Terkel, *And They All Sang,* xvii–xviii.

28. Roland Barthes, "The Grain of the Voice," in *Image—Music—Text,* trans. Stephen Heath (New York, 1977), 179–189; Walter Ong, *The Presence of the Word: Some Prolegomena for Cultural and Religious History* (New Haven, Conn., 1967), 17–110; and P. Mario Marafioti, *Caruso's Method of Voice Production: The Scientific Culture of the Voice* (1922; New York, 1981).

29. *New York Tribune,* Nov. 23, 1903, quoted in Jean-Pierre Mouchon, "Enrico Caruso: L'homme et l'artiste" (Ph.D. diss., Université de Paris–Sorbonne, 1980), 3:1001–1002 ; John Dizikes, *Opera in America: A Cultural History* (New Haven, 1993), 397.

30. Bernays, *Biography of an Idea,* 198.

31. Ibid., 129–146, quotations on 138 and 143–144; Ewen, *PR!* 8.

32. *VoV* 19 (July 1924). Emphasis in the original.

33. Q. X. Z., "The Record Makers Give a Concert in Pulaski, Virginia, 40 Years Ago," *Hobbies,* Apr. 1957, 30–35, quotation on 30; Q. X. Z., "The Record Makers Give a Concert in Pulaski, Virginia, 40 Years Ago," *Hobbies,* May 1957, 30–35, quotation on 35. This two-part article appeared as a special guest-authored column in Jim Walsh's Favorite Pioneer Recording Artists series, for many years one of the few places to find serious discussion of pre-1925 vernacular recordings. The author used a pseudonym, she explained, only because she did not want the people of Pulaski to deduce her age from the fact she had been seventeen years old at the time of the concert forty years earlier.

34. Q. X. Z., "The Record Makers," Apr. 1957, 30.

35. Dizikes, *Opera in America,* 397; Dorothy Caruso, *Enrico Caruso: His Life and Death* (New York, 1945), esp. 58–62 and 75, quotation on 58.

36. On Caruso as a symbol among African Americans, see "Record of Our Own Singers," *Competitor* 3 (Jan. 1921): 6; "Caruso's Voice," advertisement, *Crisis* 22 (Sept.

1921): 236; and advertisement from the *New York Age*, quoted in Ann Charters, *Nobody: The Story of Bert Williams* (New York, 1970), 131.

37. Tim Brooks, *Lost Sounds: Blacks and the Birth of the Recording Industry, 1890–1919* (Urbana, Ill., 2004), 437; Martin Wolfson to Jay Robert G. Teran, Nov. 30, 1971, quoted in Jay Robert G. Teran, "The New York Opera Audience, 1825–1974" (Ph.D. diss., New York University, 1974), 97–98; John Freund, "Italians at the Opera," *Musical America*, Nov. 1909, in NYPL-LOCKE106.

38. Tim Brooks, *The Columbia Master Discography*, vol. 1, *U.S. Matrix Series 1 through 4999, 1901–10, with a History of the Columbia Phonograph Company to 1934* (Westport, Conn., 1999). For an example of Columbia's Victor-like advertising, see "Grand Opera on Talking Machines in Your Own Home," advertisement, *Town & Country*, Apr. 4, 1903, a copy of which can be found in Phonographs, box 1, folder 5, NMAH-WAR.

39. Marsha Siefert, "The Audience at Home: The Early Recording Industry and the Marketing of Musical Taste," in *Audiencemaking: How the Media Create the Audience*, ed. James S. Ettema and D. Charles Whitney (Thousand Oaks, Calif., 1994), 192, 199; Siefert, "Aesthetics, Technology, and the Capitalization of Culture: How the Talking Machine Became a Musical Instrument," *Science in Context* 8 (1995): 440; DeGraff, "Confronting the Mass Market," 88–96, esp. 92; Andre Millard, *Edison and the Business of Innovation* (Baltimore, 1990). For Edison catalogues, see Thomas A. Edison, Inc., *Edison Re-Creations* (Orange, N.J., [1920]), NMAH-NTLC, and the numerous examples found in Phonographs, box 1, folder 19, NMAH-WAR.

40. Roland Gelatt, *The Fabulous Phonograph, 1877–1977*, 2nd ed. (New York, 1977), 166; DeGraff, "Confronting the Mass Market," 94; *Edison Phonograph Monthly* (July 1909): 1, quoted in Siefert, "The Audience at Home," 202.

41. *Biennial Census of Manufactures: 1925* (Washington, D.C., 1928), 1066. The number of regular player-pianos includes 4,500 automatic and electric pianos.

42. Nelson Barden, interview of Angelico Valerio, 1969, ed. Richard J. Howe, Ampico files, UMD-HC-IPA.

43. "Albums as Mileposts in a Musical Century," *NYT*, Jan. 3, 2000; Enrico Caruso, *Caruso 2000* (BMG/RCA Victor, 2000); Allan Kozinn, "Have You Heard the New Caruso? (No Kidding)," *NYT*, Feb. 20, 2000. On Caruso in novels, movies, and advertisements, see Barbara Paul, *A Cadenza for Caruso* (New York, 1974); Mayra Montero, *The Messenger*, trans. Edith Grossman (New York, 1999); *The Great Caruso*, dir. Richard Thorpe, 1951; *Fitzcarraldo*, dir. Herzog; Paris Garters advertisement, *Literary Digest*, June 23, 1934, 29.

5. Musical Properties

1. *Arguments before the Committees on Patents of the Senate and House of Representatives, Conjointly, on the Bills S.6330 and H.R. 19853, to Amend and Consolidate the*

Acts respecting Copyright, June 6–9, 1906 (Washington, D.C., 1906), 23 (hereafter cited as *Hearings,* June 1906); Neil Harris, "John Philip Sousa and the Culture of Reassurance," in *Cultural Excursions: Marketing Appetites and Cultural Tastes in Modern America* (Chicago, 1990), 198–232.

2. Story quoted in Paul Goldstein, *Copyright's Highway: From Gutenberg to the Celestial Jukebox* (Stanford, Calif., 2003), 6; Jane M. Gaines, *Contested Culture: The Image, the Voice, and the Law* (Chapel Hill, N.C., 1991).

3. Morton J. Horwitz, *The Transformation of American Law, 1870–1960: The Crisis of Legal Orthodoxy* (New York, 1992), 145–167, quotations on 145, 147, 156, and 165; Kenneth J. Vandevelde, "The New Property of the Nineteenth Century: The Development of the Modern Concept of Property," *Buffalo Law Review* 29 (1980): 325–367.

4. Martin J. Sklar, *The Corporate Reconstruction of American Capitalism, 1890–1916: The Market, the Law, and Politics* (New York, 1988), esp. 43–51; Horwitz, *The Transformation of American Law,* 65–107; Alan Trachtenberg, *The Incorporation of America: Culture and Society in the Gilded Age* (New York, 1982). On the abstraction of market relations underpinning this shift, see Jean-Christophe Agnew, *Worlds Apart: The Market and the Theater in Anglo-American Thought, 1550–1750* (Cambridge, 1986).

5. David F. Noble, *America by Design: Science, Technology, and the Rise of Corporate Capitalism* (New York, 1977), 10, 83–108; Roland Gelatt, *The Fabulous Phonograph, 1877–1977,* 2nd ed. (New York, 1977), 132; Howard W. Hayes to Thomas A. Edison, Feb. 27, 1903, reel 188, *TAE;* Peter Martland, "A Business History of the Gramophone Company Ltd., 1897–1918," (Ph.D. diss., Cambridge University, 1992), 38; Tim Brooks, *The Columbia Master Discography,* vol. 1, *U.S. Matrix Series 1 through 4999, 1901–10, with a History of the Columbia Phonograph Company to 1934* (Westport, Conn., 1999), 4–6; [B. L. Aldridge], "Untitled Chronology [I]," box 1, folder "VTM—Chronology, General," HAG-PEN; Siva Vaidhyanathan, *Copyrights and Copywrongs: The Rise of Intellectual Property and How It Threatens Creativity* (New York, 2001), 92–93.

6. *Leeds & Catlin Co. v. Victor Talking Machine Co.,* 213 U.S. 301 (1909).

7. Eldridge R. Johnson, "The Recent Supreme Court Decision; Its Effect; and the Future of the Talking Machine Business," *VoV* 4 (July 1909): 5. (Emphasis in the original.)

8. The overview given here is based on Carla Hesse, "The Rise of Intellectual Property, 700 B.C.–A.D. 2000: An Idea in the Balance," *Daedalus* 131 (Spring 2002): 26–45; Martin Kretschmer and Friedmann Kawohl, "The History and Philosophy of Copyright," in *Music and Copyright,* 2nd ed., ed. Simon Frith and Lee Marshall (New York, 2004), 21–53; and Hillel Schwartz, *The Culture of the Copy: Striking Likenesses, Unreasonable Facsimiles* (New York, 1996), 243.

9. Goldstein, *Copyright's Highway.* On common property and private property, see C. B. Macpherson, "The Meaning of Property," in *Property: Mainstream and Critical Positions,* ed. C. B. Macpherson (Toronto, 1978), 1–13.

10. Mark Rose, "The Author as Proprietor: *Donaldson v. Becket* and the Genealogy

of Modern Authorship," in *Of Authors and Origins: Essays on Copyright Law,* ed. Brad Sherman and Alain Strowel (Oxford, 1994), 23–56.

11. See William Lichtenwanger, "Music and Copyright Law in the United States," in *Music Publishing and Collecting: Essays in Honor of Donald W. Krummel,* ed. David Hunter (Urbana-Champaign, Ill., 1994), 69–94.

12. On piracy in England, see James Coover, comp., *Music Publishing, Copyright and Piracy in Victorian England* (London, 1985).

13. William W. Fisher III, "The Growth of Intellectual Property: A History of the Ownership of Ideas in the United States," 20, www.tfisher.org (accessed Oct. 22, 2007). For a current perspective, see Fisher, *Promises to Keep: Technology, Law, and the Future of Entertainment* (Stanford, Calif., 2004).

14. Michael Perelman, *Steal This Idea: Intellectual Property Rights and the Corporate Confiscation of Creativity* (New York, 2002), 10. On Copyleft, see Vaidhyanathan, *Copyrights and Copywrongs,* 153–159.

15. Lichtenwanger, "Music and Copyright Law in the United States," 72, 80–82; Gaines, *Contested Culture,* 42–83; *Bleistein v. Donaldson Lithographing Co.,* 188 U.S. 239 (1903).

16. Herman Finkelstein, "The Copyright Law: A Reappraisal," *University of Pennsylvania Law Review* 104 (June 1956): 1025; Lichtenwanger, "Music and Copyright Law in the United States," 84.

17. Data are taken from *Biennial United States Census of Manufactures: 1921* (Washington, D.C., 1924), 614, 1145, adjusted for inflation by using the Inflation Calculator at www.westegg.com/inflation (accessed Sept. 17, 2008), based on the Consumer Price Index. Figures for music printing and publishing were classified under the heading "Printing and Publishing" and were not included in "Musical Instruments and Phonographs." See also the data and summary in Department of Commerce and Labor, Bureau of the Census, *Manufactures, 1905* (Washington, D.C., 1908), 3:713, 800, and 4:239–251, 264–265.

18. Lucia S. Schultz, "Performing-Right Societies in the United States," *Notes,* 2nd ser., 35 (Mar. 1979): 513.

19. *Biennial United States Census of Manufactures: 1921,* 1145.

20. David Nasaw, *Going Out: The Rise and Fall of Public Amusements* (New York, 1993); Lewis A. Erenberg, *Steppin' Out: New York Nightlife and the Transformation of American Culture, 1890–1930* (Chicago, 1981), James P. Kraft, *Stage to Studio: Musicians and the Sound Revolution, 1890–1950* (Baltimore, 1996), 7.

21. Richard A. Posner, "The Law and Economics of Intellectual Property," *Daedalus* 131 (Spring 2002): 7.

22. The following account is based on *Hearings,* June 1906; *Arguments before the Committees on Patents of the Senate and House of Representatives, Conjointly, on the Bills S.6330 and H.R. 19853, to Amend and Consolidate the Acts respecting Copyright,* Dec.

7–11, 1906 (Washington, D.C., 1906), 23 (hereafter cited as *Hearings,* Dec. 1906); *Hearings before the Committees on Patents of the Senate and House of Representatives on Pending Bills to Amend and Consolidate the Acts Respecting Copyright,* Mar. 26–28, 1908 (Washington, D.C., 1908); memorandum from the National Piano Manufacturers Association of America, the National Phonograph Company (Edison), the Columbia Phonograph Company, and the Victor Talking Machine Company to U.S. secretary of state [Elihu Root], Oct. 1908, reel 216, *TAE;* Isidore Witmark and Isaac Goldberg, *From Ragtime to Swingtime: The Story of the House of Witmark* (New York, 1939), 295–311; *MT* 35 (Apr. 4, 1908): 1; *MT* 35 (Apr. 11, 1908): 43; *MT* 37 (Mar. 13, 1909): 5–6; *MTR* 46 (Apr. 11, 1908): 23; *MTR* 48 (Mar. 13, 1909): 44; Craig H. Roell, *The Piano in America, 1890–1940* (Chapel Hill, N.C., 1989), 59–64.

23. *Hearings,* June 1906, 26–31, 139–146; *Hearings,* Dec. 1906, 201–212, 233.

24. *Hearings,* June 1906, 77, 97, 110, 151, 156; *Hearings,* Dec. 1906, 26, 233.

25. Witmark and Goldberg, *From Ragtime to Swingtime,* 300.

26. John Philip Sousa, "The Menace of Mechanical Music," *Appleton's Journal* 8, no. 3 (1906): 278–284; Victor Talking Machine Company, *Victor Disk Talking Machine,* 1900, HAG-TR; Victor Talking Machine Company, *New Victor Records,* 1903, HAG-TR; *Hearings,* June 1906, 30–31; Frank Byrne, "The Recorded Sousa Marches—Story and Sound," liner notes for *Sousa Marches Played by the Sousa Band: The Complete Recordings* (Crystal Records, 2000), 29–30; untitled liner notes, *The Bicentennial Collection: Celebrating the 200th Anniversary of "the President's Own" United States Marine Band* (United States Marine Band, 1998), 56; "Victrola and I," *VoV* 16 (Apr. 1921): 76.

27. Lisa Gitelman, "Reading Music, Reading Records, Reading Race: Musical Copyright and the U.S. Copyright Act of 1909," *Musical Quarterly* 81 (Summer 1997): 265–290.

28. *Copyright Act of 1909,* Public Law 320, *U.S. Statutes at Large* 35 (1909): 1075–1088; Harry Von Tilzer, "Mr. Tin Pan Alley, Himself," 1942, p. 90, box 1, folder 13, LC-HVT; *MT* 37 (Mar. 13, 1909): 42.

29. Gitelman, "Reading Music, Reading Records, Reading Race." On the problems posed by sound recordings for conventional copyright issues, see Benjamin Kaplan, "Publication in Copyright Law: The Question of Phonograph Records," *University of Pennsylvania Law Review* 103 (Jan. 1955): 469–490.

30. On "authorship" as prerequisite for copyright, see Gaines, *Contested Culture,* 51.

31. This play on words comes from Hillel Schwartz's analysis of copying in Western visual art. Schwartz, *The Culture of the Copy,* 248.

32. Hand quotation from *Gross v. Van Dyk Gravure Co.* (1916), in Ronald Cracas, "Judge Learned Hand and the Law of Copyright," in *Copyright Law Symposium* 7 (New York, 1956): 65–70, quotation on 68–69. See also Benjamin Kaplan, *An Unhurried View of Copyright* (New York, 1967), 41–47.

33. Cyril Ehrlich, *Harmonious Alliance: A History of the Performing Rights Society*

(Oxford, 1988); Raymond Hubbell, "From Nothing to Five Million a Year! The Story of ASCAP," typescript, n.d., Music Division, New York Public Library; David Ewen, *All the Years of American Popular Music* (Englewood Cliffs, N.J., 1977), 300–303; Schultz, "Performing-Right Societies in the United States," 513. On international copyright, see Simon Frith, ed., *Music and Copyright* (Edinburgh, 1993); and Simon Frith and Lee Marshall, eds., *Music and Copyright,* 2nd ed. (New York, 2004).

34. W. C. Handy, *Father of the Blues: An Autobiography,* ed. Arna Bontemps (1941; New York, 1985), 264; Witmark and Goldberg, *From Ragtime to Swingtime,* 373–376; Arnold Shaw, "The Vocabulary of Tin Pan Alley Explained," *Notes* 3 (1949–50): 38; Ewen, *All the Years of American Popular Music,* 300–303; Schultz, "Performing-Right Societies in the United States," 532.

35. Schultz, "Performing-Right Societies in the United States," 513–514.

36. Marks and Liebling, *They All Sang,* 187–188; *Herbert v. Shanley Co.,* 242 U.S. 591 (1917). Holmes quoted in Schultz, "Performing-Right Societies in the United States," 514.

37. Edward Samuels, *The Illustrated Story of Copyright* (New York, 2000), 41–43; *M. Witmark & Sons v. L. Bamberger & Co.,* 291 F. 776 (D.C. N.J. 1923); Kraft, *Stage to Studio;* Schultz, "Performing-Right Societies in the United States," 516, 518.

38. Nolan Porterfield, *Jimmie Rodgers: The Life and Times of America's Blues Yodeler,* rev. ed. (Urbana, Ill., 1992), 90–101; William Howland Kenney, *Recorded Music in American Life: The Phonograph and Popular Memory* (New York, 1999), 109–157.

39. Lyman Ray Patterson, *Copyright in Historical Perspective* (Nashville, Tenn., 1968), 226; Scott Reynolds Nelson, *Steel Drivin' Man: John Henry, the Untold Story of an American Legend* (New York, 2006); Cecil Brown, *Stagolee Shot Billy* (Cambridge, Mass., 2003).

40. Samuels, *Illustrated Story of Copyright,* 43; David Bernstein, "Music Royalties Rise, Even as CD Sales Fall," *NYT,* Jan. 26, 2004; Andrew Jacobs, "Music's Hottest Star: The Publisher," *NYT,* Apr. 24, 2006.

41. Leonard Feist, *An Introduction to Popular Music Publishing in America* (New York, 1980), 8–9; Ben Yagoda, "Lullaby of Tin Pan Alley," *American Heritage* 34, no. 6 (1983): 94. On Dreyfus, see S. N. Behrman, "Profiles: Accoucheur," *New Yorker,* Feb. 6, 1932, 20–24.

6. Perfect Pitch

1. *The Jonas Chickering Centennial Celebration* (New York, 1924), 34–43, quotations (whose order has been modified) on 35, 36, 37, and 43; "Celebration to Honor Jonas Chickering," *NYT,* Apr. 1, 1923. Portions of Coolidge's speech were reprinted in "Bring the Best Music to the People, Urges President Coolidge," *Musician* 28 (Sept. 1923): 8.

2. John Tasker Howard, untitled memoir, pp. 79–80, n.d., box 4, folder 12, NYPL-

JTH; Craig H. Roell, *The Piano in America, 1890–1940* (Chapel Hill, N.C., 1989), 69–97, 282. The figures for phonographs, which exclude phonographic dictation machines, and for pianos are based on Frederick O. Barnum III, *"His Master's Voice" in America: Ninety Years of Communications Pioneering and Progress: Victor Talking Machine Company, Radio Corporation of America, General Electric Company* (Camden, N.J., 1991), 90; *Biennial Census of Manufactures: 1921* (Washington, D.C., 1924), 1165; *Biennial Census of Manufactures: 1925* (Washington, D.C., 1928), 1066, 1082. Victor's record sales grew from 1.7 million discs in 1902 to 40.5 million in 1923, for a total of more than 373 million during this interval. The average of more than 20 percent annual increase in sales is skewed slightly by a 97.8 percent jump from 1905 to 1906, by far the sharpest increase, but the annual increase was between 20 and 55 percent ten times. In six instances, growth was between 3.6 percent and 15.9 percent, and only in four years did sales actually contract; although when they did, they fell off sharply (a 31.7 percent drop from 1907 to 1908, 11.6 percent from 1908 to 1909, 22.4 percent from 1917 to 1918, and 32.3 percent from 1921 to 1922). See Record Accounting Department, "Record Unit Sales, Domestic and Export, 1901–1945," Mar. 4, 1946, folder "Hit Records, Etc.," CCHS-VTM.

3. *Regulation of Prices: Hearings before the Committee on Interstate and Foreign Commerce of the House of Representatives, Sixty-fourth Congress, Second Session, on H.R. 13568, to Protect the Public against Dishonest Advertising and False Pretenses in Merchandising—January 5 to 11, 1917* (Washington, D.C., 1917), 248–250, quotations on 249.

4. B. L. Aldridge, "Confidential History," 34, series 1, box 1, HAG-ALD; Barnum, *"His Master's Voice" in America*, 79.

5. *VoV* 5 (Sept.–Oct. 1910): 2 (emphasis in the original); *VoV* 5 (Mar.–Apr. 1910): 16; *VoV* 11 (Aug. 1916): 154 (emphasis in the original); *VoV* 4 (Jan. 1909): 3.

6. *VoV* 9 (Aug. 1914): 148; *VoV* 8 (Jan. 1913): 12. Aldridge, "Confidential History," 273–275. Other management-related articles noted by Aldridge include "Masters of Store Management," "Yesterday's Methods Won't Do Today," "First Principles of Successful Merchandising," and "Why Some Dealers Make Money and Others Don't."

7. William Leach, *Land of Desire: Merchants, Power and the Rise of a New American Culture* (New York, 1993), 112–150; Susan Porter Benson, *Counter Cultures: Saleswomen, Managers, and Customers in American Department Stores, 1890–1940* (Urbana, Ill., 1986); Charles F. McGovern, *Sold American: Consumption and Citizenship, 1890–1945* (Chapel Hill, N.C., 2006), 96–131; Aldridge, "Confidential History," 273–274; *VoV* 11 (Jan. 1916): 227; *VoV* 21 (Jan. 1926): 12.

8. Leach, *Land of Desire*, 39–70; Aldridge, "Confidential History," 276; *VoV* 5 (Sept.–Oct. 1910): 14; *VoV* 4 (Sept. 1909): *VoV* 7 (Apr. 1912): 6.

9. *VoV* 5 (Sept.–Oct. 1910): 14; *VoV* 7 (Feb. 1912): 15, 16; *VoV* 7 (Mar. 1912): 15; *VoV* 7 (Apr. 1912): 13; *VoV* (May 1929).

10. *VoV* 4 (Sept. 1909): 3; Aldridge, "Confidential History," 274–275. On "Good Advertisements Made Better," see, for example, *VoV* 8 (Feb. 1913): 15.

11. *VoV* 20 (Dec. 1925): 12. On salesmen, see Walter A. Friedman, *Birth of a Salesman: The Transformation of Selling in America* (Cambridge, Mass., 2004).

12. *VoV* 20 (Dec. 1925): 3; *VoV* 5 (Sept.–Oct. 1910): 4–5; *VoV* 6 (May–June 1911): 8.

13. David Kapp, "Reminiscences of David Kapp" [1958–1959], p. 1976, CU-OHROC; *VoV* 2 (May 1907): 4; *VoV* 2 (Nov. 1907): 3.

14. *Columbia Record* 2 (May 1904); Babson Bros., *Edison Phonograph Distributors* (Chicago, [1907]); "Phonograph Sales Show Big Growth," *NYT*, Jan. 22, 1922; "Phonograph Rivals Motor Car's Vogue," *NYT*, Mar. 12, 1922; *VoV* 17 (Sept. 1922): 163; "Have You Tried the Installment Plan?" *VoV* 2 (May 1907): 4; "The Victor Installment Educational Campaign," *VoV* 2 (Nov. 1907): 3; Lizabeth Cohen, *Making a New Deal: Industrial Workers in Chicago, 1919–1939* (Cambridge, Mass., 1990), 103–104.

15. *VoV* 9 (June 1914): 103 (emphasis in the original). On assumptions about consumers, see *VoV* 3 (July 1908): 2; *VoV* 9 (Mar. 1914): 48; *VoV* 5 (Sept.–Oct. 1910): 5.

16. *VoV* 5 (Sept.–Oct. 1910): 5; *VoV* 3 (Nov. 1908): 3.

17. For the cultural resonance of "mind cure," see Leach, *Land of Desire*, 225–260; William James, *The Varieties of Religious Experience* (New York, 1958), 87–108; Johan Huizinga, *America: A Dutch Historian's Vision from Afar and Near* (1928; New York, 1972), 187–204.

18. *VoV* 5 (Mar.–Apr. 1910): [3]; *VoV* 3 (Nov. 1908); *VoV* 7 (Mar. 1912): 2; *VoV* 3 (July 1908).

19. Frank H. Holman, "Applying 'New Thought' or Psycho-Therapy to the Dealer," *Printers' Ink* 72 (Aug. 25, 1910): 36.

20. Milt Gabler, "Reminiscences of Milt Gabler," Nov. 1959, pp. 1–2, CU-OHROC; Aldridge, "Confidential History," 278; *VoV* 7 (Dec. 1912): 5.

21. *Victor Talking Machine Co. v. The Fair*, 123 F. 424 (7th Cir. 1903); Aldridge, "Confidential History," chap. 7; *VoV* 2 (Nov. 1907): 9; *VoV* 11 (Dec. 1912): 8–9, 11; *Straus v. Victor Talking Machine Co.*, 243 U.S. 490 (1917). For discussion of or reference to Victor in the congressional hearings on price regulation, see *Regulation of Prices*, esp. pp. 5, 13, 18, 21, 175, 191, 249, 263, 272, 303, 334, 540–564, and 613–614. Victor's vice president, Leon Douglass, described Victor's legal strategy in his unpublished memoirs, but his account is filled with inaccuracies and should be used with caution; see Leon Douglass, "Memoirs of Leon Forrest Douglass (Condensed)," box 2, folders 50–53, HAG-ALD. On the history of retail price maintenance, see Andrew N. Kleit, "Efficiencies without Economists: The Early Years of Resale Price Maintenance," *Southern Economic Journal* 59 (Apr. 1993): 597–619.

22. "Memorandum in Matter of United States vs. Victor Talking Machine Company et al." DOJ 60–23–0, box 243, National Archives II, College Park, Md.; Aldridge, "Confidential History," 57, 66, 243, 278; Barnum, *"His Master's Voice" in America*, 79. On

duties performed by salesmen, see Friedman, *The Birth of a Salesman;* Susan Strasser, *Satisfaction Guaranteed: The Making of the Mass Market* (New York, 1989), 23; and Richard S. Tedlow, *New and Improved: The Story of Mass Marketing in America* (New York, 1990), 22–112.

23. Frances Elliott Clark, Address to Victor Dealers and Distributors, Dec. 1911, pp. 6, 11, 15, 18, series 1, box 1, folder 1.3.1, UMD-FEC.

24. W. L. Hubbard, *History of American Music* (New York, 1908), 199–200; Charles L. Gary, "The Dawn of a New Frontier," in *Music in American Schools, 1838–1988,* ed. Marie McCarthy and Bruce D. Wilson (College Park, Md., 1991), 73–76; Shannon L. Green, "'Art for Life's Sake': Music Schools and Activities in U.S. Social Settlements, 1892–1942" (Ph.D. diss., University of Wisconsin–Madison, 1998).

25. *VoV* 6 (Oct. 1911): 1–5; *VoV* 6 (May–June 1911): 6–7.

26. *VoV* 5 (Sept.–Oct. 1910): 5; W. A. Willson, "The Advertising Value of the Child in the Retail Talking Machine Trade," *TMW* 15 (Dec. 15, 1919): 70.

27. Clark, Address to Victor Dealers and Distributors, 3; *VoV* 2 (Nov. 1907): 3, 8.

28. J. S. Parsons, "The Talking Machine Assumes the Part of Pedagogue Most Successfully," *TMW* 15 (Dec. 15, 1919): 25; S. Dana Townsend, comp., *The Victrola in Correlation with English and American Literature* (Camden, N.J., 1922), NMAH-NTLC; James N. Weber, *The Talking Machine: The Advertising History of the Berliner Gramophone and Victor Talking Machine* (Midland, Ont., 1997), 130–131; Aldridge, "Confidential History," 48. Quotations from *VoV* 6 (May–June 1911): 6–7. See also Clark, Address to Victor Dealers and Distributors, 21.

29. Branson M. DeCou, *The Organization of an Education Department,* undated pamphlet, box 2, folder 56, HAG-ALD; *VoV* 9 (June 1914): 109.

30. *VoV* 9 (Aug. 1914); *VoV* 17 (Sept. 1922): [166–167] (emphasis in the original); Mark Katz, "Making America More Musical through the Phonograph, 1900–1930," *American Music* 16 (Winter 1998): 457.

31. Ampico Corporation, *How to Sell the Ampico to Schools: A Supplemental Unit of the Course in Ampico Salesmanship* (New York, 1926), UMD-HC-MMI; Howard, untitled memoir, 96.

32. Parsons, "The Talking Machine Assumes the Part of Pedagogue Most Successfully," 25.

33. "Leo Feist" (obituary), *Variety,* June 25, 1930; Barnum, *"His Master's Voice" in America,* 84–85; *VoV* 14 (Feb. 1919): 35.

34. Barnum, *"His Master's Voice" in America,* 85–89. Dorothy Caruso, *Enrico Caruso: His Life and Death* (New York, 1945), 67; *NYT,* May 2, 1918. On Elman, see *New Victor Records,* Oct. 1918 (monthly catalogue supplement), 27.

35. Glenn Watkins, *Proof through the Night: Music and the Great War* (Berkeley, 2003); Edwin Wildman, "Leo Feist: The Man Who Put Music in the War," typescript, n.d., box 2, folder 6, NYPL-LFP; *VoV* 13 (Jan. 1918).

36. William J. Fitzgerald, "How Talking Machines Play a Prominent Part in the History of the World War," *TMW* 14 (June 1918): 27.

37. F. W. Gaisberg, *The Music Goes Round* (New York, 1942), 78; Roell, *The Piano in America,* 19; "Women Ready to Patrol Camp against Vice," *Chicago Daily Tribune,* May 10, 1917.

38. "Phonographs on the Firing Line," *Independent* 96 (Oct. 1918): 126.

39. *My Beloved Poilus* (St. John, N.B., Canada, 1917), www.vlib.us/medical/canadian/cnurse.htm, accessed Sept. 25, 2008.

40. Gaisberg, *The Music Goes Round,* 78. On Tin Pan Alley during the war, see Watkins, *Proof through the Night;* Edward B. Marks and Abbot J. Liebling, *They All Sang: From Tony Pastor to Rudy Vallee* (New York, 1935), 189–193.

41. Roell, *The Piano in America,* 188–190, Wilson quoted on 189; William Tonk, *Memoirs of a Manufacturer* (New York, 1926), 212–216; *TMW* (June 15, 1917): 111; *TMW* (Dec. 15, 1917): 8; *TMW* (Dec. 15, 1919): 8; *1919 Supplement to U.S. Compiled Statutes: Compact Edition, Embracing the Statutes of the United States of a General and Permanent Nature from June 14, 1918, to March 4, 1919* (St. Paul, Minn., 1919), 133.

42. John Dizikes, *Opera in America: A Cultural History* (New Haven, Conn., 1993), 407; *TMW* (June 15, 1917): 8; Aldridge, "Confidential History," 64; Barnum, *"His Master's Voice" in America,* 84; Record Accounting Department, "Record Unit Sales, Domestic and Export, 1901–1945."

43. "Record Unit Sales, Domestic and Export, 1901–1945." Exports accounted for approximately 5 percent of the total.

44. *Biennial Census of Manufactures: 1921,* 1163.

45. Katz, "Making America More Musical Through the Phonograph," 461–475; Charles D. Isaacson, "A New Musical Outlook—and the War," *Musical Quarterly* 6 (Jan. 1920): 1–11; Clara T. Nichols, "Music in Our Public Schools," *Musical Quarterly* 4 (Oct. 1918): 535–541; Cora Conway, "Community Songs and Singing," *Music Supervisors' Journal* 5 (Sept. 1918): 26, 28; J. Lawrence Erb, "Music for a Better Community," *Musical Quarterly* 12 (July 1926): 441–448; Peter W. Dykema, "The Spread of the Community Music Idea," in "New Possibilities in Education," special issue, *Annals of the American Academy of Political and Social Science* 67 (Sept. 1916): 218–223; "Industrial Music Bureau Formed," *TMW* 15 (Dec. 15, 1919): 77; Francis G. Couvares, *The Remaking of Pittsburgh: Class and Culture in an Industrializing City, 1877–1919* (Albany, N.Y., 1984), 117. The description of the Heinz auditorium comes from Robert Alberts, *The Good Provider: H. J. Heinz and His 57 Varieties* (Boston, 1973), quoted ibid.

46. Frances Elliott Clark, "Talk by Mrs. Clark on Educational Work," 1924, series 1, box 1, folder 1.1.8, UMD-FEC; "Chimes and Choirs Today to Usher in Music Week," *NYT,* Feb. 1, 1920.

47. *VoV* 11 (Apr. 1916), cover (emphasis in the original); Elise K. Kirk, *Musical Highlights from the White House* (Malabar, Fla., 1992), 87–101.

48. *Biennial Census of Manufactures: 1921* (Washington, D.C., 1924), 1153; *Fifteenth Census of the United States: Manufactures, 1929* (Washington, D.C., 1933), 1330; *The Jonas Chickering Centennial Celebration,* 42.

49. Actual exports made up only a small percentage of Victor's overall business, however. On the effect of World War I on the international phonograph business, see Peter Martland, "A Business History of the Gramophone Company Ltd., 1897–1918," (Ph.D. diss., Cambridge University, 1992), 414–466.

7. The Black Swan

1. Jon Pareles, "Post Mergers: A Modest Proposal," *NYT,* Feb. 6, 2000.

2. Edmund E. Day and Woodlief Thomas, *The Growth of Manufactures, 1899 to 1923: A Study of the Indexes of Increase in the Volume of Manufactured Products* (Washington, D.C., 1928), 173–174.

3. Ronald C. Foreman, Jr., "Jazz and Race Records, 1920–1932: Their Origins and Their Significance for the Record Industry and Society" (Ph.D. diss., University of Illinois, 1968), 11–54; William Howland Kenney, *Recorded Music in American Life: The Phonograph and Popular Memory* (New York, 1999), 65–87, 109–134; American Folklife Center, *Ethnic Recordings in America: A Neglected Heritage,* Studies in American Folklife, no. 1 (Washington, D.C., 1982). On coon songs, see James H. Dormon, "Shaping the Popular Image of Post-Reconstruction American Blacks: The 'Coon Song' Phenomenon of the Gilded Age," *American Quarterly* 40 (Dec. 1988): 450–471. For technical reasons, many of James Reese Europe's recordings were not playable on most phonographs; see Foreman, "Jazz and Race Records," 19–21.

4. David Levering Lewis, *When Harlem Was in Vogue* (New York, 1981), 3–24; Nathan Irvin Huggins, *Harlem Renaissance* (New York, 1971), 6–7; *Chicago Defender,* May 31, 1919.

5. Tim Brooks, *Lost Sounds: Blacks and the Birth of the Recording Industry, 1890–1919* (Urbana, Ill., 2004), 464–470.

6. For most of its existence, the actual company name was Pace Phonograph Corp., and the label name (trade name) was Black Swan. Eventually the two were combined as the Black Swan Phonograph Company. For the sake of simplicity, I will use only the Black Swan name.

7. Du Bois proposed the establishment of a "Negro Business Men's League" at the conference and worked in the months that followed to draft a list of proposed members. When political wrangling forced Du Bois out of the project, he surrendered his work to Washington, who used it at least in part in founding the NNBL. Louis R. Harlan, *Booker T. Washington: The Making of a Black Leader, 1856–1901* (New York, 1972), 266–267. For examples of Du Bois's continued support for the development of black business, see [W. E. B. Du Bois, ed.,] *The Negro in Business* (1899; New York, 1968); [W. E. B. Du

Bois, ed.,] *Economic Cooperation among Negro Americans* (1907; New York, 1968); [W. E. B. Du Bois, ed.,] *Efforts for Social Betterment among Negro Americans* (1910; New York, 1968).

8. On Garvey and business development, see Judith Stein, *The World of Marcus Garvey: Race and Class in Modern Society* (Baton Rouge, La., 1986), 61–88.

9. Jeffrey Melnick, *A Right to Sing the Blues: African Americans, Jews, and American Popular Song* (Cambridge, Mass., 1999), 45–52.

10. Regarding the professional opportunities that African Americans did secure, see David A. Jasen and Gene Jones, *Spreadin' Rhythm Around: Black Popular Songwriters, 1880–1930* (New York, 1998); Thomas Riis, *Just Before Jazz: Black Musical Theater in New York, 1890 to 1915* (Washington, D.C., 1989); Eileen Southern, *The Music of Black Americans: A History,* 3rd ed. (New York, 1997). The single black-owned publishing firm was the Gotham-Attucks Music Publishing Company, discussed in Chapter 1. See Wayne D. Shirley, "The House of Melody: A List of Publications of the Gotham-Attucks Music Company at the Library of Congress," *Black Perspective in Music* 15 (Spring 1987): 79–112.

11. W. E. B. Du Bois, *The Souls of Black Folk* (1903; New York, 1989), 3; Robert M. W. Dixon and John Godrich, *Recording the Blues* (New York, 1970), 8; Foreman, "Jazz and Race Records," 11–16, 34–41, 55–65; Roland Gelatt, *The Fabulous Phonograph, 1877–1977,* 2nd ed. (New York, 1977), 189–190; Perry Bradford, *Born with the Blues: Perry Bradford's Own Story: The True Story of the Pioneering Blues Singers and Musicians in the Early Days of Jazz* (New York, 1965), 114–129. Bradford quotations on 114, 116, and 118.

12. Harry H. Pace to W. E. B. Du Bois, Dec. 27, 1920, reel 9, *WEBD*. The account of Pace's personal life and business and political activities in these years is based on Joseph J. Boris, ed., *Who's Who in Colored America* (New York, 1927), 152; Miriam DeCosta-Willis, "DuBois' Memphis Connection," *West Tennessee Historical Society Papers* 42 (Dec. 1988): 30–38; Paul G. Partington, "*The Moon Illustrated Weekly*—The Precursor of the *Crisis,*" *Journal of Negro History,* 48 (July 1963): 206–216; John N. Ingham and Lynne B. Feldman, eds., *African-American Business Leaders: A Biographical Dictionary* (Westport, Conn., 1994), 501–517; David Levering Lewis, *W. E. B. Du Bois: Biography of a Race, 1868–1919* (New York, 1993), 324–328; George W. Lee, *Beale Street: Where the Blues Began* (1934; College Park, 1969), 290; Herbert Aptheker, ed., *The Correspondence of W. E. B. Du Bois,* vol. 1, *Selections, 1877–1934* (n.p., 1973), 179; *Chicago Defender,* July 31, 1943, 5; and Walter White, *A Man Called White: The Autobiography of Walter White* (New York, 1948), 30–32.

13. On African American business, see Juliet E. K. Walker, *The History of Black Business in America: Capitalism, Race, Entrepreneurship* (New York, 1998), 187; Walter B. Weare, *Black Business in the New South: A Social History of the North Carolina Mutual Life Insurance Company* (Urbana, Ill., 1973); Merah S. Stuart, *An Economic Detour: A*

History of Insurance in the Lives of American Negroes (New York, 1940); Robert E. Weems, Jr., *Black Business in the Black Metropolis: The Chicago Metropolitan Assurance Company, 1925–1985* (Bloomington, Ind., 1996); Alexa Benson Henderson, *Atlanta Life Insurance Company: Guardian of Black Economic Dignity* (Tuscaloosa, Ala., 1990); Robert C. Puth, "Supreme Life: The History of a Negro Life Insurance Company" (Ph.D. diss., Northwestern University, 1967).

14. Handy, *Father of the Blues*, 125–127, 186–200, quotation on 199; Pace quoted in Roi Ottley and William J. Weatherby, eds., *The Negro in New York: An Informal Social History* (New York, 1967), 232. The Handy compositions for which Pace wrote the lyrics include "In the Cotton Fields of Dixie," "The Girl You Never Have Met," "In the Land Where Cotton Is King," and "Thinking of Thee."

15. Although Handy's well-crafted memoirs appeared many years after the fact and may have been heavily modified by the editor, Arna Bontemps, the substance of his recollections is corroborated by Perry Bradford and others. Handy, *Father of the Blues*, 199–200; Harry H. Pace, "The Pace Recording Company," a speech given to the National Association of Negro Musicians [1921], quoted in Willis C. Patterson, "A History of the National Association of Negro Musicians (NANM): The First Quarter Century, 1919–1943" (Ph.D. diss., Wayne State University, 1993), 79.

16. *Chicago Defender,* July 13, 1920, 4, quoted in Foreman, "Jazz and Race Records," 66.

17. Harry H. Pace to W. E. B. Du Bois, Dec. 27, 1920, reel 9, *WEBD*. See also Len Kunstadt, "Black Swan," *Record Research* 1, no. 5 (Oct. 1955): 5; Southern, *The Music of Black Americans,* 103–104. Somewhat similarly, another African American concert vocalist, M. Sissieretta Jones (1869–1933), was known as Black Patti, in reference to the leading prima donna of the Gilded Age, Adelina Patti. In the late 1920s another short-lived black-owned record company followed the Black Swan example when its founder, Mayo Williams, chose to name the label Black Patti.

18. On musical uplift, see Joseph Horowitz, *Wagner Nights: An American History* (Berkeley, Calif., 1994), 5, 24–25, 30; George Willis Cooke, *John Sullivan Dwight, Brook-Farmer, Editor, and Critic of Music: A Biography* (1898; New York, 1969); Joseph A. Mussulman, *Music in the Cultured Generation: A Social History of Music in America, 1870–1900* (Evanston, Ill., 1971), esp. 84–103; Lawrence W. Levine, *Highbrow, Lowbrow: The Emergence of Cultural Hierarchy in America* (Cambridge, Mass., 1988), 104–146.

19. Ronald Radano, "Denoting Difference: The Writing of the Slave Spirituals," *Critical Inquiry* 22 (Spring 1996): 516–517; Du Bois, *The Souls of Black Folk.*

20. Mannes quoted in Reid Badger, *A Life in Ragtime: A Biography of James Reese Europe* (New York, 1995), 61.

21. *Chicago Defender,* May 10, 1919, quoted in Badger, *A Life in Ragtime,* 211.

22. Harry H. Pace, "Public Opinion and the Negro," typescript, June 29, 1921,

pp. 1–2, 9, box 5, series B, group 1, *Papers of the NAACP,* University Publications of America, 1982–, reel 8.

23. Harry H. Pace to W. E. B. Du Bois, Dec. 27, 1920, reel 9, *WEBD;* "Phonograph Records," *Crisis* 21 (Feb. 1921): 152; "The Black Swan," *Crisis* 21 (Mar. 1921): 212–213; W. E. B. Du Bois, "Criteria of Negro Art," in *The New Negro Renaissance: An Anthology,* ed. Arthur P. Davis and Michael W. Peplow (New York, 1975), 496.

24. At different times, the board included John E. Nail, the Harlem real estate pioneer (and James Weldon Johnson's brother-in-law); Truman K. Gibson, an insurance and banking executive; Godfrey Nurse, a doctor and real estate developer; Viola Bibb, a Chicago society figure and daughter-in-law of the Yale- and Harvard-educated cofounder of the *Chicago Whip;* Matthew V. Boutté, a pharmacist; W. H. Willis; and the accountant John P. Quander. Harry H. Pace to W. E. B. Du Bois, Nov. 10, 1925, reel 14, *WEBD;* Ted Vincent, "The Social Context of Black Swan Records," *Living Blues,* 20 (May–June 1989): 36; Ted Vincent, *Keep Cool: The Black Activists Who Built the Jazz Age* (East Haven, Conn., 1995), 99; and Boris, *Who's Who in Colored America,* 14, 19, 148.

25. W. C. Handy, "A Brief History of Black Swan," typescript, 1948, box 1, W. C. Handy Collection, National Museum of American History; Pace Phonograph Corporation advertisement, *Crisis* 23 (Apr. 1922): 284.

26. "Record of Our Own Singers," *Competitor* 3 (Jan. 1921): 6; *Norfolk Journal and Guide,* Jan. 15, 1921, 1; untitled photograph with caption, *Crusader* 3 (Feb. 1921): 15; *Chicago Broad Ax,* May 7, 1921, 1; *Chicago Defender,* June 4, 1921, 6; *Washington Bee,* June 4, 1921; Patterson, "A History of the National Association of Negro Musicians," 80; Vincent, *Keep Cool,* 98–99. Sources reveal little about the perpetrators of these "boycotts," but orchestra leaders, theater directors, recording managers, and individual performers all made decisions about repertoire and therefore would have been in a position to exert pressure on a music publisher.

27. Doris Evans McGinty, "Conversation with Revella Hughes: From the Classics to Broadway to Swing," *Black Perspective in Music* 16 (Spring 1988): 81–104; Vincent, *Keep Cool,* 134–137; Robert A. Hill, ed., *Marcus Garvey and Universal Negro Improvement Association Papers,* vol. 2, *27 August 1919–31 August 1920* (Berkeley, Calif., 1986), 322, 471, 583. After Garvey's notorious entente with the Ku Klux Klan, Pace joined with a number of other African American leaders in an appeal to U.S. Attorney General Harry M. Daugherty to have Garvey incarcerated, which was successful. See, for example, Richard B. Moore, "The Critics and Opponents of Marcus Garvey," in *Marcus Garvey and the Vision of Africa,* ed. John Henrik Clarke with Amy Jacques Garvey (New York, 1974), 228.

28. *Chicago Defender,* June 6, 1921, 6; Tim Brooks, *The Columbia Master Discography,* vol. 1, *U.S. Matrix Series 1 through 4999, 1901–10, with a History of the Columbia Phonograph Company to 1934* (Westport, Conn., 1999), 26.

29. *Norfolk Journal and Guide,* Jan. 15, 1921, 1. My evaluation of Black Swan's best-

selling titles is based on advertisements and Fred W. Boerner & Co., "Selected List of Most Popular Black Swan Records," dealer's list, record catalogues collection, Recorded Sound Reference Center, Library of Congress. The estimation of the percentage of popular recordings among all Black Swan releases is based on a record-by-record analysis of every record listed in Helge Thygesen, Mark Berresford, and Russ Shor, *Black Swan: The Record Label of the Harlem Renaissance: A History and Catalogue Listing Including Olympic Records and Associated Labels* (Nottingham, Eng., 1996). Where possible, I have listened to actual recordings, either original 78 rpm records or compact disc reissues, at the Library of Congress, Rutgers University's Institute of Jazz Studies, the New York Public Library, or in my personal collection. I classified all titles into one of six categories—blues/jazz; popular/vaudeville vocal; serious or sacred vocal, including spirituals; dance instrumental; novelty; and Hawaiian—on the basis of known information about the artist, the composition, the composer, or any other label markings given in the discography.

30. For more on these distinctions, see, for example, William Barlow, *"Looking Up at Down": The Emergence of Blues Culture* (Philadelphia, 1989).

31. Ethel Waters with Charles Samuels, *His Eye Is on the Sparrow: An Autobiography* (Garden City, N.Y., 1951), 141–147; quotations on 141 and 142.

32. Waters, *His Eye Is on the Sparrow,* 141; Dixon and Godrich, *Recording the Blues,* 13–14; Ottley and Weatherby, *The Negro in New York,* 233; "$104,628.74 Paid for 'Black Swan' Records," *New York Age,* Jan. 28, 1922, 6; Kunstadt, "Black Swan," *Record Research* 1, no. 4 (Aug. 1955): 4–5; *Chicago Defender,* Dec. 24, 1921, 7, quoted in Walter C. Allen, *Hendersonia: The Music of Fletcher Henderson and His Musicians* (Highland Park, Ill., 1973), 26; undated and untitled press release, typescript, 1924, folder 28, box 144–29, Percival Leroy Prattis Papers, Moorland-Spingarn Research Center, Howard University, Washington, D.C.

33. *Chicago Defender,* June 2, 1923, 7; "The Golden Age of Blues-Recording," *Record Research* 2, no. 5 (Jan.-Feb. 1957): 3–4; Samuel B. Charters and Leonard Kunstadt, *Jazz: A History of the New York Scene* (1962; New York, 1981), 101–102; *TMW,* Feb. 15, 1922, 149.

34. Pace and Walton had connections on many levels—political, professional, social. Both served as high-ranking members of the Benevolent and Protective Order of Elks (BPOE), for instance. See, for example, Harry H. Pace to Lester A. Walton, Oct. 13, 1916, folder 2, box 6, Lester A. Walton Papers, New York Public Library.

35. Allen, *Hendersonia,* 24–35; *Chicago Defender,* Feb. 11, 1922, 7, quoted ibid., 27. For tour manager Lester Walton, traveling through the South marked the turning point in his career, ended his involvement in the entertainment business and laid the groundwork for his full commitment to the fight for civil rights. Indeed, he was so moved by his experiences with the Troubadours that in 1922, after the tour, he retraced with the Tuskegee

Institute's Robert Russa Moton (successor to Booker T. Washington) the route taken by the group. The two held public talks and information-gathering meetings as they went, and Walton subsequently dedicated himself exclusively to the fight for civil rights. In 1933 he was appointed to serve as U.S. envoy to Liberia, a post he held until 1946, and in 1955 he became a charter member of the New York State Human Rights Commission. Vincent, *Keep Cool,* 45–46.

36. Frank C. Taylor with Gerald Cook, *Alberta Hunter: A Celebration in Blues* (New York, 1987), 52; "Black Swan Artists Broadcast," *TMW,* May 15, 1922, 43; "Ethel Waters Sings for the Radiophone," *Negro World,* May 13, 1922, 3. See also *Chicago Defender,* Apr. 29, 1922, 7, and *Savannah Tribune,* Apr. 27, 1922, 1, quoted in Allen, *Hendersonia,* 29. On other early performances by African Americans on radio, see Stanley Dance, *The World of Earl Hines* (New York, 1977), 25, 134.

37. Handy, "A Brief History of Black Swan"; Paul Oliver, *Bessie Smith* (London, 1959), 1; Chris Albertson, *Bessie* (New York, 1972), 37. Isabelle Washington's recording of "I Want To" (1923) can be heard online at http://www.journalofamericanhistory.org/teaching/2004_03/sources.html (as can numerous other Black Swan recordings), or on *Fletcher Henderson and the Blues Singers,* vol. 1, compact disc (Document Records, DOCD-5342; n.d.). Washington was later married to Adam Clayton Powell, Jr.

38. Waters, *His Eye Is on the Sparrow,* 146–147; Garvin Bushell, as told to Mark Tucker, *Jazz from the Beginning* (Ann Arbor, Mich., 1988), 31; Lewis, *When Harlem Was in Vogue,* 172.

39. Quoted in Patterson, "A History of the National Association of Negro Musicians," 80–81.

40. Hazel V. Carby, "It Jus Be's Dat Way Sometime: The Sexual Politics of Women's Blues," *Radical America* 20, no. 4 (1987): 8–22; Carby, "Policing the Black Woman's Body in an Urban Context," *Critical Inquiry* 18 (Summer 1992): 738–755; Sandra R. Lieb, *Mother of the Blues: A Study of Ma Rainey* (n.p., 1981); Daphne Duval Harrison, *Black Pearls: Blues Queens of the 1920s* (New Brunswick, N.J., 1988).

41. Vincent, *Keep Cool,* 93.

42. Thygesen, Berresford, and Shor, *Black Swan,* 7; Kunstadt, "Black Swan," *Record Research* 1, no. 4 (Aug. 1955), 5.

43. *TMW,* May 15, 1922, 128. The Swanola name was of course a play on the Victor Talking Machine Company's industry standard Victrola, whose name by the 1920s was a virtual synonym for "phonograph." A Black Swan catalogue from 1923 shows the Dunbar model of the Swanola, named for poet Paul Laurence Dunbar, and an advertisement in *Crisis* promoted the L'Ouverture model, named for Haitian revolutionary Toussaint-Louverture. See Thygesen, Berresford, and Shor, *Black Swan,* 74; *Crisis* 22 (Oct. 1921): 284.

44. *Chicago Defender,* Nov. 5, 1921, 7; *New York Age,* Jan. 21, 1922, 6; *Negro World,* May 20, 1922, 6.

45. Jeff Todd Titon, *Early Downhome Blues: A Musical and Cultural Analysis* (Urbana, Ill., 1977), 225–269; Foreman, "Jazz and Race Records," 211–264.

46. *Crisis* 23 (Jan. 1922): 137; *Crisis* 26 (July 1923): 140; *Crisis* 25 (Jan. 1923): 139.

47. Pace quoted in Patterson, "A History of the National Association of Negro Musicians," 81. On consumer campaigns against child labor, see Kathryn Kish Sklar, *Florence Kelley and the Nation's Work: The Rise of Women's Political Culture, 1830–1900* (New Haven, Conn., 1995).

48. *Crisis* 26 (May 1923): 42.

49. *Chicago Defender,* Oct. 29, 1921, 7, quoted in Allen, *Hendersonia,* 31–32; Carl Kendziora, Jr., and Perry Armagnac, "The Labels behind Black Swan," *Record Research,* no. 221–222 (Apr. 1986): 1, 4; Len Kunstadt, "The Labels behind Black Swan: The Black Swan/Olympic Connection," *Record Research,* no. 229–230 (June 1987): 4–5; *TMW,* July 15, 1922, quoted in Allen, *Hendersonia,* 32. Pace acquired the pressing plant in partnership with a white record business veteran named John Fletcher, who had worked for Olympic. There is some question whether it was Pace or Black Swan that technically went into partnership with Fletcher on the Olympic plant. Walter Allen, in *Hendersonia,* suggests it was Pace personally, apart from Black Swan, but the *Chicago Defender* announcement of April 29, 1922, implies otherwise. See Allen, *Hendersonia,* 32; Barry Kernfeld, ed., *The New Grove Dictionary of Jazz* (New York, 1988), 112–113; Thygesen, Berresford, and Shor, *Black Swan,* 91. For Fletcher, see "John Fletcher: From Sousa's Band to Black Swan and Beyond," *Mainspring Press: Research in Historical Recordings,* www.mainspringpress.com/fletcher.html, accessed Sept. 4, 2008.

50. *Chicago Defender,* Apr. 29, 1922, quoted in Thygesen, Berresford, and Shor, *Black Swan,* 10; "To the Investing Public" (advertisement), *Crisis* 24 (Oct. 1922): 282; "To the Investing Public" (advertisement), *Crisis* 25 (Nov. 1922): 44; Harry H. Pace to Black Swan Board of Directors, Oct. 21, 1925, p. 4, reel 14, *WEBD.*

51. Vincent, *Keep Cool,* 96.

52. Vincent, "The Social Context of Black Swan Records," 35.

53. Black Swan's "Blind Man Blues," for example, sung by Katie Crippen, inspired copycat versions issued by Columbia (sung by Mary Stafford) and OKeh (sung by Sara Martin), two companies with much bigger advertising budgets than Black Swan had. Thygesen, Berresford, and Shor, *Black Swan,* 7.

54. *NYT,* Jan. 22, 1922, sec. 2, p. 13; *NYT,* June 18, 1922, sec. 2, p. 10; "How Retailers Are Merchandising Radio," *TMW* (Dec. 15, 1923): 20; Erik Barnouw, *A Tower in Babel: A History of Broadcasting in the United States,* vol. 1, *To 1933* (New York, 1966), 125; Susan Douglas, *Listening In: Radio and the American Imagination* (New York, 1999), 86; B. L. Aldridge, "Confidential History," 70, series 1, box 1, HAG-ALD; *VoV* 20 (Aug. 1925): 6; Record Accounting Department, "Record Unit Sales, Domestic and Export, 1901–45," folder "Hit Records, Etc.," CCHS-VTM; Ottley and Weatherby, *The Negro in New York,* 234.

55. Harry H. Pace to the board of directors of Black Swan, Oct. 21, 1925, reel 14, *WEBD*. See also W. E. B. Du Bois, John E. Nail, Jr., and Matthew V. Boutté to Stock Holders of the Black Swan Phonograph Company [1925], reel 14, *WEBD*.

56. Thygesen, Berresford, and Shor, *Black Swan*, 17, 53; Allen, *Hendersonia*, 33; Kendziora and Armagnac, "The Labels behind Black Swan," 1, 4; Kunstadt, "The Labels behind Black Swan," 4–5.

57. A fuller discussion of the ethics and business dynamics of the white reissues would bear the following factors in mind (none of which alters my basic conclusions): First, Black Swan also reissued records by African American artists, and it leased its *own* masters to other companies. Second, many of the pseudonymous records were in styles such as popular dance music, Hawaiian, and comedy, which did not compete directly with the high-class music Black Swan was trying to promote or with the vocal blues records that were the company's bread and butter. Third, the pseudonymous records made up a large percentage of the *titles* in the catalogue, but advertisements do not suggest that they played a big part in promotions or sales. For details, see Thygesen, Berresford, and Shor, *Black Swan*, 9, 90; Robert M. W. Dixon, John Godrich, and Howard Rye, comps., *Blues and Gospel Records, 1890–1943* (Oxford, 1997), xxxvi–xxxvii; Kendziora and Armagnac, "The Labels behind Black Swan," 4; Kunstadt, "Black Swan," *Record Research* 3, no. 4 (Jan.–Feb. 1957): 11.

58. Advertisements in the trade journal *Talking Machine World*, which had appeared monthly, ceased even earlier, in October 1922.

59. See Walker, *The History of Black Business in America*, 201–208.

60. Thygesen, Berresford and Shor, *Black Swan*, 7. A list of such artists would include Essie Whitman, the singing member of the celebrated Whitman Sisters song and dance troupe; Eddie Gray, who starred in the 1923 musical *Runnin' Wild*, which introduced the Charleston; Henry Creamer, an important songwriter and cofounder of the Clef Club, the pioneering Harlem-based music association and booking agency; and Georgette Harvey, whose remarkable thirty-five-year stage career included a twelve-year stint in Russia (1905–1917), several years in Southeast Asia, and a role in the original stage production of *Porgy*, the dramatic play on which the milestone opera *Porgy and Bess* was based.

61. *Chicago Defender*, Nov. 4, 1922, quoted in Vincent, *Keep Cool*, 93; Darius Milhaud, *Notes without Music*, quoted in Jervis Anderson, *This Was Harlem: A Cultural Portrait, 1900–1950* (New York, 1982), 179; Catherine Parsons Smith, *William Grant Still: A Study in Contradictions* (Berkeley, Calif., 2000); Robert Bartlett Haas, ed., *William Grant Still and the Fusion of Cultures in American Music* (Flagstaff, Ariz., 1995), 5; Leopold Stokowski, quoted in Southern, *The Music of Black Americans*, 431.

62. *Chicago Defender*, May 17, 1924, sec. 1, p. 7, and sec. 2, p. 14; Chandler Owen, "The Neglected Truth," *Messenger*, Jan. 1926, quoted in Theodore G. Vincent, ed., *Voices of a Black Nation: Political Journalism in the Harlem Renaissance* (1973; Tren-

ton, N.J., n.d.), 256; Harry H. Pace, "Black Swan Not Like the Standard," *Baltimore Afro-American,* Jan. 16, 1926, 3; Ottley and Weatherby, eds., *The Negro in New York,* 232–233, 235. On Paramount and the New York Recording Laboratory, see Dixon, Godrich, and Rye, *Blues and Gospel Records,* xxxvi–xxxvii; Rick Kennedy and Randy McNutt, *Little Labels—Big Sound: Small Record Companies and the Rise of American Music* (Bloomington, Ind., 1999), 20–37; David Luhrssen, "Blues in Wisconsin: The Paramount Records Story," *Wisconsin Academy Review* 45 (Winter 1998–1999): 17–21; Sarah Filzen, "The Rise and Fall of Paramount Records," *Wisconsin Magazine of History* 82 (Winter 1998–1999): 104–127.

63. LeRoi Jones (Amiri Baraka), *Blues People* (New York, 1963), 128; Harold Cruse, *The Crisis of the Negro Intellectual* (1967; New York, 1984), 25–26; James Weldon Johnson quoted on 25.

64. Kevin K. Gaines, *Uplifting the Race: Black Leadership, Politics, and Culture in the Twentieth Century* (Chapel Hill, N.C., 1996).

65. John Vickers, "The Problem of Induction," *The Stanford Encyclopedia of Philosophy* (Winter 2006 edition), ed. Edward N. Zalta, http://plato.stanford.edu/archives/win2006/entries/induction-problem, accessed June 4, 2008.

66. Alain Locke, ed., *The New Negro: An Interpretation* (1925; New York, 1997); Samuel A. Floyd, Jr., ed., *Black Music in the Harlem Renaissance* (Westport, Conn., 1990); Paul Allen Anderson, *Deep River: Music and Memory in Harlem Renaissance Thought* (Durham, N.C., 2001).

8. The Musical Soundscape of Modernity

1. Emily Thompson, *The Soundscape of Modernity: Architectural Acoustics and the Culture of Listening in America, 1900–1933* (Cambridge, Mass., 2002); Karin Bijsterveld, "The Diabolical Symphony of the Mechanical Age: Technology and Symbolism of Sound in European and North American Noise Abatement Campaigns, 1900–40," *Social Studies of Science* 31 (Feb. 2001): 37–70; Raymond W. Smilor, "Confronting the Industrial Environment: The Noise Problem in America, 1893–1932" (Ph.D. diss., University of Texas at Austin, 1978); Derek Vaillant, *Sounds of Reform: Progressivism and Music in Chicago, 1873–1935* (Chapel Hill, N.C., 2003). See also Karin Bijsterveld, *Mechanical Sound: Technology, Culture, and Public Problems of Noise in the Twentieth Century* (Cambridge, Mass., 2008), which was published as this book was going to press.

2. *Victor Records, 1925* (Camden, N.J., 1925), HAG-TR; Daniel Gregory Mason, "The Depreciation of Music," *Musical Quarterly* 15 (Jan. 1929): 8, 15.

3. MacDonald Smith Moore, *Yankee Blues: Musical Culture and American Identity* (Bloomington, Ind., 1985); Carol Oja, *Making Music Modern: New York in the 1920s* (New York, 2000).

4. Augustus Zanzig, *Music in American Life: Present and Future* (Washington, D.C., 1932), 2.

5. Michael Denning has noted this paradox as it applied to radio and cinema. Michael Denning, "The End of Mass Culture," *International Labor and Working Class History* 37 (Spring 1990): 4–18.

6. Ernest Newman, *The Piano-Player and Its Music* (London, 1920); Carroll Brent Chilton, "A Musical Caliban," *Independent* 62 (Apr. 11, 1907): 838, 839, 841. The Taylor quotation comes from "The Wonder of the Duo-Art," a testimonial advertisement published by the Aeolian Company as an insert in numerous national periodicals in 1922 (for example the *Atlantic,* Oct. 1922). Aeolian claimed that Taylor's text first appeared as an article in the *New York World,* for which he served as music critic. See also George Hamlin, "Popular Songs Bad, Insists George Hamlin," *Musical America,* July 13, 1912, 36.

7. Henry C. Lomb, "Standardization in the Music Industries," in "Standards in Industry," special issue, *Annals of the American Academy of Political and Social Science* 137 (May 1928): 176–180; H. H. Stuckenschmidt, "The Mechanization of Music" (1925), in *German Essays on Music,* ed. Jost Hermand and Michael Gilbert (New York, 1994), 149–156, quotation on 156; Rudhyar D. Chennevière and Frederick H. Martens, "The Rise of the Musical Proletariat," *Musical Quarterly* 6 (Oct. 1920): 500–509. Chennevière was better known later as the composer and writer Dane Rudhyar.

8. Arthur Whiting, "The Mechanical Player," *Yale Review* 8 (July 1919): 831; Mason, "The Depreciation of Music," 8. See also "Against Mechanical Music," *NYT,* Dec. 30, 1908.

9. H. G. Wells, *Tono-Bungay* (1908; New York, 1935), 381; P. J. Meahl, *The Player-Piano: How and Why* (n.p., 1914), 10–11; F. S. L., "A Gramophone Method of Singing," *Musician,* Sept. 1910, 618; William Saroyan to William Gaddis, Oct. 8, 1946, box 158, folder 639, WUSTL-WG.

10. The first Stravinsky quotation is from *Current Opinion,* March 1925, the second from the *Etude,* August 1926, both quoted in David Silverman, "Igor Stravinsky," *AMICA News Bulletin,* n.d., subject clippings file "Player-piano," Music Division, New York Public Library. Toch quoted in Jürgen Hocker, liner notes to *Player-piano 4: Piano Music without Limits: Original Compositions of the 1920s* (Musikproduktion Dabringhaus und Grimm, 2007, MGD 645-1404-2).

11. Mark Katz, *Capturing Sound: How Technology Has Changed Music* (Berkeley, Calif., 2004), 99–113; Douglas Kahn, *Noise, Water, Meat: A History of Sound in the Arts* (Cambridge, Mass., 1999), 92–93, 127–128.

12. Kahn, *Noise, Water, Meat,* 56–67, 124–126; Thompson, *The Soundscape of Modernity,* 130–144; Henry Cowell, "The Joys of Noise" (1929) in Henry Cowell, *Essential Cowell: Selected Writings on Music,* ed. Dick Higgins (Kingston, N.Y., 2001), 249–252.

13. Le Corbusier, *Towards a New Architecture* (New York, 1960), 115. The first English translation appeared in 1927.

14. E. M. Forster, "The Machine Stops," in *The Machine Stops and Other Stories* (1947; London, 1997), 87–118. On the concept of the "keynote" of a soundscape, see R. Murray Schafer, *The Soundscape: Our Sonic Environment and the Tuning of the World* (Rochester, Vt., 1993), 9–10. Forster's was not the only fantasy world in which recorded sound was an unsettling presence; L. Frank Baum imagined a particularly grating personified phonograph in Oz. See L. Frank Baum, *The Patchwork Girl of Oz* (Chicago, 1913), chap. 7. Thanks to Peter Hanff for alerting me to this source.

15. Robert S. Lynd and Helen Merrell Lynd, *Middletown: A Study in Modern American Culture* (New York, 1929), 244, 269. A survey of small-town Kansas households, skewed towards middle- and upper-class residents, conveys a more modest picture—34 percent owned phonographs, 53 percent pianos (including player-pianos), and 34 percent radios—but little rigor appears to have been applied to the determination of the sample, and these data should be treated with some skepticism. Mary E. Hoffman, *The Buying Habits of Small-Town Women* (Kansas City, 1926), 71–74. See also Lizabeth Cohen, "Encountering Mass Culture at the Grassroots: The Experience of Chicago Workers in the 1920s," in *Consumer Society in American History: A Reader,* ed. Lawrence B. Glickman (Ithaca, N.Y., 1999), 147–169.

16. Steve Craig, "How America Adopted Radio: Demographic Differences in Set Ownership Reported in the 1930–1950 U.S. Censuses," *Journal of Broadcasting and Electronic Media* 48 (June 2004): 179–195; Johnson's study is quoted in Paul Oliver, *Songsters and Saints: Vocal Traditions on Race Records* (Cambridge, Mass., 1984), 274; William Faulkner, *As I Lay Dying* (1930; New York, 1987), 219–220, 241–242.

17. T. Carl Whitmer, "The Energy of American Crowd Music," *Musical Quarterly* 4 (Jan. 1918): 98–116.

18. Rick Altman, "Film Sound—All of It," *iris* 27 (Spring 1999): 31–48.

19. Susan J. Douglas, *Inventing American Broadcasting, 1899–1922* (Baltimore, 1987).

20. Susan Smulyan, *Selling Radio: The Commercialization of American Broadcasting, 1920–1934* (Washington, D.C., 1994), 19, Sarnoff quoted on 37.

21. William Arms Fisher, "The Radio and Music," *Music Supervisors' Journal* 12 (Feb. 1926): 14, 16.

22. Mason, "The Depreciation of Music," 8n2; Constant Lambert, *Music Ho! A Study of Music in Decline* (n.p., 1934), 168, 169; *Washington Post* cited in David Goodman, "Distracted Listening," in *Sound in the Age of Mechanical Reproduction*, ed. David Suisman and Susan Strasser (Philadelphia, forthcoming).

23. Carl Van Vechten, "On Hearing What You Want When You Want It," *Musical Quarterly* 7 (Oct. 1921): 559; George Jean Nathan and H. L. Mencken, *The American Credo: A Contribution toward the Interpretation of the National Mind* (New York, 1920), 28.

24. Katz, *Capturing Sound,* 61–67; Anne Shaw Faulkner, "Phonographs and Player Instruments," *National Music Monthly* (Aug. 1917), quoted ibid., 61.

25. J. Lawrence Erb, "Musical Appreciation," *Musical Quarterly* 11 (Jan. 1925): 1–7, quotation on 2; Arthur Hinton, "The Gift of Musical Appreciation," *Musical Quarterly* 1 (Oct. 1915): 560–568; Max Schoen, "The Teaching of Appreciation in Music" *Musical Quarterly* 13 (Jan. 1927): 39–58; *NYT,* Feb. 12, 1909; Clara T. Nichols, "Music in Our Public Schools," *Musical Quarterly* 4 (Oct. 1918): 538; Constantin Von Sternberg, "Music and Its Auditors," *Musical Quarterly* 9 (July 1923): 343–349, quotations on 344 and 348. See also Theodor Adorno, "Analytical Study of the NBC *Music Appreciation Hour,*" *Musical Quarterly* 78 (Summer 1994): 325–377.

26. Isaac Goldberg, *Tin Pan Alley: A Chronicle of American Popular Music* (1930; New York, 1961), 100. He makes the almost identical point on p. 13.

27. Theodor Adorno, "On the Fetish-Character in Music and the Regression of Listening" (1938), in *Essays on Music,* ed. Richard Leppert (Berkeley, Calif., 2002), 288–317.

28. Lambert, *Music Ho!* 169; Mason, "Depreciation of Music," 9; Theodor Adorno, "The Radio Symphony: An Experiment in Theory," in *Essays on Music,* ed. Richard Leppert (Berkeley, Calif., 2002), 261–263. A number of the leading authorities on Satie's work and career (for instance, Rollo Myers and Robert Orledge) maintain that the label of *musique d'ameublement* can be applied to much of Satie's work beginning in 1916 or 1918, but the term was not used formally until 1920. Rollo H. Myers, *Erik Satie* (London, 1948), 59–60; Ornella Volta, ed., *Satie Seen through His Letters,* trans. Michael Bullock (London, 1989), 175–177; Nancy Perloff, *Art and the Everyday: Popular Entertainment and the Circle of Erik Satie* (Oxford, 1991), 170; Robert Orledge, *Satie the Composer* (Cambridge, 1990), 133, 143; James Harding, *Erik Satie* (New York, 1975), 196–203. Recordings of Satie's furnishing music can be heard at ubuweb.com/sound/satie_conceptual.html.

29. Eleanor Selfridge-Field, "Experiments with Melody and Meter; or, The Effects of Music: The Edison-Bingham Music Research," *Musical Quarterly* 81 (Summer 1997): 291–310, quotation on 297.

30. Agnes Savill, "Music and Medicine," *Music and Letters* 4 (July 1923): 282–289; Charles M. Diserens, *The Influence of Music on Behavior* (Princeton, N.J., 1926); Max Schoen, *The Effects of Music: A Series of Essays* (New York, 1927).

31. Kenneth S. Clark, *Music in Industry* (New York, 1929); Frank H. Williams, "Phonograph Reduces Labor Turnover," *Industrial Management* 62 (July 1921): 60.

32. Joseph Lanza, *Elevator Music: A Surreal History of Muzak, Easy-Listening, and Other Moodsong* (New York, 1994), 22–30, 39–44; Jerri Husch, "Music of the Workplace: A Study of Muzak Culture" (Ph.D. diss., University of Massachusetts, 1984), 124, 145; the former Muzak vice president is quoted in Ronald Radano, "Interpreting Muzak: Speculations on Musical Experience in Everyday Life," *American Music* 7 (Winter 1989): 450. On music and work, see Ted Gioia, *Work Songs* (Durham, N.C., 2006).

33. Erik Barnouw, "Introduction," in *Wonderful Inventions: Motion Pictures, Broadcasting, and Recorded Sound at the Library of Congress,* ed. Iris Newsom (Washington, D.C., 1985), ix.

34. James Parakilas, "The Piano Institutionalized," in *Piano Roles: Three Hundred Years of Life with the Piano,* by James Parakilas et al. (New Haven, Conn., 1999), 317; James P. Kraft, *Stage to Studio: Musicians and the Sound Revolution, 1890–1950* (Baltimore, 1996), 35–39.

35. Altman, "Film Sound—All of It," 31–48; Craig H. Roell, "The Development of Tin Pan Alley," in *America's Musical Pulse: Popular Music in Twentieth-Century Society,* ed. Kenneth J. Bindas (Westport, Conn., 1992), 117. For the figures on musicians' employment in movie houses and AFM membership, see Robin D. G. Kelley, "Without a Song: New York Musicians Strike Out against Technology," in Howard Zinn, Dana Frank, and Robin D. G. Kelley, *Three Strikes: Miners, Musicians, Salesgirls, and the Fighting Spirit of Labor's Last Century* (Boston, 2001), 126.

36. Kelley, "Without a Song," 131; Kraft, *Stage to Studio,* 43. On film sound before 1926, see also James Lastra, *Sound Technology and the American Cinema: Perception, Representation, Modernity* (New York, 2000), 92–122.

37. On *The Jazz Singer,* see Michael Rogin, *Blackface, White Noise: Jewish Immigrants in the Hollywood Melting Pot* (Berkeley, Calif., 1996), esp. 73–120; Scott Eyman, *The Speed of Sound: Hollywood and the Talkie Revolution, 1926–1930* (New York, 1997).

38. Emily Thompson, "Wiring the World: Acoustical Engineers and the Empire of Sound in the Motion Picture Industry, 1927–1930," in *Hearing Cultures: Essays on Sound, Listening and Modernity,* ed. Veit Erlmann (Oxford, 2004), 196. On Warner Brothers, see Robert Sklar, *Movie-Made America: A Cultural History of American Movies* (New York, 1975), 152.

39. Lucia S. Schultz, "Performing-Right Societies in the United States," *Notes,* 2nd ser., 35 (Mar. 1979): 520; Goldberg, *Tin Pan Alley,* 313–314; "Who Became Us," www .warnerchappell.com/wcm/wcm_help/ourhistory.jsp, accessed Jan. 11, 2009. On modernist émigré composers, see Joseph Horowitz, *Artists in Exile: How Refugees from Twentieth-Century War and Revolution Transformed the American Performing Arts* (New York, 2008); Anthony Heilbut, *Exiled in Paradise: German Refugee Artists and Intellectuals in America from the 1930s to the Present* (Berkeley, Calif., 1997).

40. Kelley, "Without a Song," 126, 132–133; Kraft, *Stage to Studio,* 48–50. On unemployment during the Depression, see Cheryl Lynn Greenberg, *Or Does It Explode? Black Harlem in the Great Depression* (New York, 1997); Alice Kessler Harris, *Out to Work: A History of Wage-Earning Women in the United States* (New York, 2003).

41. Francis Bacon quoted in Thomas L. Hankins and Robert J. Silverman, *Instruments and the Imagination* (Princeton, N.J., 1995), 180; Edward Bellamy, *Looking Backward, 2000–1887* (1888; New York, 1915), 88–89; "To Manufacture Music by Electri-

cal Device," *NYT,* Mar. 11, 1906; "The Democracy of Music Achieved by Invention," *Current Literature* 42 (June 1907): 670–673.

42. Erik Barnouw, *A Tower in Babel: A History of Broadcasting in the United States to 1933,* vol. 1 (New York, 1966), 185–193, 220–224; Smulyan, *Selling Radio,* 37–64; Kraft, *Stage to Studio,* 69–71.

43. Edward Samuels, *The Illustrated Story of Copyright* (New York, 2000), 41–43; Schultz, "Performing-Right Societies in the United States," 516, 518.

44. American Society of Composers, Authors, and Publishers, *The Murder of Music* (New York, [1933]); American Society of Composers, Authors, and Publishers, *Nothing Can Replace Music* (New York, n.d.); Leonard Allen, "The Battle of Tin Pan Alley," *Harper's Magazine,* Oct. 1940, 514–523; Russell Sanjek and David Sanjek, *Pennies from Heaven: The American Popular Music Business in the Twentieth Century* (New York, 1996), 184–211; Robert Miller, "Reminiscences of Robert Miller," 1958, pp. 4–5, CU-OHROC.

45. *VoV* 19 (Feb. 1924); B. L. Aldridge, "Confidential History," 70, series 1, box 1, ALD-HAG; *VoV* 20 (Aug. 1925): 6.

46. The following account of the introduction of electrical recording and the integration with radio is based on Aldridge, "Confidential History," 70, 71a; Frederick O. Barnum III, *"His Master's Voice" in America: Ninety Years of Communications Pioneering and Progress: Victor Talking Machine Company, Radio Corporation of America, General Electric Company* (Camden, N.J., 1991), 112–114; Roland Gelatt, *The Fabulous Phonograph, 1877–1977,* 2nd ed. (New York, 1977), 248.

47. *TMW* 22 (Dec. 1926): 3. On mergermania, see William Leach, *Land of Desire: Merchants, Power and the Rise of a New American Culture* (New York, 1993), 263–297.

48. Aldridge, "Confidential History," 241–242.

49. Gelatt, *The Fabulous Phonograph,* 177; Robert M. W. Dixon, John Godrich, and Howard Rye, *Blues and Gospel Records, 1890–1943,* 4th ed. (Oxford, 1997), xxxii–xxxiii; Aldridge, "Confidential History," 71b.

50. In the period from 1906 to 1926, exports accounted for only 4 percent of the total value of the sale of machines (6 percent of the units sold) and 5 percent of the total value of the sale of records (again, 6 percent of units). See [B. L. Aldridge], "Untitled Chronology [I]," box 1, folder "VTM-Chronology, General," HAG-PEN.

51. Bertolt Brecht, "The Radio as an Apparatus of Communication," in *Radiotext(e),* eds. Neil Strauss and Dave Mandl, *Semiotext(e)* 16 (New York, 1993): 15; Kenney, *Recorded Music in American Life,* 140, 226n24; Richard A. Peterson, *Creating Country Music: Fabricating Authenticity* (Chicago, 1997).

52. Mark Booth, *The Experience of Song* (New Haven, Conn., 1981), 186, citing the critic Peter Reilly, originally quoted in Henry Pleasants, *Great American Popular Singers* (New York, 1974). Lawrence W. Levine and Cornelia R. Levine, comp., *The People and the President: America's Conversation with FDR* (Boston, 2002).

Epilogue

1. Dave Soldier, liner notes to Komar & Melamid and Dave Soldier, *The People's Choice Music* (compact disc, Dia Center for the Arts, 1997). "Eine Kleine Naughtmusik: How Nefarious Nonartists Cleverly Imitate Music," in "Pleasure," special issue, *Leonardo Music Journal* 12 (2002): 53–58. Both recordings are available online at www.ubu.com/sound/komar.html. The project was an offshoot of a similar project about people's taste in paintings. See JoAnn Wypijewski, ed., *Painting by Numbers: Komar and Melamid's Scientific Guide to Art* (Berkeley, Calif., 1997).

2. Michael Denning, "The End of Mass Culture," *International Labor and Working Class History* 37 (Spring 1990): 4–18.

3. On *The Anthology of American Folk Music,* see Robert Cantwell, *When We Were Good: The Folk Revival* (Cambridge, Mass., 1996).

4. Theodor Adorno, "Music in the Background," in *Essays on Music,* ed. Richard Leppert (Berkeley, Calif., 2002), 508.

5. Arthur Whiting, "The Mechanical Player," *Yale Review* 8 (July 1919): 831.

6. Ted Gioia, *Work Songs* (Durham, N.C., 2006), 231–239.

7. Alex Cummings, "Collectors, Bootleggers, and the Value of Jazz, 1930–1952," in *Sound in the Age of Mechanical Reproduction,* ed. David Suisman and Susan Strasser (Philadelphia, forthcoming); Rick Kennedy and Randy McNutt, *Little Labels—Big Sound* (Bloomington, Ind., 1999); Tony Olmsted, *Folkways Records: Moses Asch and His Encyclopedia of Sound* (New York, 2003), xi.

8. John Avery Lomax, *Adventures of a Ballad Hunter* (New York, 1947); John Avery Lomax and Alan Lomax, comp., *American Ballads and Folk Songs* (New York, 1934).

9. *Biennial Census of Manufactures, 1931* (Washington, D.C., 1935), 1127; Roland Gelatt, *The Fabulous Phonograph, 1877–1977,* 2nd ed. (New York, 1977), 255.

Acknowledgments

This book would not have been possible without the help and encouragement I received from a great many people and institutions. For their help tracking down and procuring several images for the book, I wish to thank Charles Amirkhanian, Shinji Kanki, Paul Lehrman; Stephan Saks of the New York Public Library; and especially Edward Samuels. Much of the material in Chapter 7 appeared in slightly different form in the *Journal of American History* in March 2004 in an article titled "Co-Workers in the Kingdom of Culture: Black Swan Records and the Political Economy of African American Music." I am grateful for permission to reprint it here.

Two fellowships from the Smithsonian Institution allowed me to conduct research at the National Museum of American History and the Library of Congress and to take a valuable research trip to the British Library and the EMI Archives in England and the Bibliothèque Nationale in Paris. The Smithsonian was an immensely stimulating environment in which to work, and I wish to thank Pete Daniel, Laura Burd Schiavo, Sarah Johnson, Jason Weems, Georgine Clarsen, Alexander Russo, and David Sanjek for taking time from their research and writing to talk with me about my own.

A General University Research Grant from the University of Delaware supplied funding to work on revisions to the manuscript, and an invaluable yearlong fellowship from the National Endowment for the Humanities enabled me to complete them. At the University of Delaware I am lucky to have fine colleagues and help from a great support staff, especially Douglas Tobias. I am indebted to George Basalla, who alerted me to several helpful sources, and especially to Susan Strasser, who read the entire manuscript and has offered much sage advice.

The Department of History of the University of California, Berkeley, hosted me as a visiting scholar in the Bay Area for a year and a half, a connection that would have been impossible without the kind intervention of Rebecca McLennan. During that time, I also participated in the Affiliate Artist Program of the Headlands Center for the Arts, located in a sublimely beautiful spot whose peculiar acoustics deepened my understanding of soundscapes. Thanks especially to Holly Blake and Linda Samuels for arranging this affiliation and to Juliette Delventhal for many wonderful meals. At the Headlands, my thinking about the argument of *Selling Sounds,* and about its audience, benefited from conversations with many artists, musicians, and writers, including Chris Bell, Michael Fiday, Noria Jablonski, Pawek Kruk, Daniel McCormack, Danielle Nelson Mourning, and especially Hadi Tabatabai and Lisa Hamilton.

Eric Foner helped me immensely as this project developed, and his thoughtful, sometimes skeptical counsel helped me at every stage. Without Betsy Blackmar's insight and compassion, the manuscript would never have come together or reached completion; her combination of curiosity and rigor continues to inspire me. Timothy Taylor read countless drafts and pressed me to think through numerous subjects. Richard Bushman, Barbara J. Fields, Daryl Scott, Herb Sloan, Anders Stephanson, and the late Mark Tucker also read parts of this work or talked with me about it in useful ways. Alan Brinkley read and commented on an entire draft at an earlier stage, as did Robin Kelley. At Columbia University, where the seeds of this project were first sown, I benefited from conversations with and comments from my outstanding colleagues, including Michael Bernstein, Chris Capozzola, Sam Haselby, Thea Hunter, Martha Jones, Adam Rothman, and especially my dear friends Margaret Garb and Eliza Byard.

Since 2000 I have been a sometime disc jockey at WFMU, a freeform radio station in Jersey City, New Jersey, which comprises the most creative group of people I have known. They continue to challenge my ideas about music, sound, and noncommercial culture on a regular basis, and this book is far richer for all the aural channels WFMU has opened up for me, both as a DJ and as a listener. The world of sound is lucky to have in it such wonders as Ken Freedman, Brian Turner, Scott Williams, Bryce Kretschmann, Bethany Ryker, Jason Engel, and Ken Goldsmith.

It was a pleasure to work with Joyce Seltzer at Harvard University Press. Her enthusiasm for this book never flagged, even as numerous deadlines came and went, and the finished product is far better for her critical suggestions. Susan Abel's careful editing tightened the manuscript in innumerable ways and helped me steer clear of many errors. Two anonymous outside readers offered salutary suggestions that pushed me to clarify several important points. I am also grateful for the comments by another outside reader, Charles McGovern, whom I first met in 1999, when he and Pete Daniel sponsored me as a fellow at the Smithsonian. Since that time, Charles has read numerous complete drafts of this work, and I have learned immensely from his piercing critical insights, boundless knowledge of music and American culture, and deep humanism.

In the more than ten years that I have been at work on this project, countless people have offered me food, shelter, good cheer, and other forms of sustenance. Those who deserve my gratitude include Tucker Nichols, Melissa Axelrod, Amira Day, Lew Stringer, Elana Bober, Jon Nichols, Rayna Kalas, Bill and Linda Link, Annie Link, Marina Rustow, Michael Sappol, Nora Jaffary, Derrick Rossi, Anshu Srivastava, Tracy Rolling-Brunar, Erik Brunar, Michael Dorian, Heidi Nakashima, Cynthia Joyce, Ed Park, David Sampliner, Sam Zalutsky, Ed Boland, and Vera and Vica Popescu. Rachael Stryker offered some extremely useful thoughts about writing, and Bob Guldin generously brainstormed ideas for the book's title.

Conversations with Emily Thompson, Douglas Kahn, and Elena Razlogova enhanced my thinking about all things sonic and aural; and for their comments on different parts of this book at earlier stages, I wish to thank the late Lawrence Levine, David Nasaw, Jackson Lears, Barry Shank, Michelle Hilmes, Roger Horowitz, Jeffrey Melnick, and Douglas H. Daniels. Joshua Freeman generously passed on to me some helpful sources about New York opera audiences. The late Lee Buckley Suisman revealed to me, at a young age, that it was possible to think both seriously and passionately about music. In more recent years, my understanding of music, culture, and capitalism also was enriched by many hours of talking with Michael Carter, Karl Hagstrom Miller, and Florin Popescu. Early in the development of this project, Adina Popescu helped me shape and refine many of my ideas and drafts of numerous early sections. In the late stages, Jeremy Braddock talked with me about issues I had not yet resolved and generously offered his reactions to drafts of several newer sections.

I owe an inexpressible debt of gratitude to my family, especially Sherry Suisman, Charlie Suisman, and Michael and Elsa Suisman. My mother, Janet Schecter Suisman, was always my most loyal, tireless champion, and she showed great enthusiasm for the early parts of this project. I feel a great sadness that she did not live to see the completion of the book; I think she would have liked it. Finally, I want to thank Holly Link for her unfailing confidence in this book and in me, for buoying my spirits when they sagged, and for indulging me with her love and patience.

Index

Academy of Music (New York City), 284

Adams, Samuel Hopkins, 120

Adorno, Theodor: on sight, 14; "On the Fetish-Character in Music and the Regression of Listening," 255; "The Radio Symphony," 255–256; on background music, 276

Advertising, 11, 60; sound as, 11, 60, 73, 88; invasive, 14; and radio, 14, 265, 267, 278; and music publishers, 22, 25, 27, 41, 44, 49, 51–52, 60, 61, 67, 74–75; and player-pianos, 97, 98, 102, 194; and phonograph companies, 104, 106–107, 109–110, 111, 112–113, 114–117, 118, 119–121, 122, 123, 128–129, 130, 131, 133, 134, 135, 136, 137, 142–144, 146, 147, 148, 149, 179–183, 184, 185–189, 190, 191–195, 205, 213, 219–220, 223–229, 231, 232, 236, 262, 266, 267, 279; Red Seal as, 113, 122; and pianos, 114, 129, 130. *See also* Music education; Plugging

Advertising Age, 182

Aeolian Co., 92, 96–99, 102, 165, 167, 189, 194, 231, 233, 244

Aeolian Hall, 98

African Americans: and spirituals, 19, 208, 214, 218, 221; pianos and organs among, 19–20; as compared with Jews, 37; discrimination against, 37–38, 39–40, 206, 207–208, 209–210, 212–213, 214–215, 220–221, 224, 225, 226, 275; and coon songs, 37–38, 54–55, 206, 209; as songwriters, 37–41; as musicians, 37–41, 48, 139, 145, 206, 207, 208, 209, 210, 212–216, 217–222, 223, 224, 230, 231, 235, 238, 263, 276; in Tin Pan Alley, 37–41, 274; and ragtime, 39–41, 54–55, 56, 207, 209, 219, 227; as consumers, 207, 208, 210, 213, 223, 224, 226–227, 232, 236, 237, 249; and World War I, 207–208, 209; attitudes toward black-owned businesses, 208–209, 215–216, 217, 226, 236–237; lynching of, 220–221. *See also* Black Swan Records

"After the Ball," 28–30, 31, 47–48, 55, 87

"Ain't My Baby Grand?" 65, 66

Ajax Record Co., 225, 231

Albee, E. F., 80, 81, 84

"Alexander's Ragtime Band," 53–55, 202

Alhambra (music hall), 71

"Always Take Mother's Advice," 27

Amateur music making, 275

American Federation of Musicians (AFM), 162, 260, 264

American Music Publishers Association, 165

American Music Stores, 86

American Piano Company (Ampico), 179, 194–195, 205

American Record Corporation (ARC), 269

American Society of Composers, Authors, and Publishers (ASCAP), 171–175, 176, 263, 266, 271

Antheil, George, 244; *Ballet Mécanique*, 245, 246

Anthology of American Folk Music, The, 276

Anti-Semitism, 32, 35

Aristotle, 12
Armour, Philip, 97
Armstrong, F. Wallis, 114
Armstrong, Louis, 231, 276
Arnoth, D. G., 32
Arrangers, 38–39, 41, 42–43
Art songs, 18
ASCAP. *See* American Society of Composers, Authors, and Publishers
Asch, Moses, 280. *See also* Folkways Records
AT&T, 251, 261, 267
Attali, Jacques, 5
Authors' and Composers' Copyright League of America, 162
Automobiles, 186, 240
Ayer, N. W., 114–115

Bacon, Francis: *New Atlantis,* 264
Barnum, P. T.: humbug principle of, 60, 70; circus parades of, 79; and Lind, 129
Barraud, Francis: *His Master's Voice,* 119–120, 121
Barrel organs, 73, 74, 92, 96, 250
Barrymore, John, 261
Barthes, Roland, on consumption, 94
Baum, L. Frank: *Wonderful Wizard of Oz,* 188, 333n14
Beatles, the, 282
Bechet, Sidney, 126
Beck, Martin, 80
Beecher, Henry Ward, 185
Bell, Alexander Graham, 3
Bell, Chichester, 4
Bellamy, Edward: *Looking Backward,* 264
Bell Telephone, 201
Benjamin, Walter: on the senses, 13; on technology, 13; on mechanical reproduction, 111
Berlin, Irving, 35; and Tin Pan Alley, 21, 52; rules for writing a successful popular song, 45–46, 47; attitude toward novelty, 47; "Alexander's Ragtime Band," 53–55, 202; "That Mysterious Rag," 55; on professional copies, 61; "The Popular Song," 86–87; and ASCAP, 171; and copyright law, 174
Berliner, Emile, 16, 124; gramophone of, 4–6, 101–102; and Deutsche Grammophon, 269–270
Bernays, Edward, 129; on Caruso, 142–143
Bernstein, Louis, 32, 44, 45; on plugging, 72; on vaudeville, 82
Bingham, Walter Van Dyke, 256–257

Black Seal records. *See* Victor Talking Machine Co.
Black Swan Records, 205–206, 216–224, 233–239; and Du Bois, 206, 208, 209, 211, 213, 215–216; and Pace, 206, 208–209, 210, 216–217, 218–219, 221, 222–224, 230, 231, 233, 234, 236, 238–239; racial/cultural uplift promoted by, 207–209, 213, 214–215, 219, 220, 221–223, 226–228, 230, 231, 234–235, 236–237, 238–239, 280; advertising by, 213, 219, 220, 223–224, 225, 226–227, 228, 229, 230, 231, 232, 234–235; origin of name, 213–214, 216; and Fletcher Henderson, 216, 218, 220, 222, 235; board of directors, 216–217, 236; and Ethel Waters, 218–219, 220–221, 222, 224, 230, 235, 238; class conflict within, 218–219, 221–223, 238; and blues, 218–223, 224, 227, 231, 237, 238, 279; and Trixie Smith, 220; Black Swan Troubadours, 220–221; and Bessie Smith, 221; expansion of, 230–231, 234; impact of radio on, 231, 233–234; reissues of records by white musicians, 234–235; compared with Victor, 238
Blakeley, David, 129
Bleistein v. Donaldson, 157–158
Bloom, Benny, 64–65
Bloom, Sol, 82
Blues, 19, 169, 208, 212, 225, 226, 230, 236, 271; and Black Swan Records, 218–223, 224, 227, 231, 237, 238, 279
BMI, 176
Board of Music Trade, 25
Bonwit Teller, 202
Book-of-the-Month Club, 123
Bourseuil, Charles, 4
Bradford, Perry, 210, 213
Brecht, Bertolt, on radio, 271
British Invasion, 281
Broome Records, 208
Brownie cameras, 123
Brunswick-Balke-Collender, 267
Brunswick Co., 231, 233
Bryan, William Jennings, recordings of, 5, 289n5
Burkan, Nathan, 162, 167, 171, 172, 174
Burleigh, Harry T., 37, 171
Burr, Henry, 144
Bushell, Garvin, 222

Caesar, Irving, 35; on songwriting, 45; "Tea for Two," 45; "Swanee," 83
Cage, John, 276; *Imaginary Landscape No. 1,* 244

Index

Cahill, Thaddeus, the telharmonium, 264

Calvé, Emma, 105

Camera Work, 112

Cameron, S. T., 162

Capitol Theatre (New York City), 260

Carl Fischer, 262

Carnegie Hall, 98, 202, 246

Carnegie Institute of Technology, 256

Carson, Fiddlin' John, 175

Carter Family, 175

Caruso, Dorothy, 145, 219

Caruso, Enrico: Victor recordings made by, 106, 107–110, 114, 115, 116, 124, 125–126, 128–132, 133, 134, 136, 137, 140–141, 142, 143, 145, 148–149, 182, 202, 227, 229, 280; recollections of, 113–114, 125–126, 140, 142–143, 144, 145; as celebrity, 125–126, 128–132, 133, 134, 135, 136, 137–142, 144–145, 148, 149, 168–169; and Helen Keller, 126, 127; royalties paid to, 130; personality of, 134, 137–140, 142, 144–145; Monkey House Incident, 138–139, 145; during World War I, 197; and "Vesti la Giubba" from *I Pagliacci,* 261

Castle, Vernon and Irene, 207

Castle Tremaine, Irene, 219, 220

Catchings, Waddill. *See* Muzak

Celebrity, 110, 115, 125–130, 135, 137–139, 142–148; Hollywood star system, 128

Cell phones: musical ring tones for, 8; and copyright law, 176

Chaliapin, Fyodor, 105

Charisma, 129, 142

Charivari, 13

Chennevière, Rudhyar D., 243

Chicago Defender, 208, 210, 220, 225, 230–231; "Jazzing Away Prejudice," 214–215

Chickering, Jonas, 178–179

Child, Francis James, 50, 275

Chilton, Carroll Brent, 90; on the player-piano, 242

Choruses: importance in popular music, 49–50, 275, 277; chorus slips, 62, 63, 67, 72, 88; chorus slides, 67

Christian Science, 187, 188

Christie, Agatha, 121

Christmas songs, 279

Church, John, 32

Ciardi, John, on Caruso, 140

Cinema. *See* Motion pictures

Claques, 70, 73, 88

Clark, Alfred C., 105

Clark, Carroll, 207, 217–218, 227, 229

Clark, Frances Elliott, 191–192, 193, 195, 201

Cohan, George M.: "Over There," 195

Cohen, Morris: "Property and Sovereignty," 152

Cole-Talbert, Florence, 227

Collins, Arthur, 144

Columbia Broadcasting System (CBS), 265, 266, 269

Columbia Graphophone Co., 269

Columbian World Exposition (Chicago, 1893), 30, 87

Columbia Phonograph Co., 217–218, 221, 231, 268–269, 278–279; and National, 102, 104, 106, 153, 210, 267; and Victor, 104, 114, 145–146, 153, 162–163, 194, 210, 267; advertising by, 106, 114; and CBS, 265, 269

Comic songs, 45, 49, 208, 215, 218, 227, 228–229

Commodification of music, 9–17, 240–242; consumer credit, 11, 186; attitudes toward songwriting, 20, 21–22, 23, 44–45; and local advertising, 179–183; professional musical salesmanship, 180, 182–183, 185; commodity fetishism, 204–205; and multidimensional character of music, 280. *See also* Music publishers; Plugging; Tin Pan Alley; Victor Talking Machine Co.

Community music movement, 201–202, 203

Computers, 282–283

Computer software, 16

Condorcet, marquis de, 155

Conreid, Heinrich, 139

Consolidated Film Industries, 269

Consumer capitalism: novelty in, 10; role of consumer desires in, 10, 15, 51–52, 57–58, 60; production of consumer desires in, 10, 57–58, 60; advertising in, 11; consumer credit, 11, 186; and women, 46; role of large corporations in, 153, 204–206, 259, 268–269, 270, 271, 274–275; invisibility of music industry, 204–206; centralization of cultural production, 241–242, 263; development of, 253–254. *See also* Commodification of music; Popular music

Cook, Will Marion, 37, 171; "Clorindy, or the Origin of the Cakewalk," 38

Coolidge, Calvin, 202, 203; on music and democracy, 178–179

Coon songs, 37–38, 40, 54, 106, 206, 207, 209, 277

Copland, Aaron: *Appalachian Spring,* 7

Copyleft movement, 157

Copyright law: and music as intellectual property, 3, 8, 9, 150–153, 154–177, 280; and music publishers, 3, 8, 159–160, 163–164, 167, 175–177, 280; performance right in, 3, 159, 160, 162, 167, 170–175, 176; Copyright Act of 1891, 25; enforcement of, 27–28, 157–159, 170, 172–175, 283–284; mechanical right in, 75, 167, 168, 175, 176; defined, 151; and U.S. Constitution, 151–152, 162, 165; contrasted with patent law, 153–154; and private versus common property debate, 154–155, 156–158; and *Donaldson v. Becket,* 155; and Statute of Anne (England), 155; Copyright Act of 1790, 155–156, 157; copyright law of 1831, 156; and sheet music, 156, 159, 160–162; and foreign copyrights, 156–157; and Berne Convention of 1886, 157; and Copyleft movement, 157; and *Bleistein v. Donaldson,* 157–158; relation to technology, 157–158; Copyright Act of 1909, 159–165, 166–177; and Victor, 162–163, 175; as protecting expression of ideas rather than ideas themselves, 163; and *White-Smith v. Apollo,* 165, 166, 167; compulsory license in, 167; copyright term, 167, 177; amendment of 1971, 168; music as product rather than process in, 168–169; and originality, 169; dramatic works as product rather than process in, 169–170; and revenue of licensing organizations, 176; and public domain, 177; international agreements regarding, 270; Digital Millennium Copyright Act of 1998, 282–283

Corbin, Arthur L., 152

Corbusier, Le: *Towards a New Architecture,* 245, 247

Corporations and consumer capitalism, 153, 259, 270, 271, 274–275; invisibility of corporations, 204–206; mergers of corporations, 268–269

Cover songs, 167

Cowboy songs, 19

Cowell, Henry, 245; *Aeolian Harp,* 276

Crisis, 211, 215, 226, 228, 229, 231, 232

Cros, Charles, 4

Crosby, Bing, 272

Cultural capital, 104, 111, 148

Cultural hierarchy, 110–111, 123

Damrosch, Leopold, 20, 34

Damrosch, Walter, 20, 34, 214

Dance halls, 10, 64, 71, 79, 158, 160, 250

Davis, Gussie, 38

Debussy, Claude, 99

De Koven, Reginald, 23

DeMille, Cecil B., 67

Democratic values, 123–124, 178, 182, 195, 238, 240, 242, 271, 282

Department stores: music in, 10, 14, 46, 64–65, 66, 75, 76, 77–78, 80, 85, 88–89, 110, 181, 189, 250; Macy's, 64, 85, 119, 191, 202; Siegel-Cooper's, 64–65, 78, 85, 110; Wanamaker's, 75, 76, 77, 78, 115; Gimbel's, 78; Montgomery Ward, 115; Bamburger's, 174–175; Fair Department Store, 189

Depew, Chauncey, 109

De Sylva, Brown & Henderson, 262

Dett, R. Nathaniel, 218

Deutsche Grammophon, 269–270

Dewey, John, 192

Diderot, Denis, 155

Digitization, 282

Dippel, Andreas, 141

Ditson, Oliver A., 32

Division of labor, 41–44, 49; at M. Witmark and Sons, 3

Dizikes, John, on Caruso, 141, 144

Dogiel, Johann, 258

Donaldson v. Becket, 155

Don Juan (motion picture), 261

Douglass, Leon, 113, 115

Doyle, Arthur Conan, 121

Dreams, popular songs about, 47

Dreiser, Theodore, 34; on music industry, 38, 73

Dresser, Paul, 34, 36

Dreyfus, Max, 32, 33; on copyrights, 176–177

Dry Goods Economist, 77

Du Bois, W. E. B.: relations with Pace and Black Swan Records, 206, 208, 209, 211, 213, 215–216; *The Souls of Black Folk,* 210, 214; on art and public opinion, 215–216; "Phonograph Records," 215–216

Dunbar, Paul Lawrence, 37; "Clorindy, or the Origin of the Cakewalk," 38

Dwight, John Sullivan, 20

Dwight's Journal of Music, 214

Dyer, Frank L., 113

Dylan, Bob, 276

Eastman, George, 123

Easton, Edward, 102

Edison, Thomas: phonograph of, 4–6, 91, 102, 104, 106, 128; as celebrity, 146; and studies on the psychological effects of music, 256–257. *See also* National Phonograph Co.

Egypt, phonograph record sales in, 16

Eisler, Hanns, on sight, 14
Electrical and Musical Instruments Ltd. (EMI), 269
Ellington, Duke, 276
Elman, Mischa, 197
Emerson, Ralph Waldo, 185
Emotion and music. *See* Feeling and music
England: *Donaldson v. Becket*, 155; Statute of Anne, 155; Copyright Act of 1911, 171; Performing Rights Society (PRS), 171. *See also* United Kingdom
English songs, 19, 20, 23, 27
Erb, J. Lawrence, 254
Europe, James Reese, 207, 214–215

F. A. Mills, 30
Farrar, Geraldine, 115
"Fatal Night of the Ball, The," 47–48
Faulkner, William: *As I Lay Dying*, 249–250
Feeling and music, 11–12, 14–15, 45, 51, 140, 143, 144, 149, 192, 256–258, 270, 277, 280
Feist, Leo, 32, 33, 53, 74–75, 167, 176, 195
Feist, Leonard, 176
Fichte, Johann Gottlieb, 155
Finland, phonograph record sales in, 16
Firth, Thaddeus, 32
Fisher, William Arms, on song sharking, 51
Fletcher, Alexander, 150
Folk songs, 169, 176, 275–276, 280; compared with popular songs, 18, 50, 57
Folkways Records, 276, 280
Formulas, in popular song, 48–50, 51–52
Forster, E. M.: "The Machine Stops," 247, 249, 264
Foster, Stephen C., 7, 49, 59, 87; "Old Folks at Home" ("Way Down upon the Swanee River"), 22, 23, 24, 54; income of, 22–23, 24
France, 256; copyright law of 1783, 155
Franklin Institute, 4, 7
Freund, John C., 46
Futures markets, 152–153
Futurists, 245

Gabler, Milt, 189
Gaddis, William, 244
Gaisberg, Frederick, 105–106, 107–108, 109, 197
Garnes, Antoinette, 227
Garvey, Marcus, 209, 213, 217, 223
General Electric, 251
Gennett Records, 231
George Steck & Co., 98

German Americans, 33–36
Germany: phonograph record sales in, 16; player-pianos in, 98
Gershwin, George, 35, 176; "Rhapsody in Blue," 7; and Tin Pan Alley, 21, 52; as plugger, 61, 64; "Swanee," 83
Gershwin, Ira, 35
"Get on the Raft with Taft," 75
Gilbert, L. Wolfe, 35, 44
Girdner, J. H.: "The Plague of City Noises," 73
Goldberg, Isaac, 255; on filling the air with music, 11; on arrangers, 43; on influence of women, 46; on music publishing before 1893, 58; on marketing of songs, 58–59
Goldberg, Rube, 247, 248, 249
Gospel music, 221, 279
Gotham-Attucks Music Publishing Co., 39
Gould, Glenn, 282
Gounod, Charles, 218
Gramophone Co. Ltd., 102; and Victor, 104–107, 109, 112–113, 114, 119, 121, 122, 123, 125–126, 131–132, 203, 268–269, 270; and EMI, 269
Gramophones versus phonographs, 4–6
Great Depression, 241, 252–253, 263, 266, 267, 281
Greenfield, Elizabeth Taylor, 213–214, 216
Griffith, D. W., 67
Grigsby-Grunow Co., 269
Gulbransen Co., 98, 100, 205
Gurney, Edmund: *The Power of Sound*, 12–13
Guthrie, Woody, 7

Hager, Fred, 210
Haggard, Merle: "An Okie from Muskogee," 7
Hall, G. Stanley, 192
Hall, William, 32
Hammerstein, Oscar, II, on ASCAP, 172
Hand, Learned, 172; *Fred Fisher v. Dillingham*, 169
Handy, W. C., 212–213, 215, 217
Hansen, Ellis, 183
"Happy Birthday to You," 8
Hardin, Lil, 72–73
Harding, Frank, 27
Harding, Warren G., 178, 202
Harlem, 214, 218–220; blues contest at Manhattan Casino, 219–220
"Harlem Hellfighters" regiment, 207
Harms, Alex, 27
Harms, Tom, 27
Harriman, Mrs. Oliver, 219

Harris, Charles K., 22, *33*, 36, 274; "After the Ball," 28–30, 31, 47–48, 55, 87; on musical structure, 49; on song titles, 49; on song choruses, 50; on song slides, 65, 67; on paid plants, 70
Haviland, Frederick Benjamin, 33
Hawthorne, Nathaniel, 13
Hayes, Roland, 139, 145
Hearst, William Randolph, 128
Hedgeland, F. W., 163
Hein, Silvio, 171
Helmholtz, Hermann, 4
"He May Be Your Man (But He Comes to See Me Sometimes)," 222
Henderson, Fletcher, 216, 218, 220, 222, 235
"Henrietta! Have You Met Her?" 26
Herbert, Victor, 34, 171; and copyright law, 162, 163, 172–173, 174; "Sweethearts," 172–173
Herreld, Kemper, 227
Herzog, Werner: *Fitzcarraldo,* 126
Higginson, Henry Lee, 20
Hindemith, Paul, 244
Hip-hop, 281
Hirsch, Louis A., 171
Hit songs, 15–16, 44, 58, 89; "After the Ball," 28–30, 31, 47–48, 55, 87; "All Coons Look Alike to Me," 38; "Alexander's Ragtime Band," 53–55, 202
H. J. Heinz Co., 201
Hobbies, 143–144
Hogan, Ernest: "All Coons Look Alike to Me," 38
Holiday, Billie: "Strange Fruit," 7
Holmes, Oliver Wendell, Jr.: on performing rights and *Shanley* decision, 14, 172–174, 175, 176; majority opinion in *Bleistein v. Donaldson,* 158; concurring opinion in *White-Smith v. Apollo,* 167
Homer, Winslow, 59
"Honey You Sho' Looks Bad," 228, 230
Hoover, Herbert, 153; and "The Star Spangled Banner," 202–203
Howley, Patrick, 33
Howley, Haviland Co., 30
Hubbard, W. L.: *History of American Music,* 28, 43
Hubbell, Raymond, 171
Hughes, Charles Evans, 165, 189
Hughes, Revella, 217, 219
Hume, David, on induction, 237–238
Hunter, Alberta, 221, 235
Hymns, 19, 279

Immigrants, 107, 145, 207, 241, 270
Independent, 90
Industrialization, 52, 270–272, 280; and volume of sound, 12, 13, 240–241, 245, 247, 248–250, 251–254
Industrial music movement. *See* Music-in-industry movement
Industrial Workers of the World (IWW), 278; *The Little Red Song Book,* 278–279
Internationalization of music industry, 203, 269–270, 272
Internet, the, 282
iPods, 8
Ireland, 23
Irwin, May, 30
Ives, Charles, 87–88, 176, 276

Jackson, Aunt Molly: "Kentucky Miner's Wife," 279
Jazz, 56, 169, 214–215, 218, 230, 231, 236, 276, 279, 281
Jazz Singer, The, 261–262
Jerome, William, 174
Jerome H. Remick & Co., 30, 32, 33, 64–65, 85, 262
Jews: anti-Semitism, 32, 35; in Tin Pan Alley, 32–35, 37, 241; in Hollywood, 35; as compared with African Americans, 37
John Church & Co., 172
"John Henry," 176
Johnson, Charles S., 249
Johnson, Eldridge Reeves, 101–102, 119, 130, 189, 268; attitudes toward music, 104, 114, 124, 238; and Red Seal series, 106–107, 113, 114; on *Leeds & Catlin Company v. Victor Talking Machine Company,* 154
Johnson, James P., 219; "Desperate Blues," 220
Johnson, James Weldon, 37, 171; *Black Manhattan,* 236–237
Johnson, J. Rosamond, 37, 171
Johnson, Nicholas, 52
Jolson, Al, 202, 272; and "Swanee," 83; relations with music publishers, 83, 84; as celebrity, 168–169; "My Mammy," 261; in *The Jazz Singer,* 261–262
Jones, LeRoi: *Blues People,* 237
Joplin, Scott, 40
Jose, Dick, 30
Journal of American Folklore, 50
Jukeboxes, 96, 281
J. & W. Seligman, 268

Index

Kapp, Dave, 186
Keith and Albee's Circuit, 80, 81, 84, 284
Keller, Helen, 126, 127
Kerker, Gustave, 171
Kern, Jerome, 176; at Tin Pan Alley, 21; as plugger, 61; and ASCAP, 171
Kinetoscopes, 95, 264
Komar and Melamid, *People's Choice Music, The,* 273–274
Krehbiel, Henry, 20, 34; on Caruso, 141

La Guardia, Fiorello, 219
Lambert, Constant: *Music Ho! A Study of Music in Decline,* 252–253, 255
Leeds & Catlin Company v. Victor Talking Machine Company, 153–154
Leo Feist Publishing Co., 30, 61, 74–75, 195, 262; slogan "You Can't Go Wrong with a Feist Song," 75
Lessing, Gotthold, 155
Libbey, James Aldrich, 30, 31
Liebling, A. J., on Caruso, 125–126, 144
"Lift Ev'ry Voice and Sing," 218
Lincoln, Abraham, 185
Lind, Jenny, 129, 131
Lippmann, Walter: *Public Opinion,* 215
Listening versus hearing, 255–259
Liszt, Franz, 129
"Little Annie Rooney," 20
Locke, John, on property, 154–155, 156
Lomax, Alan, 281
Lomax, John, 281; *Cowboy Songs and Other Frontier Ballads,* 50
Lomb, Henry C., on standardization of music, 242–243
Lord & Taylor, 78
Loudspeakers, electrical, 241, 250, 251, 252, 253, 264, 267
Louisiana Purchase Exposition (Saint Louis, 1904), 39–40, 87
Lynd, Robert and Helen Merrell: *Middletown,* 249, 254
Lyon & Healy, 113
Lyricists, 41, 45, 49, 171

MacDonough, Glenn, 171
Mack, Cecil. *See* McPherson, R. C.
Macy's, 64, 85, 119, 191, 202
Magnetic tape, 123, 282
Mahler, Gustav, 99
Malaya, phonograph record sales in, 16
Mannes, David, 214

Marconi, Guglielmo, 251
Marks, Edward, 32, 33, 42, 53, 80, 84; on songwriting for the market, 44; on plugging, 59, 71, 72, 81–82, 86; and song slides, 65; on nickelodeons, 67; on vaudeville, 81–82
Marshall Field, 201
Martens, Frederick H., 243
Martin, Riccardo, 148
Martinelli, Giovanni, 261
Marx, Groucho, 126
Marx, Karl: on the senses, 12; on commodity fetishism, 204
Mason, Daniel Gregory: "The Depreciation of Music," 240–242; on mechanical music, 243, 255; on radio, 252, 253
Mason, Lowell, 191, 241
Mason & Hamlin, 241
Maxwell, George, 171
Maxwell, William, 256
McCall's Magazine, 202
McCormack, John, 132, 135, 144–145
McPhail, Lindsay, 234
McPherson, R. C., 171; "Teasing," 38; and Gotham-Attucks Music Publishing Co., 39
Mechanical Orguinette Co., 96
"Meet Me Tonight in Dreamland," 47
Melba, Nellie, 97, 98, 115
Mencken, H. L.: *The American Credo,* 254
Messenger, The, 226, 228
Metro-Goldwyn-Mayer, 262, 263
Metropolitan Opera, 119, 128, 139, 141, 145, 261
MICC. *See* Music Industries Chamber of Commerce
Middle class, 25, 40, 91, 154, 201, 237; contrasted with working class, 12, 19–20, 35, 113–114, 145, 221–223, 249
Milhaud, Darius, 235
Miller, Nathan L., 219
Miller, Robert, 62, 83
Mills, F. A., 167
Mind cure groups, 187–188
Minstrel shows, 3, 36, 40, 54, 79–80, 207, 209, 261, 284
Modernism, 88, 263, 269; and mechanical music, 244–245, 246, 247. *See also* Ives, Charles
Modern Methods, 182
Moholy-Nagy, László, 244
Moody and Sankey hymns, 19
Moon Illustrated Weekly, 211
Mora, Helen, 30
Morgan, J. P., 97, 269

Morton, Jelly Roll, 231, 276

"Most Wanted Song, The," versus "The Most Unwanted Song," 273–274

Motion pictures: music in, 10, 16; talking pictures, 16, 142, 261–263; Hollywood, 21, 35, 43, 53, 128, 261–263, 284; versus song slides, 67, 70; stars, 139, 142; and patent pools, 153; and copyright law, 157, 158, 176; and phonographs, 259–260, 262, 270; and live musicians, 259–261, 263, 264; Vitaphone technology, 261; *The Jazz Singer,* 261–262; musicals, 262–263, 281; and radio, 263–264

Movie theaters: plugging in, 64, 65, 67, 250; and ASCAP, 175

MTV music videos, 67

Murdock, John J., 80

Murray, Billy, 144

Music, as intrinsic to community and nation, 7, 178–179, 191–192, 195, 197–203

Music, as property: and copyright law, 3, 8, 9, 150–153, 154–177, 280; relation to financial stakes, 151; versus physicalist conceptions of property, 152–153; versus writing, 155–156, 162, 165, 166, 168

Musical improvisation, 169, 275

Musical notation, 91

Musical theater, 19, 158, 250, 277

Music appreciation movement, 241, 254–255

Music boxes, 92

Music education, 180, 191–195, 203, 214, 238, 241, 254

Music halls: in England, 20, 27, 62; in New York, 71

Musicians, 49; payment of, 5, 23, 27, 29, 30, 38, 40, 43–44, 130; relations with music publishers, 15, 29–30, 43–44, 61; African Americans as, 37–41, 48, 139, 145, 206, 207, 208, 209, 210, 212–216, 217–222, 223, 224, 230, 231, 235, 238, 263, 276; contracts, 38, 44, 45, 84, 116, 130, 132, 219, 220, 231; arrangers, 38–39, 41, 42–43; street musicians, 73, 74, 88, 250; inspiration of, 154; American Federation of Musicians (AFM), 162, 260, 264; demand for, 259–260, 263, 264–265, 266, 277; audiences, 277

Music Industries Chamber of Commerce (MICC), 179, 199–200, 250

Music-in-industry movement, 201, 257, 258

Music memory contests, 201–202, 203

Music publishers: and copyright law, 3, 8, 159–160, 163–164, 167, 175–177; separation of music production and consumption by, 5–6,

10, 15, 17, 282; advertising and promotion by, 11, 13–14, 25, 27, 29, 31, 41, 42, 56–89, 160, 205; relations with musicians, 15, 29–30, 43–44, 61; revenue of, 16; in New York City, 20–22, 27, 30, 32, 53, 64–65, 70–72; in Philadelphia, 22; in Chicago, 25, 27, 82; and ragtime, 39–41; role in Tin Pan Alley, 41–42, 43, 53; and song sharking, 51; and prices for sheet music, 85–86; and ASCAP, 171; and radio, 266. *See also* Hit songs; M. Witmark and Sons; Popular music; Tin Pan Alley

Music Publishers' Association (MPA), 162, 163

Music Publishers' Protective Association, 84

Music Publishing Holding Corp., 262

Music School Settlement for Colored People, 214

Mutoscopes, 95

Muzak, 257–259

M. Witmark and Sons, 1–3, 27–28, 32, 44, 70, 262, 283–284; Minstrel Department, 36–37; coon songs published by, 37, 38; advertising by, 46, 65, 74; Chicago office, 82; and copyright law, 164, 167; and ASCAP, 171, 175

"My Mammy," 261

"My Man Rocks Me (with One Steady Roll)," 222

NAACP. *See* National Association for the Advancement of Colored People

Nail, John, 236

Nancarrow, Conlon, 244

Nast, Thomas, 59

Nathan, George Jean: *The American Credo,* 254

National Association for the Advancement of Colored People (NAACP), 208, 212; *Crisis,* 211, 215, 226, 228, 229, 231, 232

National Association of Negro Musicians (NANM), 222, 227

National Broadcasting Corporation (NBC), 265

National Music Show, 202

National Music Week, 179, 202

National Phonograph Co., 113; and Columbia, 102, 104, 106, 153, 210, 267; and Victor, 104, 106, 121–122, 146, 181, 210, 267; advertising by, 106, 146, 147, 148; and patents, 153. *See also* Edison, Thomas

National Phonograph Records Recruiting Corps, 197–198

Nesbit, Evelyn, 138

Newell, William Wells: *Games and Songs of American Children,* 50

Newman, Ernest, on mechanical music, 242

Newspapers, 74–75; African American, 232, 236

New Thought, 187, 188

New York Recording Co., 236

Nickelodeons, 65, 67

Night at the Opera, A, 126

Noise: environmental, 73, 240, 245, 247–248, 253; phonograph record surface, 108, 141

N. W. Ayer & Son, 114–115

Ohio Federation of Colored Women's Clubs, 40

OKeh Records, 210, 224, 231

Olman, Adolph, 45, 64; on pluggers, 71

Olympic Disc Record Corp., 230–231, 234

Opera, 10, 16, 123; and Gaisberg, 105–106, 107–110; and quality of sound recordings, 107–109, 271; *Victor Book of the Opera,* 117; Metropolitan Opera, 119, 128, 139, 141, 145, 261. *See also* Caruso, Enrico; McCormack, John; Tamagno, Francesco

Operettas, 19

Organs, 19–20

Ornstein, Leo, 202

Ossman, Vess, 144

Ostendorf, Berndt, 33, 34

"Over There," 195

Owen, Chandler, 226, 228, 236

Owen, William Barry, 102, 112, 119, 122

Pace, Harry H.: relationship with Handy, 39, 212–213, 217; relationship with Du Bois, 206, 208, 209, 211, 213, 215–216; and Black Swan Records, 206, 208–209, 210, 216–217, 218–219, 221, 222–224, 230, 231, 233, 234, 236, 238–239; "Public Opinion and the Negro," 215; relationship with Garvey, 217; on racial uplift, 222–223, 227; on impact of radio, 233

Pace & Handy Music Co., 39, 212–213, 217

Paderewski, Ignacy Jan, 97, 98, 99, 108, 131; and Steinway, 129, 130

Paramount Records, 236

Paramount Studios, 263

Pastor, Tony, 25, 27

Patent law, 153–154, 189, 200, 210, 280

Pathé Frères, 106, 233

Patten, Simon, 188

Payola, 83–84, 281. *See also* Plugging

Peer, Ralph, 175

Periodical Publishers Association of America, 120

Personality, 126, 129, 134, 137, 139–140, 312n22

Peru, phonograph record sales in, 16

Pettit, Horace, 162–163

Phonograph records: cylinders versus discs, 4–5, 101–102, 146; sales of, 16, 95, 104, 200, 231, 233, 266–267, 270, 281; versus musical instruments, 90–96, 276–277; repetition with, 91, 111, 149, 277; sound quality, 104, 107–109, 128, 146, 267, 272, 277, 278; prices of, 105, 112–113, 114, 122, 189, 191; of Caruso, 106, 107–110, 114, 115, 116, 124, 125, 126, 128–132, 133, 134, 136, 137, 140–141, 142, 143, 145, 148–149, 182, 202, 227, 229, 280; royalties for, 130, 162, 164–165, 167; and copyright law, 151, 158, 159–160, 161–163, 164, 167–168, 170, 175; sleeves of, 205; orthophonic recordings, 267–268; export of, 270; 45 rpm singles, 282; long-playing records, 282; sound recordings as artificial, 282. *See also* Columbia Phonograph Co.; National Phonograph Co.; Victor Talking Machine Co.

Phonographs: Edison's, 4–6, 91, 102, 104, 106, 128; Berliner's gramophone, 4–6, 101–102; versus radio, 5, 250–251, 266–268, 270, 271; sales of, 16, 122, 200, 231, 233, 249–250, 270, 271, 281; versus player-pianos, 90–101, 113; the Victrola, 92, 94, 121, 126, 154, 179, 185–186, 188, 200, 278; horns of, 94, 119, 120, 125, 251, 257, 270–271; prices of, 189, 191; in schools, 191–195, 203; attitudes of critics toward, 242–244, 247, 248, 254–255; rate of ownership, 249; versus motion pictures, 259–260, 262, 270. *See also* Columbia Phonograph Co.; National Phonograph Co.; Victor Talking Machine Co.

Photography, 112, 123, 157, 158, 263

Pianolas, 92, 96, 244. *See also* Player-pianos

Pianos: in parlors, 10, 40, 94; manufacture of, 16–17, 19–20, 74, 153, 178–179, 203, 241, 269, 281; in homes, 19–20, 178–179, 249; and ragtime, 40; sales in department stores, 77, 78; rate of ownership, 249. *See also* Player-pianos

"Picture Turned toward the Wall, The," 27

Plançon, Pol, 105

Plants, paid, 70, 73, 88

Player-pianos, 10, 29, 123, 151, 202, 207, 242, 266; manufacture of, 16–17, 148, 203, 281; versus phonographs, 90–101, 113; Aeolian Co., 92, 96–99, 102, 165, 167, 189, 194, 231, 233, 244; reproducing player-pianos, 93, 99–100, 148, 244; advertising of, 97–98, 102; Gulbransen, 98, 100, 205; piano rolls and copyright law, 158, 159–160, 161, 164, 165, 166, 167–168, 170, 175; American Piano Company (Ampico), 179, 194–195, 205; in schools, 195; packaging of, 205; attitudes

Player-pianos *(continued)*
    of critics toward, 242–244, 247, 248, 254–255;
    and modernist composers, 244, 246
Plessy v. Ferguson, 37
Pleyel, 244
Plugging, 59, 78, 81–84, 88–89, 160; pluggers,
    41, 60–62, 64–65, 70–72, 73, 77, 79, 250;
    chorus slips, 62, 63, 67, 72, 88; song slides, 65,
    67, 68, 69, 70, 75; versus print advertising,
    74–75; payments to vaudeville performers,
    83–84; on radio, 86, 266
Pond, William A., 32
Popular music, 3, 6–7, 18, 26; ubiquity of, 8–9,
    10, 11, 12, 13–14, 17, 56, 57, 72–73, 78–79,
    88–89, 240–242, 249–250, 251–253, 255,
    257–259, 274; as opposed to classical or
    "serious music," 10, 19–20, 57, 87–88, 90–91,
    110–111, 123–124, 241, 242, 244, 255;
    catchiness of, 10, 41, 49, 50; contrasted with
    folk music, 18, 50, 57; styles and genres, 19,
    21–22, 39–41, 223, 277; as ephemeral, 20, 50,
    58, 60, 86–87, 110, 275; simplicity of, 23, 28,
    29, 45, 46, 49, 51, 54, 57, 58, 277; song
    popularity, 23, 28–30, 36, 45–46, 56–89;
    syncopation in, 41, 54; as impersonal, 43–44;
    song lyrics, 45, 46; comic songs, 45, 49, 208,
    215, 218, 227, 228–229; Berlin's rules for
    popular songs, 45–46, 47; musical structure,
    49, 255; song titles, 49–50; as chorus-oriented,
    49–50, 62, 63, 277, 278; national market for,
    58, 60, 79–85, 89; duration of songs, 123–124,
    277, 279; *The People's Choice Music* project,
    273–274. *See also* Hit songs; Music publishers;
    Songwriters; Tin Pan Alley
Porter, Eleanor: *Pollyanna,* 188
Powers & Armstrong, 114
"President Cleveland's Wedding March," 1, 7
Printers' Ink, 75, 188
Proctor & Gamble, 115
Production of music versus consumption of
    music, 5–6, 10, 15, 17, 60, 282
Pryor, Arthur, 83
Public parks and music, 62, 79, 96, 250
Pulitzer, Joseph, 128

Rachmaninoff, Sergei, 145
Radio, 10, 16, 64, 221, 247, 248; versus
    phonographs, 5, 250–251, 266–268, 270, 271;
    advertising on, 14, 73, 278; oldies on, 57;
    plugging on, 86, 266; determination of content
    on, 94; and patent pools, 153; and copyright
    law, 174–175, 176; impact on phonograph

business, 230, 231, 233–234; commercial
    development of, 231, 233–234, 250–253;
    electrical loudspeakers, 241, 250, 251, 252,
    253, 264, 267; rate of ownership, 249; sales of
    radio sets, 251, 281; musical content on,
    251–253, 264–267, 270, 277–278; attitudes of
    critics toward, 252–253; and live musicians,
    259, 264–265, 266; versus motion pictures,
    263–264; NBC, 264–265; CBS, 265, 266;
    sound quality, 267, 272, 278; Roosevelt's
    Fireside Chats, 272; standardization in
    programming, 278; transistor, 282
Radio Corporation of American (RCA), 251,
    264–265, 268, 269
Ragtime, 39–41, 53–55, 56, 207, 208, 209, 219,
    227
Railroads, 95, 153, 154
Rainey, Ma, 223, 231
Randolph, A. Philip, 226, 228
Ravel, Maurice, 99
Recording Industry Association of America
    (RIAA), 282
Red Seal records. *See* Victor Talking Machine Co.
Red Star Publishing Co., 262
Religious songs, 18, 19, 208, 214, 218, 221, 279
Remick, Jerome, 30, 32, 33, 64–65, 85, 262
Remington Phonograph Corp., 230–231
Reproducing player-pianos, 93, 99–100, 148
Restaurants: music in, 10, 14, 64, 71, 79, 88–89,
    172–174, 175, 176, 250, 276; and copyright
    law and *Shanley* decision, 14, 172–174, 175,
    176
Revenue Act of 1921, 200
Rhythm and blues, 237
Ricordi, 171
RKO, 262
Robbins, 262
Robeson, Paul, 139
Rock and roll, 277
Rodgers, Jimmy, 175
Rodgers, Richard: as plugger, 61; on Dreyfus, 177
"Roll, Jordan, Roll," 7
Rolls-Royce, 115
Ronald, Sir Landon, 105
Roosevelt, Franklin, 53; Fireside Chats, 272
Roosevelt, Theodore: recordings of, 5; on
    copyright law, 158–159; music programs of,
    202
Root, George Frederick, 23, 32
Rosenfeld, Monroe, 21
Rosenthal, Moriz, 97
Rossiter, Will, 25, 27, 33

Roxy Theatre (New York City), 260
Royalties, 5, 23, 27; for public performance, 3, 159, 160, 162, 167, 170–175, 176; for songwriters, 23, 38, 40, 44; for mechanical reproduction, 75, 162, 164–165, 167, 168, 175, 176; for phonograph records, 130, 162, 164–165, 167
Rubicam, Raymond, 114
Rubinstein, Arthur, 202
Russia, 105–106
Russolo, Luigi: *The Art of Noises,* 245

Saint Louis World's Fair, 39–40, 87
Saint-Saëns, Camille, 99
Sarnoff, David, 251
Saroyan, William, 244
Satie, Erik, and *musique d'ameublement,* 256, 268
Saturday Evening Post, 115, 116
Schafer, R. Murray, 249, 291n28, 333n14
Schauffler, Robert Haven: on popular songs, 51–52; on machine-made music, 90, 91
Schivelbusch, Wolfgang, on machine ensembles, 95
Schools, music education in, 180, 191–195, 203, 214, 238, 241, 254
Schumann-Heink, Ernestine, 115
Scott de Martinville, Edouard-Léon, 4
Scotti, Antonio, 105, 109, 133
Scriabin, Alexander, 99
Seidl, Anton, 20, 98
Seldes, Gilbert, 52
Senses, 12–13; hearing versus sight, 14
Shanley's Restaurant, and performing rights, 172–174, 175, 176
Shapiro, Maurice, 32, 33
Shapiro, Bernstein & Co., 30, 65, 82
Sheathing, 94
Sheet music: sales of, 22, 44, 176, 207, 266; covers of, 24, 26, 27, 30, 31, 37, 41, 44, 59–60, 65, 66, 67, 205; prices for, 57–58, 85–86; versus phonograph records, 93–94, 134–135; and copyright law, 156, 159, 160–162. *See also* Music publishers; Plugging
Siegel-Cooper's, 64–65, 78, 85, 110
Silverman, Sime, 84
Sing-alongs, 62, 63, 67, 79
"Singer in the Gallery, A," 70
Singer sewing machines, 115
Sissle, Noble, 219
Small phonograph companies, 279–280
Smith, Bessie, 221, 222, 223, 231
Smith, Harry, 276

Smith, Mamie, 210, 213, 220, 225
Smith, Trixie, 220, 235
Snyder, Ted, 32, 54
Société des Auteurs, Compositeurs, et Editeurs de Musique (SACEM), 170–171
Society of European Stage Authors and Composers (SESAC), 176
Solberg, Thorvald: *Copyright in Congress,* 158
Soldier, Dave: "The Most Unwanted Song," 273–274; "The Most Wanted Song," 273–274
Song sharking, 51
Song slides, 65, 67, 68, 69, 70, 75
Songwriters, 18, 20, 21–24, 27, 28–30; payment of, 22–23, 24, 38, 40, 43–44; royalties for, 23, 38, 40, 44; Jews as, 32, 36; African Americans as, 37–41; staff songwriters, 38–39, 43–45; as unknown, 43–44; relations with music publishers, 43–44; attitudes toward songwriting among, 44–52; women as, 46–47; amateurs as, 51; and song slides, 67; and copyright law, 163, 164; and ASCAP, 171. *See also* Berlin, Irving; Harris, Charles K.; Kern, Jerome; Tin Pan Alley; Von Tilzer, Harry
Sonneck, Oscar, 34
Sony, 269
Sousa, John Philip, 34, 98, 104, 106, 161; and "After the Ball," 30; at Columbian World Exposition in Chicago, 30; as celebrity, 129, 130; on laws, 150; and copyright law, 162, 163, 164–165, 172, 174; and Victor, 164; "The Menace of Mechanical Music," 164–165; "From Maine to Oregon," 172
Speyer & Co., 268
Spirituals, 19, 208, 214, 218, 221
Squier, George Owens. *See* Wired Music
"Stagger Lee," 176
Standard Life Insurance Co., 212
Stanley, Aileen, 234
Stark, John, 40
"Star Spangled Banner, The," 202–203
Steinway Hall, 98, 284
Steinway & Sons, 97, 98, 115, 129, 130, 269
Sterling, Louis, 269
Stern, Joseph, 30, 32, 33, 46, 65, 80
Stieglitz, Alfred, 112
Still, William Grant, 216, 235
Stokowski, Leopold, 77, 235
Story, Joseph, 152
Strauss, Richard, 75, 99
Stravinsky, Igor, on the player-piano, 244
Street musicians, 73, 74, 88, 250
Stuckenschmidt, H. H., 243

Successful Farming, 115
Swayne, Noah H., 152
"Sweetheart of My Dreams," 47

Taft, William Howard, 202, 289n5
Tainter, Charles Sumner, 4
Tamagno, Francesco, 109, 112–113
Tape recorders, 123, 282
"Ta-ra-ra Boom-de-ay," 20
Taylor, Deems, on the player-piano, 242
Taylor, Frederick Winslow, 53
T. B. Harms and Co., 27, 42, 65, 262
Ted Snyder, Inc., 53–54
Telegraph, 93, 153, 263–264
Telephone, 93, 153, 247, 248
Television, 16, 52, 247; and copyright law, 176
Terkel, Studs, on Caruso, 113–114, 126
Theater Exhibitors' Chamber of Commerce,
   260
Theosophists, 187
Thomas, Theodore, 34
Tindale, J. L., 163
Tin Pan Alley: and Hollywood, 21, 35, 43, 53,
   262–263, 284; origins of, 21–22, 28, 30, 32,
   284; Jews in, 32–35, 37, 241; and minstrel
   shows, 36–37; and coon songs, 37, 38, 206;
   African Americans in, 37–41; division of labor
   in, 41–44, 49; as song factory, 41–55; Berlin's
   rules for popular songs, 45–46, 47; and
   women, 46–47, 72; attitudes toward innovation
   and standardization in, 47–49, 163, 274, 275;
   and ragtime, 39–41, 56; and song titles, 49–50;
   attitudes toward consumers in, 51–52, 57–58,
   60, 73; success of, 56–58; attitudes toward, 89,
   90, 110–111, 156–157; and copyright law, 163;
   and ASCAP, 171; during World War I, 195,
   197; and *The Jazz Singer,* 261. *See also* Music
   publishers; Popular music; Plugging
Tivoli Dance Orchestra, 234
Toch, Ernst, 244
Tompkins, Gilbert, 57
Tremaine, Harry B., 96–98, 102
Tremaine, William B., 96
Twain, Mark, 121
Twentieth Century Fox, 262, 263
Tyers, Will H., 171

Union Square (New York City), 283–284
United Kingdom, phonograph record sales in, 16.
   See also England
United Music Stores, 86
United States, 9, 16, 98, 155

Universal Negro Improvement Association
   (UNIA), 209, 217
U.S. Patent Office, 153
U.S. Supreme Court: *Herbert v. Shanley Co.,* 14,
   172–174, 175, 176; *Plessy v. Ferguson,* 37;
   *Leeds & Catlin Company v. Victor Talking
   Machine Company,* 153–154; *Bleistein v.
   Donaldson,* 157–158; *White-Smith v. Apollo,*
   165, 166, 167; and Victor's pricing policies,
   191

Valentino, Rudolph, 139
Vanderbilt, Cornelius, 97
Van Vechten, Carl, 254
Varèse, Edgard, 235; *Amériques,* 245; *Hyper-
   prism,* 245
Vaudeville, 10, 29, 30, 34, 36, 79, 158, 202, 275;
   origin of, 25; role in promotion of popular
   songs, 42, 43, 60, 67, 70–71, 80–85, 250; in
   New York City, 80; Koster and Biel's, 80;
   Martin Beck's Orpheum Circuit, 80; Pastor's,
   80; Western Vaudeville Association, 80; Keith
   and Albee's Circuit, 80, 81, 84, 284; big-time
   circuits versus small-time circuits, 80–81; Sun
   Circuit, 81; decline of, 86; and ASCAP, 175;
   and *The Jazz Singer,* 261
Veblen, Thorstein: on modern businesses, 21–22;
   on profit, 21–22
Verdi, Giuseppe, 218
Victorian values, 28–29, 53, 78, 85
Victor Talking Machine Co., 101–102, 104–117,
   162, 251; the Victrola, 92, 94, 121, 126, 154,
   179, 185–186, 188, 200, 278; and Johnson,
   101–102, 104, 106–107, 113, 114, 119, 124,
   130, 154, 189, 238, 268; picture of, 103; Red
   Seal series, 104, 105–114, 115, 117, 119–120,
   121, 122, 123, 126, 131–132, 133, 134, 136,
   144, 145, 146, 148, 192, 205, 262, 270, 277,
   279; and National, 104, 106, 121–122, 146,
   181, 210, 267; advertising by, 104, 106–107,
   109–110, 111, 112–113, 114–117, 118,
   119–121, 122, 123, 128–129, 130, 131, 133,
   134, 135, 136, 137, 142–144, 146, 148, 149,
   179–183, 184, 185–189, 190, 191–195, 205,
   262, 266, 267, 279; and Columbia, 104, 114,
   145–146, 153, 162–163, 194, 210, 267;
   trademark image "His Master's Voice," 104,
   116, 118, 119, 205; and Gramophone Co.
   Ltd., 104–107, 109, 112–113, 114, 119, 121,
   122, 123, 125–126, 131–132, 203, 268–269,
   270; Caruso's recordings, 106, 107–110, 114,
   115, 116, 124, 125–126, 128–132, 133, 134,

136, 137, 140–141, 142, 143, 145, 148–149, 182, 202, 227, 229, 280; and Douglass, 113, 115; *Victor Book of Opera,* 117; Black Seal series, 122, 144, 149; *Voice of the Victor,* 127, 133, 181–183, 184, 185–189, 190, 191, 192–193, 194, 196, 202, 203, 266; Victor News Service, 143; *Leeds & Catlin Company v. Victor Talking Machine Company,* 153–154; and patents, 153–154; and copyright law, 162–163, 175; and Sousa, 164; dominance of, 179, 203, 210, 233, 262; local influence on, 179–183, 184, 185; relations with dealers and retail stores, 180, 181–183, 184, 185–189, 190, 191, 192–194, 196, 197, 201–202, 203, 266, 267; Education Department, 180, 191–195, 201–202, 238; Window Display Service, 183; *How to Sell Victors on Installments,* 186; pricing policies, 189, 191; Traveling Department, 190, 191; *Music Appreciation for Little Children,* 193; *What We Hear in Music,* 193; during World War I, 195, 196, 197, 200; blues and jazz recordings, 231; compared with Black Swan, 238; and Warner Brothers, 262; and RCA, 265, 268, 269; orthophonic recordings introduced by, 267–268; the Victrola-Radiola, 268
Victor Talking Machine Co. of Brazil, 268
Victor Talking Machine Co. of Canada, 268
Victor Talking Machine Co. of Chile, 268
Victor Talking Machine Co. of Japan, Ltd., 268
Video games, and copyright law, 176
Virgin Megastore (New York City), 283
Vocco, Rocco, 82
Vodery, Will, 219
Von Sternberg, Constantin, 255
Von Tilzer, Albert: "Teasing," 38
Von Tilzer, Harry, 21, 33, 36, 84, 171, 174, 274; on music as commodity, 20, 22, 23, 44–45; and Tin Pan Alley, 21

Wagner, Richard, 109
Wallace Downey Dance Orchestra, 234
Walsh, Arthur, 146
Walton, Lester, 220
Wanamaker's, 75, 76, 77, 78, 97, 202
Warner Brothers, 261, 262, 264
Warner Music Group, 8
Warner Theater (New York City), 261
War Revenue Act, 199–200
Washington, Booker T., 20, 212, 230; recordings of, 5; Atlanta Compromise, 37; National Negro Business League (NNBL), 209

Washington, George, 157
Washington, Isabelle, 221–222
Waters, Ethel, and Black Swan Records, 218–219, 220–221, 222, 224, 230, 235, 238
Waterson, Henry, 54
WEAF (New York City), 264–265
Weber Piano Co., 98
Weill, Kurt: "Tango-Angèle," 244
Wells, H. G.: *Tono-Bungay,* 243
Western Electric, 261, 267
Westinghouse, 251
Whistler, James Abbott McNeill, 59
White, Stanford, 138
White, Walter, 212
Whiteman, Paul: *Jazz,* 50
Whiting, Arthur, on mechanical music, 243
Whitman, Walt: "I Hear America Singing," 7–8
Williams, Bert, 37, 48, 207, 217; "Nobody," 39
Williams, Raymond, on structure of feeling, 12
Willis Woodward & Co., 27
Wilson, Woodrow, 202; on music during World War I, 199
Window displays, 89, 117, 119, 181, 183, 184, 191, 267
Winner, Septimus, 22
Wired Music, 258
Witmark, Eddie, 1–2, 27, 36. *See also* M. Witmark and Sons
Witmark, Frank, 1–2, 27, 36. *See also* M. Witmark and Sons
Witmark, Isidore, 1, 3, 7, 27, 30, 32, 33, 36, 38, 164, 167. *See also* M. Witmark and Sons
Witmark, Jay, 1–2, 3, 27, 32, 171. *See also* M. Witmark and Sons
Witmark, Julius, 1–2, 3, 16, 27, 32, 33, 36. *See also* M. Witmark and Sons
Witmark, Marcus, 1
Witmark Amateur Minstrel Guide and Burnt Cork Encyclopedia, 36
WJZ (New York City), 265
Wolfson, Martin, on Caruso, 145
Wood, Charles Winter, 228, 230
Woodward, Willis, 27
Woolworth's, 86
Working class: versus middle class, 12, 19–20, 35, 113–114, 145, 221–223, 249; and Black Swan Records, 221–223, 238; labor songs, 278–279
Workplace music: Muzak, 257–259; work songs, 18, 19, 258. *See also* Music-in-industry movement
World War I, 245, 251; pluggers during, 62; music and morale during, 178–179, 195,

World War I *(continued)*
  197–200, 257–258; "Over There," 195; Victor
  during, 195, 196, 197, 200; Tin Pan Alley
  during, 195, 197; Caruso during, 197; War
  Revenue Act, 199–200; and African
  Americans, 207–208, 209

"Yankee Doodle," 7
Yellen, Jack, 44

Youmans, Vincent, 61
Young, Edward, 155

Zanzig, Augustus: *Music in American Life,* 241
Zonophone, 106

Harvard University Press is a member of Green Press Initiative (greenpressinitiative.org), a nonprofit organization working to help publishers and printers increase their use of recycled paper and decrease their use of fiber derived from endangered forests. This book was printed on recycled paper containing 30% post-consumer waste and processed chlorine free.